Part 2:

Individual rights

Part 2:

Individual rights

3. Your contract of employment

What is a contract / why it's important / where to find the law / who has a contract of employment / before you make a contract / what's in the written part / written particulars, pay statement, collective agreements, Wages Council orders, works rules / what's unwritten / custom and practice, employers' and workers' general obligations / ending the contract / how to claim for breach of contract / collective action / and a summary.

What is a contract?

You make contracts every day. Some look more formal than others, such as an agreement to buy a house or an insurance policy, but they are basically the same as agreements to buy bread or travel on a bus. The essential feature is a binding agreement in which an offer by one person is accepted by someone else. It involves a benefit to one of them or a detriment to the other, or an exchange of benefits. **It is a promise that can be enforced in the courts.**

Not all promises can. You wouldn't think friends should be able to sue you if you promise to babysit while they go to the pictures, and you go back on your word. Neither of you intended that a *legal* obligation should arise. If you promise to make a donation to a charity it cannot sue you if you later refuse, unless the promise is in writing and witnessed formally. This is because the charity has not, in exchange for your promise, given you any benefit or acted to its detriment on your behalf. Your promise is a gift, and is entirely one way. So without a written 'deed' it is not enforceable in the courts (but in Scotland it might be).

Contracts need not be written or signed. If you buy a second-hand car there is usually no paperwork except the registration book. You may get a receipt saying how much you paid but the agreement is unwritten. It is no less binding in law because of it. But proving there was an agreement, or what was intended at the time of sale, is a lot easier if you have drawn up a list of the main points – such as, is there a guarantee, how many miles has it done, is it in good running order, and who is going to pay for the dent in the wing?

How important is your contract of employment?

The contract of employment is the starting point for many aspects of your working life. You can't discuss the effect of strikes, of refusing to accept instructions, discipline, sacking, lay-offs or equal pay without the lawyers forcing you back to your contract, examining what it says and, equally importantly, telling you what is unwritten. Even union rights won through organisation are enforced by reference to individual contracts of employment.

Although the contract is so important, the amount of information written, or even discussed, at the time you take up employment is often very limited. Only in 1963 did it become obligatory to put into writing certain details of contracts of employment. If you are not in a union, and not subject to any collective agreement, this is the only piece of written data you get. Yet there are enough unwritten rules for the judges to tell you exactly where you stand.

Despite the obvious and continuing inequality of bargaining power between a worker and an employer, the courts treat your contract as if every item is suggested, discussed, negotiated, compromised and agreed. The very essence of all the rules that follow in this chapter is that there is an *agreement* made by willing equal parties. It may not make sense to treat an employment contract like a contract to buy a used car, but the courts do.

Where to find the law

Much of the law on contracts of employment is made by judges. The Employment Protection Consolidation Act 1978 (EPCA

1978) defines 'employee' (section 153) and deals with written particulars and pay statements (sections 1–11); time off for public duties (section 29); and minimum notice (section 49). The Sex Discrimination Act 1975 (SDA 1975) and the Race Relations Act 1976 (RRA 1976) outlaw discrimination. The Rehabilitation of Offenders Act 1974 (ROA 1974) entitles you to live down a conviction.

Who has a contract of employment?

Workers and employees

There is a difference between a worker and an employee. The difference is generally ignored in this book because almost all workers are employees, most of the individual rights apply only to employees, and worker and employee are used interchangeably by most people. All employees have contracts of employment. Some people work for themselves or are in partnership; some are directors of companies; some are neither workers nor employees – police officers, for instance, who 'hold office'. The main group of non-employee workers consists of self-employed 'independent contractors'. It is important to recognise the difference because being an employee has a number of consequences:

- You are entitled to most of the statutory rights in this book – time off, redundancy pay, protection against unfair dismissal, etc.
- You and management are subject to the unwritten general obligations of a contract of employment.
- You are both liable to pay social security contributions.
- Management deduct tax from your pay.
- Management must be insured against claims by you for personal injury.
- Management are subject to levies, for example, for industrial training in certain industries, and must notify the Department of Employment (DE) of certain impending redundancies.

The difference between an employee and an independent contractor is easier to see than to define. For example, a taxi driver and a full-time company chauffeur do the same work but the taxi driver is often self-employed. There is a similar distinction between a freelance writer and a newspaper reporter, or a casual window-cleaner and a permanent caretaker, or a jobbing electrician and an electrical fitter in a big factory.

The courts have not laid down a clear rule about how to tell whether a person is employed or self-employed. The key question is: are you in business on your own account? If you are, you are self-employed and work under a **contract for services**. If not, you are an employee and work under a **contract of service**.

In deciding this question you must look at the realities of the relationship, not simply what the worker and the employer say or write.

■ Michael Ferguson was hired as a labourer on a building site. He agreed to a labour-only sub-contract (Lump). He was injured and successfully claimed £30,000 in damages. The Court of Appeal (CA) said that the reality of the situation was employer–employee, so his employers were liable as they did not provide a guardrail where he was working. The employers told Mr Ferguson where to work, provided him with tools, told him what work was to be done and paid him wages. This in reality meant that he was an employee not a self-employed contractor. *Ferguson v Dawson* 1976 (CA)

Section 153 of the EPCA 1978 defines an employee as someone who has entered into, works under or has worked under a contract of employment or apprenticeship. The definition of a worker in TULRA 1974 is wider. This includes employees, potential employees, self-employed people (except self-employed members of the 'professions'), civil servants and trainees on the Youth Training Scheme. Excluded are the police, prison officers and the armed services.

If you knowingly participate in an illegal act, for example, if you are paid cash-in-hand to avoid tax and national insurance, you will not be entitled to claim under the employment legislation.

■ J. Newland worked for a Kensington, West London, hairdressers where she was paid £50 out of the till every Saturday. She believed her employer grossed up and paid the tax and NI. He produced books showing he paid her £48 gross, £37 net. Her P60 annual statement showed that she was not receiving £50 net and that her assumption that tax had been deducted was incorrect. Nevertheless, the EAT accepted that she did not know her employer's purpose was to defraud.

His illegality did not deprive *her* of her status as an employee. She successfully claimed unfair dismissal (although her compensation was reduced by half for other reasons). *Newland v Simons & Willer* 1981 (EAT)

Co-operatives

Members of a workers' co-operative can be owners and, at the same time, employees entitled to use the EPCA. If the co-op is registered as a limited company it exists separately from its individual members and can sack them. So can a co-op registered under the Industrial and Provident Societies Acts 1893–1965.

■ A group of metalworkers formed a co-op which registered as a limited company. At one meeting, Colin Johnson led a move to tighten up on absenteeism which required signing an attendance book, the penalty for falsifying it being dismissal. At a subsequent meeting many complaints were upheld against him and he was sacked. The EAT said the co-op did have power to sack one of its members and the dismissal was fair as Johnson helped to formulate the dismissal policy. *Drym Fabricators v Johnson* 1980 (EAT)

The EAT went on to say that even an unregistered co-op would have the same collective powers of employment. But some co-ops are clearly a grouping of *self-employed* people. For example, member–shareholders of an orchestra might employ a manager but not each other or other freelance musicians called in for a sessional fee and expenses – *Addison v London Philharmonic Orchestra* 1981 (EAT)

Crown employment

The legal theory behind Crown employment is that you can't sue the Crown and you are employed only as long as the Crown wants you. This has led to civil servants being treated differently from other workers. They are not employees and have terms of employment, not contracts. Nevertheless, much of the employment legislation applies to them – itemised pay statements, guarantee and medical suspension pay, maternity and union membership rights, unfair dismissal and written reasons for dismissal. Time off for some public duties may be restricted (see page 55).

You are not entitled to written particulars, minimum notice or redundancy pay (EPCA section 138).

Staff at the House of Commons are treated in the same way; but the House of Lords, as in many things, is a law unto itself. Its staff are covered by no legislation.

National Health Service
NHS workers are not Crown employees and are specifically covered by all the EPCA except redundancy pay. Some senior NHS who *are* regarded as working for the Crown are not entitled to written particulars or minimum notice (EPCA section 138).

Homeworkers
Homeworkers or outworkers are often employees protected by the employment and health and safety legislation, but this depends on the reality of the relationship with the employer.

■ Delia Cope had assembled shoes at home for a Yorkshire company for seven years. The company trained her, advised on safety precautions, supplied all materials and tools, delivered and picked up the product five days a week and paid her for shoes satisfactorily assembled. She got no sick or holiday pay and paid no tax or NI. The company said there was no obligation on their part to send or on her part to accept work so she was in business on her own account and not an employee. The EAT said that the parties' conduct established a continuing (not a daily) contract of employment. *Airfix Footwear v Cope* 1978 (EAT)

If the work is done sporadically, such as on an occasional week a few times a year, the outworker may be a new employee on each of those separate occasions, or may not be an employee at all.

Government training schemes
Trainees on Youth Training Schemes are not employees but do have certain rights – see page 460. The Health and Safety at Work Act 1974 (HSWA 1974) sections 4 and 6 impose duties on employers and manufacturers to take reasonable measures to ensure their premises and products are safe for workers, including trainees, to use. From 1983 trainees are covered by the race and sex discrimination laws.

■ Jean Daley went on a YOP (Youth Opportunity Programme) work experience scheme and was placed in Lipton's grocery shop in Peterborough. She complained of racial discrimination. The CRE argued that Liptons had the same right to accept or reject her, to give her instructions, to control what she did, to dictate her attendance hours and to discipline her as they had over regular employees. She was paid by Liptons on behalf of the MSC so the CRE said she was employed either by Liptons, or by the MSC, or she was a contract worker. The EAT decided she had no contract of employment and was not an employee but a trainee. Only certain bodies providing training are covered by the Race Relations Act, and MSC sponsors were not included until 1983. *Daley v Allied Suppliers* 1983 (EAT)

Apprentices

A contract of apprenticeship is regarded as a contract of employment (EPCA section 153) although it has some differences. It must be in writing and be signed by the apprentice, a parent (or guardian) and the 'master'. Archaic statutes still allow magistrates to try disputes between a 'master' and apprentice.

An apprentice cannot give notice and leave, nor be sacked for misconduct unless the contract specifically says so. Nevertheless if the 'master's' conduct shows that s/he is not prepared to carry out his/her essential obligations to teach and maintain, the apprentice can sue for breach of contract. Here the damages would go beyond the normal limits of notice money. In *Dunk v George Waller* 1970 (HC) these included loss of earnings and teaching for the remaining 15 months of a four-year contract and for loss of future prospects as a time-served skilled worker. Circumstances which would justify summary or fair dismissal of an *employee* may not justify the sacking of an *apprentice* unless the contract says so, or the apprentice's conduct makes it impossible for the 'master' to carry out his/her teaching obligations, such as 'serious and habitual neglect of duties' or habitual theft. In other words, a sacked apprentice could lose a claim of unfair dismissal but win a claim for breach of contract. Once your time is up, you have no legal protection if you are not kept on as a skilled worker, unless your contract says so – see page 197.

Self-employment in the building industry

The 'Lump' is the name given to labour-only sub-contracting in the building and civil engineering industries. Typically, it takes the form of a group of workers, each self-employed, who agree with a sub-contractor that the sub-contractor will find work for them with a main contractor. There are other forms. In all cases the main feature is that the worker is paid a lump sum, and is supposed to pay income tax and social security contributions out of that sum.

The Lump has advantages for workers and employers. It enables both of them to evade the legal liabilities imposed on them.

It undermines union organisation in a badly organised industry, and contributes to its appalling safety record. Despite union pressure over many years no effective measures were taken to crush the Lump. In 1977 a system of certification was introduced. Limited companies and self-employed workers in the building industry must carry certificates with photographs. Tax must be deducted by employers from every payment made unless a valid certificate is produced. Weekly tax returns must be made by sub-contractors. But the lack of union organisation and the haphazard nature of building work mean that abuses continue.

Before you make a contract of employment

Legal consequences can arise even before you enter into your contract.

1. Discrimination on the grounds of race, sex and being married is outlawed. Employees, potential employees and independent contractors have equal rights.

2. Under the Disabled Persons (Employment)Acts 1944 and 1958, employers with more than 20 regular workers must employ a quota of registered disabled workers (usually 3 per cent), and if they are employing less than their quota, they cannot fill a vacancy with a non-disabled person unless exempt. The penalty is a fine of £500, but prosecutions are extremely rare.

3. Women and workers under the age of 18 are prevented by the Factories Act 1961 and the Mines and Quarries Act 1954 from working certain hours and in certain occupations.

4. The Employment Agencies Act 1973 makes it a criminal offence to run an employment agency without a licence, or to charge fees to prospective employees.

5. Under the Rehabilitation of Offenders Act 1974 (ROA 1974) you are entitled to forget some 'spent' convictions. When applying for most jobs you can forget about convictions for various crimes for which you got less than two-and-a-half years in prison and which occurred some time ago, if you have not subsequently been convicted of another offence. The length of the period of rehabilitation varies according to the sentence and your age on conviction.

For example

Imprisonment for between 6 and 30 months	10 years' rehabilitation
Imprisonment for less than 6 months	7 years' rehabilitation
Fine	5 years' rehabilitation
Conditional discharge, probation, binding-over	1 year or date on which order expires (whichever is longer)

The above periods are halved for offences committed by juveniles (under 17).

Although the words of the Act are strong, there is no direct remedy if you have action taken against you on account of a conviction which has become spent. Your remedy for dismissal would be a claim for unfair dismissal, but not all workers can make a claim (see page 208).

ROA section 4 says:

a conviction which has become spent or any circumstances ancillary thereto, or any failure to disclose . . . shall not be a proper ground for dismissing or excluding a person from any office, profession, occupation or employment or for prejudicing him in any way in any occupation or employment.

There are numerous exceptions (see SI 1975 No 1023) which mean that you have to disclose your convictions if you are applying for a job as: a doctor, lawyer, accountant, dentist, vet, nurse, midwife, optician, chemist, law clerk, constable, traffic warden, probation officer, teacher, health or social worker or if you deal with people under 18 years old; or if you need a licence to carry on your trade. In all other cases you are entitled to say you have no record. See also *Property Guards v Taylor and Kershaw* page 236 for a specific example of unfair dismissal.

Making the contract

Once you accept an offer of a job, the contract is made. The details are known as **terms and conditions**. You may have talked about the basic elements of the work – the pay and the hours – but many other details are often included because of collective agreements or legislation, such as pension rights, training, union rights and sickness.

There are also many obligations that you and management are required to adhere to because they are automatically considered to be part of every contract of employment unless they are expressly excluded. These are **implied terms** under the common law. In this chapter they occur as custom and practice, and general obligations imposed on employers and employees. Common law implied terms include management's duty to pay you and provide a safe system of working. For your part, you must work and co-operate, obey reasonable instructions within the scope of your contract and be trustworthy.

The time to object to any aspect of the deal is at the time you are offered the job. This may be relevant advice for managers and senior staff, but for most workers the chances of objecting individually to bits of a contract are virtually nil. After you accept the job, it is too late to start demanding different terms, unless you are organised and can apply sanctions.

Your contract may be made up of:

1. Terms expressly agreed – your written statement is often evidence of what these are.
2. Terms included from collective agreements.
3. Terms included because of a Wages Council Order, or an award of the Central Arbitration Committee.
4. Works rules.
5. Terms implied by custom and practice in your trade.
6. Terms implied by the common law which impose general obligations on employers.
7. Terms implied by the common law which impose general obligations on employees.

All of these are dealt with in the following sections.

The written part of your contract

1. Written statement of terms

The EPCA 1978 (section 49) lays down minimum periods of notice that every worker is entitled to. (See page 195.) Section 1 requires employers to give employees a list of the main terms of the contract of employment. The rationale of this part of the Act is that workers should be told exactly how they stand on the main points of their contracts, so it is easier in a dispute to prove what the terms are.

Section 1 of the Act applies to all employees except: part-timers who work less than 16 hours a week (plus exceptions – see page 468); registered dockers; seafarers; overseas workers; Crown and some National Health Service workers; and employees whose *entire* contract is written (very rarely found).

Within 13 weeks of starting work management must give you your own copy of a written statement setting out the following particulars.

1. Identity of the employer (such as the company name, or what it trades as) and employee.

2. Date employment began, whether any previous service counts as continuous and if so when it began. There are clear rules about strikes, illness, lay-off and transfer, but a note that previous service counts will prevent employers subsequently denying that this is true.

3. Job title. This is not a conclusive description of what you actually do. In considering, for example, suitable alternative work if you are redundant or pregnant it is what you actually do that is important, not what it's called. The Act does not require a job description, but it should show the nature of the work you are employed to do in accordance with your contract and the capacity and place in which you are employed – EPCA 1978 section 153.

4. Rate of remuneration, or method of calculating it. Remuneration includes *all* forms of pay. This is crucial as redundancy and other payments depend on contractual entitlement to pay. Overtime rates should be specified.

5. Whether paid weekly, monthly or at some other interval, and whether you work a week or month in hand.

6. Hours of work, and normal working hours.

7. Annual, public and other holidays, rights to holiday pay and to accrued holiday pay on termination.

8. Provision for sickness and injury – for example, when a doctor's note must be given, and entitlement under occupational and statutory sick pay schemes.

9. Pension rights (unless you belong to a scheme established by statute, as do NHS and local authority workers).

10. Amount of notice you must give, and are entitled to receive. Even if this is the same as the minimum under the EPCA 1978 the periods must be spelt out.

11. Disciplinary rules that apply to you.

12. The name or description of a person you can apply to if you are dissatisfied with *any* disciplinary decision against you, or if you want to bring up a grievance, and how to apply.

13. The procedure following such an application.

14. Whether or not a contracting-out certificate under the Social Security Pensions Act 1975 is in force.

15. If the contract is for a fixed period, the date it expires.

Points to note about the statement

Instead of specifying the information in paragraphs 1–11 and 13, the statement can refer you to a document which you have a reasonable opportunity to read while at work. So you may see a reference to a collective agreement, or to the works rules, or to the EPCA (for minimum notice periods) provided it is accessible to you at work, or to the pension scheme deeds.

If there are no details to be given in paragraphs 1–10, the written statement must say so. If you don't get normal pay for holidays, for instance, this must be recorded. But you must be given the information required in paragraphs 11–15.

Paragraphs 11–13 do not apply to rules, procedures and decisions relating to health and safety. So there is no obligation to give you details about disciplinary action that might be taken against you if you break safety rules. This sort of thing must be covered by management's policy statement under the Health and Safety at Work Act 1974 (HSWA 1974).

It must be stressed that the statement is *not* your contract or even *conclusive evidence* of what its main points are. It is important to realise the difference. As we shall see, there is far more to a contract than the matters contained in the list above. Although the chances of saying that the written statement does not correspond to what you agreed are slim, it is still possible to overturn the statement by evidence from custom and practice or of what was said. The statement is of *written particulars* of your contract, and other facts can be brought up to show that something else was intended.

The President of the EAT said in *System Floors v Daniel* (1981):

> The status of the statutory statement is this. It provides very strong prima facie evidence of what were the terms of the contract between the parties, but does not constitute a written contract between the parties. Nor are the statements of the terms finally conclusive: at most, they place a heavy burden on the employer to show that the actual terms of contract are different from those which he has set out in the statutory statement . . . The document is a unilateral one merely stating the employer's view of what those terms are.

How to get a written statement of terms

If you do not get a written statement within 13 weeks of starting work, or if you dispute the accuracy of it, you can apply to an industrial tribunal for an order that management should supply one. See page 490 for the procedure. You can apply while you are employed, or up to **three months** after you have left the job.

The tribunal's powers are limited, however, to recording what the agreed terms are. It can look at all the facts surrounding the employment relationship including what would have been agreed had you discussed it, and what you and your employer have done in practice since you were taken on. It has also been suggested in the Court of Appeal that if this does not resolve the issue, the tribunal can decide what *should* have been agreed between you and, because it is management's failure to observe the EPCA 1978 which causes the claim, any doubt should be resolved in your favour.

■ A worker's written statement said nothing about sick pay. He was off for seven months before he resigned on health grounds. He applied for a declaration that his contract required management to pay him during sickness. The court said that as there was no agreement, what happened in practice could give a guide. No one else in the firm got sick pay, he had never asked for it until after he left and he did not regularly send in sick notes. This indicated that there was no entitlement. But if there were no indication from factors like these, there is a presumption that wages will continue during sickness. *Mears v Safecar Security* 1982 (CA)

This presumption is important in establishing entitlement to better rights than those applying to statutory sick pay (see page 64).

On the other hand, a tribunal cannot determine what, for example, is 'reasonable' notice if that is what your written statement gives you. For that sort of interpretation you must go to the county court.

Signing the statement

Nothing in the EPCA 1978 requires you to sign the written statement, although in practice you are often asked to sign one copy and keep the other yourself. You do not benefit from signing the statement or signing that you have received it. In fact, it could be to your disadvantage. The Court of Appeal told John Mercer, a gas conversion fitter who claimed redundancy pay based on a 54-hour week, that by signing a written statement fixing a 40-hour week he had formed a written contract that could not be varied (see page 318).

This was because he confirmed in writing that he had received a new contract of employment setting out the terms and conditions of his employment. The decision has been widely criticised and the EAT's view in *System Floors* reflects current thinking:

> In the absence of an acknowledgement by the parties that the statement is itself a contract and that the terms are correct (such as that contained in the *Mercer* case), the statutory statement does not itself constitute a contract in writing.

In *System Floors* itself, an employer successfully challenged his own statement as to the date a worker started employment by producing other information which showed the worker's service was a week short of the one year required for a claim of unfair dismissal.

If you refuse to sign and are sacked you can claim unfair dismissal, as a bartender at Yates's Wine Lodge in Blackpool did. He consulted his union and refused to sign a statement foisted on to him after seven months' service. He was sacked, not uncoincidentally, after he started organising for USDAW (*Turner v Yates Bros* 1972 (IT)).

If you sign, make sure management sign too.

Changing the statement
No change in your contract can be made unless you agree, or agree to changes being made automatically following collective agreement with your union. But once changes have been agreed the EPCA requires management to notify you formally within one month. They must give you a written note or show it to you and keep it in a place that is reasonably accessible to you. **Demand your own copy**.

If your original statement says that changes will be recorded automatically in some specific way – for example, following a Joint Industrial Council (JIC) agreement – it is not obligatory to inform you, although you are still entitled to see all the changes made. You should insist on your union giving you the information.

2. Itemised pay statement
Most workers have the right to get an itemised pay statement. Merchant seafarers, share fishers and people who work less than 16 hours a week (plus exceptions – see page 468) are excluded. It is not explained why such workers should not have an equal right to know where their money goes.

Section 8 of the EPCA 1978 says you must get an itemised pay statement every time you are paid. The statement must set out:

- gross wages
- fixed deductions
- variable deductions
- net wages
- method and amounts of payment if it is not all paid in the same way.

If you have several fixed deductions, such as union contributions, rent, or payments under an attachment-of-earnings court order, management need not specify each separate amount. They must state the total amount of all your fixed deductions each payday *and* give you a standing written statement once a year specifying the amount of *each* fixed deduction, the intervals at which it occurs and its purpose.

How to get a pay statement
If you do not get a statement, or think the statement is inaccurate, you can apply to an industrial tribunal **within three months** to get a declaration of what particulars should be given.

If management make any deduction without giving you a pay statement, even if they have not broken your contract the tribunal can order them to repay any amount deducted in the 13 weeks prior to your claim. A threat of legal action could therefore be useful in getting a pay statement.

■ A local government worker was advanced £111 for exam fees. He knew that if he failed, or resigned within a year, he would have to pay it back. He gave notice but objected to paying back the money all at once. The employers deducted the £111 from one of his salary cheques under the heading of 'miscellaneous deductions'. This was not a properly itemised pay statement and therefore the deduction was unlawful. As he suffered no financial loss (he knew he had to pay) the tribunal ordered the employers to pay him £25. *Milsom v Leicestershire C.C.* 1978 (IT)

3. Collective agreements

As we shall see (page 316), bits of a collective agreement can be sucked into your own contract if you have agreed to this. This generally happens with wages, hours, holidays and other **substantive terms.** It does not usually apply to purely **procedural terms** of the collective agreement specifying, for example, a health and safety grievance procedure, or the procedure for avoiding disputes. Consequently, it would be difficult to say you broke your contract if you did not carry out procedure. But the law is unclear on this point and the courts could conceivably decide against you.

Changes in terms and conditions negotiated in a substantive collective agreement will change the individual contracts of employment. But a unilateral change in, or termination of, the agreement does not automatically change contracts and you can challenge any attack on your conditions.

■ Meter readers and collectors employed by North Thames Gas received an incentive bonus of about £400 a month, amounting to more than one-third of their total pay. The scheme was negotiated by their union (GMB/MATSA) and was referred to in the written statement of terms of each employee. Management gave the union six months' notice to terminate the agreement embodying the scheme. The union members said this was a breach of contract and successfully urged the Appeal Court to stop this change. *Robertson v British Gas* 1983 (CA)

The importance of individual contracts was stressed by Lord Justice Ackner:

> It is true that collective agreements . . . create no legally enforceable obligation between the trade union and the employers. Either side can withdraw. But their terms are in this case incorporated into the individual contracts of employment, and it is only if and when those terms are varied collectively by agreement that the individual contract of employment will also be varied. If the collective scheme is not varied by agreement, but by some unilateral abrogation or withdrawal or variation to which the other side does not agree, then it seems to me that the individual contracts of employment remain unaffected.

4. Wages Councils, arbitration awards and incomes policy
Wages Councils and Statutory JICs can make orders for minimum rates that must be observed. These are automatically incorporated into your contract if you are in an appropriate industry.

Terms and conditions awarded by the Central Arbitration Committee (CAC) take effect as part of every affected worker's contract. The CAC awards terms and conditions in claims for equal pay and disclosure of information.

The government's incomes policy can also affect your contract of employment. Under the incomes policies of 1972–74 and 1975–78 employers were protected from some actions for breach of contract.

5. Works rules
The law on works rules is a mess. Sometimes they form part of your contract, sometimes they don't. Because they are so varied it is impossible to give anything but general guidelines.

The rules are likely to be in your contract if you sign them, or if they are posted in notices in your workplace. They can also be **implied terms** of your contract if they are so well-known in the trade in your area that both you and management are assumed to know they will form part of your contract. If you do not abide by contractual works rules you are breaking your contract.

If you don't sign the rules, or if you register your objection to, say, some of the disciplinary offences, you may prevent them forming part of your contract. Even if you do sign the rules, they don't always become contractual. In the railway workers' work-to-rule in 1972 (see page 387) the courts considered the British Rail rules. The Court of Appeal said that although the rules were signed by every worker they were not contractual. **But they were instructions about how the railway workers should do their job.** Provided they were lawful and reasonable they had to be obeyed.

The differences between a contractual rule and a lawful instruction are:

- A contractual rule can be altered only with your consent. Instructions can be changed without consultation or agreement.
- By sticking to a contractual rule, you are merely *carrying out* your contract. If you disobey instructions which are lawful and reasonable you are *breaking* your contract.
- If you interpret instructions in a way which is so unreasonable that it creates chaos, or in a way which has the effect of 'wilfully disrupting the system the efficient running of which you are employed to ensure', you are breaking your contract – for instance, the railway workers' work-to-rule.

Since you are likely to be bound by works rules either because they are contractual, or because they are reasonable and lawful instructions, it is often advisable for your union to negotiate with management over them. You can in this way also negotiate rules which are binding on management – to test machinery, supply safety equipment, and guarantee rest periods, for instance.

6. Custom and practice
In many jobs custom and practice govern workplace relations as effectively as written agreements. A custom may be so well known that it is not worth putting in writing, or it may suit management and unions to keep the arrangements relatively loose. In law, a custom can be binding if it meets three conditions.

- It must be 'notorious' so that it is almost universally observed and everyone involved knows about it;

- It must be reasonable (although the courts have often taken the employers' view of this); and
- It must be so certain that you know exactly what effect the custom has on you.

The major areas in which custom and practice are relevant are dealt with as they arise elsewhere in this book, so a brief look here at some examples is sufficient.

On *discipline*, lower wages were to be paid to Lancashire weavers for bad work. This practice was even supported by the weaving unions, who obtained a special exemption from the Truck Acts which would make these deductions illegal (see page 48). In 1931 Thomas Sagar challenged the practice but the Court of Appeal said he had gone to work fully knowing of it, as did every weaver in the trade in Lancashire. The practice was reasonable and its application was clear. So the management were able to refuse to pay full wages for work *they* considered sub-standard.

On *notice*, the old cases show that workers in some trades and domestic service are entitled to a month's notice, to be given on the first day of the month. This custom overrides the right to minimum notice under the EPCA if it provides longer notice.

On a custom of *negotiating* rates, Charles Wallace showed that there was a custom for negotiations over rates to precede any pipe-bending work he did and successfully claimed unfair dismissal when management refused to negotiate (see pages 223–24).

A custom of *providing work* was acknowledged by the courts in 1906. Mr Devonald, a steelworker on piece-work, was laid off for two weeks during slack trading, and then given four weeks' notice, as required by agreement. Management tried to show that by custom and practice they had a right to lay off workers whenever they felt trade was bad. But the Court of Appeal conceded that 'the workman has to live', and should be given the opportunity of piece-working during his notice – *Devonald v Rosser* 1906 (CA).

7. Employers' general obligations
There are general obligations under the common law that are *implied* in every contract of employment, even though nothing is written or even mentioned. These include the duty:

- to pay wages and salaries
- not to make unauthorised deductions
- (in some cases) to provide work
- to provide a safe system of work
- to obey the law
- to allow time off.

There is no duty to provide holidays or references.

Wages and salaries

If you have done the work, you are entitled to be paid. If you are hired and then not taken on, or given only a few days' work, you are entitled to be paid the amount you would have received had management not broken their contract – at least up to the value of your notice money.

The way in which 'a week's pay' is calculated for assessing your entitlement to many of the rights in this book is explained in chapter 19.

Failure to pay wages or to pay on time is usually a fundamental breach of contract equivalent to tearing it up, although management's *intentions* are relevant. A management consultant who quit because his pay cheque was a month late could not claim that he had been constructively dismissed, because he knew his employers were anxious to pay and that his pay was dependent on them receiving a payment from Argentina (*Adams v Charles Zub Associates* 1978 (EAT)). On the other hand, a representative paid a salary and a percentage commission on sales was entitled to claim when management unilaterally substituted a scheme based on reaching specific targets. This altered the basis of remuneration in a way which went to the root of the contract and was therefore unlawful (*R.F.Hill v Mooney*1981 (EAT)).

Backdated pay increases

Negotiations on pay increases often carry on after the normal settlement date. In most cases the agreement, when made, is backdated to the settlement date. If you are working on both these dates you will get your back pay either because the agreement specifically provides for this, or because it is a long-established custom, but if you leave before the agreement is concluded you may not be entitled to your money. The absence of an authoritative court decision probably indicates that most workers who apply for increased back pay get it. The legal position is, however, unclear.

Once your contract is ended there is nothing on which the subsequently-negotiated pay rise can bite. Nor is it likely that a court would imply a term into your contract that you should be paid some higher but unknown rate, because there is too much uncertainty. In the *Leyland* case (below) the EAT said union members got increased back pay only because of the clear agreement to this effect made at the time the wages were settled, and not because they worked each week both for the old rate and also under an implied agreement for a subsequent increase.

There are several ways to ensure you get the money. In collective agreements you should specifically provide for leavers to receive back pay. You could also seek agreement with management before you leave. Or you could agree individually to accept the employer's latest offer. If a Wages Council order has been made but not implemented before you leave, you are entitled to the new rate as this is automatically incorporated into your contract. If you are covered by a national or regional agreement which has been reached but not implemented, you can claim the increase. All of these methods avoid the legal problem created by not knowing exactly what the new rate is.

The position is different, however, when you are claiming increases in payments made under the EPCA 1978, for example, for maternity, unfair dismissal basic awards, redundancy and notice pay. Here, the EAT has said that the rate in force at the time you leave is conclusive.

■ Five workers at BL Bathgate took voluntary redundancy in March, 1980, with payments based on the then current rates. The annual wage negotiations were settled in April, backdated to January. BL mailed them the difference in back pay on the new rates. The EAT said that, *for the purposes of notice and redundancy pay*, EPCA Schedule 14 required the calculation to be based on 'the week's pay which is payable under the contract of employment' on the date they left. It rejected the argument that this was the old rate of pay plus £x i.e. the increase subsequently negotiated, because at the time of leaving this figure was not known and couldn't therefore affect the contract then in force. *Leyland Vehicles v Reston* 1981 (EAT)

The EAT could not use EPCA 1978 to stretch the workers' service by the length of their statutory notice to a date beyond the settlement date and so get the increased pay. Section 90 (3), designed to stop employers sacking you before you qualify for unfair dismissal or redundancy rights, affects length of service, but the rate of pay on the date you leave is still the figure for calculating statutory pay settlements.

Deductions

Deductions from wages must be made for PAYE income tax, social security contributions and attachment-of-earnings court orders.

Deductions from your pay may be outlawed by the Truck Acts. Dating from 1831, these prevent employers paying in kind (truck) for work done, and allow deductions to be made only for certain specified purposes. Payments in tickets exchange-able only at the company store – the old butty shop – is illegal. The Acts today give rise to a number of problems: **1.** who is covered, **2.** how payment is made, **3.** exceptions and **4.** enforcement.

1. The Acts apply only to 'artificers' and 'workmen engaged in manual labour'. It is often difficult to draw the line if you do manual and non-manual work but a (rather unhelpful) rule has been laid down that you are covered if the manual work you do is your 'real and substantial' employment, but not if it is merely incidental or accessory to it. In other words, is the manual part more important than the mental? So the courts have applied the Acts to sewing machinists, bus drivers who do some repair work, and TV repairers, but not to bus conductors, typists, hairdressers, railway guards and shop assistants, although some parts dealing with deductions and fines *do* apply to shop assistants.

2. The 1831 Act says how wages are to be paid:

> The entire amount of the wages earned by or payable to any artificer . . . in respect of any labour done by him . . . shall be actually paid to any such artificer in the current coin of this realm, and not otherwise; and payment . . . by the delivering to him of goods or otherwise than in the current coin . . . is hereby declared illegal null and void.

It can be paid in notes, but payment by cheque, postal order or money order or into a bank account is forbidden unless you request it in writing and management agree. And an Act of 1883, expressing the worst of Victorian fears, says: 'No wages shall be paid to any workman at or within any public-house, beer-shop or place for the sale of any spirits, wine, cyder or other spirituous . . . liquor.' Bar staff are exempt.

3. There are many exceptions. You can agree to a deduction if the amount is forwarded direct to someone you appoint – your union, or a charity, or a Christmas club, for instance. Management are entitled to make deductions for medicine, fuel, tools, materials, rent, food and hay for your horse! But the sums must be agreed in writing, reflect the true value of the goods and, for tools, be audited every year. Wages Councils can specify maximum lodging allowance deductions. Deductions for fines and damaged goods are subject to stricter controls – see page 93. No deduction can be made for supplying equipment needed under safety legislation (HSWA 1974 section 9).

4. The Acts are enforced (if that is the right word) by the Wages Inspectors of the DE. On conviction in the magistrates court management can be fined £200 for each offence. But this doesn't give *you* any money. You have to sue in the county court for your proper wages. The fact that you may have agreed to deductions being made does not prevent you suing. Such agreements are illegal.

Similar laws to the Truck Acts apply to seafarers and textile workers.

Cashless payment of wages has long been encouraged by employers as a means of saving costs and increasing working time. Support was given to this drive by a county court judge in *Brooker v Charrington Fuel Oils* (1981) who said that payment by Giro-cheque or cash cheque was equivalent to cash. A union had agreed in principle to cashless payment and 70 per cent of the members had acceded, but a supervisor who refused had it imposed on him. The judge rejected the arguments that a cheque cashable at a post office or bank is not the same as cash and that the new system was inconvenient. This is clearly a wrong interpretation of the Truck Acts. But since the case concerned a supervisor not covered by the Acts, and since county court judgments are not binding in other courts, the decision has no force.

The Payment of Wages Act 1960 permits you to agree in writing to cashless pay, but you can revoke this by giving four weeks' notice. Section 6 of the Act says it is unlawful for management to make agreement to cashless pay a condition of employment. A unilateral change would entitle you to claim you had been constructively dismissed.

The government proposed to repeal the Truck Acts and bring in limited tribunal protection for all workers by 1985.

If you are not protected by any statute you can sue in a county court for any improper deductions, but management are not guilty of a criminal offence. So all white-collar and many blue-collar workers are at risk. Your rights to written particulars of your contract, and itemised pay statements, are no substitute for a clear and well-policed Act preventing deductions from every worker's wages. The Truck Acts are a shambles and should be replaced by an Act applying to all workers enforceable in tribunals and criminal courts.

The Attachment of Earnings Act 1971 allows a court to order your employer to make deductions to pay a fine, family maintenance or judgment debt. The court decides your minimum earnings level which must be protected. Management are entitled to deduct up to 50p for administration and must give you a written statement of the total deduction – see also page 41 for itemised pay statements.

The Act does not apply to Scotland, where the Wages Arrestment Limitation Acts 1870 and 1960 permit limited deductions for debt.

Following the amendment of EPCA 1978 section 23 by the 1982 Employment Act, the deduction of a sum equivalent to union dues is victimisation for refusing to join a union (page 337).

Overpayment

If you are *overpaid* one week due to a clerical error, it may be unreasonable for management to recoup the whole amount the following week. Certainly, you are obliged to pay it back but management cannot use their control over your wages to extract what is in fact a civil debt. Mistakes of this kind are generally rectified by agreement to staged deductions over a period of time. Every deduction must be properly itemised – see page 41.

There are circumstances, however, where it is unfair for management to reclaim all or part of the overpayment. These are when

1. you are led to believe you are entitled to the money *either* by the fact that you have been paid it, *or* by management's statement that it is due to you;
2. without knowing about the mistake, you changed your position in that you spent more money than you otherwise

would either on normal living expenses and day-to-day bills, or on commitments involving a change in your normal way of life; and

3. you are not to blame for the mistaken overpayment.

■ Because of a clerical error in programming the payroll computer, Harold Howlett, a council gym teacher, was overpaid £1,007 during two years of sickness prior to his retirement in 1976. He had spent most of it by the time the council told him of the mistake and asked for it back. It had gone on normal living expenses, a new suit and a better second-hand car worth £470 on HP. His higher income had precluded him from claiming social security benefits. The judges said it would be unfair to demand the money back – he had been led to believe the money was his and he had made commitments on the strength of it. Nor did he have to prove that he had spent all of the money. *Avon County Council v Howlett* 1983 (CA)

You are also entitled to hold on to money paid to you if management has made a mistake *of law*. For example, if they think you are entitled under the EPCA 1978 to 10 weeks' maternity pay (instead of six) or to guarantee pay above the £9.50 daily rate (1983/4), they have no legal right to require you to correct their mistake by handing back the difference.

Providing work

There is no right to work. Mr Justice Asquith said in 1940:

Provided I pay my cook her wages regularly she cannot complain if I choose to take all or any of my meals out. *Collier v Sunday Referee*

There are, though, three groups of workers who may be entitled to complain if they are not provided with work, even when they are being paid:

1. **Workers whose earnings vary according to their performance and attendance:** Anyone paid by results or commission, or on variable shift premiums or given the contractual opportunity to work overtime needs the physical opportunity to work. They work for basic wages and for the chance to earn extra.(See *Devonald v Rosser* page 45.)

2. **Skilled workers:** When Joseph Langston resigned from the AUEW at Chryslers in 1972, and was suspended on full pay for almost two years, he suceeded in his claim for a right to work.

He was held to be in category **1.** above, but Lord Denning in the Court of Appeal said that it was arguable that:

> in these days an employer, when employing a skilled man, is bound to provide him with work. By which I mean that the man should be given the opportunity of doing his work when it is available and he is ready and willing to do it. *Langston v AUEW* 1974.

3. Performers and writers: An actor or singer promised a leading part and then prevented from performing, and an editor not allowed to write, both lose the opportunity to gain publicity and enhance their reputation. They work for that as much as for the money in some cases.

Providing a safe system of work
Management are required to take reasonable care for your safety. This means providing:

- a safely operating system of work
- safe tools, plant and materials
- adequate supervision
- trained, efficient personnel

Management must take care not to expose you to risks that could be foreseen by a reasonable person. They will be liable for all the reasonably foreseeable consequences (such as injuries and loss of earnings) of any failure to take this care. They have a general contractual obligation to act reasonably in dealing with safety, and complaints must be investigated 'promptly and sensibly'. These duties exist in addition to the duties imposed by the health and safety legislation.

■ Mrs Austin's work changed so that she needed to wear protective goggles. Because she wore glasses, she found the goggles impossible and asked for them to be made to her prescription. The company safety officer said he would look into it. After six months, nothing had happened so she resigned. The EAT said she had been constructively dismissed because the employers had not properly investigated her complaint, and she could no longer put up with the danger. *British Aircraft Corporation v Austin* 1978 (EAT)

■ Mrs Firth, aged 54, was a grinding machine operator in a small engineering factory. For two months during the bad winter of 1978/79 she had to work in temperatures found by a Health and Safety Inspector to be below 49°F. (The Factories Act 1961 requires at least 60°F.) After being kept outside for 25 minutes she quit, 'owing to freezing working conditions which I have to work in', she told management. The EAT said management had broken her contract in a fundamental way by failing for so long and in so serious a manner to provide a proper working environment. *Graham Oxley Tool Steels v Firth* 1980 (EAT)

They are also responsible for defective equipment that they have bought from some other firm if you are injured and can show that the defect was due to someone's fault elsewhere, even if you do not know whose – Employer's Liability (Defective Equipment) Act 1969.

If you are injured by the negligence of a fellow-worker you can also claim against your *employer* provided the act occurred in the course of employment. Since the Employer's Liability (Compulsory Insurance) Act 1969, all employers have to be insured against claims by injured workers.

Protecting your property

You are not covered if your property is stolen or damaged while you are working, unless management have failed to act following a number of similar incidents. If you want to protect your property against theft or breakages, and your employer's own insurance doesn't cover it, you could ask him/her to take out a separate policy, or force him/her to give you an undertaking to reimburse you.

A works rule or a notice on the wall or in the car park saying management are not responsible for loss or damage to your property is not always binding on you. They can escape liability for *negligence* only if it is 'reasonable' for the notice to apply, and this depends on your relative bargaining position, your awareness and what happens in practice – Unfair Contract Terms Act 1977.

All employers have a general duty to provide welfare arrangements that are, so far as is reasonably practicable, safe (HSWA 1974 section 2).

If you work in a factory, office or shop management must provide 'adequate and suitable accommodation' for non-working clothes (Factories Act 1961 section 59; Offices, Shops and Railway Premises Act 1963 section 12). This does not guarantee safety, but frequent thefts and damage would make the lockers 'inadequate'. You can sue and your employer can be prosecuted by the health and safety inspectors, or ordered to improve the arrangements.

Obeying the law

Management must obey the law. They are under a personal obligation to *you* which requires them to observe statutes.

■ Thomas Hill collided with a motor-cyclist while driving his employer's lorry. When the motor-cyclist was awarded damages, the court said Thomas's employer had to pay because he was legally obliged to comply with the law requiring compulsory insurance, and to indemnify his employees against losses. *Gregory v Ford* 1951 (HC)

The judge in this case said:

> There must be an implied term in the contract of service that the servant shall not be required to do an unlawful act . . . [and] that the employer will comply with the provisions of the statute.

This implied obligation can be very useful in situations where enforcement of the law by the authorities is minimal. If, for example, management are legally bound to you not to break the Health and Safety at Work Act, they are breaking your contract if they don't comply with it.

Time off

Lay representatives and members of recognised independent unions have the right to time off for union activities (see page 318). A legal right to time off is given in two other situations. Redundant workers can look for new work, or retrain (see page 273). And you can have time off for certain public duties.

Section 29 of the EPCA 1978 says employers must give you time off so that you can carry out your duties if you are a member of a

- magistrates' bench
- local authority
- tribunal
- health authority
- governing body for any maintained school or college
- water authority.

Duties include attending meetings of committees, sub-committees and other approved functions. No mention is made of time off for training for these duties, but you could argue that training is a necessary activity. The right does not extent to seafarers or to people who work less than 16 hours a week (plus exceptions, see page 468). Nor does it cover those (even quite lowly) civil servants whose terms of employment restrict their right to take part in certain political activities which may conflict with their official functions – EPCA section 138.

The amount of time you can get is that which is 'reasonable in all the circumstances', bearing in mind:

1. the amount of time required generally to carry out the duties, and any particular duty on any given day;

2. the amount of time off you have already had for union duties and activities; and

3. the effect of your absence on your employer's business.

Employers may use this catch-all phrase to try to stop working people taking up public positions. You could ensure fair treatment if you put these rights into collective agreements. British Nuclear Fuels, for example, agree to 24 *paid* days off a year for councillors and JPs.

The Act says nothing about pay for the days off you take. In most cases you receive payment from the body you attend. **But again you should use collective agreements to guarantee average earnings.**

How to claim time off for public duties

If you don't get time off you can apply to a tribunal **within three months.** See page 490 for the procedure. The tribunal can award compensation which relates to your loss and to your management's 'default'. Compensation in this case is small since you are not likely to have suffered a financial loss by being refused time off, but non-financial hardship can be considered.

Holidays

Wages Councils, Agricultural Boards and Statutory JICs fix holidays. In other industries in Britain there is no statutory right to *any* holidays, with or without pay, not even to bank holidays. Some Acts (such as the Factories Act) do require women and young people to be given days off, but nothing is said of payment, and anyway other days can be substituted. Holidays and holiday pay depend entirely on collective bargaining and management benevolence.

There is one exception. If you are given minimum notice which covers your holiday period, you can get holiday pay (EPCA 1978 schedule 3 para 2).

It has been decided by a county court that an hourly-paid employee is entitled to a day off on a statutory holiday, with pay if s/he is entitled to a guaranteed weekly wage, provided there is no contractual term or custom and practice saying otherwise.

■ BL agreed with the unions nationally that there would be local agreements on a shut-down of plants for the week over Christmas. At Swindon this was agreed to be done by transferring August and New Year's bank holidays, and taking a day's annual leave. Two TGWU members objected from the start, saying the company should concede the week anyway, took their August and New Year's holidays, and sued for normal pay on the days during Christmas week. The judge said they were entitled, despite a ballot and agreement from the majority of unions locally. The employers could not sack them for absence, or change the men's contracts which gave bank holidays or the written assurance they had previously received that no change would be made without the agreement of all local unions. *Tucker v BLMC* 1978 (Swindon County Court)

References

You have no legal right to a reference. If management write a false reference, you may not be able to sue them for libel because this type of correspondence is often protected. They could, however, be prosecuted under the Characters of Servants Act 1792. If they tell the truth, there is nothing you can do.

You do have a right to a **written statement** giving particulars of the reasons for your dismissal if you are sacked – see page 248.

Workers' general obligations

To work and co-operate

Your primary obligation is to turn up for work and personally do what you have agreed to do. You are not obliged to do more than your contract requires, so you do not have to work cheerfully, or with goodwill, or do overtime if you are not required by your contract to do so.

In the railway workers' case (page 387), Lord Denning found that workers are under an implied obligation 'not wilfully to disrupt' their employer's business. This is probably wrong because it is so wide and subjective ('wilfulness'). But it is a possible weapon for employers in a dispute.

Section 7 of the Health and Safety at Work Act says, in relation to any legal duty of your employer, that you must 'co-operate with him so far as is necessary to enable that duty to be . . . complied with'. This section has been desperately overplayed by employers. **Co-operation applies only to legal duties that are laid down in some Act or regulation.** Nevertheless, threats of legal action by employers against workers and safety representatives who refuse to submit to, say, new machinery or new working practices have ocurred. Employers say they are fulfilling their *general* duty to take reasonable care by introducing new, safer equipment. **But you should not allow them to override custom and practice without agreement.** Section 7 does not require you to co-operate in this way.

To obey orders

The courts say you must obey any lawful and reasonable instructions management give you. You are not required: **1.** to obey orders that are unlawful in that they involve you in some criminal or civil wrong, or **2.** to work on unsafe machinery, or **3.** to go outside the strict boundaries of your contract – working voluntary overtime, for instance.

Sackings following refusal to obey orders are a major source of unfair dismisal complaints. See page 221 for examples. The courts have occasionally upheld the sacking of workers refusing to obey an instruction to do something outside their contracts when the refusal was, in the employers' and courts' views, unreasonable. This *might* arise if in a temporary crisis you object to helping out on duties beyond the normal terms of your contract.

To take reasonable care

You must take reasonable care in the way you go about your work. If you do damage or cause injury because of your carelessness, and your employer loses money, you can be ordered to pay compensation. You are most unlikely to be sued for such losses but it has happened.

■ One day in 1949, Martin Lister, a Romford lorry driver, was reversing in a yard. He backed into his father, Martin Lister senior. People said he was negligent. Martin senior claimed against his employer on the grounds that he was responsible for the acts of his employees. Knowing that the company was insured, he expected to be paid. The company refused to pay so Martin senior went to court. The judge found that Martin junior had been careless, and that the company was responsible for his acts while in the course of his employment. He awarded £2,400 and costs, but said that Martin senior was himself partly to blame so he cut down the damages by a third to £1,600. The company then claimed off their insurance, which paid up. But then the *insurance company* forced the employers to sue Martin junior for the £1,600. He had an **obligation to take reasonable care** and to reimburse his employers if they lost money due to his lack of care. A majority of the House of Lords said OK. Martin junior was forced to pay his employers the amount *they had paid to his father*. *Lister v Romford Ice* 1957 (HL)

The practical impact of this case on industrial injuries is now minimal since most insurance companies have agreed not to force legal actions like this. It is bad for public relations. But as a principle it remains operative, and as an illustration of the judges' inhumanity it is a classic.

To be trustworthy

If you give away secret information about management's business you are breaking your contract which requires 'faithful service'. Information about your own conditions can be disclosed and is often essential to union organisation.

■ A union official as part of a campaign wrote to members who were pub managers asking 16 questions about their conditions and livelihood. A brewery complained that disclosure by the managers was a breach of their contractual duty of fidelity. The court said the members were free to pass on any information about their terms and conditions, but not to answer two questions about the pubs' takings or the wage bill of the managers' staff. *Bent's Brewery v Hogan* 1945 (HC)

Management and security staff have no special powers to deal with crime. *Any* citizen can arrest you if s/he reasonably suspects you are committing or have committed or attempted to commit an arrestable offence such as theft. S/he must call the police in immediately. If s/he is mistaken you can sue for damages or prosecute for false imprisonment.

If you are considered to be untrustworthy **your employer and** his/her security staff **are not entitled to search you unless you have agreed**, either generally in your contract, or on the occasion in question. You can resist with reasonable force. Only the police have the (limited) right to search.

Patents, copyright, inventions and your own work

You must work only for your employer during working hours. Your own time belongs to you, but this can be bought out if you agree that you won't work for anyone else while being employed by one employer. You can even agree to restrictions on your freedom to work once you leave. It is one of the many contradictions of capitalism that although the free market is paramount, workers who pick up experience, skill and ideas can be prevented from working for employers or from setting up on their own. Only if a written stipulation in your contract has the effect of starving you out will the courts say the restriction is an unjustifiable 'restraint of trade'.

■ In 1977 the English and international cricket authorities changed their rules and banned from Test and county cricket any player who signed for Kerry Packer's cricket circus. Three players and Packer challenged these rulings. The High Court said that the bans were in restraint of trade. They prevented players from earning a living during the winter months even though the cricket authorities guaranteed them no employment. The unlimited bans could not be justified in the interests of the players and the cricket authorities, or in the public interest. *Greig v Insole* 1977 (HC)

While you are working you are bound to pick up knowledge, experience and know-how and there is nothing to stop you using this for yourself or in a subsequent job. The law does not stop you competing with your former employers, only from using your personal knowledge of their secrets and customers to their disadvantage (*Spafax v Harrison* 1980 (CA)).

Many scientists, research workers, writers and teachers create new material, and there is often a clause in their contracts saying who owns what. If there is no such stipulation, the general rule for written material is contained in the Copyright Act 1956. This says management have the copyright over everything you write in the course of your employment. Newspaper writers, though, retain their own copyright.

For inventions and patents, management get the benefit, but *only* if you are employed on your normal duties, or duties specifically given to you, and it is expected that an invention might occur, or if you have a *special obligation* to further management's interest (Patents Act 1977). If the invention is of outstanding benefit to management you have the right to claim a *fair share* of the profits. If the invention is just a minor part of your work, you own it even though you created it while at work for your employer.

Ending the contract

A very serious breach of contract, which goes to the root of the contract or shows that one side does not intend to be bound any longer by one or more of its essential terms, does not *automatically* end the contract. It gives the innocent party the option of going on with the contract *or* regarding the other side as having ended it. See pages 199–202 for examples. This is repudiation, or if management do it it is often called constructive dismissal. The contract can end if it is frustrated by an unforeseen event. It can end by termination, with or without notice, by either party. All of these are dealt with in chapter 10. If it is for a fixed period or for a specific task, the contract ends when this is completed.

Even though your contract is brought to an end by management giving you proper notice, you may still be entitled to claim a statutory right – discrimination, unfair dismissal, redundancy pay. See chapters 8, 10, 11.

Claims for breach of contract

For organised workers, the response to management's breach of contract should be negotiations or direct action. If you want to bring a legal claim you must sue in the county court or the High Court. You may get Legal Aid for advice and representation.

Since tribunals deal with statutory rights, common law claims by workers are rare. The courts have the power to order management to pay damages for losses you suffer for breach of contract. If you are dismissed, you can claim only the amount of notice money due to you. But for a *breach* of contract while you are still employed you can claim damages for any loss you sustain, and for physical or mental hardship which results from the breach.

■ Glyn Cox had been employed as an engineer for 20 years by

the same firm. When he complained about his salary level he was immediately given a job with less responsibility and vague duties but on the same pay. He became depressed, anxious, frustrated and ill, and was pressurised into resigning. He got five months' pay in lieu of notice as required by his contract. When he claimed damages the court said that as he had been paid his notice entitlement he could not get damages for the dismissal. But he got £500 for the distress he suffered when management broke his contract by changing his responsibilities. *Cox v Philips Industries* 1975 (HC)

Very rarely, the courts have given remedies to workers which have had the effect of continuing contracts of employment. In one case, a worker's contract was ordered to continue because the relationship of 'mutual trust' had not been broken – *Hill v Parsons* 1971 (CA). Or the correct procedure may not have been followed – see page 99. People who are 'office-holders', like police officers and some trade union officials, have also got the courts to give them the right to continue in office, instead of merely getting damages. But section 16 of TULRA 1974 prevents courts from making orders to compel people to work, and in practice courts don't order employers to keep workers on. Tribunals have power to order reinstatement (see page 246) but if management refuse to comply they can't be forced to take you back.

The Lord Chancellor and the Scottish Secretary have power to extend the jurisdiction of tribunals to cover some breach of contract claims. These are claims when you are also claiming some other right – for example, written particulars of your contract; or if you quit or are sacked – for example, arrears of wages (EPCA section 131).

Some breaches of contract are also criminal offences – orders to work with unsafe machinery, illegal deductions, underpayment in Wages Council industries. In these cases, inform the Health and Safety Inspector, or the Wages Inspector, and your union.

Management can sue you if you break the contract. In practice this rarely happens. The Coal Board did it in 1956 following a ban on Saturday working, and other employers have got injunctions in disputes (see page 398).

Collective action

The law of contract is concerned only with individuals. *In fact*, employment contracts depend heavily on collective agreements and custom and practice established by organised workers. **Your only hope of getting any movement towards equality of bargaining power in contracts of employment is by collective action.** The courts treat all aspects of your contract as though they have been agreed. By union organisation you can ensure that all aspects *are* negotiated and agreed.

Summary

1. Every employee has a contract of employment, even though there may be nothing written or signed.

2. You have rights before you make a contract of employment – rights connected with disablement, discrimination and 'spent' convictions.

3. Your contract may include some written terms – set out in a statement, collective agreement, Wages Council order, arbitration award or works rules.

4. Unwritten terms of contract can be implied from custom and practice in your industry.

5. Every contract of employment contains, unless specifically excluded, unwritten general obligations on employers – to pay wages, not to make deductions, to provide safe conditions.

6. Employees have general obligations too – to work, co-operate, obey reasonable instructions, take care and be trustworthy.

7. A contract can end by resignation, dismissal (with or without notice), very serious breach of contract which you decide you cannot tolerate, a totally unforeseen event which makes the contract impossible to carry out, or completion of the agreed task.

8. You can claim damages in the courts for breach of contract, but the courts rarely give you the right to be reinstated if you are sacked.

9. As an individual worker, the law of contract is stacked against you. Realistic steps towards control over your contractual conditions can be made only through collective action.

4. Sick pay and medical suspension

Your statutory and contractual right to be paid when sick / suspension on health and safety grounds / offers of alternative work away from hazards / how to claim your pay / collective action / and a summary.

Medical reasons may prevent you working in several ways. You may be incapable of work, or be advised by your doctor not to work, or you may decide that conditions are so unsafe that you refuse to work. Or you may be suspended by your employer for health and safety reasons.

Until 1983, sickness was regarded as a problem for the worker and not the employer. You had rights to social security benefits but no general claim against management for sick pay. In April 1983 the Tories introduced Statutory Sick Pay (SSP) as part of a campaign to cut civil service jobs and to privatise central government functions. The change was condemned by the TUC as being wholly inadequate and by employers' representatives for involving them in organising payments to sick workers.

If you are off work for medical reasons you have the right to social security benefits (see chapter 12) and pay from your employer in the following ways:

- under the SSP rules
- according to your contract of employment
- according to your rights under the Employment Protection Consolidation Act 1978 (EPCA) while you are suspended on medical grounds
- according to your rights under the EPCA if you are pregnant – see chapter 7.

Where to find the law

Statutory sick pay (SSP) is found in the Social Security and Housing Benefits Act 1982, the Statutory Sick Pay (General) and (Adjudication) Regulations 1982, SI Nos 894 and 1400; the right to written particulars of sick pay entitlement is given by the Employment Protection Consolidation Act 1978 (EPCA 1978) section 1; and medical suspension is covered by EPCA 1978 section 19 and schedule 1.

Statutory Sick Pay

In April 1983 the government introduced a radical new method of paying for short-term sickness. The Social Security and Housing Benefits Act 1982 and the detailed Regulations issued under it continued the government's commitment to breaking up the welfare state. The scheme provides a flat rate benefit of up to £40.25 (from April 1983), according to earnings, for most workers off sick for up to eight weeks. In this section the levels and duration of benefit should be regarded by organised workers as minimum rights with scope for substantial improvements to be negotiated. Many aspects of the scheme are expressly left to be negotiated and agreed between workers and employers.

SSP rarely provides better benefits than freely negotiated sick pay arrangements which operate in tandem with DHSS sickness benefit. Indeed, the introduction of SSP meant a decrease in take-home pay to most workers, because you pay tax and national insurance on SSP but not on sickness benefit. Although all SSP payments are reimbursed to employers, they too pay national insurance on your SSP, whereas none is due on sickness benefit, and they shoulder the additional administrative burdens of running the scheme for the government.

Who gets SSP?

As a general rule you get SSP when you are off sick for four days. This is a period of incapacity for work (PIW) but the first three are waiting days and do not generate payment. If you do not get SSP, or have exhausted your entitlement, you may get DHSS sickness benefit if you have paid the appropriate amount of social security contributions.

Workers are excluded from SSP in the following circumstances:

1. Low earnings: people who earned on average in the eight weeks before going sick less than the 'lower earnings limit'. This is the level below which you do not pay social security contributins and from April 1983 it was £32.50. Part-timers, particularly women, are most at risk.

2. Casual or short-term contracts: these are contracts for a specified period of three months or less. If you actually work beyond this you are covered. If you have two short contracts separated by eight weeks or less you can aggregate them to give you SSP from the date you *agree to*, or in fact work, more than 13 weeks.

3. Over pension age: 65 (men) or 60 (women) at the *start* of your PIW. You are still covered if your birthday occurs while you are off sick.

4. Pregnancy: SSP is not payable during the time that maternity allowance (see page 120) is available, that is for 18 weeks following the 11th week before your expected week of confinement. If you work during this time you do not get SSP or maternity allowance.

5. Recent claims: if you claimed sickness, invalidity, maternity or (very rarely) unemployment benefits in the 57 days before sickness you will be notified by the DHSS that SSP is not available. Chapter 12 explains these benefits.

6. Industrial action: if you go sick during a stoppage of work you get no SSP unless you have no direct interest in the dispute. If your PIW started before the stoppage you do get SSP. Since some PIWs are linked together, you may get SSP if a stoppage occurs between two spells of sickness – see below.

7. Abroad: you can get SSP if you are abroad in an EEC country (including Gibraltar) but not elsewhere.

8. SSP exhausted: once you have used up your entitlement in any tax year your SSP stops.

9. No work done: you are excluded if you have done no work at all under your contract. As soon as you do even a few minutes' work, you qualify for SSP.

After you have been off for four days in any of the above circumstances management must let you know if you are excluded from SSP. They must hand or post you a form SSPI (E) within seven days. The form requires them to say why they are not paying and it contains a form on which you can claim DHSS sickness benefit. See page 287 for industrial injuries.

How long does SSP last?

It is payable on the fourth *qualifying day* (QD) of sickness, as explained below, and it lasts for up to eight weeks in any tax year. You cannot get more than eight weeks' SSP in any one PIW, so sickness straddling April 5 does not entitle you to, say, 16 weeks. Two or more PIWs can be linked to form a single PIW if the gap between them is no more than two weeks. Each PIW must of course be of at least four days.

Qualifying days

You get SSP only on days when you are incapable of work and the day is agreed as a qualifying day. Only QDs count as waiting days. Frequently, QDs are the same as the days you normally work, for example Monday to Friday, but they can be any combination of days. If you decide – and it is a matter for negotiation and agreement – that you will have seven QDs, Sunday to Saturday, you will get through your three waiting days (which must be QDs) more quickly. But the daily amount of SSP will be one seventh of the weekly rate for periods of less than one week. In general the scheme is less confusing if you agree *either* the same specified days each week, *or* the days on which you are required to work, which will vary according to shift patterns. You must have at least one QD a week, and you can have QDs while on holiday.

Notification and certification

These are separate issues. You must *notify* management, in whatever way they specify, that you are sick. They may then require reasonable evidence to *certify* you are sick. Notification can be required by telephone, or by a friend, or in writing but not by a specific time or before the first QD, nor more than once a week.

If you are late in complying with management's rules on notification for SSP, they are entitled to withhold SSP for the late qualifying days. This is management's option, not a requirement on them, and they can withhold pay only if they think you have no 'good cause' for lateness.

The way in which you prove you were sick is not specified in the SSP rules. Management can require 'reasonable evidence' and the DHSS says that self-certification introduced in 1982 is reasonable for days 4 to 7 and a medical certificate thereafter. Self-certification on either DHSS forms or forms drawn up by your employer can be used for SSP, but only the DHSS form is appropriate for DHSS sickness benefit.

If management dispute your incapacity they can refuse to pay. You should use the grievance (or disciplinary) procedure to challenge the decision and immediately involve your union, as it might be part of a wider attack on other workers' absences. You can demand a written statement of their reasons and you have rights of appeal to a DHSS insurance officer, local tribunal and Social Security Commissioner (see page 293).

Management cannot demand a report from your or any other doctor without your consent. The DHSS says that a medical certificate is usually conclusive unless there is evidence to the contrary. See, for example, *Hutchinson v Enfield*, page 220. Special rules apply after you have had four spells of self-certified absence during any 12-month period. If management doubt that your absences are genuine they can report you to the DHSS. The DHSS will write to you saying that you should see your doctor the next time you are sick. With *your* consent your doctor will be asked to send a report to the DHSS regional medical officer.

The next time you are sick, that is the fifth spell, management can suspend SSP if they think your absence is not genuinely due to sickness. The DHSS doctor will report to the insurance officer and you have the usual rights of appeal. This procedure clearly involves substantial collusion between employers and the government in the control of workplace absence. You should therefore be conscious of the consequences of repeated self-certified sickness. Remember that the procedure is not automatic – management decide whether your absence is genuine, and whether to report you after four absences. You should challenge this action through your grievance (or, possibly more appropriately, disciplinary) procedure.

Certificates from people other than medical practitioners, such as osteopaths, homeopaths, Christian Scientists, acupuncturists and midwives, are 'reasonable evidence' of incapacity. You can get SSP if as a precaution you are advised by a doctor not to work. This includes pregnant women and carriers of infectious diseases.

In all cases the incapacity must be for a whole day, so you are not eligible if you are taken ill after you have started work. For night-shift workers on shifts spanning midnight, your working day is deemed to be the day on which the shift *started*.

Employers are required to keep records of all sickness absences of four days or more and of each employee's QDs in each of these periods. All SSP payments must be recorded and a return filed with annual statements of pay, tax and national insurance. You can demand a written statement of your SSP over any past period.

How much SSP?
From April 1983 the levels of SSP depended on earnings as follows:

Normal weekly earnings	Weekly rate of SSP
Less than £32.50	—
£32.50 to £48.49	£27.20
£48.50 to £64.99	£33.75
£65.00 and over	£40.25

The value of SSP for fractions of a week depends on how many QDs you have agreed for that week.

When SSP ends
You are not entitled to SSP after you leave your job, or after your annual SSP entitlement is exhausted. In these cases management must smooth the transition to DHSS sickness benefit by giving you a transfer form – SSP1 (T) – on which you can make a claim. If management sack you to avoid paying SSP you have a right to the money. A sacking in these circumstances would also be an unfair dismissal – see page 211.

SSP and occupational sick pay
Since most workers are covered by an occupational sick pay scheme negotiated by unions or granted by employers the relationship between it and SSP is important. Employers are required to 'offset' SSP against any contractual earnings payable for a period of sickness. If your agreement provides more money than SSP, you do not get SSP on top. If your agreement provides less than SSP you get the full SSP and management can offset the whole of your occupational sick pay against it. Offsetting is required only if 'contractual remuneration' is payable on the days when SSP is due. So discretionary payments are not offset – you can get SSP *on top* of an *ex gratia* payment.

You can also get SSP on top of *contractual* payments if you have more QDs than working days.

■ **Example:** You work a five-day week. Sick pay is £15 a day, £75 a week. But you have agreed to seven QDs a week so you are entitled to SSP for seven days in any week. You go sick on Wednesday 1 June and return to work on Monday 13 June. Wednesday 1 to Friday 3 are three waiting days under SSP and your contractual scheme. Saturday and Sunday do not count for contractual sick pay but *do* qualify for SSP at 2/7ths of the weekly rate. Management must offset the remaining 5/7ths against the £75 contractual sick pay from Monday 4 to Friday 10.

W Th F	S S	M T W Th F	S S
waiting days	£5.75 £5.75	£15 £15 £15 £15 £15	£5.75 £5.75
	(SSP)	(offsetting £28.75 SSP)	(SSP)

As can be seen, you are better off by £23 SSP if, in the above work pattern, you have agreed to seven instead of five QDs.

Contractual rights to sick pay

The contractual position is that **if sick pay is provided for by your contract – whether it is specified in writing, orally agreed, implied from custom and practice or incorporated from a collective agreement – the courts will uphold your legal right to sick pay.**

We have seen (page 38) that management must give you written particulars of any terms and conditions relating to sickness and injury. If there are no such terms, the statement must say that. If you don't get a written statement, or disagree with one you do get, you can complain to a tribunal.

Collective bargaining has achieved some basic entitlement to sick pay for about 80 per cent of all workers. The rest must rely on common law or the 'charity' of their employers.

If you can't get sick pay through collective bargaining, or by drawing attention to the fact by demanding written particulars, the courts can use their power to decide that you are covered. When the Lord Chancellor gives tribunals the jurisdiction to hear breach of contract claims, *tribunals* will decide this (EPCA section 13).

Courts and tribunals firstly ask about what was discussed at the time you were hired, what in fact occurred to you and others at your workplace, and then look at custom and practice in the industry. If that fails to show whether or not sick pay is provided, courts and tribunals *may* assume that pay should continue as usual during sickness. One judge said that a production manager in a skirt factory was entitled to be paid his basic rate and his bonus while he was off sick for two months. The judge said:

> Where the written terms of the contract of service are silent as to what is to happen in regard to the employee's rights to be paid whilst he is absent from work due to sickness, the employer remains liable to continue paying so long as the contract is not (terminated) by proper notice, except where a condition to the contrary can properly be inferred from all the facts and the evidence in the case. If the employer – and, of course, it will always be the employer – seeks to establish an implied condition that no wages are payable, it is for him to [prove it]. *Orman v Saville Sportswear* 1960 (HC)

That strong statement was modified in *Mears v Safecar* (page 40), so that sick pay is to be assumed only if there is no contrary conclusion to be drawn from the circumstances of your employment and from what your employer and you in fact did. In the same way as courts and tribunals can say what period of lay-off is reasonable (see *Dakri v Tiffen* page 77), they can also say that when management are obliged to pay sick pay it will continue for a *reasonable* period of time. In the absence of a specified period in your contract you can look at the practice and agreements in your industry, and factors such as your length of service are relevant in deciding what is reasonable – *Howman & Son v Blyth* 1983 (EAT).

So in the absence of any definite evidence about what is to happen during sickness, you are entitled to the benefit of the doubt.

Sick pay and social security benefits

Courts have held that social security benefit for sickness is **additional to,** not **instead of,** any contractual rights. The DHSS can't reduce your benefit if you get sick pay. Many employers, however, insist on deducting social security benefit from sick pay, despite the fact that you have paid for your social security benefit with your contributions. You should therefore fight any attempt by management to offset social security benefit against sick pay.

Sickness while under notice
Regardless of your contractual position, or of your rights to SSP, management are under a *further* statutory obligation to pay you during sickness when

- you are entitled to the minimum notice under the EPCA 1978 or up to one week extra
- you are given notice and
- you go sick while serving your notice (EPCA section 50 and schedule 2).

■ **Example:** You have been employed for four-and-a-half years. You are entitled to a minimum of four weeks' notice under the Act. If your contract gives you five weeks or less, you can get paid for all those weeks, even if you are sick and even if your contract gives no right to sick pay. But if your contract gives you a right to six or more weeks' notice (that is, more than one week above the minimum) you don't have a right to sick pay under the EPCA 1978.

Suspension on health and safety grounds

Suspension or dismissal?
What if management tell you not to come to work for the sake of your own or other people's health? You can claim reinstatement or compensation for unfair dismissal (see page 216). If you are sacked following a doctor's examination under regulations listed in the EPCA 1978 schedule 1 (as amended by the Employment Protection Medical Suspension Order 1980 SI No 1581) dealing with lead, rubber, chemicals and radioactive substances, or approved codes, you can claim unfair dismissal, provided you have one month's service (not one year as usually needed for unfair dismissal). These regulations generally require employers to remove workers from exposure to certain substances following examination by a medical adviser from the Employment Medical Advisory Service (EMAS).

For example, in the case of ionising radiation, workers must be taken off their normal job if their film-badges show that certain limits have been exceeded. An EMAS doctor must tell your employer if your health would be endangered by continued exposure to lead or other chemicals.

Dismissal following a doctor's recommendation under one of the regulations or codes may be unfair, since suspension will be the more reasonable solution. If the plant is closed down as a result of many of you being suspended, you may get **redundancy money** and **medical suspension pay.**

The rules on suspension are just the same as those applying to suspension for discipline and shortage of work. **Employers have no right to suspend without pay unless your contract allows this.** See page 76. If it does and you are suspended, you may be entitled to medical suspension pay under the EPCA 1978.

Who can claim medical suspension pay?

Section 19 of the EPCA 1978 entitles you to be paid if you are suspended from work, or from work you normally do, by an employer who is acting in accordance with a doctor's report made under one of the regulations or codes described above. You have a right to medical suspension pay provided you have been employed for one month or more. Contracts for a fixed term of three months, or not expected to last more than three months, are excluded unless you actually work more than three months (section 19 of the EPCA 1978).

It is important to realise that this right is extremely limited. It does not come into operation if you are suspended for medical reasons not falling under one of the specific regulations. It may not apply to suspension following a prohibition or improvement notice issued by a Health and Safety Inspector, or situations where workers demand closure of part of a plant for safety reasons. You may have to negotiate *ad hoc terms* in these circumstances but if you are suspended you can argue:

1. You have a contractual right to be paid unless your contract says otherwise. Failure to pay is breach of contract and it may be the grounds for claiming constructive unfair dismissal (page 46).

2. If you refuse to work in conditions which violate a code of practice under Schedule 1 of the EPCA 1978, you can treat yourself as suspended.

3. If management force you to work in unsafe conditions contrary to the HSWA 1974 or any regulation, they are breaking your contract and you can claim as in **1.** above and report them to the Health and Safety Inspector.

You can claim medical suspension pay if you have been employed for four weeks or more. If you are actually incapable of work you are excluded. In other words, the right applies only if you are suspended because further exposure may be dangerous, and does not apply if things have got so bad that physically you cannot work. You have to claim sick pay under your contract, SSP and social security benefits. These may be worth less than medical suspension pay.

Alternative work
You won't get paid if management offer you suitable alternative work, whether or not it is work within your contract, and you unreasonably turn this down (section 20). Guidance on what this means can be found in the cases on redundancy (page 268). A general rule is that you are not obliged to take a cut in wages. But tribunals may say it is unreasonable to refuse a lower paid job on a *temporary* basis.

You may also lose your right to pay if you do not fall in with reasonable requirements your employer imposes for making sure you are available. Clearly, there is a danger here that established working arrangements could be disturbed under the threat of withdrawal of medical suspension pay, but the key word is 'reasonable'. For example, management may insist you don't go on holiday, or that you report regularly to your workplace. These might be reasonable requirements.

How much can you get?
You can get 'a week's pay' (see page 474) every week for up to 26 weeks. Management can offset this by any money they are bound to give you under your contract. *Ex gratia* payments can't be offset. If you are still not authorised to go back to your normal job, your statutory right runs out. It might be advisable to insert a clause in your collective agreement providing for pay during suspension on health and safety grounds. Payments under an agreement like this would be offset against your right under the Act, but they could last beyond the 26-week period.

Temporary replacements
If your job is taken over by another worker hired specifically for this purpose, s/he can be sacked when you return, provided s/he

was informed **in writing** at the time s/he was taken on that s/he would be sacked on your return. But management must still show they acted reasonably in actually carrying out the sacking – they must look for alternative vacancies, etc. However, if the replacement has not worked for more than one year s/he can't claim unfair dismissal.

How to claim

If you are refused pay you can make a claim to a tribunal **within three months.** See page 490 for the procedure. If you suceed, the tribunal must order management to pay you.

Collective action

The rights provided by the common law are not judge-proof and the statutory rights are puny. You can take sick pay out of the area of employer benevolence and into the area of workers' rights if you are organised. Only by union action can you guarantee your rights.

SSP is limited in value and scope, making the need for negotiated sick pay schemes paramount. Additional protection is required for **industrial injury**, and for workers laid off as a result of health and safety checks.

Summary

1. Your EPCA written statement must say what rights you have to sick pay.

2. At common law courts have said in that in the absence of any contrary evidence, employers are obliged to pay you during sickness for a reasonable time.

3. Under SSP you are entitled to eight weeks a year at levels which depend on average weekly earnings. But many workers, particularly part-timers and women, are excluded from SSP.

4. If you are not entitled to SSP you will be entitled to DHSS sickness benefit if you meet the conditions relating to social security contributions. **No contributions are required for industrial injury or disease, since benefit is available to all workers.**

5. You have a right to be paid for 26 weeks if management suspend you from your normal work following a doctor's report made under certain health and safety laws.

5. Lay-off and short-time

Your right to pay during a lay-off / where to find the law / contractual rights / guarantee payments / when you can claim them / who can claim / how much you get / suspending the guarantee / industrial disputes / collective agreements / how to claim a guarantee payment / the effect on social security benefits / trade union demands / lay-offs leading to redundancy / collective action / and a summary.

Many industries are covered by collective agreements which guarantee wages during temporary periods when work is not available. In fact, these agreements define the occasions when employers can *escape* paying wages. They apply mainly to manual workers.

The Employment Protection Consolidation Act 1978 (EPCA) gives workers the right to a minimum payment if they are laid off in certain circumstances. Longer term lay-off gives you the option of claiming redundancy pay.

Whether you negotiate collective agreements, or make *ad hoc* arrangements, or use your legal rights, your argument is the same. **Loss of production and disruption is a business risk assumed by employers. Workers should not suffer from lay-offs or wage cuts** when employers refuse to accept the consequences of the risk they have voluntarily undertaken in the name of profit.

Agreements or legal rights guaranteeing income security stand or fall according to three tests:

- do they provide adequate levels of remuneration while employment lasts?

- can they be suspended? and
- in what circumstances and with what warning can they be suspended?

Where to find the law

The 1978 Act deals with rights to guaranteed wages (sections 12–18) and redundancy pay following lay-off or short-time (sections 87–89).

Contractual rights

Your employer has no right to suspend you from work, to cut your minimum rate, to put you on short-time working or to lay you off unless this is provided for in your contract. See page 41. Without your agreement, management's action is a breach of contract, and in some cases you can treat this as grounds for claiming unfair dismissal and redundancy pay.

■ G. Smith, a supervisor, was told by management on 8 February 1974 that he was being suspended for two or three weeks and it might be the beginning of April before he would be back at work. On 20 February 1974, Mr Smith got work elsewhere. On 25 February 1974 he asked for and received his cards. He claimed redundancy pay. Lord McDonald said his contract didn't allow management to suspend him, he hadn't agreed to it, and it amounted to a sacking. *An employer is not entitled unilaterally to suspend his/her employee unless there is some provision express or implied in the contract of employment permitting him/her to do so* said the judge. G. Smith got his redundancy pay. *McKenzie v Smith* 1976 (Scottish Court of Session)

You can claim unfair dismissal and redundancy pay, or, if you go back to work, you have the right to be *paid* for the days you were suspended. If you agree to the suspension, or if your contract is governed by a collective agreement which gives management the right to suspend, their action is *not* illegal.

■ The engineering national agreement gives employers the right to suspend workers in certain circumstances. Burroughs Machines left the Engineering Employers' Federation (EEF). During a strike in one part of the company, workers were laid off in another. They claimed that as they were no longer covered by the national agreement, the company had no right to suspend them and that this amounted to dismissal. The court decided that the men's contracts still depended on the EEF as it was in force when they had been hired. So the employer could legally suspend them. *Burroughs Machines v Timmoney* 1977 (Scottish Court of Session, Inner House)

If the length of the permitted lay-off period is not specified, the courts will say it lasts only for a reasonable time, and this depends on the nature of the industry, the level of wages and the likely amount of your savings.

■ The contracts of nine women employed in the London rag trade allowed the company to lay them off 'temporarily' without pay if there was a shortage of work due to circumstances beyond its control. After four weeks off they wrote to the company saying they were entitled to redundancy pay and the following week registered tribunal claims. They slipped up in the technical procedure (see page 86) by not giving one week's notice. But the EAT said that the contract gave management the right to lay off only for a *reasonable* time. As they were on low wages, with limited savings, more than four weeks was unreasonable. They were therefore constructively dismissed and entitled to redundancy pay following the normal definition of dismissal on the grounds of redundancy. *A Dakri & Co v Tiffen* 1981 (EAT)

In contracts where employers do have the right to suspend workers or put them on short-time you have the right to claim a **guarantee payment** under the Act.

Guarantee payments

You can claim a guarantee payment from management under section 12 of the EPCA in two situations.

- your employer's need for the kind of work you do (or can be required to do) is lessened,
- an 'occurrence' affects normal working in relation to your job.

These situations include a fall in orders, bankruptcy of a customer, lack of raw materials and sudden temporary setbacks such as power failures, floods, fires, bad weather and some industrial disputes. But they don't seem to cover redundancy occurring as a result of your employer *ceasing* to carry on business. Here you would claim redundancy pay (see chapter 11) and it may be worth claiming a guarantee payment as well. If redundancy follows a lay-off, claim both.

If, as a result of one of the above events, you are not given work, you are entitled to payment. You must be deprived of work for a whole working day because the Act talks of 'workless days'. **This gives employers the chance to avoid payments.** All they have to do is call you in and give you work for a short period of time. This means you are not deprived of work throughout a normal working day so no payment is due, even though your earnings for the time you work are minimal. Refuse to leave the site, and claim your contractual right not to have your earnings reduced.

Payments are made for workless days, each day leading to a separate payment. This is sometimes going to be more beneficial than arrangements providing for a guaranteed weekly earnings level, because you could be laid off for two days and yet receive more for three days' work than you would under the weekly guarantee in your collective agreement. Under a daily assessment each day is treated as entitling you to the statutory payment. A day means from midnight to midnight, but if your working day would normally spread over midnight there are special rules. If you would normally work more hours before midnight than after, for instance on a 6 p.m. to 2 a.m. shift, the first day is regarded as the workless day. If you would normally work 8 p.m. to 4 a.m., or work more hours after midnight than before, the second day counts instead.

If the lay-off or short-time working continues you should bear in mind the circumstances in which this can itself constitute redundancy – see page 86.

Who can claim?

Share-fishers, dockers, and people who mainly work outside Great Britain can't claim. Some *groups* of workers are also deprived of the right to claim. These are:

- workers who have less than one month's continuous employment;
- part-time workers (that is, less than 16 hours a week with exceptions – see page 468);

- workers hired on fixed-term contracts of three months or less;
- workers who are hired for a particular job which is not expected to last more than three months.

If you actually work more than three months you *can* claim whatever your contract says or you previously were told by management. If you have no normal working hours on the day in question, such as a school cleaner during the school holidays or a sales rep, you are also excluded.

Why are all these workers excluded from the right to guarantee pay? The loss of a normal day's pay is no less serious just because you are on a short contract or have recently started a job, and indeed it is *more* serious since you may have been unemployed for some time previously.

The *practical* effect of these exclusions is that industries which are notoriously prone to insecurity and a high labour turnover such as building, civil engineering, ship-repair and catering remain uncovered by the law. Without union opposition, short-term contracts and early dismissals may actually increase as employers try to escape the obligation to make payments. So remember:

- A series of short-term contracts counts as continuous employment.
- If you work one year you can claim unfair dismissal. You will win if you can show management intended by short-term contracts to avoid their obligations – see *Terry v Sussex C.C.* (page 196).

How much is guaranteed?

Payments are not based on earnings but on a day's pay using the formula for 'a week's pay' (see page 474). The method is different for different workers.

1. If you work a regular number of hours each week. Take your basic rate and any bonus, commission and conditioned (that is, guaranteed) overtime and divide that figure by the number of hours you are required to work. This gives you your 'guaranteed hourly rate'. Your guarantee payment for any workless day, subject to the government maximum, is that rate multiplied by the number of hours you would normally have worked on that day.

■ **Example:** You get £2 an hour for a basic week of 39 hours. This comes to £78 + 10 per cent bonus (£7.80) + £3 attendance allowance. You work four days of eight hours and one day of seven hours. Your guaranteed hourly rate is:

$$\frac{78 + 7.80 + 3}{39} = £2.28$$

Your normal pay is £2.28 × 8 (or 7) or £18.24. But this is subject to the maximum figure in force (£9.50 in 1983/4). So you get only £9.50.

2. If your hours vary from day to day. Many office workers work flexitime or nine-day fortnights. They can work any hours (usually during the day, between say 8 a.m. and 8 p.m.) provided they do the stated number of hours each week, or fortnight or month. If you are laid off and your employer disputes the number of hours you would have worked you have to prove your entitlement.

3. If you are on shift, or regularly work different numbers of hours each week. Find your guaranteed hourly rate as in **1.** above, but instead of taking one week as the starting point, you look back over the 12-week period that ended the week before you were laid off. Calculate the average hourly rate. If you have recently started and therefore do not have 12 weeks' service you can look at the average hours you could have *expected* to work, and the hours done by comparable fellow-employees of your employer. If you have been absent through sickness, holidays or lay-off in the 12-week period you can look further back to make up 12 full weeks.

If you work nights, and you do more hours before midnight than after, you are deemed to be laid off on the day when you would have worked the longer hours.

■ **Example:** if you are laid off from 10 p.m. on Thursday to 8 a.m. on Friday the 'workless day' is Friday. This may operate against some workers, especially in engineering, who work four long nights and one short. You can't claim if you are laid off on your (short) Friday night as you have already claimed for the night before.

Altering normal hours
Sometimes contracts are altered temporarily during a lay-off by

agreement between management and unions. If this has happened, and you have to calculate your guarantee payment, all references are to the old contract, not the new one. So your right is based on working hours in normal conditions.

Limits on guaranteed pay
Your rights are subject to the strict financial limitations imposed by EPCA 1978 and annual revisions.

1. The maximum you could get in any day was £9.50 in 1983/4, so if your calculations show that you would have got more than this you are prevented from claiming the surplus over £9.50 (see example on page 80).

2. You can only claim a maximum of five days in any three-month period. The period begins on the first day off and is a 'rolling' three-month period. If you normally work less than five days a week, for example, if you work four days at 10 hours a day, you can claim a guarantee for only four days a quarter. If your week varies you take the average number of days worked over each of the previous 12 weeks.

These limits on money and days can be increased each year by the Employment Secretary, who has to take account of the economic situation and average earnings in the country.

When these levels are compared with arrangements already existing in organised workplaces they look fairly insignificant – see page 85.

3. You are not entitled to the full guarantee payment if you receive any *contractual* payment for the days in question. This must by offset and you cannot claim your full contractual entitlement if you have been paid the guaranteed amount.

■ **Example A:** you are covered by an agreement providing guaranteed weekly earnings or minimum time rates of £90. You normally earn £150 a week. You are laid off after earning £90 in three days. The agreement does not come into operation – you have already earned your £90. But for the two idle days you can claim under the 1978 Act.

■ **Example B:** on the other hand, if you earn less than the agreement guarantees you – say only £75 for the three days worked – you are contractually entitled under your agreement to a further £15. When you claim your guarantee under the Act for the two idle days, management can say: I have already paid you £15 according to the agreement and this works out at £7.50 for each of the idle days. So I can offset this against my statutory obligation. You can claim only the difference between £7.50 and the amount of the statutory guarantee.

To get the most money in this situation don't claim your statutory rights. You can claim for only five days in the three-month period. Better not to waste one of these days in claiming less than the statutory maximum. Instead claim only if you have already earned more than your agreement guarantees (as in Example A above) or where for some reason the agreement is suspended.

Suspending the guarantee

Suspension of the right to a guarantee payment is the term used in many collective agreements to show when employers can avoid payments. Under the 1978 Act your right is suspended in three broad situations:

- if you don't take alternative work;
- if you don't comply with reasonable requirements; and
- if there is an industrial dispute involving your employer or an associated firm. These are dealt with separately.

Alternative work

Section 13 of the EPCA 1978 says that the guarantee is not payable if an employer has offered to provide alternative work 'which is suitable in all the circumstances, whether or not work which the employee is under his contract employed to perform, and the employee has unreasonably refused that offer'.

This is similar to the rule used in redundancy cases. It means you consider both the *objective* nature of the work itself and the *personal* reasons you may have for refusing to do it. There is no requirement that you *must* work on different jobs at lower wages. If management threaten to suspend the guarantee if you refuse to take the new work, threaten legal action.

Section 13 may give your employer scope unilaterally to change custom and practice and working arrangements.

S/he may say that rules of demarcation don't apply, and s/he may threaten to suspend the guarantee if you don't accept new working rules, or even if you refuse them pending negotiations. Section 13 might be taken by tribunals to mean that 'in all the circumstances' of a temporary recession it is reasonable to refuse to do alternative work even though this cuts right across existing practices and agreed procedures. Tribunals may look sympathetically on a worker who is faced with an ultimatum of either permanently changing his/her job within the same company, or losing his/her redundancy payment. They may be less sympathetic to workers who refuse to help their employer in a difficult period by accepting alternative work for a few days. **So use your industrial strength to counter any threat by management to suspend the guarantee.**

Reasonable requirements

The guarantee can be suspended if a worker does not 'comply with reasonable **requirements imposed by his employer** with a view to ensuring that his services are available', (section 13, emphasis added). This may mean that you can be required to be available at different locations or to clock in every day. We have seen that if you do some work you lose your right to a guarantee payment, since it is only available for 'workless' days. In this case, you should refuse to work or argue that your contract gives you the right to be paid in full. If the requirement is unreasonable, threaten legal action to get the guarantee.

Industrial disputes

Your employer can suspend the guarantee if you are laid off due to a dispute involving any employee of his/hers, or of any associated employer.

This exclusion strengthens the hand of employers engaged in a dispute. It attempts to ensure that no pressure is brought to bear on them by other employers complaining that, as a result of the dispute, they have to make guarantee payments to their workers. More to the point, it has the effect of dividing workers from each other at a time when they should be closing ranks. Consequential lay-offs due to industrial disputes in the motor industry, and the media's treatment of them, frequently turn laid-off workers against those in dispute.

During some disputes you lose the right to a guarantee payment but you can still claim social security benefit, for example if you are not participating in or directly interested in a dispute at your place of work (see page 285).

Collective agreements

All the parties to a collective agreement or Wages Council can apply to the Employment Secretary to have their agreement override the EPCA guarantees. The only requirement is that the agreement must allow for reference to an industrial tribunal or an independent arbitrator if any worker claims a disputed payment. Since there is no requirement that the agreement be more favourable than the EPCA, and since you can take advantage of whichever of the guarantees (that is, in the Act or in the agreement) suits you better, there is no point in closing the door to this choice by seeking exemption from the Act. The TUC has advised unions not to apply but by 1982 exemptions were granted in 30 industries including civil engineering, demolition, building (England and Wales), refractories, fireboard, footwear, multiwall sack and carton manufacture, together with several individual company exemptions.

How to claim a guarantee payment

If you have not been paid your guarantee in accordance with the Act you can apply to a tribunal. See page 490 for the procedure. The claim must be filed **within three months** of the day for which you are claiming.

If a tribunal hears the claim and agrees with you, it must order your employer to pay you the full amount under the Act. If s/he cannot pay because s/he has gone bust you can apply to the Department of Employment. (See page 277.)

Lay-offs and social security

You can't claim unemployment benefit for a day when you receive a guarantee payment. Careful timing by agreement on short-time working and lay-offs can give you the maximum combination of guarantee and social security payments. See chapter 12 for rules on social security.

If management dispute your right to guarantee pay, you can claim unemployment benefit and the amount of guarantee pay is subsequently recouped if they are found liable to pay you.

Lay-offs and continuity

A temporary cessation of work does not break your continuity of employment. In fact, the time when you are laid off counts as part of your continuous employment. See page 470.

Trade union demands

Many workers are already covered by collective agreements which provide better protection than the EPCA. The statutory right to a guarantee arises in many more circumstances than in most agreements. For example, in chemicals and electrical cable making the guarantee is suspended if there are circumstances 'beyond the employer's control'. While many agreements provide for suspension, this can only be done with notice (e.g. two weeks in chemicals) or by agreement (for example, engineering). The Act guarantees are automatically suspended without the need for notice or agreement.

Most existing agreements require you to be available for work and exclude you from payment if you are sick, on holiday, or are not ready and willing to work. The National Working Rules for the building industry, for example, require you to be available for work in your own or 'any other suitable building industry occupation, or at any other site where work is available', a very onerous stipulation.

Exemptions during disputes are found in almost every collective agreement. In some the guarantee is suspended whenever there is a dispute *anywhere*, or in any firm which is covered by the agreement – as in engineering, shipbuilding and repairing, and building. Perhaps the best is the British Steel agreement which disqualifies workers only if there is a dispute at the same *plant*.

The value of the statutory guarantee is small when compared with arrangements already existing in organised workplaces. In engineering you are guaranteed 39 hours at the minimum time rate, and there is no maximum duration. At Fords you get 80 per cent of your personal hourly rate for up to 15 days during any one lay-off. In the building industry you get your standard weekly rate for your normal hours (but after one entirely workless week this can be suspended). The rubber industry agreement provides payments for a year.

By juggling social security payments and collective agreements you can usually do better than the EPCA. **Payments under the Act are taxable.**

If you are negotiating a guaranteed pay agreement you should demand the following:

- No suspension except by agreement or after long notice
- Pay should be given in a dispute to all workers not involved
- The EPCA should not be taken as a guide on the amount or duration of payments.

Redundancy through lay-off/short-time

You can claim redundancy pay in some periods of lay-off or short-time working (LOST). If management have no right in the contract of employment to lay you off, you can claim unfair dismissal and redundancy pay. If there is a right to lay-off, claim a guarantee payment. You can in addition claim redundancy pay while your contract is still alive.

This section applies **only to employees who are entitled by length of service etc. to claim redundancy pay.** For details see pages 208, 253. The usual definition of redundancy does not apply to LOST situations. Instead, section 88 of the EPCA says you can activate the complex procedure if you have been laid off or put on short-time (or a combination of both) for

- four consecutive weeks, or
- six weeks in any 13-week period.

The definitions are important: lay-off means you receive no pay at all. Short-time means you receive half of a 'week's pay' (see page 474) or less. Guarantee pay under the EPCA 1978 does not count, but any negotiated fall-back pay or guarantee does. LOST caused by a strike or lock-out, whether you are involved in it or not, does not qualify, but if the cause is lesser industrial action, such as boycotting, you can claim.

You can start the ball rolling on a claim for redundancy pay following this timetable:

1. LOST continues for the appropriate period, that is four or six weeks.

2. Not later than four weeks after this period you tell management in writing that you intend to claim redundancy pay.

3. Within seven days your employer must give you written counter-notice that you can resume work. It must state that, within the next four weeks, work will be resumed for a minimum of 13 continuous weeks without any LOST.

4. Whether or not your employer gives notice, if there is no resumption within four weeks of your notice, you must claim redundancy from management and give notice of termination according to your contract.

5. If your employer does not give you redundancy pay, you apply to a tribunal for it. See page 490 for the procedure.

There are many pitfalls in this technical procedure, see *Dakri* case, page 77, and you should consider the consequences of giving notice to terminate. It may be a useful tactic for you to give notice of your claim, but giving notice to terminate is very risky.

Collective action

The statutory rights are no substitute for direct action to attack unilateral changes in job security. Rearrangement of hours of work, and loss of earnings, can be stopped by union action.

Summary

1. Unless your contract allows it, management can't suspend you or lay you off without your agreement.

2. If they do you can claim for breach of contract, unfair dismissal and redundancy pay.

3. If they do have the right to lay you off, you can claim a guarantee payment under the EPCA, or you may want to claim dismissal if the period of lay-off is unreasonably long.

4. The right to pay can be suspended if you aren't available for work, don't comply with reasonable instructions, or if there is an industrial dispute involving your employer or an associated employer.

5. Many collective agreements provide better protection. You can claim the best of both rights if you have an agreement.

6. You can claim social security benefit during some lay-offs.

7. You can claim redundancy pay after lay-off or short-time working over a specified period.

6. Discipline

Management's view of discipline at work / your protection against action for taking part in union activities / discipline which is discriminatory on the grounds of race, sex or a previous conviction / your contractual rights on discipline / rules and procedures / the Code of Practice / the forms of discipline – warnings, reprimands, fines, deductions, suspension, demotion and transfer / special rules for police, armed forces, merchant seafarers, apprentices, and the professions / whether you should negotiate disciplinary rules / what to include in your agreements / disciplinary action against management? / and a summary.

The extent to which your employer is able to take disciplinary action against you is directly related to your organisation and bargaining strength. Shopfloor discipline is one of the areas of labour law *least* affected by statutory rights and *most* affected by workers' resistance. In well-organised workplaces no disciplinary action is carried out if there is organised dissent.

The Tories have long recognised this. In 1968 they put forward a plan to regulate discipline and to stop strikes *(Fair Deal at Work)*, in which they said (on page 42):

> about two-fifths of all stoppages and about one-fifth of days lost through strikes stem from disputes about 'the employment or discharge of workers and other working arrangements, rules and discipline'.

Number two on the Tories' list of 'main causes' of disputes, after pay claims, was 'dismissal or disciplining of fellow-workers'.

Disputes over discipline are a more serious threat to management than disputes over wages. Employers expect workers to want more money than they are prepared to pay, and bargaining, together with industrial action, are essential features of industrial relations. A dispute over disciplinary action taken against a worker has, though, two dangerous implications for employers. It shows an outright resistance to management prerogative, and it demonstrates the extent of workers' solidarity over what management see as purely an individual matter.

Successive governments have tried recently to mould discipline into a manageable form. They have done this by encouraging agreed disciplinary procedures rather than by direct legal intervention. Whether or not unionised workers should get involved in agreements relating to disciplinary procedures or disciplinary rules is discussed at the end of this chapter.

Disciplinary action is taken to be management's response to an individual's fault, either as a punishment or as an attempt to correct it. Such statutory rights as there are – the law of contract and the Code – all treat discipline in this personal way. **Discipline should, however, be regarded as a single example of an action that could be taken against all other workers. For this reason collective support is as important as it is in enforcing every other right.**

The scope of this chapter is disciplinary action short of dismissal. For dismissals, see chapter 10.

Where to find the law

The Employment Protection Consolidation Act 1978 (EPCA) section 1 requires written particulars of rules; the Advisory, Conciliation and Arbitration Service (ACAS) Code of Practice on Disciplinary Practice and Procedures ('the Code') gives the framework. The Truck Acts 1831–96 deal with fines and deductions. The Sex Discrimination Act 1975 (SDA) section 4, Race Relations Act 1976 (RRA) section 2, EPCA section 53 and the Rehabilitation of Offenders Act 1974 (ROA) outlaw discrimination.

Trade union activity

As we shall see (page 301) you have the right under section 23 of the EPCA not to have action taken against you by your employer if the purpose is to prevent or deter you from being a member of an independent trade union, or joining in its activities at an appropriate time. Penalising you in any way, or subjecting you to disciplinary action, would entitle you to claim at a tribunal an unlimited amount of compensation.

It doesn't matter what form the deterrence or penalisation takes. If you are denied a Christmas bonus because you took part in union activities (which might include your campaigning in pursuit of your union's objectives) you can complain, even though the bonus was a non-contractual gift from management which you could not demand as of right. Management must show why they took action against you.

Union representatives also have the right under the Code (see below) not to be disciplined until their full-time official or senior representative has been involved.

Racial and sex discrimination

Discrimination is dealt with in chapter 8 but it should be noted here that victimisation because you brought a claim, or intended to, or gave evidence at a hearing, is specifically outlawed (SDA section 4 and RRA section 2).

Living down a conviction

We have seen (page 35) that you are under no obligation to disclose spent convictions when answering questions. If management discover that you have a record which you are entitled to regard as spent any disciplinary action taken against you is unlawful, **even if your contract permits it** (for example, suspension). Section 4 of the ROA makes it unlawful for an employer to 'prejudice (a worker) in any way in any occupation or employment'.

How do you exercise this right? Parliament drafted this legislation without *specifically* providing either a remedy for you or a punishment for your employer. This means that you can challenge 'prejudicial' action (short of dismissal) only by alleging breach of contract or suing for defamation. For dismissal see page 236. Collective action, therefore, is the only effective method.

Your contractual rights

Management can take action short of dismissal only if it is provided for in your contract or if it does not affect your contractual rights. In your hands, theoretically at least, is the extent to which you let disciplinary action happen. If you do not concede the right, there is none. If you allow management to write work rules establishing penalties for breach of them, or if a collective agreement deals with them, you are liable to be disciplined. You can't stop action that doesn't strictly affect your contractual rights. If a non-contractual benefit is withheld, for example, you have no legal cause for complaint, unless it is victimisation for union activity.

The general advice, therefore, is: **don't agree to disciplinary penalties in a contract or agreement.** Operating against you if you take this line is the fact that the EPCA requires a written statement of rules.

Written rules and procedures

The EPCA requires employers to give written particulars to most workers – see page 38. These must spell out 'any disciplinary rules applicable . . . or refer to a document which is reasonably accessible . . . and which specifies such rules'. The purpose of this section is to introduce clear rules which would cut down the number of disputes over discipline, and would restore to management their right to discipline. It also has the effect of encouraging employers to introduce a contractual duty on workers to submit to discipline. In fact, the Act does not allow employers to make *new* rules – it simply says that if they exist, they must be set down.

If you don't have clear rules and management's power to discipline is regulated by your collective resistance, there is often no point in accepting a written statement of the rules. If rules actually exist and are operating to your satisfaction, there is no harm in having them in writing. But if they are only periodically enforced, or do not exist, **you should not accept a codification in a written statement as this will usually become contractual.** If you carry on working without protest after new disciplinary rules have been proposed you may be deemed to have accepted them. If the only alternatives to accepting changes are resignation or dismissal a tribunal is unlikely to uphold the unilateral imposition as a contractual change. Always ensure that your objection is explicit.

The EPCA says you must be told of the disciplinary procedure and that you have a right of appeal from any disciplinary decision (although there must presumably be a limit on this) to a specifically designated person. The form and content of agreed procedures are not laid down in the Act, and are dealt with below.

The Code of Practice

The Code of Practice encourages negotiated procedures for dealing with discipline. The Code lists 'essential features' for any agreement. It should: be speedy; be written; state the range of disciplinary actions and who they apply to; say who has authority to discipline; provide for notice of any complaint, and for a right to state a case and be accompanied by a representative; require management to investigate the case carefully and to give the reasons for any penalty; ensure that no dismissal occurs for a first breach of discipline except for gross misconduct; and give a right of appeal to a level not previously involved.

The Code recommends (paragraph 12) that the following steps should be taken in all cases except those for which the rules allow instant dismissal:

- formal oral warning, or, for 'more serious issues'
- written warning, setting out the nature of the offence and the likely consequences of further offences
- final written warning saying further misconduct will lead to suspension, or dismissal, or some other penalty
- transfer or suspension (if contract allows) or dismissal.

Details should be given in writing to the worker, who should be told of his/her right of appeal. Records should be kept, but breach of discipline should be removed from records after an 'appropriate period of satisfactory conduct'.

Special provisions should be make for **people working nights,** or working in **isolated places** who don't have access to someone in authority. **Union representatives** should not be disciplined beyond a possible oral warning until the case has been discussed with a full-time official or senior representative.

What kind of disciplinary action?

Warnings

Warnings, either oral or written, can be given even if there is no mention of them in your contract. This is because they do not detract from your basic contractual rights. Cumulatively they may do, in that they can lead to dismissal, but since they are not contrary to any of your rights under your contract, management can give them out.

The steps laid down in the Code should be followed. Warnings should be unambiguous and clearly specify the offence, and the consequences of further offences.

Reprimand

Unless some penalty infringing your contractual rights is attached, a reprimand is within the scope of every employer's prerogative.

Fines and deductions: all workers

It follows from the law of contract that management cannot fine you or make a deduction from your wages unless there is a very clear rule or custom allowing this. If such a rule exists, management in fining you does not go outside the contract and you have no legal right to object, except when the fine is larger than the one permitted, or made in inappropriate circumstances. Otherwise, failure to pay wages due to you amounts to a breach of contract. You have a choice of *legal* remedies: **1.** you can stay at work and sue for the money due to you as a result of this breach; or **2.** you can claim that this breach is so serious that it shows management are not prepared to carry on with the contract, and leave. You can then claim that this amounted to constructive unfair dismissal.

Fines and deductions: manual workers and shop assistants

We know (page 48) that 'workers covered by the Truck Acts must be paid the whole of the wages they have earned in 'current coin of this realm'. Only specified exceptions are allowed. Disciplinary fines or deductions therefore constitute offences. The 1896 Truck Act, however, introduced a relaxation which gives any employer the power to levy fines, and to make deductions for 'bad or negligent work or injury to the materials or other property of the employer'. The power is fairly tightly regulated by the Act and the following conditions must be met:

- You have signed a written contract, or you have access to a notice in a prominent place showing the terms of your contract, which provides for fines or deductions.
- Any fine or deduction made is in accordance with this contract.
- Written particulars of the 'offence' and the amount of the fine or deduction are given to you on each occasion.

In addition to these conditions, a *fine* can be imposed only if:

- your contract specifies events that can lead to a fine and the amount
- the particular event causes or is likely to cause loss or hindrance to your employer
- the amount is reasonable; and
- management keep a register of all fines;

and a *deduction* can be made only if:

- it does not exceed the loss caused to management by you or workers you are responsible for; and
- the amount is reasonable.

Deductions for bad work are still common in the textile trades. Disciplinary fines, for example for bad time-keeping, are common in many industries. Some of these are expressly excluded from the requirements of the 1896 Act. Despite this legal control on employers' powers – and these all ultimately derive from an agreement in your contract to accept them – the courts have allowed employers to abuse the law.

In one case it was decided that a worker was paid to do *good* work, and if he did *bad* work he got a lesser price. In other words there was one wage for bad work and one for good work, rather than a deduction from the normal wages:

■ Thomas Sagar, a Lancashire weaver, produced cloth by the piece. One week he received 1s. less because of carelessly produced work. When he claimed under the Truck Act the Court of Appeal said that there had been no deduction. His work had not been up to scratch so he got paid only what the defective goods were worth. He had not actually earned the full amount he would have got if the work had been good, so there could be no deduction from it. *Sagar v Ridehalgh* 1930 (CA)

This pedantic distinction does not apply only to piece-workers. If you are entitled to a good timekeeping bonus, it can't be 'deducted' until you have achieved full attendance. So you can't claim under the Truck Act until the bonus becomes due and is withheld.

Suspension with pay
Management can suspend you on full pay. If you are in one of those rare groups of workers who have a right to be provided with work – piece-workers, skilled workers, performers and artists – management can't suspend you. See page 51.

Suspension without full pay
Suspension on anything less than full pay is unlawful unless you have agreed to this in your contract, or by custom. See page 76. If you turn up for work and are locked out or if you are disciplined by means of temporary suspension, you are entitled to claim for the wages due to you or even to resign and claim you have been unfairly dismissed. **Don't accept a right to suspend for disciplinary reasons in your contract or agreements** unless you feel that it is useful to have a middle road between warnings and a sacking. Without such a right, suspension is a breach of the contract to provide wages to a worker who is ready and willing to work.

■ Mr Hanley took a day off work so management suspended him without pay for a day. He claimed 6s. 2d. The High Court said his employers could have sacked him, or claimed damages from him. Instead, they did neither. They treated the contract as still alive, and 'took upon themselves to suspend him for one day; in other words to deprive the workman of his wages for one day, thereby assessing their own damages for the servant's misconduct. . . . They have no possible right to do that'. *Hanley v Pease & Partners* 1915 (HC)

You can claim your wages, but it would be most unlikely that a court would force management to take you back to work (TULRA section 16). You might think that suspension without full pay is also an offence under the Truck Acts, as a fine or deduction. But the courts have applied the law to protect employers of piece-workers from this suggestion. They say you are entitled to all the wages you have earned. If you don't work because management have suspended you in accordance with your contract, you are not entitled to wages, so there can be no deduction from them. If there is no deduction, management do not infringe the Truck Act. But, if you have not conceded the right to suspend, and you are not on straight piece-work, suspension *will* be an offence under the Truck Act.

Demotion and transfer
Demotion, or transfer to a job not covered by your contract, is a breach of contract. It will often be a breach so serious that management are really showing that they are tearing up the contract. You can claim unfair dismissal if you quit after refusing a move not authorised by your contract. That is constructive dismissal.

This does not apply if you have accepted a flexibility or mobility agreement. A disciplinary transfer may not be a breach of contract if you are covered by this kind of agreement. **Be wary of negotiating flexibility agreements.**

Workers subject to special discipline

The police and armed forces
The services are covered by stringent disciplinary rules. These rules are archaic, unnecessarily strict, and undemocratic. The right to go before a civil court with a jury, and be represented by a lawyer are excluded. The powers given to the authorities go far beyond the powers of any employer and include corporal punishment, imprisonment and physical labour. The police are subject to internal disciplinary bodies and, for senior officers, local watch committees.

Merchant seafarers
Seafarers are subject to the Merchant Shipping Act 1970, which made reforms in ship discipline. Most of a captain's power to discipline can be taken over by ship disciplinary committees. In fact, experiments with such committees proved unsuccessful.

Workers didn't want to serve on them, and others preferred to be disciplined by their skipper. A captain still retains the right to arrest and fine.

Apprentices
Ancient rules allowing 'masters' to 'chastise' apprentices are now obsolete. Apprentices are more protected than other workers against disciplinary action, particularly dismissal.

The professions
There are special disciplinary bodies in all the professions. They have various powers including disqualification. Teachers, doctors, dentists, lawyers, nurses, opticians and architects all have their own rules, enforced by a disciplinary authority.

Should you negotiate disciplinary agreements?

The Code positively encourages joint regulation of both rules and procedures. It also envisages the possibility of joint adjudication. There are pros and cons in this approach. On balance you are better off not negotiating rules, while at the same time agreeing **procedures.**

In a well-organised workplace, you are giving up your control over discipline if you put the rules in writing. If the views of your workmates are usually accepted in disciplinary matters, so that no disciplinary action or sacking takes place unless it is deserved, you gain nothing by agreeing to written rules. In less organised sectors, the codification of rules can be detrimental when it comes to challenging disciplinary action or making a claim for unfair dismissal. This is because flexibility in treatment is reduced, and employers can easily show to a tribunal an offence specifically covered by an agreed rule. Furthermore, the absence of agreed rules (and procedures) will make it harder for employers to show they acted reasonably.

If you choose to have a set of rules, the advantages are that you always know where you stand, and if they are followed there is no scope for favouritism or victimisation.

Workers may be more inclined to observe them if they are arrived at through negotiation rather than by management decree.

Procedures are different. It is usually in your interest to be guaranteed a right to warnings, an appeal and representation. There is no ideological bar to trade unionists negotiating a procedure, but there may be if you jointly fix rules and penalties. The only time it may benefit you *not* to have an agreed procedure is when you are claiming unfair dismissal. Tribunals don't like employers who neither have procedures nor follow the Code.

If you already have a fairly long procedure which is better than that in the Code it is still advisable to put it in writing. Otherwise management may convince a tribunal that they have followed procedure if they merely take the (minimum) number of steps set out in the Code, but fail to exhaust the *agreed* procedure.

On adjudication, many trade unionists feel that it is better to have disciplinary matters decided by a body which includes workers. This is probably right, but there are few procedures which leave decisions to an appeal body with a *majority of workers* on it. For the most part, workers are involved only to give credibility to a decision.

Improving on the Code
The Code sets out to give practical advice. It is extremely influential, whether or not a procedure is agreed, in setting standards against which disciplinary action can be judged.

It has many shortcomings, though. If you are going to negotiate rules and procedures, you can aim a lot higher. The Code represents a minimum, not an optimum, or even a norm. The following are realistic bargaining objectives:

1. Steps in the procedure. These should be increased to include more warnings. Suspension should be accepted as a penalty only if you think it is the only way of avoiding a dismissal. A suspended worker should be given the right to return to work to interview witnesses and collect evidence.

2. Instant dismissal. This should be regarded in organised workplaces as obsolete. All potential dismissals should go into procedure. If the offence is bad enough, you are less likely to win a claim for unfair dismissal if management sack you on the spot, and this right is written into a procedure.

3. Records. These should be destroyed if you have had no similar offences for six months.

4. Special workers. The procedure should apply to all. Probationary workers and new starters are particularly vulnerable as they may not know the ropes, and they should have all the protection of the procedure.

5. Rules. If often reduces flexibility if you specify rules and offences.

Enforcing procedures

Jointly-agreed procedures should be enforced by trade union action. Disciplinary procedures incorporated into individual contracts of employment can, however, be enforced in the civil courts. An injunction might be given if the proper procedure for dismissal has not been carried out, depriving you of your right to a hearing.

■ Harold Jones was head of a small Catholic primary school in Gloucestershire. He and another teacher both got divorces and married each other. She left the school. The school managers sacked him on the grounds that his conduct was incompatible with the Catholic faith. The Court of Appeal granted him an injunction to stop the dismissal since his contract gave him a right to a hearing in front of, and a decision by, the county council education committee. *Jones v Lee and Guilding* 1980 (CA)

The High Court made it clear in *R v BBC (Lavelle)* 1982 that it will intervene to suspend or set aside a disciplinary decision if procedural guarantees have not been observed. It can do so in four circumstances:

- You 'hold office' or are in a job which has an element of public status. The rules of natural justice apply – a right to a hearing, etc.
- You are in a job where, despite a decision to sack you, 'mutual trust' under the contract still continues, e.g. *Hill v Parsons* page 61.
- Your contract requires a procedure or an investigation prior to disciplinary action.
- When criminal proceedings are pending, a prior disciplinary hearing raising the same issues might create a real danger of injustice.

Disciplinary action against management?

In some circumstances you could take action against management. If they infringe the Truck Acts or the Health and Safety at Work Act, or fail to take action on hazards quickly enough, you could 'warn', or take direct action, or inform the authorities. Management have a contractual obligation to you to observe the statutes – see *Gregory v Ford* (page 54). Why not take disciplinary action against management if they break your contract?

Summary

1. Disciplinary action is illegal if it shows discrimination on the grounds of sex, race, trade union activity or spent convictions.

2. Disciplinary action must be authorised by your contract. It is illegal if it affects your contractual rights.

3. Workers covered by the Truck Acts can agree to disciplinary deductions and fines. If you don't agree, or if they aren't customary, they are illegal. Strict rules regulate deductions and fines until 1985 – see page 50.

4. The Code of Practice lays down minimum guidelines that should be followed, including warnings, appeals, representation and the form of procedures that should be negotiated.

5. The EPCA says management must give you written particulars of disciplinary rules, and who you can appeal to.

6. Disciplinary action against one worker, if it is unchallenged, can become a threat to others. It is essential for organised workers to establish rights of representation and appeal, and to take collective action in support of colleagues unfairly disciplined.

7. Maternity

The need for maternity rights for working women /
the law and collective bargaining / summary of
your rights / table showing legal protections /
dismissal connected with pregnancy / ante-natal
care / maternity grant / the right to alternative
work / how to claim unfair dismissal / maternity
pay / social security maternity allowance / payment /
how to claim pay / maternity leave / refusal to
take you back / how to claim the right to return /
temps / pitfalls / specimen letter to your employer /
recommended timetable for claiming your rights /
collective action.

Men can't have babies. This overworked statement of fact has
been the reason for unequal treatment of men and women, and
for the lack of job and income security of pregnant workers.
Before 1976 protection for women workers was provided, if at
all, only by collective and individual agreements. Social security
benefits are available to those women who have paid the necessary number of contributions, but these don't guarantee job
security. Parliament was slow to give legal rights, but this is
related to the lack of interest shown in the past by industry.
Well-organised workers have a lot to answer for. The national
agreement for the engineering industry, for example, covering
probably 200,000 women workers, says nothing about maternity leave or pay.

This inadequacy of collective bargaining will be remedied
only when the campaign for maternity rights ceases to be

regarded as a woman's issue and becomes a demand affecting the whole of the working class. Since Conservative government policies increased unemployment and reduced real income from wages and social security, a woman's income and job-security are crucial to many families – even more so if she is a single parent. So while maternity rights can be exercised only by women, they are in fact rights won for all workers. Collective bargaining must improve on the legal rights and make good the defects noted below.

1. There are no rights on paternity in the UK. Other countries recognise paternity rights, such as Sweden, where nine months' leave can be taken, by either the mother or the father or alternately.

2. The law excludes large numbers of working women from the right to maternity pay and to return to work. You need to have worked continuously for over two years in the same job. Since many women of child-bearing age will have entered employment quite recently, or will have changed employers within that period of time, the rights are restricted.

The reason for excluding so many women is purely financial. As with the original unfair dismissal laws, which also required two years' service before they could be activated, the main object is to satisfy the demands of the labour movement by conceding the principle of maternity rights, while making sure that the financial effect of this concession on employers and government is minimal.

3. It could be said that **the social security system has imposed a rigidity** on agreements and now on the maternity rights in the Employment Protection Consolidation Act 1978. Payments can be claimed only during the 11 weeks before and seven weeks after confinement. This is quite inconsistent with a woman's need to choose when to begin and end her leave.

The maternity rights introduced in 1975 generated a degree of hostility from employers out of all proportion to their practical effect. Independent research into a sample of women workers (*Employment Gazette*, May 1980) showed that 3.6 per cent of women stop work on account of pregnancy. Just over half of these qualify for the EPCA rights. Of those entitled, less than one fifth gave notice that they would be exercising their right to return. Of those who did go back, only 20 per cent went on the basis guaranteed by the Act.

Added to this is the exclusion of many women from the right

to claim unfair dismissal because they do not have the one year's service now necessary to make a claim. The research showed that since the Tories doubled the service qualification:

> it appears that the increase will have placed substantially more women at risk of dismissal owing to their pregnancy. Indeed the number at risk will have more than doubled.

Nine per cent had less than six months' service, but 23 per cent had less than a year's service.

A survey by the Labour Research Department of comparative EEC legislation showed (*Bargaining Report* No 8 1980) that the UK's was the worst in almost every way. This is the only country which requires a qualifying period of employment. Only Ireland has a lower rate of pay, and only Belgium pays for a shorter period.

Where to find the law

The Employment Protection Consolidation Act 1978 (EPCA 1978) deals with time off for ante-natal care (section 31A); dismissal (section 60); maternity pay (sections 35–47); the right to return (sections 45–48). Maternity grant is contained in the Social Security Act 1980 section 5 and maternity allowance in the Social Security Act 1975 section 22.

Summary of rights

The table on page 104 shows what rights you have. Regardless of how long, and for how many hours a week, you have worked, and regardless of age, you have:

1. the right to take time off for ante-natal care
2. the right to state maternity grant.

If you have been working for the same employer for one year at 16 or more hours a week (plus the usual exceptions – see page 468) you have:

3. the right not to be dismissed simply because you are or have been, pregnant or for any reason connected with this
4. the right to be given suitable alternative work if you become incapable of doing your normal work, and a vacancy exists
5. if your contract is suspended while you take maternity leave, the right to claim unfair dismissal if you are sacked while on leave.

Table 1: Maternity rights

Right	Who can claim	When does protection begin	When does protection end	Extension
State maternity grant	Women in the UK for 26 out of last 52 weeks	Claim 14 weeks before or up to 3 months after birth	—	—
Time off for ante-natal care	All working women	On pregnancy	On confinement	—
Social Security maternity rights	Women with sufficient contribution record	11th week before expected week of confinement	18 weeks later	None
Maternity pay	Women with 2 years' service at 11th week before confinement	11th week before expected week of confinement	6 weeks later	The 6 weeks can be taken any time after 11th week before confinement
Right to return to work and to claim unfair dismissal if refused	Women with 2 years' service at 11th week before confinement. See Note 3	11th week before expected week of confinement	29th week after week of confinement	See notes 1 and 2 below
Right to claim redundancy pay if refused right to return due to redundancy	Women with 2 years' service at 11th week before confinement	11th week before expected week of confinement	29th week after week of confinement	See Notes 1 and 2 below
Rights not to be dismissed for reasons connected with pregnancy	Women with 1 year's service at date of dismissal. See Note 4	On pregnancy	Indefinite	—
Right to be offered suitable available vacancy if incapable of normal work	Women with 1 year's service at date of dismissal	On pregnancy	Indefinite	—

Note 1: **Employer** can extend once for 4 weeks on giving specific reasons. Employee can extend once for 4 weeks on giving medical certificate.
Note 2: **Employee** can extend if it is unreasonable to expect her to return e.g. because of industrial action. Must return within 14 days of action ending.

Note 3: Except firms with 5 or fewer employees.
Note 4: 2 years' if 20 or fewer employees.

If you have been working for the same employer for two years by the 11th week before your expected week of confinement you have:

6. the right to take maternity leave starting any time after the 11th week before confinement

7. the right to maternity pay for the first six weeks of absence whether or not you intend to return to work

8. the right to return to work at any time within 29 weeks of the week of confinement

9. if redundancy arises while on leave, the right to be offered any suitable alternative work which exists when you return to work

10. the right to claim unfair dismissal if you are not allowed to return to your old job after your absence.

If your contract or collective agreement deals with maternity:

11. the right to take advantage of any term that may be better than the EPCA.

If you have made sufficient social security contributions:

12. the right to maternity allowance.

Ante-natal care

During the passage of the 1980 Employment Bill, the government adopted a new clause giving women the right to paid time off to attend ante-natal care appointments.

This right, embodied in EPCA section 31A, applies to almost all women workers. Unlike the requirements for other maternity rights, you do not need to have been employed for two years in order to be entitled to time off, and part-timers who work less than 16 hours a week are included.

You have the right to take time off if you are pregnant to attend an arranged appointment for ante-natal care. If management request it, you must produce a medical certificate showing that you are pregnant and either your appointment card or some other document. These are not required if you are seeking time off for the first appointment during your pregnancy. The right applies only if you are pregnant, so if you turn out not to be management may stop payment.

Once you comply with any request by management for evidence, they must not 'unreasonably' refuse to let you go, or to pay you. There is no limit on the number of times you can go, where you can go to, or the length of your stay, providing you

are attending for ante-natal care. Tribunals will judge the
reasonableness of any refusal and we can expect employers to
object to giving paid leave at short notice, or for several days'
duration as might occur in unstable pregnancies.

Relaxation classes, exercises or hospital babycraft sessions
might also be covered. The only stipulation in the Act is that
you are attending an ante-natal care appointment **on the advice
of** a doctor, midwife or health visitor.

You are entitled to be paid your normal hourly rate. If management refuse to let you go, or to pay you, you can complain
to an industrial tribunal within three months of the date of the
appointment.

Maternity grant

The Social Security Act 1980 released the government from the
duty to upvalue social security benefits annually by the same
percentage as either prices or earnings, whichever was greater.
Now the sole indicator is prices.

In taking a small part of what the Treasury saved by this
revision, the Tories removed the conditions applying to the £25
maternity grant so that **all** women can receive it.

Dismissal connected with pregnancy

Who can claim?

Provided you have one year's **continuous employment** and fulfil
the usual conditions for protection against unfair dismissal (see
page 207) you can complain to a tribunal if you are sacked while
you are pregnant. Management must give a reason for sacking
you (other than pregnancy) and the tribunal must judge the
fairness of their actions in the normal way. However, because
you may have difficulty in doing some jobs, and will want time
off for hospital visits, and because you are going to cost money
and demand the right to maternity leave, you are likely to be
extremely vulnerable to dismissal at this time. Some **additional
protection** is given by the EPCA whether or not you qualify for
maternity pay or **maternity leave**.

If you are sacked because of pregnancy, even though you are
quite capable of carrying on at work, you are automatically considered as unfairly dismissed. Management must give their
reason for dismissing you (if you request it – EPCA 1978 section

53). They must prove some reason other than pregnancy. If they can't, you are unfairly dismissed. They may even be quite open about it – pregnant models, air stewardesses or sales representatives do not conform to the image put over by sexist employers. Protection against being dismissed for other reasons, such as having a child (rather than being pregnant) is given by the general law on unfair dismissal:

■ Genevieve Pillet, an unmarried marketing assistant, was sacked while pregnant. She wasn't entitled to statutory maternity leave and was refused even three months' leave. Management said she wouldn't be able to do her job properly if she had a child. Ms Pillet got £2,023 compensation. *Pillet v Land Settlement Association* 1977 (IT)

Management might try to sack you for reasons *connected with* your pregnancy. They might object, for example, to your having sick leave or time off to attend hospital classes, or because you have psychological problems which may affect your work (concentration, for example), or because you need to take time out to nurse the baby, or because you can't work long hours, or stand, or do heavy work, or adjust to shift-working. You can claim unfair dismissal in these and similar situations, but management can use the defence given in section 60 of the EPCA 1978.

Section 60 says that management *can* sack you for a reason connected with pregnancy if:

● you can't adequately do the work you are employed to do;
or
● you can't carry on doing that work without breaking the law.

But, if a suitable vacancy exists, they must offer it to you.
This means:
1. Management must prove that you are incapable. Incapacity justifying dismissal is assessed in terms of skill, aptitude, health and mental and physical qualities (EPCA 1978 section 57), and may include incapacity due to repeated absences. But because pregnancy involves only a short-time incapacity, dismissal on those grounds might be unreasonable.
2. If you can do the job to some extent, management may be

unreasonable in sacking you, because it is only reasonable to sack you if you can't *adequately* do the job. You will have to challenge any attempt to redefine performance levels at your workplace.

3. In any event the test is whether management acted reasonably in all the circumstances in sackng you.

4. Management *must* offer you a suitable alternative job if a vacancy exists. If they don't they must **prove** that no suitable vacancy exists.

Suitable vacancy means that it must be suitable for you to do and appropriate in the circumstances. If you are given a new contract, the terms and conditions must be 'not substantially less favourable' than in the previous one, particularly those affecting the capacity and location in which you worked. If you are offered less money or different hours, you will have to weigh up whether it is substantially less favourable. Management must prove a job was offered and it was suitable.

Vacancies with associated employers don't count. The obligation to offer work applies if there is a vacancy with the employer you work for (or a successor if the firm is taken over). So although workers who are affected by an industrial dispute involving employees of an associated employer cannot claim guarantee payments (see page 83), there is no corresponding *obligation* on employers to offer women work with associated employers. Employers are required to behave reasonably though, so you might succeed in showing that it was reasonable to expect management to look for vacancies among associated employers in the same group – see *Vokes v Bear* page 243.

Since you may not have access to the files on whether vacancies exist or are likely to arise even in your own firm, constant exchange of information between workmates is essential. You could also try a claim for disclosure of information under the EPA 1975 (see chapter 15).

The situations in which a law prevents an employer from keeping on a worker who is, or has been, pregnant are few. Section 60 applies only where an Act of Parliament or a specific regulation forbids employment. It does *not* apply to your employer's own rules or custom and practice. The fact that in your firm women workers habitually quit, or are required by an agreement to quit, in the 11th week before confinement does not mean your employer is complying with a *law*. The kind of regulation envisaged is section 75 of the Factories Act which requires employers to take women off the job if a medical adviser of the Employment Medical Advisory Service (EMAS) says they are exposed to lead, or radioactivity, or under other regulations. But in these situations workers who are not given alternative work and are temporarily laid off are entitled to 26 weeks' pay for **medical suspension** (see chapter 4). Faced with this alternative, employers may be acting unreasonably in sacking a woman worker when suspension is all that is needed to comply with the doctor's order.

When must the offer be made?
Finally, the offer of new work must be made before you are sacked, and the work must start immediately after the old work finished.

How to claim unfair dismissal
Claim unfair dismissal **within three months.** See page 490 for the procedure. If you would have been entitled to maternity pay and maternity leave had you not been sacked, tell management (in writing is best) before you leave, or as soon as is reasonably practicable, that you intend to claim the right to return to work with them.

Remedies for dismissal
If you are unfairly dismissed you preserve your rights to maternity pay and to return to work. If you are fairly dismissed because, for example, you are incapable of adequately doing your job and no vacancy exists, your rights are also preserved. But in both these cases the rights are preserved only if you would have had two years' continuous service by the 11th week before the week you expect your baby. If that is not the case, you may get compensation or even reinstatment according to the normal powers of tribunals when dealing with unfair dismissal (see page 246).

Sex discrimination
The EAT blocked one avenue of redress for women who are sacked because they are pregnant. The court dismissed a claim under the Sex Discrimination Act by women sacked from a south London department store.

■ Kim Turley was sacked while she was pregnant. She did not have sufficient length of service (now one year) necessary for her to bring an unfair dismissal claim. She said she was sacked because she was pregnant; only women can get pregnant; so she was sacked because she was a woman. This was illegal under the Sex Discrimination Act. Although the trade union member of the EAT agreed with her, the two male members rejected the appeal. They said 'she was no longer simply a woman, but a woman carrying a child, so she cannot get by the back door of the Sex Discrimination Act the relief she cannot get by the front door' of the unfair dismissal law. *Turley v Allders Department Stores* 1980 (EAT)

This is an astonishingly thoughtless decision and ignores the possibility that dismissal for pregnancy could constitute unlawful indirect discrimination. In similar circumstances a favourable decision is more likely following the 1981 case *Hurley v Mustoe* (page 126).

Maternity pay

Who can claim?
In order to qualify for maternity pay under section 33 of the EPCA you must fulfil certain conditions.

The starting point is the week you are expecting your baby to be born. That week is known as the 'expected week of confinement'. The previous week, ending on the Saturday night, is the first week before the expected week of confinement. (Confinement means the birth of a living child, or a still-birth after 28 weeks' pregnancy). **Your rights depend on your status at the beginning of the 11th week before the expected week of confinement.** In order to claim maternity pay and the right to return to work you must:

1. have had two years' continuous employment by the beginning of the 11th week

2. still be 'employed' (even if you are not actually working) at the end of the previous week. You are 'employed' even if you are fairly or unfairly dismissed (see above) before this date

3. normally work at least 16 hours a week (plus the usual exceptions – see page 468)

4. inform management that you intend to be absent because of pregnancy. They can request that you put it in writing, and anyway it is advisable to do this. You must give at least 21 days' notice of your intention.

5. if they request it, provide them with a doctor's or widwife's certificate showing the expected week of confinement.

Conditions **1.** to **3.** are compulsory. If you don't comply with **4.** because it was not reasonably practicable – you might be off sick or your baby might be unexpectedly early – you must provide the information as soon as possible. If you fail to provide it or to give a certificate when requested, your employer can withhold payment until you do – but then it must be backdated (EPCA section 34). **You can get maternity pay whether or not you return or intend to return to work after the birth.**

How much is due?

The EPCA aims to give you six weeks at 90 per cent of your 'week's pay' (see page 474). Management must make up the difference between social security maternity allowance and 90 per cent of a week's pay. **You get the same amount from management whether or not you are entitled to social security maternity allowance.** Maternity pay is taxable if your contract continues. If your contract has ended PAYE can't be deducted but you would be required to show this as untaxed income in your (or your husband's) annual tax return.

If you have two jobs, you can claim maternity pay from each employer provided you have the necessary service, etc., with each. Maternity allowance is deducted twice, even though you receive it only once. When earnings-related supplement was payable on top of maternity allowance you got roughly 100 per cent of your week's pay. But the Tories stopped this entitlement in 1981. The Employment Secretary has power to increase the 90 per cent figure up to 100 per cent (EPCA 1978 section 35) but still had not done so at the time of writing.

Your week's pay is worked out on the basis of the arrangements in force just before your absence. If, because of your condition, you have been forced to accept alternative work with the same employer but at a lower rate, it is the lower rate that applies for working out maternity pay. This is completely unjustified in that you may have worked, say, for five years on one set of rates and been on reduced rates for only four weeks. It is also inconsistent with guarantee payments (page 80), where your rights are not prejudiced if you accept lower rates for a while during a recession.

Contractual rights

If they are already making payments to you in accordance with your contract or a collective agreement which covers you, management are entitled to offset this amount against maternity pay during the first six weeks. Only *strictly contractual* or collectively-agreed payments count. An *ex gratia* payment or an annual bonus that isn't guaranteed by your contract does not affect your statutory right to maternity pay.

If your own arrangements are better than those in the Act you can claim on them. If they are not as good you can go for the better terms. And if some terms are better, some worse, you can be choosey and get both the full EPCA rights and any better terms under the agreement. Local authorities once used to provide four weeks at full pay and 14 at half pay. So you could get four weeks at full pay, then two weeks at 90 per cent under the Act, and 12 weeks at half pay.

How is it paid?

The right is to payment for the **first six weeks** of absence due to pregnancy or confinement. They can be taken any time after the 11th week, and they need not be taken consecutively, but if you do not quit at the 11th week you will lose some state maternity allowance (see page 120).

The Act does not say how the maternity pay is to be paid. It could be paid weekly or monthly or as a lump sum. The DE says 'the intention behind maternity pay is to maintain earnings during the weeks of absence. The payment of a lump sum at the end of six weeks would be contrary to this intention' (EPCA Leaflet 4). Ideally you want your money at the beginning.

The Maternity Pay Fund is financed by an additional 0.05 per cent on employers' social security contributions. The load is spread evenly across all employers and they cannot object to hiring women on the grounds that it will expose them to claims of maternity pay. Your employer makes the payment and then claims **a full rebate from the fund.** If s/he pays you according to your own contract or collective agreement, s/he can recoup the amount of the statutory rebate, provided that you would be entitled to claim under the Act.

How to claim

You should write to your employer as soon as possible saying you intend to be absent because of pregnancy. You must tell him/her **three weeks** before you are absent or as soon as is reasonably practicable. See specimen letter on page 121. If s/he refuses to pay, you can claim to a tribunal **within three months** of the last day on which you should have been paid. See page 490 for the procedure.

If you get a tribunal award in your favour and management still refuse to pay up, or if they have gone bust, you can apply directly to the Employment Secretary for payment out of the Fund. The Fund pays you direct, and claims against management if they don't have a reasonable excuse for not paying you. In view of the small amounts due, it is hard to envisage what excuses could be reasonable.

Maternity leave

Many agreements provide for maternity leave. The EPCA talks instead of a 'right to return to work' (section 45). The two are not quite the same but the effect of the Act is to give a period during which you can be absent from work and be protected if you are sacked, made redundant or refused work, to the same extent as if you were not absent. See also page 470.

Who can claim?
To claim this right you must meet the same conditions as for maternity pay on page 110. In addition you must say you intend to exercise your right to return to work with your employer.

How long does leave last?
The EPCA 1978 gives you the right to return to work at any time during the period stretching from the 11th week before confinement to the end of the 29th week after the week of your confinement. **There is nothing in the Act to force you to quit work at any specified date before confinement.** You will lose some social security maternity allowance, though, if you work after the 11th week.

The date of return can be postponed in three different situations.

1. You can postpone your return by up to four weeks after the date you said you would be returning – the 'notified day of return' – even if this takes you beyond 29 weeks. You can do this only if you send your employer a medical certificate saying you are incapable of work 'by reason of disease or bodily or mental disablement'. You can only do it once. So **you should make absolutely sure you are fit before you tell management the date you are returning.**

2. After you've notified management of the date you intend to return, they can postpone it by up to four weeks, even if this means extending the period of absence over the 29-week limit. They must specify their reasons for doing this when they notify you of the postponement. But the power to fix the date of return is yours – your employer can postpone it only for a limited period.

3. You can postpone your day of return because of an interruption of work which would make it unreasonable for you to be expected to return during it. A strike, for instance, would entitle you to put back your notified day of return, or to extend it beyond the 29th week if you have not already notified management. Your leave is extended indefinitely, even beyond the 29th week. Once the strike or other interruption is over you have **two weeks** in which to return to work.

These are the only situations when you can postpone your return date having once notified your employer or having gone beyond the 29 weeks. So you must be quite certain your health and commitments will enable you to return on the notified day. It also means **you should resist your employer's pressure at the start of your absence to say in advance when you will be back.** If this means employers are unable to plan their personnel requirements, it is the result of the EPCA. There is no reason why women workers should be prejudiced by it.

Return to what?
The right is to return to work with your employer (or successor if s/he has sold out or merged) in the job in which you were employed under your original contract. According to section 45, this means that the **capacity and place** in which you **could be required to work** and **the nature** of the work must be the same as those in your regular contract. The terms and conditions must be 'not less favourable' than you would have had if you had not been absent. So if there has been a pay increase while you have been away, you come back on the new rate. For all your statutory rights, like redundancy, unfair dismissal, notice and maternity pay, you have continuity of employment throughout your leave, so you are treated as never having been

away. For non-statutory rights that you have negotiated, such as pensions, holidays and seniority, section 48 is ambiguous. You can argue that you are coming back to 'not less favourable' terms only if your absence counts for all these purposes to.

You go back to the work that you could be required to do under your original contract. If you accepted alternative work before confinement under a different contract, the right to return applies to work under your original contract.

The scope for employers to avoid their obligation to returning mothers was extended by the 1980 Employment Act so that your right to return can be denied in two cases:

- Management say it isn't 'practicable' because of redundancy to have you back. You have a right to suitable alternative work **if a vacancy exists.**
- Management say it isn't 'reasonably practicable' for any other reason to have you back. They must offer you suitable alternative work.

The EPCA 1978 gives no indication of what circumstances would make it not reasonably practicable to take you back on your original contract, but two defences are likely to be used.

■ **Example:** Management say that they cannot sack the person who replaced you while you were away. They say they could not get a temporary replacement (for whose dismissal or redeployment EPCA section 61 makes specific provision) and expect you, rather than the replacement, to transfer. You argue that these are not sufficient reasons to deprive you of your right. They should offer alternative work to the replacement.

■ **Example:** Management say that since you left, the work has been reorganised and the nature of the work has changed substantially. You can demand the same terms and conditions, and to be employed in the same capacity (e.g. clerical assistant or packer) in the same place.

In both these examples you will be at a disadvantage because you may have been away for nine months and be out of touch with what has happened at work. For this reason, it is crucial to keep up with your colleagues and union representatives. It is management, though, who have the burden of proving that it is not reasonably practicable to give you back your job. In other cases you will know more than they do.

■ **Example:** You have postponed your return to work for medical reasons. Management leap at this opportunity to say that you are unfit to do your job and therefore it is impracticable to take you back. You might welcome lighter or less intense work for a while, but you and your doctor will have the best idea of what you can and cannot do.

If your old job is out, management or an associated employer must offer you alternative work which:

- is suitable to you (e.g. your kind of work, and your grade)
- is appropriate for you in the circumstances (i.e. because of your health and domestic commitments)
- is 'not substantially less favourable' to you, meaning the capacity in which you are employed, where you work and all your terms and conditions of employment *and*
- would be unreasonable for you to refuse (i.e. you have no personal reasons for objecting to it).

This gives management some scope to move you around and to alter your terms of employment. Tribunals judge whether there is a substantial deterioration in your conditions. What may seem a trivial change of duties to management and tribunal members who never see or do the work, may to you be a major worsening of the job.

If you accept alternative work because of redundancy, you are entitled to a four-week trial period in the new job. It is arguable, but not clear in the Act, that this trial period applies where other reasons force you into a new job. You or your union should get this agreed before you start back.

Small firms

'The government are anxious to ease the burden on small firms of the employment protection legislation,' said the Tories' 1979 *Working Paper on Proposed Amendments to the Employment Protection Legislation*. So employers with **fewer than six** employees (including those in associated firms) are exempt from the return-to-work provisions.

There is no evidence for the Tory view – indeed the independent research commissioned by the Department of Employment shows that small firms are not disproportionately affected by the labour laws (*Employment Gazette*, July 1979, May 1980). Of 300 small businesses surveyed, only 4 per cent had experienced maternity leave, and none had found it 'troublesome'.

A firm with fewer than 10 employees will on average have one woman stop work through pregnancy every three years. But the statutory right will be exercised only once in 30 years. The survey also found that there was 'a substantial failure to receive entitlement' to maternity pay in small firms. Yet the myth of the small firm's burden remains prevalent, no doubt fostered by the electoral promise to the small business (including farming) lobby.

Management must prove that it is not reasonably practicable to take you back or for them or an associated employer to offer suitable work. If you challenge their refusal to give you work, you can take your case as unfair dismissal to an industrial tribunal. But there's a catch there, for after 1980 the law requires the tribunal to consider the 'size and administrative resources' of an employer facing an unfair dismissal charge (EPCA 1978 section 57). In labour law these days, small is indeed beautiful.

Giving notice to management
Since 1980 all notices must be given **in writing**. These provisions make the arrangements for taking maternity leave more technical, and you could lose your rights if you don't follow the new requirements precisely.

In the first place you must now inform management in writing at least 21 days before you want to begin your maternity leave. This must include the date of the expected week of confinement, i.e. the week when your baby is due. **You must say that you intend to return to work after the birth.** Management can then get you to provide a medical certificate confirming the date.

You can return to work at any time up to 29 weeks after the week of confinement. But before that, you will have to comply with two further requirements. Firstly, seven weeks (or later) after the end of the week of your baby's birth, management can write asking you if you still intend to return to work. The letter must say that you will forfeit your rights if you don't reply in writing within 14 days.

If you miss this date, or give less than the 21 days' original notice of your absence, you won't necessarily lose your rights.

If it is 'not reasonably practicable' for you to meet these dead-lines, you must nevertheless send in your notices as soon as is reasonably practicable after the deadline. Bear in mind, when planning your arrangements, that while you are pregnant and shortly after the birth of your child you may have other things on your mind and overlook the dates.

The second requirement before you go back is that you must give management written notice at least 21 days before the date you intend to return. Once you give this date, or once the 29-week period is up, you can postpone your return only in the circumstances described on page 113.

The notification requirements were heavily criticised by the EAT, who thought they were 'of inordinate complexity exceeding the worst excesses of a taxing statute; we find that especially regrettable bearing in mind that they are regulating the every-day rights of ordinary employers and employees' (*Lavery v Plessey* 1982).

Recommended timetable

Assuming you become pregnant in week 1 and the expected week of confinement is week 40:

- **Any time during week 1 to week 40:** request time off with pay to attend ante-natal care appointments;
- **Week 25:** notify your employer in writing that you are leaving, of the expected week of confinement (for which s/he can require you to produce a medical certificate) and that you intend to return to work;
- **Week 26:** claim on Form BM4 the social security mater-nity grant and maternity allowance;
- **Week 29:** (this is the 11th week before the expected week of confinement) leave work. Employer starts to pay maternity pay. Social security maternity allowance starts;
- **Week 35:** your statutory right to pay runs out;
- **Week 40:** baby born;
- **Week 47:** maternity allowance runs out;
- **Week 48:** any time from now, employer may request writ-ten confirmation of intention to return;
- **Week 50:** (or within 14 days of receiving request), reply with written confirmation of intention to return;
- **Week 66:** last date for notifying management in writing of your date of return. Must give 21 days' notice;

- **Week 69:** you must return to work or get a postponement on medical grounds (for four weeks) or because of a strike at work.

Dismissal, redundancy and refusal to reinstate

Suppose you have told your employer the date you are coming back and s/he says you are redundant. As you have been away a while you may not know the facts and you may not be in a position to rally support for resistance. If you are forced to rely on your legal rights, they are these:

1. You have a right to be offered any suitable alternative vacancy in the firm or associated firms. This is not the same as the employer's *defence* to a redundancy pay claim by which s/he can avoid payment by offering suitable alternative work. Under the EPCA it is expressed as your right to claim any suitable work appropriate for you to do. If there is such a vacancy and you are not given it, this is automatically unfair and you may get a reinstatement order or compensation.

2. If suitable alternative work is not available, you will get a redundancy payment if you are not re-hired, with your continuous employment being reckoned to your notified day of return, or the date redundancy occurred.

3. If management simply refuse to have you back and there is no evidence of redundancy, you can claim unfair dismissal and you may get an order for reinstatement or compensation.

4. Your contract may say that while on leave your contract continues and all your rights under it still apply. So if you are declared redundant or dismissed at any time after the 11th week before confinement and before you have had a chance to give a notified day of return, you can claim. You are employed (although absent from work) up to the dismissal date and may get an order for reinstatement or compensation. These rights exist *in addition to* your maternity rights so you can claim again later on if your right to return is not observed.

How to claim

Claims for refusal to allow a return to work must be made **within three months** of the notified day of return. If you are dismissed or made redundant before you fixed a date you should claim within three months, (six months if there is a genuine redundancy and no other work is available – better to be safe with three months). See page 490 for the procedure.

Temporary replacements

Employers can take on men or women to fill vacancies temporarily created by a woman on maternity leave. These workers are extremely vulnerable since they will often not reach the one year's service required for (legal) protection against unfair dismissal unless they are replacing two women on leave consecutively.

Under EPCA 1978 section 61 there are three restrictions on an employer's freedom to sack a temp:

1. The temp must have been told **in writing** at the time s/he was hired that s/he would be sacked when a woman returned to work.

2. The temp must in fact have been sacked in order to make it possible to give work to the returning woman.

3. The employer must show s/he acted reasonably in sacking the temp when the woman returns. This means that s/he is expected to look for work for the temp in the firm or with associated employers (*Vokes v Bear* – page 243). **It is important to protect the job-security of these workers by demanding equal treatment for all.**

Maternity allowance

You have a right to the weekly maternity allowance:

- if you have paid the appropriate value of Class 1 or Class 2 contributions – see page 283,
- if you are expecting, or have just had a baby,
- if you do no work on the days for which you are claiming, and
- even though you may be getting maternity pay from management.

Payment is made weekly for 18 weeks starting in the 11th week before the week your baby is due but if your baby is late you can make a separate claim to the allowance for six weeks after the week your baby is born. Maternity allowance is not taxable. Claim maternity benefits on form BM4, available from the DHSS and child health clinics.

You can get an increase for dependants and supplementary benefits in addition to maternity allowance.

Specimen letters to employer

Because of all the pitfalls surrounding maternity rights it may be useful to write to your employer as follows:

6 January 1983

Dear Mr/Ms Smith,

I wish to inform you that I intend to be absent on account of pregnancy.

My expected date of confinement is in the week beginning Sunday 17 April 1983 and I intend to take advantage of my rights under the Employment Protection Consolidation Act to maternity pay and to return to work. I would be glad if you could arrange for my maternity pay to be paid weekly by cheque/collected by me/paid in a lump sum on . . .

Yours sincerely,

In response to management's request for notice of intention to return, reply within 14 days:

Dear Mr/Ms Smith,
This is to let you know that I still intend to return to work.

Final notification to be sent not later than 21 days before the proposed date of return:

1 October 1983

Dear Mr/Ms Smith,
This is to let you know that I will be coming back to work on Monday, 24 October, 1983.

Collective action

The right to return to work at any time up to 29 weeks after confinement is about the only right which collective agreements rarely match. This long period should be the target for minimum rights in collective agreements. **Maternity rights will be improved only if union members recognise the importance for all workers of giving job-security to women at work.**

Summary

A summary of your rights is given in the notes and table on

pages 103-05. In claiming them you should take care to follow
the complicated formal requirements for notification and bear
in mind the following points.

Points to watch out for
- If management sack you at any time, ask for the reasons
  in writing. They must give it if you have six months' service.
- If they sack you before your baby is born and you would
  be entitled to return to work, tell them you intend to exercise this right.
- Give notice in writing of your intention to claim maternity
  pay as soon as possible. You must give this three weeks,
  or as soon as reasonably practicable, before you leave. If
  you don't, your pay can be withheld.
- Provide a medical certificate if requested.
- Give notice **in writing** of your intention to be absent and
  say that you will be returning in accordance with the
  EPCA. If you don't say this, you lose the right. At this
  stage you should not say when you intend to return.
- Notify management **in writing** at least 21 days before you
  intend to return. Make sure you will be absolutely fit by
  that day.
- If you aren't fit, get a medical certificate but don't postpone the date by more than four weeks.
- Whether or not you are entitled to the right to return,
  make sure you aren't forced into a phoney 'resignation'. If
  pressure is put on you to quit, make sure you register this
  as a dismissal or exercise your right to return to work by
  notifying management.
- Claim social security maternity grant and allowance
  between the 14th and 11th week before confinement.
- If you are sacked or are refused pay or the right to return,
  claim within three months.

8. Discrimination

Discrimination on the grounds of race, sex and
marriage / religion and political opinion / who can
claim / direct and indirect discrimination /
victimisation / segregation / how this applies to jobs /
recruitment, terms and conditions, transfer, promotion,
training, benefits, dismissal / what are
the exceptions / genuine occupational
qualifications / immigration and work permits /
discriminatory practices / inciting racial hatred /
sexual harassment / the Equality Commissions /
enforcement / how to claim / proving discrimination /
remedies / trade union action / and a summary.

Some types of racial discrimination were first outlawed in 1965.
Discrimination in employment was made illegal in 1968. Yet in
1974 the research group Political and Economic Planning (PEP)
found that:

> a coloured unskilled worker has nearly a one in two chance
> of being discriminated against when (s)he applies for a job;
> for a coloured skilled worker the chance is one in five and for
> a white collar worker about one in three. PEP estimates, on
> the basis of its samples, that 20,000 acts of discrimination in
> recruitment occur each year. The PEP report confirms over-
> whelmingly that discrimination in employment continues on
> a massive scale (Quoted in Race Relations Board (RRB)
> Report 1974, page 8).

Something had to be done. The legislative answer was the

Race Relations Act 1976 (RRA 1976), which came into effect in 1977. The labour movement's answer was a campaign against racism in 1976 and 1977.

It is clear that discrimination, more or less overt, continues. The Commission for Racial Equality's 1981 Report conceded that discrimination in employment 'continues at a very high level and there are still few employers who grasp the full seriousness of the evil'. Laws can change behaviour but not attitudes.

Racial discrimination is not constant. It can be stirred up by offensive propaganda from organisations like the National Front, which blame racial minorities for deteriorating living standards, unemployment and bad housing. It can also flare up in an irrational response to national events. An Irish worker engaged by a Cheshire company was prevented from starting because of feeling against the Irish following the IRA bombings of Birmingham city centre in 1974. He got only £29.50 in compensation (*RRB v Clays Commercial*).

Sex discrimination is outlawed by the Sex Discrimination Act of 1975. It attempts to lay the groundwork for equal treatment in employment, housing, education and services. Figures for earnings given on page 159. show just how much work this Act has still to do in employment matters.

Laws alone can't wipe out discrimination. On practically every occasion when the higher courts have dealt with discrimination, they have shown no inclination to interpret the laws so as to eliminate it, and only grudgingly apply the more liberal EEC laws when forced to do so. Trade union action can go a long way. This is suggested at the end of the chapter.

Where to find the law

Discrimination on the grounds of sex or being married: Sex Discrimination Act 1975 (SDA 1975); on the grounds of race: Race Relations Act 1976 (RRA 1976); inciting racial hatred: Public Order Act 1936 as amended by the RRA 1976; dismissal: Employment Protection Consolidation Act 1978 (EPCA 1978) section 71; equal pay and equal treatment: Treaty of Rome, Article 119 and EEC Directives 75/117 and 76/207. Employers' duties towards disabled people are dealt with on page 34. Dismissal on the grounds of being gay is dealt with on page 242. Discrimination on the grounds of political opinion or religious belief is covered only by the Northern Ireland Fair Employment Act 1976.

Statutory bodies

The Equal Opportunities Commission (EOC) deals with the SDA. The Commission for Racial Equality (CRE) deals with the RRA. It replaced the Race Relations Board and the Community Relations Commission in 1977. Their powers and functions are described below.

Race, sex and marriage

Discrimination is illegal in employment, education and in the provision of goods, facilities, services and housing, if it is based on:

- race, colour, nationality, ethnic origins or national origins
- sex
- the fact that you are married (employment only).

Discrimination on the grounds of nationality is still permitted in the immigration laws (see below).

Discrimination on the grounds of language is not included. It is contrary to the UN International Covenant on Social and Cultural Rights, which the United Kingdom has ratified, and it could lead to a charge of indirect discrimination.

Gypsies are covered if they are discriminated against on ethnic grounds. The Race Relations Board also regarded **travellers** without clear ethnic roots as being covered and they would be protected by the RRA 1976 if they could show they were a well-defined community similar to Sikhs (see below).

Discrimination against a man or woman on the grounds of sex is illegal. Marital status is included for employment matters only and applies only to married people.

■ B.C. Parsons was a child care officer at a special school. She announced her intention to get married on 31 January and was sacked on 30 January. She claimed discrimination but the Exeter tribunal said she was not married at the date of dismissal, so had no claim. *Bick v Royal West of England Residential School for Deaf* 1976 (IT)

The tribunal did not consider whether the employers would have sacked a man and therefore discriminated on the grounds of sex.

In any event, you can claim unfair dismissal if you meet the usual conditions about hours worked and length of service (see page 208) – Ms Parsons did not have the necesary service. A London tribunal gave compensation for sex discrimination as well as unfair dismissal:

■ Jeanette Johnston, a reservation clerk in a Hertfordshire travel agents, was sacked the day before she married John McLean, the assistant manager. It was 'company policy' not to have two married people working together. She successfully claimed £117 for unfair dismissal and £200 for injury to her feelings under the SDA. *McLean v Paris Travel Service* 1976 (IT)

The EEC Directive on equal treatment (76/207) says there must be 'no discrimination whatsoever whether directly or indirectly by reference to marital or family status'; this is obviously wider than the SDA. The SDA is supposed to be the UK's way of implementing the Directive, and has to be interpreted to give effect to the Treaty of Rome and the Directive. This means that the UK is in breach of its EEC obligations, and tribunals should give a wide interpretation when faced with claims which fit the Directive but not the SDA – for example, claims of discrimination on the grounds of family status. To some extent protection is given to a woman who is discriminated against because she has young children.

■ Ursula Hurley was married with four children under 11. She had worked evenings as a waitress for 10 years when she answered an ad for another 'waitress' job (in itself discriminatory) in a London bistro. After a few hours in the job she was sacked by the owner, who said women with young children were unreliable. He had not refused to employ men with small children. Even so, this policy would be discriminatory and could not be justified since there was no evidence that people with young children *were* unreliable in the running of a small business. *Hurley v Mustoe* 1981 (EAT)

And if you apply the logic of the *Price* and *Perera* cases (below), you can claim that a condition with which fewer women (or men) with children can comply amounts to indirect discrimination.

Religion and political opinion

Religious discrimination is outside the 1976 Act but it is contrary to International Labour Organisation (ILO) Convention 111 for employment matters. This has not been ratified by the UK.

The absence of such a clause in Great Britain had led to difficulties for Jews who have been discriminated against because of their religion (lawful) rather than race or ethnic origins (unlawful). Under the 1976 Act this might constitute indirect discrimination. The position of Sikhs was not settled until 1983, when the Law Lords said in a case involving school uniforms that the Sikhs are covered by the RRA as a racial group (*Mandla v Lee* 1983 (HL)).

However, the Fair Employment (Northern Ireland) Act 1976 outlaws discrimination on the grounds of 'religious belief or political opinion' in the six counties. Complaints are made to the Fair Employment Agency, whose task is to enforce the legislation by investigation, conciliation and in the county courts, and to promote equality of opportunity.

■ Tim Duffy, a Roman Catholic, unsuccessfully applied for a local council job. He had previously worked for the council and was more qualified and more experienced than the Protestant who was offered the job. At the interview Tim Duffy was asked, 'Are you loyal?'. The Fair Employment Agency took the case to the Northern Ireland Appeal Court, who declared the council discriminated on grounds of religious belief or political opinion. *Fair Employment Agency v Craigavon Borough Council* 1980 (NICA)

In 1981/82 only four out of 41 complaints were upheld. In 1981 the British government yielded to pressure and announced that any firm bidding for government work had to have an equal opportunity certificate declaring that it adhered to the 1976 Act.

Discrimination in jobs – can you claim?

Both Acts apply to employees, people seeking work and those listed in Table 2.

The main points to note are:

1. Most of the SDA applies only where there are **at least six employees** in the company or group of companies. No reason is

Table 2

	Sex Discrimination	Race Discrimination
Employees in small firms	Must be six or more employees with same or associated employer	Yes
Employees in private households	No	No
Job applicants	Yes	Yes
Employees alleging victimisation	Yes	Yes
Contract workers	Yes	Yes
Self-employed people	Yes	Yes
Crown and NHS workers	Yes	Yes
Holders of public office	Yes	Yes
House of Commons staff	Yes	Yes
Armed forces	No	Yes
Police and prison service officers	Yes	Yes
Midwives	Yes	Yes
Partners	Must be six or more in same firm	Must be six or more in same firm
Trade union members and applicants	Yes	Yes
Seafarers	Yes, but unusually exempt as GOQ (see page 141)	Yes, unless recruited abroad
Clergy	No	Yes
YTS and other vocational trainees	Yes	Yes

given for this. Certainly discrimination by an employer does not stop being discrimination simply because the number of workers employed falls below six.

2. If you work for someone who gets work on a **contract basis** from a third person ('the principal') you can complain of discrimination by the principal, for example, if s/he refuses to allow you to do the work. You don't need to show there are six contract workers employed.

3. If you get work through an **employment agency,** discrimination by the agency in not sending you for jobs, and by employers making stipulations, is illegal. Sometimes, though, discriminatory employers have been reported *by* agencies. See the *Kirby* case, page 134.

What is discrimination?

There are four kinds of discrimination in the Acts:

- direct discrimination
- indirect discrimination
- victimisation
- segregation.

In each situation the comparison you must make is between your case and that of someone else whose 'relevant circumstances are the same, or not materially different' (RRA 1976 section 3; SDA 1975 section 5).

Action taken against you because of someone else's race or sex is discrimination. If two white women entering a pub are refused drinks because they are with two black men, all can claim.

■ A white student got a part-time job in a Clapton, east London, pub. She was told not to serve blacks and, when she objected, was sacked. She claimed the employer sympathised with the National Front, and complained to the CRE, who supported her appeal. The EAT said she was treated less favourably than a person who went along with the colour bar and was therefore discriminated against on racial grounds. *Zarczynska v Levy* 1978 (EAT)

Direct discrimination

This occurs if, on the grounds of race, sex, or marriage, a person treats you 'less favourably than s/he treats or would treat other persons'. So favouring a white worker to a black in hiring or promotion, when both have the same qualifications, is unlawful if the favouritism is racial. You must show evidence that the intention behind the treatment was to discriminate against blacks. You can do this by pointing out the implications of various forms of conduct. Potential direct discrimination is illegal so you will win if you show that someone treats you less favourably than s/he would treat a person of a different race or sex, even though no actual better treatment of such a person has in fact occurred.

Indirect discrimination

Indirect discrimination is treatment which is equal in a formal sense, but which is discriminatory in its effects on one particular sex or racial group. Practices that have developed or been introduced might intentionally or unintentionally exclude groups of people on unlawful grounds. During the passage of the SDA many jokes were made about employers avoiding the law by applying conditions that would exclude women – advertisements for construction workers 'who must be prepared to strip to the waist during summer' or who must be over six feet tall, for example. In fact these are illegal unless the employer can prove they are justifiable criteria for the job.

Indirect discrimination occurs when someone applies a requirement or condition that applies equally to all people but which

1. is such that the proportion of people of your race or sex who can comply with it is considerably smaller than the proportion of people outside that race or sex who can *and*

2. the person can't justify *and*

3. is to your detriment because you can't comply with it.

So you have to answer three questions:

1. Can considerably fewer people of your sex or race comply with the condition?

The answer to this is based not on whether you can physically comply, but whether *in practice it is harder* for you to comply.

■ Belinda Price, aged 36, applied for a job advertised by the Civil Service. She was told candidates must be between $17\frac{1}{2}$ and 28 years old. She claimed this was indirect discrimination on grounds of sex. Far fewer women than men could in practice comply with this condition, because many women of that age are having or raising children. It didn't matter that there are roughly equal numbers of men and women under 28. The key issue was that **in practice fewer women would be able to meet the age requirement for the job.** The Employment Appeal Tribunal (EAT) agreed it was discriminatory and referred the case back to the tribunal to see if **considerably fewer** women than men could comply. The tribunal said the age bar was discriminatory and told the Civil Service and the staff unions to abolish or raise the age limit. *Price v Civil Service Commission* 1977 (EAT)

Absolute numbers are not important, since you are comparing proportions – the proportion of blacks (out of the total number of blacks) compared with the proportion of whites (out of the total number of whites) who can comply with the condition. This was illustrated in another challenge to civil service age barriers.

■ K.W. Perera, a Sri Lankan lawyer, came to England in 1973, found work in the civil service and passed the English bar exams. He made eight unsuccessful attempts to be promoted or given training. He did, though, win the right to see the relevant parts of the application forms made by other unidentified candidates for promotion interviewed with him. He was rejected as an administration trainee because he was over the maximum age of 32. He showed that out of 34 white employees of his grade in the Southall, west London, VAT office where he worked, 22 were under 32, whereas none of the 13 ethnic minority employees was. He argued that the age limit discriminated against him and other black workers who immigrated to England when adult, and the limited survey of his and two other local offices proved it. He was awarded compensation. He then went on to challenge the criteria used at his interview. The Appeal Court said UK experience, English language ability, British nationality or willingness to naturalise, and age were not racially discriminatory. *Perera v Civil Service Commission* 1983 (CA)

The Appeal Court's decision is inexplicable. How could a person who immigrated to England in his thirties stand an equal chance on these four factors for job selection?

It is important to have your statistics with you if you are going to win your case. Even then, you may still lose on a technicality:

■ Isabella Meeks worked as a clerical assistant at the Norwich office of the Agricultural Workers' Union. She worked 23 hours a week and got 91p an hour. Workers doing 35 or more hours got 110p for similar work. She complained of indirect discrimination in that she could not meet the conditions of a 35-hour week, *and* the proportion of women who could was considerable smaller than the proportion of men. Official statistics showed 97 per cent of male workers in Britain worked full-time whereas only 68 per cent of female workers did. So discrimination was proved. Discrimination in money is dealt with only by the Equal Pay Act. But, as there was no man doing the same work as Ms Meeks, the Act did not apply and she lost her case (see page 164 for details of this anomaly). *Meeks v NUAAW* 1976 (IT)

If there are men employed on 'like work', differential pay rates has to be justified on grounds other than sex, as is shown by *Jenkins v Kingsgate*, page 173.

It is irrelevant that management did not *intend* to discriminate.

■ A firm in Liverpool city centre told the job centre they didn't want anyone from the city centre (Liverpool 8). A school leaver from the area was refused a job and complained that the ban was racial discrimination. The tribunal accepted that 50 per cent of the area were blacks, whereas only 2 per cent of the Merseyside area were. Management claimed that 'these lads who live within walking distance of our shop have a lot of friends out of work who stand in front of the shop distracting their mates and putting customers off'. The blanket ban excluded a higher proportion of blacks than whites and was discriminatory. *Hussein v Saints Complete House Furnishers* 1979 (IT)

2. Can your employer justify the condition?

The EAT said that in deciding whether a condition is justifiable a tribunal must consider five points:

- that the onus of proof is on the employer
- that the condition must be genuine and necessary, not merely convenient
- whether there will be a discriminatory *effect* if the condition is allowed to continue
- whether the effect of the condition is balanced by the need for it
- whether the employer can achieve his/her objective by some other non-discriminatory method.

Applying these rules in Ms Steel's case, the EAT said the Post Office had discriminated against her.

■ Letitia Steel joined the Post Office as a postwoman in 1961.

Because of a Post Office rule she could not, *as a woman*, be classed as a 'permanent full-time' employee. The union made an agreement which gave women the right to this status in 1975. But prior service didn't count. Length of service is crucial when applying for new rounds, so when Ms Steel applied for a new round a man with *less* service got the job. The EAT said that the number of women who could comply with the seniority rule was considerably smaller than men, and the rule was not justifiable. *Steel v The Post Office* 1977 (EAT)

Sometimes a condition can be justified, even though it effectively excludes all members of a particular racial group. A series of cases concerning Sikhs shows that a requirement that workers in food factories should not have beards is lawful indirect discrimination.

■ H.S. Panesar, an orthodox Sikh from the Indian Punjab, was refused a job as a fitter in Nestlé's chocolate factory, west London because he had a beard and long hair (in a turban). The Appeal Court acknowledged that Sikhs from the Punjab are a religious community, are covered by the RRA, and that very few Sikhs could comply with the no-beards rule. Nevertheless the company's rules (and incidentally the 1970 Food Regulations) justified it in the interests of hygiene. *Panesar v Nestlé Co Ltd* 1980 (CA)

A trainee nurse was treated in the same way when she insisted, as a Sikh, on wearing trousers. The health authority would not allow any departure from the standard uniform. Although a uniform is not compulsory, if one *is* worn nursing regulations specify what it consists of. Since the health authority was following the statute, the discrimination against Sikhs was justified, but the EAT criticised the inflexibility of rules and practices which do not meet the deeply-held convictions of minority groups, whether racial or religious (*Kingston Richmond AHA v Kaur* 1981).

3. Is the condition to your detriment?

You can't sue unless you personally have suffered a detriment. But the Commissions can stop practices which would be discriminatory if the group it is applied to were not of the same sex or race (RRA section 28; SDA section 37). The Commissions can take action, even though no detriment has actually occurred to any particular worker, see example on page 145. The *Jeremiah* case on page 141 is an example of a detriment.

Victimisation
Victimisation in the anti-discrimination laws (RRA section 3; SDA section 4) means that someone treats you less favourably than s/he treats or would treat others on the grounds that you

- bought proceedings
- gave evidence or information in proceedings
- helped the CRE or EOC
- made allegations of discrimination, unless they were false and **not made in good faith.** This means you must take care to get reasonable grounds for any allegations you make.

The words of the Act were shown to be of little support for one anti-racist worker who did what he considered right.

■ Steven Kirby interviewed applicants in the Bristol job centre. On three occasions he observed that prospective employers tried to exclude black applicants so he reported them to the Community Relations Council. (Later, one of them was successfully prosecuted but the job centre did not know about it.) Unfortunately, one of the other job centre workers reported him and he was transferred to filing duties. The EAT agreed that he had been treated unfavourably because he had complained about racial discrimination. But as he was in breach of his duty not to disclose confidential information to outsiders, and of the Official Secrets Act, the job centre treated him in the same way as they would treat someone disclosing any other sort of information, so he lost his victimisation claim. *Kirby v MSC* 1980 (EAT)

In other words, he was disciplined for breach of confidentiality, not for complaining of racism. The judgment obstinately misses the point that this section is designed to protect those who uphold the Act, and not to help racist employers to shelter behind official secrecy.

Segregation
Segregation of people on racial grounds amounts to discrimi-

nation. Provision of separate but equal facilities, the philosophy of apartheid, is illegal. Segregation by sex is not specifically banned.

While segregation arising out of an employer's acts or policy are illegal, segregation occuring because of the absence of **positive action** may go unchallenged. It seems you must show not just the fact, but also the conscious act of segregation.

■ 16 African Asians worked in difficult conditions in the paint shop of a factory making tubular metal furniture. They complained the union was unresponsive to their demands because of their race. The EAT said the union might have been inefficient but it did not treat them any less favourably than it treated the other members, and there was no evidence of racism. On a similar complaint against the employer, the EAT said jobs in that department were filled by word of mouth among the Asians' friends and the company could not be accused of unlawful segregation by refusing to break up the racial exclusivity of the department; segregation was not the company's policy, and it did nothing to achieve it. *FTATU and Pel v Modgill* 1980 (EAT)

However, you can argue that the acquiescence of employers in this kind of segregation can be unlawful if they do nothing to stop it. A management policy of recruitment, retention and replacement of workers from a single ethnic group, ostensibly in the interests of workplace harmony and to aid communications, is in fact a policy of racial segregation.

How does this apply to jobs?

The following examples mentioned in the Acts show when discrimination in employment can occur:

- recruitment
- terms and conditions
- transfer and promotion
- training
- benefits, facilities and services
- dismissal
- other detriment.

Recruitment

It is illegal to give instructions to discriminate to a personnel officer. Arrangments made for dealing with application forms and interviews must be fair. You can complain to a tribunal even if you haven't applied for a job. You might, for example, be put off by the arrangements made – requiring you to travel a long distance or at night if you are a woman – or by the treatment you receive on the phone.

■ Ireka Francis saw an advert for a buffet assistant at Mecca's Gay Tower Ballroom in Birmingham. (The Mecca organisation appears in many RRB reports.) She was offered an interview by the catering manager but when she asked if being coloured would make a difference he said it would and put the phone down. Her claim of discrimination was upheld, the Birmingham County Court believing her story not the manager's. She was awarded £73 compensation. *Race Relations Board v Mecca* 1976 (County Court)

'Arrangements' include formal long-term arrangements for deciding who should be offered employment, and short-term decisions taken on the interview day by people responsible for hiring. They also include the questions asked at an interview which may themselves add up to, or at least be evidence of, discrimination. **Discriminatory arrangements are illegal even if no one gets the job advertised.** Nor can employers say they want to keep a **reasonable balance** between the sexes or racial groups. The old Race Relations Act allowed this, but it isn't in the present legislation:

■ Ms M. Roadburg was interviewed with three men for a vacancy as a social work organiser in Edinburgh. In fact the interviewers had already decided to appoint a man because **there were already many women in the department** and they wanted a reasonable balance. Shortly afterwards, public spending cuts were announced and the vacancy was frozen. She complained and was awarded £40 compensation by the Edinburgh tribunal for injury to her feelings. No discrimination occurred as a result of **refusing to offer** the job because the vacancy was withdrawn for economic reasons. But the prior **arrangements** not to appoint her *were* unlawful. *Roadburg v Lothian Regional Council* 1976 (IT)

Discriminatory advertisements can usually only be attacked by the Commissions. See page 146. Offers of jobs on terms different from those that are or would be offered to others, for reasons of race or sex, are unlawful. You can also complain if an employer refuses or deliberately omits to offer you a job on these grounds – RRA section 4(1); SDA section 6(1).

Terms and conditions
Discrimination between men and women in pay and in other contractual terms on which they work is covered by the Equal Pay Act. As we shall see, there is a gap between it and the SDA. An offer of contractual terms which is discriminatory under the Equal Pay Act is not discrimination unless there is a man you can compare with. Despite this loophole you might still win a case based on the terms *previously* offered to man. Discrimination in terms and conditions on racial grounds is covered by the RRA (section 4(2)).

Transfer and promotion
Management must give equal opportunities for transfer to more favourable shifts or sites. In selecting workers for promotion employers have scope for indirect discrimination. Take the Indian bus driver who was rejected three times for an inspector's vacancy because his accent was difficult to understand, (RRB Report 1973 Appendix VI). He complained that he never had any communication difficulties at work. Imposition of a strict language requirement might be indirect discrimination under the 1976 Act against workers born abroad.

You can effectively challenge this kind of discrimination by getting an agreement to see statistics on applications, promotions and qualifications of eligible workers.

Training
If you are denied opportunities for training you can complain to a tribunal.

■ Some AUEW stewards complained of racial discrimination by their employers, an electrical equipment manufacturer. If no skilled workers were available, vacancies for setters were filled by upgrading operators, many of whom were black.

The operators would be trained by the setters. The setters imposed a ban on all training to prevent upgrading of black workers, and then they went on strike. The Race Relations Board found that their shop steward incited management to discriminate. It ordered the company to pay compensation to two black (and one *white*) operators because they had been denied training. *RRB Report 1975–76 Appendix V Case 1*

Employers can take positive action to train minorities. This is lawful if there are no people of that sex or racial group or if the group is under-represented on a particular job during any time within the previous 12 months. Once trained, the workers must be selected on merit only. Positive discrimination in selection for the actual job is unlawful (RRA section 38; SDA section 48) Similar rules apply to training for union office.

The training agencies of the government are allowed to carry out selective training in special circumstances. These include **retraining of married women** who have been at home for a few years, and **training of minority groups** for particular kinds of work where these groups are under-represented.

Foreign workers seconded to a British firm for training in skills to be exercised abroad – Arab technicians, for example – are excluded from the RRA. But YTS trainees *are* included.

Benefits, facilities and services
Employers must give equal access to all fringe benefits – for example, loans, flexitime, insurance, medical and dental care, cars, parking, clothing allowances, staff status, luncheon vouchers, bonus, creche. Employers can discriminate on the grounds of sex and marriage (but not race) in pensions and provisions 'relating to death or retirement'. See page 144. However, there must be no discrimination in the **fringe benefits** offered to retired employees. British Rail's policy of giving free rail travel to wives of retired male employees was declared illegal because husbands of retired female employees did not get it – *Garland v British Rail* 1982 (ECJ and HL), page 166.

In a decision which threatened to wreck the whole of the SDA, the Court of Appeal said that it was lawful for employers to discriminate in providing benefits if the benefit is 'an administrative arrangement in the interests of safety'.

■ Automotive Products employed 4,000 manual workers – 3,530 men, 400 women and 70 disabled men. A works rule allowed the women and disabled men to leave work five minutes early to avoid the crush. Fred Peake claimed this discriminated against men, as they were denied this benefit. It amounted to two-and-a-half days a year in total. The EAT agreed, but the industrial tribunal and the Court of Appeal said that this was justifiable. Lord Denning said it was a benefit given **in the interests of safety.** *Peake v Automotive Products* 1977 (CA)

The comments in this case, particularly Lord Denning's, are full of reactionary value-judgments. He said that the Act was not designed to set aside the 'traditional chivalry and courtesy which we expect mankind to give to womankind'. Even if it was, he said, Mr Peake's complaint was so minor it could be ignored. To describe two-and-a-half days at work every year as minimal shows the insensitivity of a salaried judge to an hourly paid manual worker. Fortunately, Denning and the Appeal Court later admitted they were wrong, at least as far as administration and safety are concerned. This part of their reasoning is no longer law but the case still stands to allow discrimination in 'trivial' matters (*Jeremiah v MoD,* page 141).

If your employer – a bank or building society, for instance – offers you **the same services as are offered to the public** and you complain of discrimination, you take your claim to a county court under the non-employment provisions of the Acts. However, if the service you get is different from that given to the public, or if you have a contractual right to the service, you can complain to a tribunal. Preferential loans from a bank, cheap housing from a housing association or cheap flights from an airline are employment matters and you can take management to a tribunal if they are offered discriminately.

If management offer benefits and training given by **other organisations,** you can claim if they discriminate against you (RRA section 40; SDA section 50). For example, it would be illegal to refuse to nominate you for an external training course.

Dismissal

Discriminatory sacking and selection for redundancy are outlawed in both Acts, and a dismissal on grounds of race, sex or marital status is also unfair under the EPCA. See page 490 for the procedure.

Racial discrimination is often disguised. It is particularly difficult to prove where there are *some* grounds for sacking but the circumstances in which it occurs clearly point to racism.

■ A hospital employed white and Pakistani stokers in the boiler room. One Pakistani was sacked for leaving the boiler unattended for a short time, but in similar circumstances a white worker had not been. Racial discrimination was proved and £1,100 awarded. *RRB Report 1972 Appendix VI Case 2*

Other detriment
Both anti-discrimination Acts have a catch-all clause making it illegal for employers to subject you to 'any other detriment' on grounds of race or sex.

■ The Agricultural Wages Board increased basic rates and implemented equal pay in January 1976. The new rates were 91½p an hour and 80p an hour for people working less than 31 hours a week. Two weeks later 32 women (some with 20 years' service) employed by a firm of Kent fruit packers had their hours reduced from 40 to 30, and were renamed 'part-time casuals'. No men were treated in this way. Three members of the NUAAW brought claims under the SDA. The Ashford tribunal rejected the company's claim that the women were not on fixed hours because they were allowed to take time off for holidays and for domestic reasons. The company had subjected the women to a detriment so the tribunal told them to put all the women back on 40 hours at the full-time rate and to pay arrears. *Morris v Scott and Knowles* 1976 (IT)

Such a blatant attack on the women could have amounted to a sacking in itself (constructive dismissal).
The meaning of detriment has been clarified:

■ Seven men and four women supervised production in Glascoed ordnance factory. Only the men were required on a rota to supervise a shop making shells containing coloured dyes. The work was dusty and unpleasant, requiring protective clothing and showers and attracting an extra 4p an hour obnoxious conditions pay. The women never worked there because it would 'ruin their hair-do.' One of the men claimed he was subjected to a detriment since only men were required to work in those conditions. The Appeal Court allowed his claim, saying that anything which subjects you to a disadvantage (unless it is trivial, as was held in the *Peake* case) is a detriment. *Jeremiah v MoD* 1979 (CA)

The court decided that once a detriment was established it was not relevant to say, as the employers did, that the *women* objected to doing the work, there were no showers for them, it would cause industrial unrest and only one man had complained. Nor did the fact that he was compensated lessen the detriment. 'An employer cannot buy the right to discriminate by making an extra payment', said the court.

What are the exceptions?

Genuine Occupational Qualification (GOQ)

It is legitimate to look for workers of a particular sex or racial group in order to fill certain clearly-defined jobs. In these cases the law says that being of that sex or race is a **genuine occupational qualification.** Before looking at these jobs it is important to point out that there are limits on the GOQ exceptions.

1. Being of a particular race or sex is a GOQ for the purpose **only of recruitment, hiring, transfer, training and promotion.** Employers can't justify discrimination in the terms and conditions offered to applicants, or those on which existing employees work, or for sacking or subjecting a worker to any other detriment. In other words, once you get the job, further discrimination is illegal.

2. Management can't claim a GOQ for a job if they already employ sufficient people of the appropriate race or sex to do the job. For example, if being a women is, on the grounds of decency, a GOQ for a job as a sales assistant in a store selling women's clothes and there are already sufficient women to deal with the 'GOQ duties', discrimination against a man might be illegal.

3. Employers relying on a GOQ exception must prove it. **It cannot be used to justify victimisation or to justify discrimination against married people,** for example, saying that only single people should be considered for a job involving a lot of travel away from home.

When being a man or a woman is a qualification for the job
An employer is allowed to discriminate against a woman (or a man) on the grounds of sex (section 7) in any of the following circumstances:

- The essential nature of the job calls for a man because of his physiology – for example, a model. But greater strength and stamina can't be a justification.
- A man is required for authenticity in entertainment – for example, an actor.
- Decency or privacy requires the job to be done by a man either because there is likely to be physical contact or because there are men around 'in a state of undress' or using 'sanitary facilities' – for example, a lavatory cleaner.
- You are required to live-in, there are not separate sleeping and sanitary facilities *and* it is unreasonable to expect management to provide them – for instance, a construction site worker or a seaman.
- The job is at a single-sex establishment where people require supervision and it is reasonable to reserve the job for a person of the same sex – for example, a prison officer.
- You provide people with 'personal services' promoting their welfare or education or similar needs, and those services can 'most effectively' be provided by a man – for instance, a member of a social work team. But see the *Roadburg* case, page 142.
- The job is restricted by law to one sex – for example, night work in factories where there is no certificate allowing women to work nights. But a failure by your employer to apply for exemption after you request it might count as discrimination. In fact, in 1983 only 152,000 women were allowed to work nights and weekends in factories.
- The job involves work abroad which can be done, or done effectively, only by a man – for instance in the Middle East.
- The job is one of two which are to be held by a married couple.

When belonging to a particular race is a qualification for the job
An employer is allowed to discriminate on the grounds of race (section 5) in any of the following circumstances:

- The job involves providing one racial group with personal welfare services which can most effectively be provided by a person in the same group.

And for reasons of authenticity:

- In entertainment – for example, an actor.
- In art or photography – for example, a model.
- In a bar or restaurant with a particular setting – for example, a waiter or waitress in a Chinese restaurant.

Problems with GOQs

Although the exceptions are different, the problems of GOQs are common to sex and racial discrimination. Remember that it's the tribunals that will be the judges of 'privacy', 'decency', 'most effectively performed', 'personal services' and 'reasonable'. Few Chairmen and lay members of tribunals are women (see page 19). There are even fewer members from minority groups.

The exceptions can be very broad. Workers in social services, probation and teaching are vulnerable to the 'personal services' clause. Hospital and shop workers are liable to the 'state of undress' exception. If you think the clauses are being abused, challenge management using the official questionnaire (see below).

Immigration and work permits

Discrimination permitted by some legislation continues despite the two anti-discrimination Acts. The main exception to the Acts is the law on immigration, particularly the very restrictive 1971 Immigration Act and 1981 British Nationality Act.

The RRA does not outlaw anything contained in any other Act or done by any minister pursuant to one. Conditions applying to entry into the UK are therefore legal. These are laid down in the Immigration Rules (House of Commons Papers 1973 Nos 79–82, amended 1980).

Work permits are not required for Commonwealth citizens who had a parent or grandparent born in the UK and Irish Citizens. If you have lived here for five years, you don't need a permit. Workers from EEC countries don't need work permits in order to enter the UK to look for work. If you find work within six months, you need a residence permit (which lasts for five years, unless 'the holder is living on public funds although capable of maintaining himself')

Other Commonwealth citizens and other foreign nationals require work permits. Application is made to the Home Office and the permit – initially limited to a maximum of 12 months – is issued by the DE. It is for a specific post with a particular employer. If it runs out, management can apply for extension, but there is nothing you can do to force them to apply. If they refuse, you can't complain under the RRA. If you change jobs, you must notify the DE. Registration with the police is still required unless your stay is unlimited.

Unskilled seasonal workers – hired for holdiay camps or the harvest, for example – cannot stay beyond 31 October.

Other laws

Sex discrimination contained in the social security and tax laws continues unabated. EEC Directive 79/7 requires member states to eliminate discrimination in social security provision by 1985. Very few steps have been taken to conform to this – see page 284. Special treatment of women in the Factories Act and in specific industries such as those involving lead and radio-activity is unaffected.

Pregnancy, death and retirement

It is not unlawful under the SDA for employers to discriminate by giving special treatment to women in connection with pregnancy or childbirth, or by providing different death and retirement benefits, for example, specifying different retirement ages for men and women.

Under the Social Security Pensions Act 1975 employers must, though, provide equal access to occupational pension schemes. This means that men and women must be treated equally as regards age and length of service for admission to a scheme and in the specification of voluntary or obligatory membership.

The Law Lords limited the meaning of 'provision in relation to retirement' so that *lawful* discrimination against women in retirement benefits is restricted. In the *Garland* case (page 166) travel concessions given after retirement had to apply equally to men and women. In two other cases dealing with discriminatory treatment of women at or near retirement age the Appeal Court resolutely supported the employers' arguments that the SDA did not apply, but following the relatively sympathetic view given in the *Garland* case it is arguable that Ivy Turton's result would be different now.

■ Catherine Roberts, a cleaner, complained when she was sacked at the age of 60. She challenged her employer's policy of retirement at 60 for women and 65 for men on the grounds that discrimination in retirement age, unlike retirement benefits, was covered by the Act. The Court of Appeal upheld the EAT's view that she was excluded. *Roberts v Cleveland Area Authority* 1979 (CA)

■ A redundancy agreement gave an additional 10 weeks' pay to employees made redundant at or over the age of 60. Women had to retire at 60, so Ivy Turton claimed there was discrimination against women. They should be given the 10 weeks' pay if made redundant at or over the age of 55. Digging their heads in the sand, the Court of Appeal overturned the industrial tribunal and the EAT by saying that as it was impossible for a woman to work at the firm after 60, discrimination did not arise. *Turton v MacGregor Wallcoverings Ltd* 1979 (CA)

See also *Turley v Allders*, page 110, for an example of the courts' refusal to outlaw discrimination against pregnant workers.

Other unlawful acts

In addition to the main forms of direct and indirect discrimination, both Acts outlaw other actions. These are contained in sections 37–42 of the SDA and 28–33 of the RRA. These sections are generally enforceable only by the Commissions.

Discriminatory practices
A discriminatory practice is any indirect discrimination. A potential discriminatory practice occurs when all the elements of indirect discrimination are present except a victim.

■ **Example:** if buyers in a big store are recruited from among the sales assistants and the employer demands an English education, workers educated in the Commonwealth will suffer indirect discrimination. If the requirement proves to be such a deterrent that no one educated abroad ever applies, no case will arise. But this does not make the requirement any less offensive. It remains a potential discriminatory practice, and in this case the CRE can issue a **non-discrimination notice** (see below) to have the requirement changed, even though no one has actually complained.

Advertisements

Discriminatory advertisements are unlawful. Job titles such as waiter, salesgirl, postman and stewardess are discriminatory unless it is made clear that they are open to both sexes. If the job advertised requires applicants to be of a particular racial group and this is a valid GOQ, the advertisement is still illegal.

For example, an advertisement for white nurses to work in a South African hospital would be illegal, even though the jobs are abroad and not subject to the Act (RRA section 29). Lord Denning and the Appeal Court ruled, however, that an advertisement for nurses to work in South Africa to deal with 'all white patients' could not reasonably be seen as requiring white nurses only but was just part of the description of the job like 'all the year sunshine' (*RRB v Associated Newspapers* 1978 (CA)). There must be no trace of racial discrimination. But employers can advertise for applicants from one *sex* or the other for jobs where discrimination is permissible.

Instructions

If your supervisor, or anyone in authority over you, or whose wishes you usually implement (such as a client), instructs you to discriminate, that itself is unlawful.

■ London Industrial Art had a vacancy for a clerk/typist and contacted an agency. Details of an applicant were sent and an interview arranged. When the company saw she was black they sent her away and told the agency they did not want 'anyone from Africa' because Africans were not competent. The company was found liable and ordered to pay court costs. *Race Relations Board v London Industrial Art* 1975–76

Action taken against you because you object to an instruction to discriminate is also illegal – *Zarczynska v Levy*, page 129.

Pressure

It is unlawful to put pressure on people to make them discriminate. Pressure is defined as providing or offering benefits, or invoking or threatening a detriment. It would include a strike.

Aid

If you knowingly aid someone who is discriminating, you are both liable. You can escape liability if you had reasonable grounds for relying on an assurance that the act is lawful (for example, because they tell you there is a GOQ).

Liability of employers

If you allege discrimination by, say, a personnel officer recruiting staff for a company, you can sue both the officer and the company if the officer discriminates. Employers are liable for the acts of their employees done with or without their knowledge in the course of their employment.

It is, though, a defence for employers to show that they took all reasonably practicable steps to prevent discrimination by their staff.

Inciting racial hatred

It is an offence to do or say anything in a public place which is likely to stir up racial hatred (see pages 438, 444).

Sexual harassment

This was first recognised as a problem requiring systematic action in the 1970s in the USA. As many as 70 per cent of women in some surveys had been subjected to some form of sexual harassment at work. The US equivalent of the EOC considers it a violation of the equal rights guaranteed by the Civil Rights Act and drew up guidelines for its eradication. This is how they defined it.

> Unwelcome sexual advances, requests for sexual favours and other verbal or physical conduct of a sexual nature constitute sexual harassment when:
>
> **1.** submission to such conduct is made explicitly or implicitly a term or condition of an individual's employment,
>
> **2.** submission to or rejection of such conduct by an individual is used as the basis for employment decisions affecting such individual, or

3. such conduct has the purpose or effect of unreasonably interfering with an individual's work performance or creating an intimidating, hostile or offensive working environment.

It is not specifically recognised in the SDA, but conduct fitting this definition could amount to discrimination on the grounds of sex, since you are treated less favourably than a man would be, or subjected to a detriment that a man would not be. Furthermore, employers are liable (section 4) for anything done by their employees in the course of employment, unless they have taken reasonably practicable steps to stop them. So knowingly allowing an offensive working environment to continue could make them liable.

If you resign following sexual harassment you could claim constructive dismissal. The Appeal Court in *Western Excavating v Sharp* (page 199) said, 'Persistent and unwanted amorous advances by an employer to a female member of his staff would clearly be such conduct' entitling you to claim unfair dismissal. And in a claim of sexual harassment and sex discrimination supported by the EOC three women cleaners who were promoted to messengers and suffered abuse from male workers 'for taking men's jobs' won agreed compensation from their employer, the Daily Mirror, and their union, SOGAT 82 (*Williams v Mirror Group* 1983 (IT)).

The Equality Commissions

Duties

The Equal Opportunities Commission (EOC) and the Commission for Racial Equality (CRE) have similar but not identical duties and powers in the spheres in which they operate. Their duties are:

- to try to eliminate discrimination;
- to promote equality of opportunity between men and women and between racial groups, and to promote good race relations;
- to review the working of the two Acts and to propose amendments.

Members of the Commissions are appointed by the Home Secretary.

Members and staff are paid by the government but operate

independently. Both Commissions must publish annual reports surveying general developments.

Research and education

The Commissions can undertake or assist (financially or otherwise) research and educational activities. Grants can be given by the CRE to any organisation promoting 'equality of opportunity, and good relations, between persons of different racial groups'. But the Home Secretary and the Treasury must approve these grants.

The CRE can issue codes of practice on how to stop discrimination in employment. It must publish a draft and hear representations before sending it to the Home Secretary, who must put it before Parliament.

Formal investigations

The Commissions can investigate particular industries, practices and issues and these can be referred to them by the appropriate minister. The EOC, for example, examined the implementation of equal pay in five hundred companies. The Commissions can condust general inquiries, but a *formal* investigation must be carried out along specified lines. **A formal investigation has to be made before the Commissions can use any of their enforcement powers.** In 1981 the CRE was forced to abandon and restart five investigations following a decision of the Appeal Court that the terms of reference of its investigation into Hillingdon London Borough's housing policies were too wide.

In a formal investigation the Commissions:

1. must draw up terms of reference;

2. must give notice, usually by advertisements in the press, unless the investigation is confined to particular individuals. In cases of racial discrimination the CRE has to inform individuals about any allegations against them. They have the right to state their case and be represented by a lawyer or anyone the Commission does not consider 'unsuitable';

3. may require disclosure of information. If you suppress or destroy documents or if you refuse to attend to give evidence, you can be fined up to £400. For general investigations, the Commissions require the Home Secretary's authority in order to require disclosure;

4. must publish their report;

5. may make general recommendations on policies, procedures and the law and can issue **non-discrimination notices** (below). The earlier race laws were weak because there was no power to compel disclosure or to enforce the law. It is essential that workers ensure that the Commissions use their new powers and follow through their reports with systematic checks.

Legal assistance
You can get assistance from the Commissions for bringing cases in courts or tribunals – see below.

Codes of Practice
Both Commissions published draft Codes of Practice designed to eliminate discrimination, promote equal opportunity, guide employers to ensure their employees don't infringe the Acts and stimulate positive action programmes. The Codes can be taken into account by tribunals and in enforcement proceedings by the Commissions. At the time of writing only the CRE's Code had been approved by the Employment Secretary and Parliament. Norman Tebbit stated his intention to delay bringing it into operation until 1 April 1984.

Enforcement by the Commissions

Some parts of the legislation can be enforced only by the Commissions. Usually these are where no individual has suffered as a result of the discriminatory act or where the remedy is an injunction.

Non-discrimination notices
The Commissions can issue a non-discrimination notice if, during a formal investigation, they find evidence of unlawful discrimination. They can do this even though no proceedings have been brought already against the discriminator (RRA section 58; SDA section 67).

A notice lasts for five years. The Commissions can stop further ('persistent') discrimination within these five years by getting an injunction. This is dealt with below.

A notice can be issued if someone has

- committed direct or indirect discrimination
- applied an actual or potential discriminatory practice
- published an unlawful advertisement
- issued unlawful instructions, or
- put pressure on an employer to discriminate.

A non-discrimination notice requires the recipient
1. not to commit any discriminatory acts;
2. to change his/her practices and arrangements in order to comply with **1.**;
3. to inform the Commission that s/he has made the changes and what they are;
4. to take reasonable steps, as specified in the notice, to tell people concerned about the changes;
5. to provide information so that the Commission can verify that the notice has been complied with; and
6. to give information in a specified form and by a certain date.

Before issuing a non-discrimination notice, the Commission must tell the proposed recipient of its intention, give its reasons, give him/her at least 28 days to make written and/or oral representations, and take these into account. If it still goes ahead, the recipient can appeal, in employment matters, to an industrial tribunal within six weeks. The tribunal can quash or vary the notice only if its requirements are unreasonable or based on incorrect facts.

As soon as any appeal is dealt with, or the time allowed for appealing has run out, the notice becomes final. It is operative for five years from that date, and is entered in a register which anyone can inspect and take copies of. These registers are kept at the Commissions' offices.

The Commissions can start follow-up investigations, with all the statutory powers to compel information and witnesses, during the five-year period. **These powers are ineffective unless you report any breach to the Commissions. If you have any evidence of subsequent discrimination, report it.**

Injunctions for persistent discrimination

The Commissions can get an injunction against employers and others who discriminate or are likely to.

Breach of an injunction is enforceable as contempt of court. Robert Relf, a former Ku Klux Klan activist, was gaoled when he refused to comply with a Birmingham court order to remove his racist house-for-sale sign in May 1976.

How to claim

Before you make a claim to an industrial tribunal you may need more information about the employer's practices. This will be particularly important if you are alleging discrimination in recruitment, because you won't know much about the employer, can't get union support and are out of work.

To try to meet this problem you can use a questionnaire (see page 490) to obtain information. The form is not compulsory, but it will be used in evidence and tribunals can draw adverse inferences from an employer's failure to complete it.

Provided you have been employed for one year at 16 or more hours a week (plus exceptions – see page 468) and you have been sacked, you should claim under both the EPCA *and* the anti-discrimination Acts. Otherwise, your claim is restricted to the anti-discrimination Acts.

Claim **within three months** of the event you are complaining about. See page 490 for the procedure.

The Commissions can help you to bring a case and can provide legal aid. If you can't get union support, you should write to them and request it. Addresses on page 511. Sometimes they will provide legal representation in cases involving important questions of principle. They monitor cases, too, and occasionally offer assistance to individuals in appeals from industrial tribunals to the EAT.

Advertisements, instructions and pressure

If you are personally affected by one of these unlawful practices you can complain to a tribunal. For example, you may be interested in applying for a job which is advertised in a way which indirectly discriminates against you; or management may give instructions to your supervisor not to make overtime available to you. But the Commissions can start proceedings whether someone is directly prejudiced or not.

Proving discrimination

This is the most difficult part.

Between 1976 and 1982, the number of claims made each year under the employment provisions of the SDA declined from 243 to 150. About one-third reached a tribunal, where the success rate had steadily declined by 1981 to 20 per cent of cases heard. In 1982, however, successful results were achieved in nearly half of the applications, either through conciliation or tribunal hearings. The RRA presents a hopeless picture. Out of 280 cases heard by tribunals only 14 (5 per cent) succeeded in 1981 (*EOC and CRE Annual Reports 1981* and *Employment Gazette*, April 1983).

If you allege direct discrimination you have to bring enough evidence to show you have been treated less favourably than a person of the opposite sex or another racial group was treated, or would have been treated. This evidence must suggest that the reason was your sex or race. The employer then has to show either

- that you were not treated unfavourably, or
- if you *were*, it was not because of your sex or race.

If you allege indirect discrimination you have to go much further. **You have to bring evidence** to show the employer applied a condition or requirement which is applied to everyone but which

- you could not comply with;
- was to your detriment; and
- was such that a considerably smaller proportion of people of your sex or race than others could comply with it.

Once you have got over these hurdles, the employer must then prove that the requirement was justifiable. You will need firm evidence to avoid defeat on these vague terms – 'detriment', 'considerable', 'justifiable'. So prepare your case carefully.

If you can also bring a claim for unfair dismissal under the EPCA, the burden of proving the reason for sacking falls on management (see page 211).

An employer who says that discrimination is justified because of a GOQ must prove it.

Remedies

On an individual complaint to a tribunal the following remedies are available if the tribunal considers them 'just and equitable' (RRA section 56; SDA section 65):

- declaration
- compensation
- re-engagement or reinstatement
- recommendation of action to be taken.

Declaration
This declares your rights and says that you were unlawfully discriminated against. It is not enforceable but may have some persuasive influence.

Compensation
You can be awarded compensation for:

- actual losses, such as expenses and wages;
- future losses of wages and benefits;
- injury to your feelings.

Jeanette Johnston (page 126) was given £200 for injury to feelings. The maximum amount of compensation in 1983/84 was £7,500. But in 1982, more than half of the tribunal awards and conciliated settlements under the SDA were of less than £200, and only one successful applicant in seven got over £1,000. Tribunals can't reduce this on the grounds that you 'contributed' to the discrimination as they can in unfair dismissal cases.

■ A West Indian was sacked during his probationary period in a nationalised industry. He was a skilled mechanic and had been in the RAF and in private sector garages. Management said he needed close supervision and was sacked. A white worker had two warnings before this happened. The West Indian was awarded £805 compensation. *Race Relations Board Report 1975–76 Appendix V Case 1*.

You can't get compensation for indirect discrimination which your employer proves was unintentional (RRA section 50; SDA section 66). However, if you are claiming unfair dismissal as well, you (may) get up to £18,980 (1983/84) in total compensation (see page 477).

Re-engagement and reinstatement

Tribunals have no specific power under the anti-discrimination laws to order re-engagement or reinstatement. They can recommend action (see below). But if you link a discrimination claim to a claim under the EPCA the tribunal must ask if you want to go back. If it orders this and management refuse, additional compensation must be awarded (EPCA section 70–71).

Recommended action

A tribunal can make a recommendation that the employer should take action 'appearing . . . to be practicable for the purpose of obviating or reducing the adverse effect on the complainant of any act of discrimination'. Of course, this might include a recommendation of reinstatement, but it is weaker than a court order. A recommendation could specify, for example, changes in promotion, training and recruitment policies.

Trade union action against discrimination

Determined action by trade unionists to stamp out discrimination is the only way to make the Acts effective. You can't rely on the legislation alone – the burden of proof is itself a formidable obstacle to enforcement.

The TUC has recommended that unions should negotiate collective agreements. This is their model equal opportunity clause:

> The Parties to this Agreement are committed to the development of positive policies to promote equal opportunity in employment regardless of workers' sex, marital status, creed, colour, race or ethnic origins. This principle will apply in respect of all conditions of work including pay, hours of work, holiday entitlement, overtime and shiftwork, work allocation, guaranteed earnings, sick pay, pensions, recruitment, training, promotion and redundancy. The management undertake to draw opportunities for training and promotion to the attention of all eligible employees, and to inform all employees of this Agreement on equal opportunity.
>
> The parties agree that they will review from time to time, through their joint machinery, the operation of this equal opportunity policy.
>
> If any employee considers that he or she is suffering from

unequal treatment on the grounds of sex, marital status, creed, colour, race or ethnic origins he or she may make a complaint which will be dealt with through the agreed procedure for dealing with grievances.

This clause is not enough. To be effective, you should:

- negotiate agreements requiring a programme of 'affirmative action' to promote women and ethnic minorities
- make all members and management aware of the issues involved in sexual harassment and take up all complaints within the grievance procedure
- extend the equal opportunity clause in the first sentence to cover disability, sexual orientation, nationality, national origins and religious belief
- recruit all workers into unions and encourage immigrant workers to play an active part
- press for language training courses and point out their existence
- develop links with Community Relations Officers
- oppose racist actions and attitudes wherever they occur.

Summary

1. It is illegal for employers to discriminate against you on the grounds of sex, marriage, race, colour, nationality or ethnic or national origins.

2. Discrimination means an employer treats you less favourably than s/he would treat another person (direct discrimination), or s/he makes a requirement that applies to all workers but which it is much harder for you to comply with (indirect discrimination).

3. You can complain to a tribunal if an employer discriminates against you in recruitment, terms and conditions, transfer, promotion, training, benefits or dismissal or by subjecting you to any detriment.

4. Discrimination in pay or contractual terms between men and women doing similar work is covered by the Equal Pay Act.

5. Discrimination is permitted if employers can prove that being of a particular race or sex is a genuine occupational qualification for a particular job.

6. The Equality Commissions can take legal action against people who advertise, or give help to, or put pressure on others to discriminate. You may get legal assistance from the Commissions to bring a case yourself.

7. If you win at a tribunal it has power to award compensation and to recommend that the employer take action to prevent discrimination. If you are sacked, a tribunal can order management to reinstate you.

9. Equal pay

The problem of low pay for women / EEC law /
the basic elements of the Equal Pay Act / how it
fits in with the Sex Discrimination Act / equality
with a man in the same employment / 'like work'
and 'practical differences' / duties, hours,
responsibility, training, skill, experience, legal
bans / job evaluation / 'genuine material
differences' / location, grading, historical
anomalies and red-circling, length of service,
market forces / how to claim / proving it /
remedies / discriminatory agreements and pay
structures / how effective is the Act? / what
reforms are needed? / and a summary.

In 1888 the TUC decided unanimously that 'it is desirable in the
interests of both men and women that in trades where women
do the same work as men, they shall receive the same payment'.
A government committee in 1919 and a Royal Commission in
1946 said the same thing. Parliament finally responded in 1970
by passing Labour's Equal Pay Act.

The Act became effective on 29 December 1975. Despite this
unprecedented lead-in period of five-and-a-half years, women's
earnings are still much lower than men's, as the figures for April
1982 show. (Since, on average, men worked five hours a week
longer than women, it is more realistic to compare average
hourly rather than weekly earnings. See Table 3.)

Employers still think it is cheaper to employ women, Recognition disputes at Grunwick, 1977–78 and Chix, 1980 were as

Table 3

	1. Women	2. Men	1. as per-centage of 2.
Average weekly earnings			
manual workers	£80.10	£133.80	60
all workers	£99	£154.50	64
Average weekly hours			
manual workers	39.3	44.3	89
all workers	37.1	41.7	89
Average hourly earnings			
manual workers	£ 2.04	£ 3.02	67
all workers	£ 2.67	£ 3.70	72

Source: *New Earnings Survey 1982.*
Note: excluding workers whose pay was affected by absence.

much about low women's wages as the local authority workers' disputes in 1978–79 and the NHS dispute in 1982.

The Equal Pay Act can be measured in terms of how differentials between men and women have narrowed. Acting against it are traditional attitudes and legacies. In the past, women have had fewer skills, fewer opportunities, less training, more breaks in continuity of employment and less union organisation than men. Those facts necessarily perpetuate unequal pay, and **low pay** for jobs which have historically been for women only.

During the first six years of the Equal Pay Act, men's average earnings rose by 215 per cent, women's by 219 per cent. On the actual earnings figures given above, women will, at this rate of progress, achieve equal pay in AD 2024.

Internationally, the struggle for equal treatment has been reflected in the Universal Declaration of Human Rights, the European Social Charter, the International Covenant on Economic, Social and Cultural Rights and International Labour Organisation (ILO) Conventions and Recommendations. In the EEC, Article 119 of the Treaty of Rome requires equal pay for equal work and Directive 75/117 extends this to include by 1978 work of equal value. Equal pay for equal work has been a legal requirement since the UK joined the EEC on 1 January 1973, but no claims can be brought for arrears prior to 29 December 1975, the date the Equal Pay Act came into effect.

This chapter deals with the Act, the Treaty of Rome, and

decisions made by tribunals and courts. The Equal Pay Act **can be used strategically to improve conditions when negotiations and industrial action fail or are inappropriate.**

Where to find the law

Equal Pay Act 1970, as amended by the Sex Discrimination Act 1975 (SDA) and the Equal Pay (Amendment) Regulations 1983. The Equal Pay Act is reprinted in full in schedule 1 of the SDA. Article 119 of the Treaty of Rome and Directive 75/117.

The Act and EEC law

Article 119 requires equal pay for equal work. This takes precedence over the Act and can be enforced directly in UK courts and tribunals. In many respects it is more favourable to women and has been interpreted in a more sympathetic way than the Act. The *combined* effect of the Treaty and the Act is explained below at each stage. Directive 75/117 on equal pay tells the UK government how to implement the Treaty and it is clear that the Act is not a correct or adequate application of the Treaty's principles. Directive 76/207 says how the principle of equal treatment without discrimination on the grounds of sex, marital or family status should be implemented – see chapter 8. The Equal Pay (Amendment) Regulations 1983 are the government's response to the requirement for equal pay for work of equal value. They come into force on 1 January 1984, and even then it is arguable that they do not fulfil the UK's obligations to the EEC.

The Act's basic elements

The Act says that *in certain circumstances* men and women are entitled to be paid the same and to receive the same terms and conditions in their contracts, collective agreements and pay structures. If you don't have parity, your contract, agreement or pay structure will be amended to include the right to equal terms.

Despite its narrow title, the Act deals with **all terms and conditions contained in either a man's or a woman's contract. It applies equally to men and women,** although all the examples given in this handbook relate to women. The right to equal pay applies in any of the following three situations:

1. You are employed on like work with a man in the same employment. This means:

- you do the **same work,** or
- you do **work of a broadly similar nature** and differences are not of **practical importance** in relation to your terms and conditions.

2. You are employed on work **rated as equivalent** with that of a man in the same employment, following a job evaluation study.

3. With effect from 1 January 1984, you are employed on **work of equal value** which is not 'like work' as defined by **1.** above, and which is not covered by a job evaluation scheme (**unless you can prove that the scheme itself is discriminatory**).

Provided that in **1. 2.** and **3.** above, the variation in your terms is **not genuinely due to a material difference** between your case and his.

4. You are covered by a **pay structure** or **collective agreement** which is discriminatory.

1. 2. and **3.** are the individual aspects of the Act; **4.** is the collective aspect. Each of the basic elements is dealt with separately below (page 164 for individual aspects, page 186 for collective aspects). Diagram 3 shows the steps you must take if you have to enforce your rights by going to law.

The Equal Pay Act deals with matters of contract. It says that 'equality clauses' are deemed to be incorporated into every contract. In other words, you have a contractual right to equal treatment. If there is a dispute, the tribunals can amend contracts to provide equal terms and conditions.

Conversely, anything outside the contract cannot be remedied by the Act. For this you have to look to the SDA.

The right to equality under the Equal Pay Act applies if any term of your contract *is* or *becomes* less favourable than a man's. This means you can bring a claim if you are getting parity, but you think you should be getting better terms.

■ **Example:** A job is advertised on scale 1–5. You have outstanding qualifications and six years' experience, so you

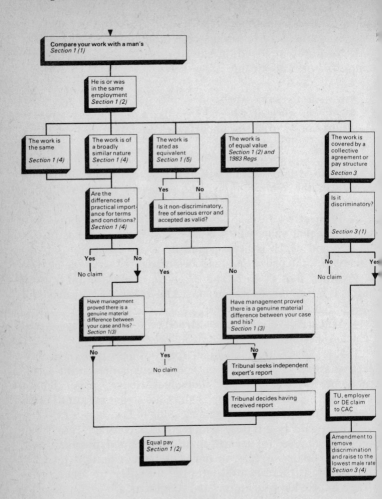

Diagram 3 **Your Equal Pay Act rights**

enter at scale 5. A man with fewer qualifications and less experience is subsequently appointed on scale 5. You are clearly entitled to *better* terms than he is. Your right to scale 5 under your contract has therefore become relatively less favourable to you. So you can claim under the Equal Pay Act. Your contract should be amended to maintain the differential obtained through your superior qualifications and experience. (Compare *Pointon v Sussex University* page 183 below, where the tribunal decided that the woman was not in fact better qualified than the man. If she was, she might have won her case.)

Sex discrimination and equal pay

There is no overlap between the SDA and the Equal Pay Act. In fact there is a *gap* in the coverage which can deprive you of all protection. The Home Office *Guide* to the SDA describes the relationship as follows (practical examples have been inserted in order to help):

- **a.** If the less favourable treatment relates to the **payment of money** which is regulated by a contract of employment, only the Equal Pay Act can apply.
  Example: You get £1.80 an hour. A male colleague gets £1.85p.
- **b.** If the employee is treated less favourably than an employee of the other sex who is doing the same or broadly similar work or whose work has been given an equal value under job evaluation and the less favourable treatment relates to **something which is regulated by the contract of employment** of either of them, only the Equal Pay Act can apply.
  Example: You are hourly paid. He is weekly paid and given the higher status accorded to white-collar staff.
- **c.** If the less favourable treatment relates to **a matter which is not included in a contract** (either expressly or by virtue of the Equal Pay Act), only the SDA can apply.
  Example: He is sent on a management training course, you aren't.
- **d.** If the less favourable treatment relates to **a matter (other than the payment of money) in a contract, and the comparison is with workers who are not doing the same or broadly similar**

work or work which has been given an equal value under job evaluation, only the SDA can apply.

Example: Men's contracts entitle them to a cheap mortgage from the employer, yours doesn't.

- **e.** If the complaint relates to **a matter (other than the payment of money) which is regulated by an employee's contract** of employment, but is based on an allegation that **an employee of the other sex would be treated more favourably** in similar circumstances (that is, it does not relate to the actual treatment of an existing employee of the other sex), only the SDA can apply.

Example: You are entitled, under your contract, to a cheap mortgage, but it must be guaranteed by your husband. You know a male employee would not have to get his wife's guarantee.

Diagram 4 illustrates the relationship between the two Acts described in the above examples.

If you have followed this tortuous trail you may have noticed the gap. Isabella Meeks (page 132) fell into it. She showed that her employers indirectly discriminated against women by paying a higher hourly rate to people who worked 35 or more hours a week. Fewer women can work full-time than men. But since the unfavourable treatment related to *money*, only the Equal Pay Act applied. Under this Act Ms Meeks had to compare herself with a man. She could find no men doing similar work to her. So she was excluded under the SD Act and was also ineligible under the Equal Pay Act.

Parliament intended that the two Acts should be complementary. But the flaw occurs when no men are available for comparison, or when they are available but a tribunal rules that you are not doing similar or equal value work. The only straw you can grasp is to complain to the EOC. The EOC can bring proceedings under section 37 of the SDA for the kind of 'discriminatory practice' that Isabella Meeks proved. But you can't get compensation this way (SDA section 73).

What is 'pay'?

The Act talks of all terms and conditions contained in your contract. The Treaty goes further and includes 'any other consideration, whether in cash or kind, which the worker receives,

WHAT DOES THE UNEQUAL TREATMENT RELATE TO?

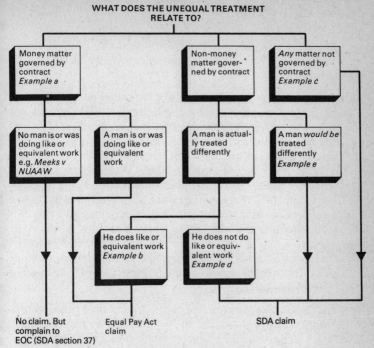

Diagram 4 **Equal Pay and Sex Discrimination**

directly or indirectly in respect of his employment from his employer'. This covers pension contributions, *ex gratia* payments, retirement benefits, indirect benefits and any other act of overt discrimination between men and women relating to pay. Indirect or covert discrimination is dealt with by the SDA.

■ Lloyds Bank's pension scheme required all men to join, but allowed women to stay out until the age of 25. In order to equalise the effective pay, the bank paid 5 per cent extra to the men, and then deducted it as pension contributions. This indirectly improved a man's unemployment benefits and entitlements under the EPCA; he also got his 5 per cent back when he left. In a test case affecting 14,000 women and worth £3 million the European Court said this was discrimination in *pay* since it affected credit, family allowances and benefits. Although employers could get away with this under the Act (because retirement arrangements are exempt) the Treaty strengthens British law and made the discrimination unlawful. *Worringham v Lloyds Bank* 1981 (ECJ and CA)

Similarly the European Court outlawed the discriminatory provision of *ex gratia* facilities for concessionary travel following retirement:

■ During employment British Rail gave travel benefits to male and female employees and their families. The concession continued after retirement for men's families. Retired women's families got nothing. Since this was a concessionary benefit, not a contractual right, the Equal Pay Act did not apply. It was claimed that the SDA, which exempts retirement provisions, did not apply either. But the European Court said the Treaty applies since these facilities are given 'in respect of employment' and are regarded as an extension of benefits given while still at work. The Law Lords were forced to agree that these were not 'provisions in relation to retirement' and that the SDA applied to make discrimination against women illegal. *Garland v British Rail Engineering* 1982 (ECJ and HL)

In both these cases the courts took the trade union position that retirement arrangements are to be regarded as deferred pay. The SDA does, though, allow for some differential retirement provisions – see page 144.

Equal with whom?

The individual part of the Equal Pay Act depends on there being men and women in the same employment. **On the assumption that we are dealing with a woman's claim** (although the same applies to men) that requirement can be broken down into two parts.

1. There must be a man
The Act requires you to find a man with whom you can compare yourself. In jobs which are traditionally female-only you can't make a claim unless you can show a male worker on like or equivalent work. You can, however, complain to the EOC. You *can* use the SDA if a man *would be* treated differently, even though none presently is.

Once you have established that a man is doing or was doing similar or equivalently-rated work, if only for a day, you have a claim. It doesn't matter if that man leaves or is promoted or is on holiday at the time – you are entitled to his terms.

■ Trust House Forte run the Post House Hotel at Heathrow Airport. In the grill room they employed six waitresses at 85p an hour and one waiter at 97½p. In order to avoid the Act, they changed the man's title to 'banqueting supervisor' on 5 January 1976. The women claimed equal pay and won – but the tribunal gave it for only the seven days between the date the Act came into force and 5 January. Ann Sorbie and the five other women appealed; so did THF. The EAT said the women's contracts had been amended with effect from the date the Act came in. **They could not be changed again simply because the man was no longer doing like work.** Nor did it matter that the grill was closed during the first week of the Act; they were still 'employed' during that week. The Act did not have a 'fluctuating effect', as THF contended. **So once you get equal pay, you don't lose it if the man leaves.** *Sorbie v Trust House Forte Hotels* 1977 (EAT)

What happens if you **take over from a man** but get less money than he was getting? This is usually grounds for a claim, but not always, the EAT has said. Joyce Nuttall (see below, page 174) took over from a man but was paid £6.50 a week less. Her claim was dismissed because the EAT said the work she did was different. Ms Nuttall could, however, have made a claim for sex discrimination in this case because she was offered work on different terms to those that would be offered to a man.

Since then the issue has been sorted out by the European Court.

■ Wendy Smith worked in a pharmaceutical warehouse in Wembley. She got £50 a week in 1976. The job had been vacant for five months and had previously been done by a man on £60 who left before the Act came into operation. She claimed equal pay. The Act did not apply because she and he were not doing the work at the same time. But the European Court said this is irrelevant under the Treaty and awarded equal pay. *Macarthys v Smith* 1980 (ECJ and CA)

This case is important because it establishes a right to equal pay under the Treaty where the Act doesn't. But it confirms that the Treaty has two other features. Firstly, **it cannot stop indirect or hidden discrimination in pay** and therefore you can't get equality by saying management *would* pay a man more than they do or would pay you. In other words you can't compare yourself with a hypothetical man – there must actually be a man who works or did work of equal value.

Secondly, while the Act does not allow financial considerations to block an equal pay claim, the Treaty does. For example, management might say they can't afford any longer to pay the rate they were paying to a former male employee. You can't claim under the Act, but under the Treaty; and the courts have said that under the Treaty economic considerations can justify equal pay to *successive* employees.

■ Ms Arnold was a clerk/typist in a small shipping office in Hull on £37 a week. Her (male) supervisor on £73 was made redundant. For nearly two years until the office was closed down she continued to do all his duties. She claimed equal pay under the Treaty. The EAT said the tribunal had to consider whether she was paid half his rate because she was a woman, or because of the firm's straitened financial circumstances. In looking at successive jobs (but not at simultaneous ones – see the *Clay Cross* case, page 183) a changing financial background is relevant and may justify unequal pay. *Albion Shipping Agency v Arnold* 1981 (EAT)

When you make your claim, **you** decide whom you want to be compared with **not** your employer, nor the tribunal. Once you decide, the comparison must be made with that man.

■ Mary Ainsworth worked in Glass Tubes's Chesterfield factory. She re-inspected glassware after it had been inspected by a man. She got about £2 a week less and claimed parity. The company found a male re-inspector on nights who was getting her rate and so the tribunal dismissed her claim. Supported by the GMWU, she appealed. The EAT said the tribunal must consider her claim for parity with the man she had nominated. It was a short-lived success, for the tribunal later held that the work was not broadly similar. *Ainsworth v Glass Tubes and Components* 1977 (EAT)

2. In the same employment

Comparison must be with a man in **the same employment** (section 1(6)). This means you are employed by the same or an associated employer at the same establishment or at establishments in Great Britain **where common terms and conditions are observed,** either generally or for workers of your 'class'.

There is no definition of 'establishment' but factors considered under other Acts are: geographical, managerial or financial separation, separate supply and servicing arrangements. In order to claim parity across different plants of the same firm or its higher-paid subsidiaries, you would have to show a common pay scale arising out of the same negotiations with the same unions. See *NAAFI v Varley*, page 179.

You can compare yourself both with employees and with self-employed workers who do work for the employer. **This could be useful if contractors are paid on a higher rate than direct labour.**

'Like work' and 'practical differences'

Section 1 (4) defines 'like work' as follows:

> A woman is to be regarded as employed on like work with men if, but only if, her work and theirs is of the same or a broadly similar nature, and the differences (if any) between the things she does and the things they do are not of practical importance in relation to terms and conditions of employment; and accordingly in comparing her work with theirs regard shall be had to the frequency or otherwise with which any such differences occur in practice as well as to the nature and extent of the differences.

These questions are important in negotiating equal pay with employers. There are five major areas where employers have tried to avoid equal pay. These involve:

- extra duties
- different hours
- responsibility
- training, skill and experience
- legal bans.

Extra duties
The most frequent abuse of the Equal Pay Act involves employers weaving extra duties into men's contracts. While

some of these abuses still exist, the end of the road for them was signalled in the *Electrolux* case.

■ All but one of 600 women working on the fridge and freezer line of Electrolux in Luton were on grade 01. The basic rate for piece-work was 4.1p. All of the 1,300 men were on grade 10, with a rate of 6.3p. The company admitted the men and women did similar work but claimed the men were obliged to accept **different duties** – to transfer to different jobs which may be less well paid or more physically demanding, to work nights and to do non-productive work. The EAT upheld the tribunal's award of equal pay. But the company later changed the women's contracts and refused to apply the ruling to any women except those who had taken their cases. There was a strike and the EOC and ACAS were called in to investigate the whole pay structure. *Electrolux v Hutchinson* 1976 (EAT)

Mr Justice Phillips said that these differences could not be regarded as important.

> For such a difference to be material . . . it must be shown that as well as being obliged to do additional, different duties the men in fact do so to some significant extent.

In other words, the key question is **what happens in practice**, not, what does the contract say? If different work *is* done by the men, the EAT says, the tribunal must then ask what is 'the nature of the work done, how often does it take place, how important is it, and so on'.

This section was interpreted in the first equal pay case to reach the EAT. The judgment was heavily critical of tribunals which take a 'too pedantic approach'.

■ Barbara Lawton worked a 40-hour week cooking lunches for 10–20 directors. She was her own boss. She claimed equal pay with two assistant chefs in the works canteen who worked a 45-hour week cooking three meals a day in two sittings (that is, 350 meals). They had to prepare meals in advance and were answerable to the head chef. The EAT upheld a Nottinghamshire tribunal's award of equal pay as the difference was not of practical importance in relation to terms and conditions. *Capper Pass v Lawton* 1976 (EAT)

Mr Justice Phillips said:

the work need not be of the same nature in order to be like work. It is enough if it is of a similar nature. Indeed, it need only be broadly similar. In such cases . . . there will necessarily be differences between the work done.

He went on to say that tribunals should use a 'broad judgment' in looking at whether work is 'broadly similar', otherwise every case would fail. He said tribunals must ask the following questions:

1. Is the work of the same or a broadly similar nature? This involves a general consideration of the type of work and the skill and knowledge required to do it. It can be answered without a 'minute examination of the detail of the differences'.

2. If it is of a broadly similar nature, are the differences of practical importance in relation to terms and conditions? Disregard trivial differences 'not likely in the real world to be reflected in terms and conditions'. Once broad similarity is established it should be regarded as like work unless the differences could be expected to result in different terms and conditions. Then take account of the frequency, the nature and the extent of these differences. In other words, **differences are important only if, in a freely and objectively negotiated pay settlement which paid no regard to sex, they would be reflected in different rates of pay.**

If there are extra duties which are of practical importance you may not be entitled to split them off from the rest of the duties which are comparable to yours, and so get equal pay for the parts which are similar. A hard line was taken by a majority of the EAT, but it may be wrong.

■ Rita Maidment and a male employee spent 90 per cent of their time packing. He got an extra £2 for his responsibility as a stock-keeper. She claimed equal pay, as for most of the time she was doing like work. Valerie Hardacre, a machine operator, compared herself with a male operator/setter. The only difference in the work they did was that he set his own machine, taking up about an hour a week. Both women lost. The jobs as a whole were different because of the extra duties. This meant they were not on like work so the Act did not apply. The EAT felt there was sex discrimination but had no power to say what the proper differential should be. *Maidment v Cooper* 1978 (EAT)

It is clearly arguable that if you are doing similar work for 90 per cent of the time the work done in the remainder is not of practical importance in your conditions. It *may* also be possible to separate the value of the common work and treat that as a contract requiring equality. It is clear that you can claim parity by separating overtime and premium-time payments if the work is the same but done during different hours.

Different hours

Some employers have argued that they don't have to give equal pay to workers who do similar work at different times of the day. To this, the EAT has said:

> in the context of the Equal Pay Act . . . the mere time at which the work is performed should be disregarded when considering the differences between the things which the woman does and the things which the man does . . . [In] applying section 1 (4) no attention should be paid to the fact that the men work at some different time of the day, if that is the only difference between what the women do and they do.

The facts leading to that judgment were:

■ Alice Dugdale and four other women worked on quality control at Kraft's food factory in Liverpool. They worked days for £32.80 basic plus £5.80 day-shift premium. Men did similar work at night and every third Sunday morning. (Women are prevented by the Factories Act from working at these times, unless exempt.) The men got £42.45 basic plus £11.60 night-shift premium, that is £9.65 on basic and £5.80 on shift rate more than the women. Supported by USDAW, the women claimed parity of basic rates. After two hearings and an EAT appeal, the tribunal said two women weren't doing similar work. One was, and got parity of basic rates. Alice and her colleague did similar work, but the men did slightly more work at night. So the women got 90 per cent of the men's basic rate, 10 per cent reflecting this real difference. *Dugdale v Kraft* 1977 (EAT)

It is easy to see discrimination in a case where the basic rates are different *and* where night shifts attract a higher premium than days. If there is no premium, but the men receive a higher basic rate, you have to apportion the rate to take acount of their availability for night. For example, if all the men work a three-shift system and get £120 a week, and all the women work a double day shift for £80, the men are effectively getting a night-shift premium of £40. It would be difficult to show that this was 'genuinely due' to the night work *alone*. You could argue that, say £30 should be treated as night-shift premium. You could then claim equality on the new notional basic of £90.

Discrimination against *part-time workers* was challenged in the European Court.

■ At a Harlow textile factory all the men worked 40 hours, apart from a pensioner re-engaged on 16 hours. All but five of the women worked 30 hours or less. The part-timers got 10 per cent less than the full-timers' hourly rate and claimed equality. The employer said the differential was justified by the need to discourage absenteeism, increase productivity and use plant to the full. The European Court said that working shorter hours *is not* itself a material difference justifying unequal pay. But a differential can be justified if in fact it does. fulfil the (non-discriminatory) stated needs of the employer – increasing productivity, etc. If the effect of these needs is discrimination, it doesn't matter that the employer did not intend it to be. *Jenkins v Kingsgate* 1981 (ECJ and EAT)

The upshot of this case is that it is unlawful to set lower rates for part-time women unless management can justify it on non-discriminatory business grounds. In most cases they will find it difficult to do this without invoking popular and unsubstantiated prejudices relating to the work of part-timers versus full-timers; and the evidence is that the majority of part-timers and a minority of full-timers are women – see *Meeks v NUAAW*, page 132.

Responsibility
Responsibility is a factor which may make a practical difference in terms and conditions. In comparing two jobs you must look at the circumstances in which they are done (which would include the degree of responsibility) and not simply at the actual

work. If a mistake by the man has a more serious effect than a mistake by the woman, he carries more responsibility. This can be a 'practical difference' under section 1 (4) of the Equal Pay Act.

■ Joyce Nuttall was a production scheduler, responsible for ordering parts and materials for the production of fork-lift trucks. She did the same work as a man, but she dealt with 2,400 items up to a value of £2.50, whereas he looked after 1,200 items from £5 to £1,000. He got £6.50 a week more. The EAT said the tribunal was wrong to disregard *the conse-quences of mistakes – responsibility is a practical difference. Eaton v Nuttall* 1977 (EAT)

The ultimate example of a difference caused by responsibility was the decision of the tribunal which found that social worker Susan Waddington, though paid less than a man, was not entitled to equal pay as she was *more* responsible.

■ Susan Waddington was a community leader paid on the national scale for social workers. She suggested opening a playground and appointed a play leader. He was paid on the youth leaders' scale and got £400 a year more, although she had overall control and was more responsible. The Nott-ingham tribunal said she could not claim parity. But the EAT said the tribunal had looked mainly at their job descriptions and contracts and not at the *similar nature* of the work they did. The EAT sent it back to be reheard, but the tribunal refused to alter its decision. *Waddington v Leicester Council for Voluntary Services* 1977 (EAT)

The tribunal's decision is clearly perverse. It could have said that Susan Waddington's contract had become less favourable than the man's (as in the example on page 161), and given her parity.

The case is also important for what was said about grading systems (see page 179 below).

Training, skill and experience
Different levels of skill and experience can make the nature of the work itself different, and so preclude equal pay under sec-tion 1 (4). (These factors might more appropriately be grounds

for personal distinctions between a man and a woman who are employed on like work, and so be a 'material difference', within section 1 (3), which is discussed below.) The nature of the work done must be quite different when performed by someone with training, skill and experience if section 1 (4) is to be used to exclude equal pay.

For example, a machine operator with three years' experience may be doing approximately the same sort of work as a new starter. But the extra experience *may* mean that he can do it more quickly, more efficiently, with fewer stoppages, and be able to recognise problems earlier and to train new starters.

Legal bans

The ban on women working in factories at nights and on Sundays (Factories Act section 93) is not itself a practical difference unless the work done by men in those hours is different from that done by women. As Alice Dugdale's case showed, the basic rate should be the same and a notional basic rate should be hewn out of a rate that embraces night work.

The ban on women working in certain processes, such as those involving lead and radioactivity, is probably a practical difference sufficient to defeat a claim for parity. Trade unionists should demand that the work should be made safe enough for both men and women to do it.

Work rated as equivalent

The second legal route to equal pay is through job evaluation. Before you get into any discussions on job evaluation it is advisable to be familiar with the trade union arguments on this management technique. See, for example, *Against the Clock* by Alan Grant (Pluto Press 1983). Many unions and the TUC provide training in this subject. Get time off to study if management propose job evaluation.

Men and women are entitled to equality if their jobs have been given an equal value

in terms of the demand made on a worker under various headings (for instance effort, skill, decision), on a study undertaken with a view to evaluating in those terms the jobs to be done by all or any of the employees in an undertaking (Equal Pay Act section 1 (5)).

The factors listed are only a few among those that can be considered. No method of job evaluation is specified – you can use any of the accepted methods such as job ranking, paired comparisons, job classification, points assessment or factor comparison. All of these are recognised by the Advisory, Conciliation and Arbitration Service (ACAS). (ACAS is required to conciliate if you make a claim to a tribunal for equal pay.)

So **like work** and **work rated as equivalent** are separate and mutually exclusive routes to equal pay. Usually a claim cannot proceed for like work or work of equal value if a job evaluation on the lines described in section 1 (5) has been carried out. The only exceptions to this rule are discriminatory schemes, or

1. if there is a fundamental error in the job evaluation, or

2. if the parties do not accept it as a 'valid' study or

3. if the study is not 'valid' because it is not 'thorough in analysis and capable of impartial application'.

The following cases illustrate these points:

■ Job evaluation was carried out by Broxtowe Council in Nottingham. The results were not accepted in full by the Council, the unions or the workers involved. So six women brought a claim on the basis of *like work*. The EAT said the tribunal was *wrong to disregard* the job evaluation and sent the case back for reconsideration. Only if there was a *fundamental error* could the study be disregarded and the claim proceed on the basis of *like work*. *Greene v Broxtowe District Council* 1977 (EAT)

This case is now relevant only for the statement that a fundamental error can invalidate a job evaluation study. Since then and more importantly, the courts have decided that the Act applies when there is a completed study, and it is complete only when the employers and employees have agreed to accept it as a valid study. In *O'Brien v Sim-Chem* 1980 (HL), a study was carried out and its results accepted by management and union, but it was not implemented as a pay structure because of government pay restraint and the employers' failure to add a merit assessment scheme. Three women who had been given an equal rating to men therefore continued to be paid unequally. The Law Lords said that once the results of the study had been accepted by both sides equal pay applied. And in *Arnold v Beecham Group* 1982 (EAT) it was confirmed that equal pay applies from the moment a study is accepted even if management and unions are unable to agree on new pay scales based on it.

In another case Joyce Nuttall, as we have seen, was claiming parity. During the appeal hearing the EAT found that there was a form of job evaluation and sent the case back to a fresh tribunal to consider this. She disputed the worth of the scheme because it took account of personal factors. Mr Justice Phillips said that for a job evaluation to be legally acceptable it must

> be possible, by applying the study, to arrive at the position of a particular employee at a particular point in a particular salary grade, without taking other matters into account, except those unconnected with the nature of the work. It will be in order to take into account such matters as merit or seniority etc, but any matters concerning the work (for example, responsibility) one would expect to find taken care of in the evaluation study. One which does not satisfy that test and which requires management to make a subjective judgment concerning the nature of the work before the employee can be fitted into the appropriate place in the appropriate salary grade, would seem to us not to be a valid study.

Your claim for equal pay will be in danger if a tribunal says that because there is a job evaluation, there can't be a claim on the alternative basis of **broadly similar work.** Management might conduct their own study, based on personal weightings and not on an objective analysis, and perpetuate existing discrimination. You can challenge that if there is a fundamental error or you can prove that the scheme is not 'valid' or if it isn't objective. But you can't claim you are doing broadly similar work. So management may try to block your access to equal pay by carrying out their own job evaluation study. The only way to stop this is by refusing to co-operate, or by requiring time off to learn about job evaluation, demanding trade union representation during all stages of the job evaluation exercise, and ensuring that the study is not complete until agreement has been reached on the scheme and on rates of pay following it.

Work of equal value

This is where the Act and the EEC law are different. The

Treaty and the Directive require equal pay for work of equal value. The EEC Commission challenged the UK government, and in 1982 the European Court ruled that the Equal Pay Act did not comply with the Treaty and the equal pay Directive (75/117). This is because the Act applies only where a man and a woman do like work. If the work is different you can claim equal pay only if a job evaluation study has been conducted, and you have no legal right to demand a study. So there was no legal way for you to get equal pay if you think your work is worth the same as a man's, and management don't agree to a method of comparing the work. The European Court judgment is binding on the government (*Commission of the EEC v UK* 1982 (ECJ)).

The government responded by passing the Equal Pay (Amendment) Regulations 1983, which apply with effect from 1 January 1984. These add a third legal route for an individual to claim equal pay and operate when she is claiming she does work which is 'in terms of the demands made on her (for instance under such headings as effort, skill and decision) of equal value to that of a man in the same employment'.

The right does not apply when you are on like work, or when both you and the man you are comparing yourself with are covered by a job evaluation scheme. In other words, the three individual routes to equal pay are mutually exclusive. You can claim here if you are comparing with a man not covered by a job evaluation scheme. There is scope for employers to argue that there is a material difference (see below) between the man's and the woman's case, but for equal value claims you have the burden of proving that the difference is due to sex discrimination. In other claims management must show that the difference was not on account of sex.

The procedure for judging equal value claims is different. If the tribunal decides you have a reasonable case it must commission a report from an independent expert on the ACAS panel. If the expert report is in favour of equal pay, the tribunal will make an award.

Genuine material differences

Once you have established that the nature of your work is broadly similar, and any differences are not of practical importance, or that it is rated as equivalent, you must then face section

1 (3) of the Equal Pay Act. Management can escape equal pay if they prove that there is a **genuine material difference,** other than sex, between your case and the man's. In other words, we are now looking at you and him, not at what the jobs involve.

Factors that may defeat your claim include:

- location
- grading
- historical anomalies and 'red-circling'
- length of service, age and qualifications
- 'market forces'.

Location
Tribunals have accepted that it is legal for employers to give different pay to workers in different locations.

■ Employees of the NAAFI in Nottingham worked a 37-hour week, whereas those in London worked 36½ hours. Robina Varley sought a reduction to 36½ hours on the grounds that men in her grade in London worked fewer hours for the same money. The EAT, overturning the Nottingham tribunal, said that the difference in hours was not due to sex but to the fact that *many industries work shorter hours in London. NAAFI v Varley* 1976 (EAT)

Grading system
Different grading systems can sometimes justify different rates of pay for men and women doing similar work. It seems bizarre that tribunals can abandon the factual question: 'what do the men and women do in practice?', just because there is an anomalous grading system. But this is what the EAT said in Susan Waddington's case (page 174). When you have 'nationally or widely negotiated' wage scales, and there is a disparity between a man and a woman on similar work, the EAT said that this disparity will generally be due to a **material difference other than sex.**

Clearly there is a danger here that spurious grading systems based on discrimination could defeat the Act. To some extent, limitations have been imposed on this by the EAT itself.

■ When Edna Wade demanded parity with a male colleague in

the same insurance office, the company claimed all employees were paid according to a fixed grading system, and this constituted a material difference. The EAT said that the company had not proved that the grading system was *not* based on sex. It was based on *personal factors*, leaving the decision to management. This kind of grading system could not provide employers with a defence under section 1 (3). The Court of Appeal reversed the decision, saying that the employer succeeded by showing a grading system which operated without reference to sex. Lord Denning said: 'A grading system according to ability, skill and experience is an integral part of good business management; and as long as it is fairly and genuinely applied irrespective of sex, there is nothing wrong with it at all'. Subjective judgment, therefore, does not invalidate a scheme. *National Vulcan Engineering v Wade* 1978 (CA)

A scheme which requires subjective treatment by management and which operates to grade people rather than jobs is unlikely to pass the test of acceptability and fairness in most trade unionists' eyes. What Lord Denning regarded as strong points in favour of employer – the exercise of personal evaluation – were factors criticised by the EAT, and viewed with hostility by unions. A scheme negotiated nationally or throughout a large company or area usually *will* constitute a material difference. This was indicated in Susan Waddington's case (see page 174), where there was a conflict between two separate national grading schemes.

Historical anomalies and red-circling
Following job evaluation, regrading or reorganisation employees sometimes find that they are getting more than colleagues in the same grade. Naturally, unions demand that these workers shouldn't be prejudiced by the change and that they should preserve their pay. A 'red circle' is drawn round them and their wages are protected at their existing rate, even though they are in the same grade and do the same work as other workers. Red-circling *may* amount to a genuine material difference between the cases of particular men and women.

■ Sylvia Snoxell and Sylvia Davies were inspectors at Vauxhall's. Though doing the same work as men, they were paid less. In 1970 male inspectors were regraded into a lower paid grade. But they were red-circled and preserved their differ-ential over the women and male new starters. No women were red-circled as no women were on the higher (male) rate. In 1976 the women claimed parity. The EAT said the employers couldn't hide behind the red circle. *It could not be a genuine material difference if it owed its existence to past sex discrimination*, that is, the fact that men got more than women. The two women got parity and arrears of pay to the date the Equal Pay Act took effect (14 months). *Snoxell v Vauxhall Motors* 1977 (EAT)

The EAT said the following rules apply when an employer refuses parity and says the difference is due to a red circle or historical anomaly:

1. The employer must prove that the red circle arrangement is unisex.

2. If sex discrimination in the past has in any way contributed to the variation in pay, the red circle is illegal.

3. It doesn't matter whether the discrimination occurred before or after the Equal Pay Act took effect.

4. The employer *may* succeed in proving that the red circle is not based on discrimination if men and women outside the red circle do similar work and are treated alike.

5. Once a legal red circle is established, it can continue in-definitely, but it is desirable that it should be phased out.

6. Introduction or continuation of a red circle, particularly if this is 'contrary to good industrial practice' or done without joint consultation, may make the red circle illegal – *Outlook Supplies v Parry* 1978 (EAT) (two-and-a-half years 'quite short').

7. To succeed, an employer must justify the inclusion of *every* member of the red circle. Once the red circle is estab-lished, subsequent entrants may make it illegal – *United Biscuits v Young* 1978 (EAT).

Length of service, age and qualifications
All of these can justify differences in pay provided they operate in a way that is genuinely unisex. Collective agreements or cus-tom and practice should be examined to prove whether this is so. In one case, an employer got away with paying higher wages to a man who was 'old and infirm' than to two fit women.

■ Two women production clerks were paid 87p and 89p an hour. A male clerk got £1.20. For 25 years this clerical job had been held by men who were old or ill and their wages were protected. When this man was transferred he lost £1 a week by going on to the rate paid to the previous incumbent, but he acquired staff status. ASTMS said this showed the rate for the job was higher than for the women's job, and was not due to 'red-circling'. The employers said the higher rate was paid to him because that was what he previously got, and he was moved on account of his age and ill-health. The court accepted this explanation and decided the differential was not due to sex discrimination. *Methven v Cow Industrial Polymers* 1980 (CA)

But blatant discrimination cannot be justified by reference to allegedly male qualifications such as the ability to sort out physical trouble.

■ Nine out of 90 of Coomes's London and south coast betting shops were considered to be in areas prone to robberies and disturbances, so they insisted on one of the two counter hands being a man in order to deal with difficult situations. In the other 81 shops there were two women. At the Pimlico shop the man was paid £1.06 an hour and the woman 92p. The employers sought to show that his ability as a 'watchdog' amounted to a genuine material difference. The court awarded equal pay, Lord Denning saying that the employers had never considered the personalities of the man and woman: 'He may have been a small nervous man who could not say boo to a goose. She may have been as fierce and formidable as a battle-axe'. The only difference was on account of sex. *Shields v E. Coomes* 1978 (CA)

Market forces
Some employers have argued that, in order to get someone to fill a vacancy, they have to pay above the going rate paid to existing workers. The EAT dealt with several claims where the existing workers are women and the higher paid new entrants are men. Employers claimed that **market forces** required them to pay higher rates, and that this was a genuine material difference. Equal value claims must still face this argument.

■ Dr Pointon, a woman lecturer with high qualifications and long experience, was appointed on scale 5. A younger, less qualified man was subsequently appointed on the same scale. Evidence was accepted that he had more experience. He was given scale 5 because his previous job in Scotland was scale 4 and **he had to be given a rise to attract him to the new job.** Dr Pointon said her contract had become less favourable than the man's because, in effect, her differential for qualifications was eroded. The EAT said the market factor, that is, giving a higher rate to the man to attract him, was a genuine material difference. The man's previous salary was not based on sex discrimination in the past so the scale 5 rate was justifiable. The Appeal Court said her contract was not worse than his – they were on the same grade and she got more pay. The grading was based on national scales and was not discriminatory, so she lost her case. *Pointon v University of Sussex* 1979 (CA)

This argument, often used by employers, threatened to wreck the Equal Pay Act. It meant that if women were getting such poor pay that men could not be attracted to the job, it was justifiable to pay new (male) applicants more. This happened to Karen Fletcher, but the courts unhesitatingly rejected the employers' argument.

■ Karen Fletcher earned £35 a week. A vacancy arose. There were three external applicants, and a man got the job. He was already getting £43 in his old job, so he demanded £43 in his new job. Following job evaluation and a £6 rise, there was still a difference of £6 between them. The EAT believed that the employer would have paid the higher rate to a **man or woman** applicant earning higher wages at the date of appointment. The economic need to attract applicants was a **genuine material difference,** provided the employers would have treated a woman applicant in the same way. But the Appeal Court said that extrinsic factors such as market forces and the fact that a man would not work for that rate are irrelevant. They awarded equal pay. *Clay Cross Quarry Services v Fletcher* 1979 (CA)

The market forces argument is therefore dead, except possibly in equal value claims after 1983. Yet if you are relying on the

Treaty to get equal pay with a previous incumbent economic factors *are* relevant – see the *Albion* case, page 168.

The EAT rejected similar arguments by the Coal Board, who claimed they had to give a male canteen worker on nights higher basic pay and concessionary coal because of recruitment problems (*NCB v Sherwin* 1978). This is clearly the correct approach under the Act.

Other factors

Tribunals have allowed employers to pay unequal rates for a range of other reasons. They include: legal bans (for example, on night work), greater skill, ability to do more profitable work and greater flexibility.

How to claim

Claims under section 1 dealing with individual complaints must be made to a tribunal either while you are still working for the employer you are complaining about, or within **six months** of leaving. See page 490 for the procedure.

Proving it

You have to prove:

- you are in the same employment with a man,
- you are doing similar work, *and*
- in practice you will have to show that any differences are not of practical importance in setting terms and conditions. (The onus of proof in section 1 (4) isn't specified, so you have to prove what you are alleging.)

Management must then prove:

- you are not doing similar work, *or*
- if you are, that the variation (that is the *whole* variation) is genuinely due to a material difference, other than sex, between your case and the man's.

Management must provide basic information. The EAT said in *Eaton v Nuttall*:

it should be regarded by employers as part of their duty . . .

to come to the hearing with the relevant information prepared in a comprehensive and readily assimilable form,
including adequate details of any job evaluation system, or
other payment method, in use.

Remedies

The tribunal has power to make a declaration that you are
entitled to equal terms and conditions and to amend your contract. It can award up to two years' arrears of pay.

Discriminatory agreements and pay structures

Claims for equal pay usually affect groups of workers, not
merely individuals. So it's right that unions should be able to
present claims on behalf of *all* their members working for the
same employer. Section 3 of the Equal Pay Act allows references to be made to the Central Arbitration Committee (CAC)
or the Northern Ireland Industrial Court where agreements or
pay structures are discriminatory.

The basis of the claim

The wording of section 3 (4) is obscure but the DE advice contained in its booklet on the Act, and decisions of the CAC,
show that a claim can be made:

1. to remove discrimination by extending to men and women
any provision applying only to one sex, and

2. to raise the women to the lowest male rate.

Since the Act came into force it has become very unusual to
see an explicit discriminatory reference in an agreement. That
doesn't mean that discrimination has stopped. The CAC says it
can look at the practice as well as the form.

■ Beckman make electrical components in Glenrothes with a
workforce of 300 hourly-paid workers. In grade 6 there were
six men and seven women; in grade 7 there were, until
August 1976, 214 women. Two men later joined. Grade 6 got
£5.50 a week more than grade 7. The AUEW successfully
claimed parity. The CAC said there was discrimination
because the theoretically unisex rate for grade 7 was **unlikely
to attract male wage earners** and the differential was anyway

three times as wide as between any other two consecutive grades. *Beckman Instruments v AUEW* 1976 (CAC)

From the outset the CAC attempted to take a broad view of its jurisdiction and do what the unions asked it – to dig below an apparently unisex pay structure and root out inequality. Its work was, however, narrowed by the High Court, which restricted the CAC's role to correcting agreements which specifically apply to men or women only.

■ Following moves to eliminate discrimination in pay before the Equal Pay Act, APEX and Hy-Mac conducted a job evaluation exercise. A unisex grading scheme was agreed, but not the wages to be paid. The union claimed that as there were no women in the top two grades, and no men in the bottom two grades, where 70 per cent of the women were, the scheme was still discriminatory. The CAC agreed and set out pay scales. The company asked the High Court to overrule the CAC, which it did and awarded costs against APEX. *R v CAC/Hy-Mac* 1979 (HC)

Only if the agreement or structure is clearly 'a sham' can the CAC go behind the words of an apparently unisex document. Obviously, in the *Hy-Mac* case, the union and the CAC considered it was a sham.

The procedure
A discriminatory agreement can be referred to the CAC by any party to it or by the Employment Secretary. Pay structures can be referred only by the employer (why should employers want to take their own pay structures to the CAC?) or the Employment Secretary. If your union doesn't have agreements and you can't get equal pay by direct action, get the union to ask the minister to refer the claim to the CAC.

The CAC invites a written statement and convenes a hearing for oral evidence and questions. It can then make an award which takes effect as part of every affected worker's contract. Or it can give 'advice' which is not binding.

Backdating is possible only to the date the reference was made to the CAC. Even that isn't common.

The effect
In the first year of the Equal Pay Act the CAC published 20

decisions. All of them gave some increase, but not all of them gave equal pay in the true sense, or even the lowest male rate. References against Beechams and Imperial Tobacco ended up with a classic arbitration solution of splitting the difference between the union's and management's claim.

In some cases the CAC made an award specifying increases in money and gave advice for future progress.

■ Jentique/Metamec Ltd make clocks and furniture in Norfolk. They follow the furniture trade agreement, but graded their workforce in a different order – journeymen, sanders (semi-skilled), labourers and *women* (whom the company started to call cushion-fillers). All 313 women were on the bottom rate. All the men were on the top three rates, meaning a difference of over £4 a week. The company claimed there was no discrimination as they paid women cushion-fillers $87\frac{1}{2}$ per cent of the craftsmen's rate as laid down in the national agreement. But the CAC raised the women in two stages to the labourers' rate and advised that job evaluation should lead to the semi-skilled rate. *Jentique/Metamec v GMWU* 1976 (CAC)

In the AUEW's claim against Babcock and Wilcox the company had changed 'female cleaners' to 'cleaning persons', but paid them £1 an hour as against £1.17 for (male) 'sanitary assistants'. The CAC said that discrimination could be stopped only by raising the women's pay to £1.17 an hour. It made two clear statements of policy.

1. A mere change of title doesn't mean that discrimination has ceased. The CAC can still intervene; and

2. You don't need to establish that men and women are doing similar work in a claim under section 3. This section is 'wider in scope and does not involve the same degree of job comparison' as section 1 (individual equal pay claims).

This was illustrated in the *Jentique/Metamec* case by the fact that an individual claim under section 1 had already been turned down at a tribunal.

In looking at pay rates you are entitled to parity on *all* components of your pay. In a factory where the majority of women were on a lower basic rate, but a higher bonus earning level, than unskilled male labourers they were awarded a higher basic rate even though their total earnings were usually higher (*Sealed Motor Construction v TGWU* 1976 (CAC)).

The value of section 3

Section 3 has proved to be useful in securing some progress towards equal pay. Its effect is limited by its accepted aim of raising female rates to that of the lowest male, and by the CAC's approach in some cases as an arbitrator rather than an interpreter of the law. Its merit is that section 3 gives unions the right to claim on behalf of their members in what is essentially a collective, rather than an individual, dispute.

How effective is the Act?

Outrageous and pedantic decisions by tribunals during 1976 got the Act off to a bad start. This, together with some celebrated equal pay strikes, had the beneficial effect of showing that going to law to enforce workers' rights must be regarded as a long shot.

Women workers at Trico-Folberth, for instance, got equal pay through a strike in 1976 *in spite of* an unfavourable tribunal ruling.

■ Women working at American-owned Trico in West Londin made windscreen wipers. Men on the same shift got higher pay. The women, members of the AUEW, came out on official strike. The *company* applied to a tribunal for a decision (section 2 of the Equal Pay Act allows employers to sue). The women, disillusioned by tribunal decisions in other cases and believing firmly in industrial action, boycotted the hearing. The tribunal said the men got a higher basic pay because they *used* to do more flexible work before their night shift was closed down. When they were transferred they did identical work but retained their higher basic rate and night-shift premium. The tribunal said this was a transitional arrangement and refused to raise the women's pay even to the men's basic rate. The strike lasted five months until the company conceded a new pay structure giving parity. *Trico-Folberth v Groves* 1976 (IT)

Success rate

Claims under the Act declined rapidly from 1,742 in 1976 to 39 in 1982, and the success rate went down to 5 per cent of all claims, or 15 per cent of cases heard (*EOC Annual Report* 1982). As the earnings figures on page 159 show, this decline is due not to any significant march towards parity, but to the restriction by the courts of the scope of the Act and individual workers' disillusionment with it as a means of achieving equal pay.

Against this background it is clear that **the most effective way to get equal pay and to remove discrimination is negotiation and direct action.**

Women on tribunals

Another major problem is the lack of women on tribunals. In 1983, in England, Wales and Scotland there were only four women out of 72 full-time Chairs, and six out of 125 part-timers. And only 22 per cent of lay members were women. Trade unions must nominate *and train* more women, if tribunals are to have any credibility in enforcing equality laws.

What reforms are needed?

While the applications may be declining and the gap between men's and women's average earnings is slowly decreasing, the major limitation on progress (apart from men) is the Equal Pay Act itself.

The TUC passed a motion in 1976 calling for equal pay for work of equal value and this was approved by the European Court. Until the government changed the Act with effect from 1 January 1984, the UK was in breach of its EEC obligations. In addition, amendments could be made to:

- section 1 (5), to prevent tribunals implementing a job evaluation scheme if an independent union objects to it
- section 2, to allow an independent union to bring a claim on behalf of its members under any section of the Act
- section 2 (1a), to prevent employers bringing cases, as Trico did
- section 3, to allow backdating of awards by the CAC
- section 3 (6), to allow an independent union to complain about a discriminatory pay structure.

Summary

1. The Equal Pay Act applies to all terms covered by your contract of employment. It applies equally to men and women.

2. You have the right to equal treatment if you are doing work which is broadly similar to that done by a man in the same employment or which has been rated as equivalent by job evaluation, or you can from 1 January 1984 claim parity if you are doing work of equal value.

3. Employers can avoid giving parity if they can prove that you aren't doing similar work or that the variation in pay is genuinely due to reasons other than sex, for example greater skill or red-circling.

4. Your union can challenge a collective agreement if the women get less than the lowest male rate or if it is discriminatory in practice.

5. You can claim to a tribunal and may be awarded up to two years' arrears of pay.

6. Organisation to eliminate low pay, and union action to secure equal pay for work of equal value, are the only effective ways to achieve parity.

10. Dismissal

The steps in claiming dismissal / what does and does not constitute dismissal / unfair and wrongful dismissal / who can claim unfair dismissal / date of dismissal / what is fair and unfair / union activity / sickness / instructions / changes in conditions / mobility / criminal acts / misconduct / capability / probationary workers / unfair redundancy / legal restrictions / how to claim / reinstatement, re-engagement, compensation / your right to written reasons / a checklist for fighting the sack / and a summary.

Legal protection against unfair dismissal was created by Parliament in 1971. Prior to its introduction, all you could complain about if you were sacked was that you were not given proper notice, that is, you could claim for the wages due to you. That is **wrongful dismissal** under common law. The right still exists but will rarely be used because claims and remedies for **unfair dismissal** are quicker, cheaper, less formal, usually more valuable and more in tune with the current climate of industrial relations. The situations where wrongful dismissal is still important are illustrated on page 206.

The suggestion to provide a remedy for unfair dismissal was made in the Donovan Report in 1968 and was taken up in the Labour government's White Paper *In Place of Strife*. It was the sugar on the pill of the rest of that White Paper, which included registration of trade unions and agreements, compulsory strike ballots, and compulsory cooling-off periods before a strike. These restrictions were defeated by the trade union movement and Labour introduced the Industrial Relations Bill 1970. This contained rights on unfair dismissal very similar to those in effect today.

That Bill lapsed and was replaced by the Tories' Industrial Relations Act, which came into effect in 1972. Again the unfair dismissal provisions were thrown in as a sop to workers and unions to try and disguise some of the savagery that was contained in that Act. Their consultative document said:

> Both on grounds of principle and as a means of removing a significant cause of industrial disputes, the government proposes to include provisions in the Industrial Relations Bill to give statutory safeguards against unfair dismissal.

It is clear that **the most effective challenge to a sacking is industrial rather than legal action. The law can be useful as a bargaining tactic or as a threat, but the organised worker's protection against sacking has always been collective support and industrial muscle.**

Following the fall of the Conservatives in 1974 the Industrial Relations Act was repealed. The parts dealing with unfair dismissal, though, were immediately re-enacted and remain substantially unaltered.

During 1981, in a reversal of the previous four years' decline, 36,276 unfair dismissal claims were made to tribunals. Many factors made this increase inevitable. While the number of people in work declined, the number of those being sacked increased. Escalating unemployment made it hard to resist a reassertion of managerial prerogatives and hard-line disciplinary attitudes. Declining union militancy meant increased reliance on legal remedies.

About one-third of applicants got some form of remedy through conciliation or private settlement and another third withdrew. Of the remaining third who went to a tribunal hearing only 1 per cent got an award of reinstatement or re-engagement. Although this was more likely to happen as a result of conciliation, only 1.7 per cent of the 36,276 got their jobs back, again a declining proportion over the years for what is supposed to be the primary remedy for unfair dismissal.

Compensation was awarded by tribunals in only 16 per cent of the cases they heard. The median amount awarded was £963, which amounted to weekly earnings at the time of about seven weeks for men and ten for women. Maximum compensation was awarded in less than 1 per cent, while the minimum basic was awarded in 10 per cent of the cases heard. Seventy-nine per cent of conciliated settlements, and 52 per cent of tribunal awards, were for £1,000 or less.

Generally speaking, these figures show you had a 40 per cent chance of getting *something* if you made an application, and a 23 per cent chance of winning if you took your case to a hearing. Both these odds considerably and steadily worsened during the period from 1976.

Where to find the law

You can find the law of unfair dismissal in the Employment Protection Consolidation Act 1978 (EPCA) sections 54–79; the Code of Practice on Disciplinary Practice and Procedures; the Sex Discrimination Act 1975 (SDA) section 6 (2); the Race Relations Act 1976 (RRA) section 4 (2); the Rehabilitation of Offenders Act 1974 (ROA) section 4. Your right to written reasons is found in the EPCA 1978 section 53.

Summary of steps

If you are considering whether to bring a claim for unfair dismissal, diagram 5 shows the steps that a tribunal must go through in dealing with your claim. Page numbers refer to pages in this chapter where the details are found.

What is dismissal?

Dismissal can take any of the following forms:

- termination of employment by your employer with or without notice
- refusal by your employer to renew your fixed-term contract that has expired
- resignation if you are already under notice and want to quit before the notice expires
- sacking due to redundancy
- refusal to re-engage you after a strike or lock-out
- refusal to allow you to return to work following pregnancy
- constructive dismissal
- 'self-dismissal'.

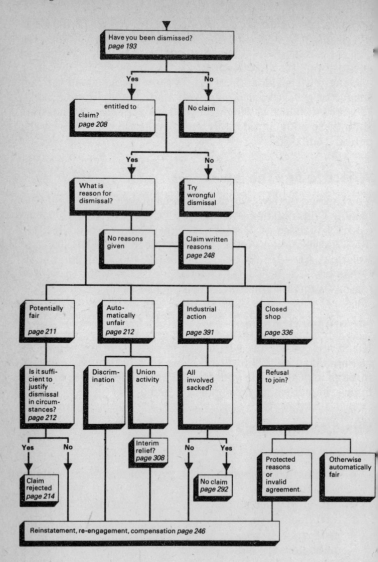

Diagram 5 **Claiming dismissal**

Termination with or without notice

Proper notice means that you receive the amount of notice laid down by your contract. This must be not less than the periods given as minima in the EPCA 1978. These are:

- Less than one month's continuous employment – not specified
- Between one month and 2 years – 1 week
- Between 2 years and 12 years – 1 week for each year of employment
- 12 years or more – 12 weeks

The Act requires *you* to give only one week's notice, regardless of your length of service. All of these minimum periods of notice can be extended by agreement, in which case the agreed period becomes your proper period of notice. The period can be *expressly* agreed or implied by the circumstances of your relationship, or by conduct, or by custom and practice.

Sacking without notice is called summary dismissal. Even if you are given proper notice or wages in lieu you can still complain of unfair dismissal. **Beware of warnings of future dismissal**. These don't constitute notice unless a definite finishing date is specified. You should also be sure that the language used clearly constitutes a sacking, not just a warning, a reprimand or hot-tempered abuse. Once notice is given, neither side can withdraw it without the other's agreement.

You can present a claim for unfair dismissal if you are working out your notice, that is, before the dismissal takes effect – EPCA 1978 section 67.

Refusal to renew a fixed-term contract

Termination of a fixed-term contract counts as dismissal if management refuse to renew it – EPCA section 55. A fixed-term contract is finite, so that both sides agree to continue it until a specified date. The Court of Appeal said that it is none the less a fixed-term contract if it can be terminated before the expiry date by either you or management giving notice (*Dixon v BBC* 1979 (CA)). This stops employers avoiding the consequences of a dismissal. It means you can claim, management must show why they did not renew the contract, and the reasons can be tested to see if they acted reasonably.

■ John Terry was employed as a physical education teacher for

one year. His contract was not renewed. He claimed unfair dismissal but the tribunal held that he was sacked for a substantial reason – that is, the expiry of the contract. Mr Terry successfully appealed and the EAT sent it back to a different tribunal. It said that sometimes the expiry of a fixed-term contract *can* be a substantial reason for sacking if the worker knew he was taken on for a specific period, for example to fill a temporary gap. But in other cases where no particular purpose is served by the fixed term, refusal to renew it will be unfair. **Workers are to be protected against being deprived of their rights through ordinary employments being dressed-up in the form of temporary fixed-term contracts,** the EAT said.
Terry v East Sussex County Council 1976 (EAT)

The real value to employers of fixed-term contracts is the exception they provide to the rule that you cannot contract out of your employment protection rights.

If you are on a fixed-term contract you *will* be able to claim unfair dismissal or redundancy pay unless:

- the contract is for a fixed term of **one year or more** (unfair dismissal) or **two years or more** (redundancy pay);
- you agreed **in writing before it expired** that you would forego your rights to claim when the contract ran out; *and*
- the dismissal consists *only* of the expiry of the fixed term.

In other words, you must agree to the exclusion of your rights and the exclusion applies only to sacking at the end of the contract. **If you are sacked before the due date, for, say, misconduct, you can claim.**

Any other agreement not to sue, unless it is made during conciliation of a claim by ACAS, is automatically void and you can ignore it (EPCA section 140).

Provided you continue to be employed without a break (or at least without any break which affects the legal definition of continuous employment – see page 468) you can claim dismissal at the end of a *series* of fixed-term contracts. For your rights to be waived, the latest of the contracts has to meet the above three requirements in every respect.

■ Susan Triesman was a technology lecturer on an 18-month contract. She agreed to extend it by seven months but was forced to agree to waive her rights to claim unfair dismissal and redundancy pay at the end of it. When the time came she claimed that the contract was for seven, not 25, months and therefore she could not sign away her rights. The EAT upheld her claim to redundancy pay. *Triesman v Open University* 1978 (EAT)

Although all your continuous working time can be aggregated in order to calculate length of service, only the latest fixed-term contract is relevant here.

Apprentices are all on fixed-term agreements. If you are not taken on as a skilled worker when you have done your time that counts as dismissal. But you may not be entitled either to unfair dismissal or to redundancy pay.

■ According to an agreement between the AUEW and a ship-repair company apprentices would be taken on as qualified fitters at the end of their time if work were available. This formed part of their contracts. Two weeks before his time was up, one apprentice was told there was no skilled job for him and he was paid redundancy money. The employers appealed when they got no rebate from the DE. The EAT said there was no redundancy. As he had never been employed as a fitter, he could not be redundant. And his dismissal could not be unfair as the reason for it was the natural ending of his apprenticeship. *N E Coast Ship Repairers v Secretary of State for Employment* 1978 (EAT)

A time-served apprentice in this position would, though, have a contractual right to be taken on as a qualified fitter if there were work, since this was the practice and the union agreement said so. Nor should the fact that the DE paid no rebate stop his/her employer paying redundancy pay.

Resignation while under notice

If you are given notice by management, and in the meantime find other work, or decide to leave for any other reason, your resignation is treated as **a dismissal on the day you leave.** Provided you give *some* notice, however short, either orally or in writing, you can leave when you like.

■ Elizabeth Walker worked in a children's home for almost 20 years. She was told at 12.30 p.m. she must leave, and was given seven weeks' notice. She was so distressed by the sud-

denness of the news that she finished her shift at 2.00 p.m.
and walked out. Despite requests to return and complete her
notice, she refused. She claimed unfair dismissal. The EAT
confirmed the tribunal's finding that she had given no notice.
She could not therefore claim dismissal. **Had she given some
notice, her resignation would count as dismissal** and she
would have been able to claim unfair dismissal. *Walker v
Cotswold Chine Home School* 1977 (EAT)

So, make sure you give *some* notice.

It may be that management are quite happy to let you go. If
so, an agreement to go early will not prejudice your claim that
you have been dismissed. It may bring forward the date of dismissal, or it might be regarded as accepting that you do not
have to work out your full notice.

There are two other situations which count as dismissal. The
first is when you are told: resign or we will sack you. (*East Sussex C.C. v Walker* 1972 (NIRC). Secondly, you can claim if you
resign in the face of a clear indication that management are
going to break your contract in a fundamental way.

■ Bernard Maher was told that the Swinton, Lancs, depot
where he worked was closing and he would be required to
work 40 miles away. Management thought this was a contractual obligation, he did not. He resigned before the date for
the move was set. The court gave him his redundancy pay,
saying that although he was not under notice because no firm
date had been given, the employers were about to break his
contract and resignation in anticipation constituted a dismissal. *Maher v Fram Gerrard* 1974 (NIRC)

Resignation does *not* count as dismissal if you are told that you
had better look for other work because in a few months there
will not be a job for you. This is merely advance warning, not
notice, because there is no specified date; and it does not indicate that management are going to break the contract because
they can lawfully terminate it by giving notice. So stay put until
the future is clear. Nor should you resign if you are given an
alternative to dismissal. An employer cannot say you resigned
voluntarily if the only alternative is the sack. But s/he may get
away with it if you have *agreed* some financial package and *then*
sign a resignation. The EAT said this in a case where a director
who knew exactly what he was doing was talking of receiving

£10,000 from his co-directors (*Sheffield v Oxford Controls* 1979 (EAT)). But a package consisting of notice money and a reference for a manual worker would not turn a dismissal into a voluntary resignation.

Redundancy
We shall see (page 253) that a dismissal must occur before you can claim redundancy pay. As such, redundancy is not really a separate kind of dismissal, but to many workers being made redundant is not the same as being sacked. In law it is.

Refusal to re-engage after a strike or lock-out
You have no claim for unfair dismissal if management sack *all* workers engaged in industrial action, or refuse to take all of you back (page 392). If only some of you are sacked, or refused re-engagement, you can claim unfair dismissal. So with lock-outs. **If there is an element of selection** you can claim.

The effects of this are far-reaching. For example, management might take the opportunity while you are in dispute to sack you for incompetence. *This* reason cannot be attacked on the grounds of unfairness or unreasonableness – the tribunal is precluded from hearing your case and looking at the merits.

Refusal to allow return to work following pregnancy
If you are refused re-employment on the date you have given as your return date, this counts as dismissal effective on that date. See page 119.

Constructive dismissal
This is forced resignation and occurs when management show by their actions or words that they **do not intend to be bound any longer by one or more of the essential terms of the contract.** It means that management are doing something which strikes at the very root of your relationship and shows that they are not prepared to abide by the agreement. (*Western Excavating v Sharp* 1977 (CA)). The most obvious example is where your **pay is cut**, or your **status is reduced**:

■ Mr Marriott was a supervisor who had been employed for eight years. Management told him that they were going to reduce his pay by £3 a week, and reduce his status because they were running down his department. He protested and they moved to a pay cut of only £1 a week. He worked at the new rate for three weeks under protest and then resigned, claiming redundancy. He was successful. The Court of Appeal said he was constructively dismissed. *Marriott v Oxford Co-op* 1969 (CA)

Constructive dismissal might also arise after **a change in shift pattern,** an order to **work with unsafe machinery** (see page 222), **unilateral insistence on a change in job duties, or in working hours, suspension without pay** where there is no prior agreement on this, an **arbitrary refusal** to give you a pay increase which everyone else got or **an order to move to other premises:**

■ L.H. Goff and his son worked in the furniture trade in London. One day he was ordered to report on the following day to other premises two-and-a-half miles away involving an extra fifteen minutes' journey each way. He and his son worked there for three weeks, took their two weeks' holiday, returned to work and gave one week's notice. The Industrial Court said that they had not **voluntarily agreed** to change their terms but had been dismissed, because they were faced with changed conditions. *Shields Furniture Ltd v Goff* 1973 (NIRC)

In all cases of constructive dismissal *you* must show that the following essential ingredients are present:

the employee terminates that contract, with or without notice, in circumstances such that he is entitled to terminate it **without notice** by reason of the employer's conduct (EPCA section 55) (emphasis added).

This means that the conduct must be so bad that you are entitled to quit without notice – a kind of 'gross misconduct' by your employer. In deciding whether to quit, the EAT has said that you must look *solely* at the contract and the effect on it of management's conduct. The surrounding circumstances may be relevant in assessing this.

■ Michael Lynn was promoted to Retail Stock Controller of a large firm of clothes distributors. Soon afterwards, he got a warning letter and suffered a breakdown. He complained that he had been accused, in front of junior members of staff, of negligence, inefficiency and lack of intelligence. The company refused to meet his ASTMS official and didn't allow him a right of appeal (as required by the company's rules). He claimed this amounted to constructive dismissal as it undermined his authority. The EAT agreed that the company's conduct showed that they no longer intended to be bound by their contract with Michael Lynn. *Wetherall v Lynn* 1977 (EAT)

The EAT has also made it clear that if you are going to claim constructive dismissal **you must positively assert that you are going to exercise your right to terminate the contract.** As we have seen (page 60), you have the option of continuing the contract *or* regarding management as having terminated it.

In assessing the seriousness of management's breach of contract you can count a series of minor attacks, some of which may be contractual, some not, but which, taken together, amount to constructive dismissal. This has been described by the EAT as 'squeezing out' – a process of gradual and persistent pressure either to get you to leave or to accept changes in your conditions. A build-up of pressure can be a breach of the term implied in every contract that employers will not 'conduct themselves in a manner calculated or likely to destroy the relationship of confidence and trust between employer and employee'. Your employer's conduct as a whole can be examined to see whether it is so bad you cannot be expected to put up with it. So a minor harassment might be the last straw.

■ Vilma Woods had worked as a secretary to a garage owner for 27 years when he sold out to new owners who guaranteed to keep her on on no less favourable terms. Over the first four months the new owners tried to cut wages, increase hours and volume of work, change job title, job content and contract of service, and gave her verbal and written warnings. Each time she resisted they withdrew and tried another tactic. She was told finally that if she rejected a new job specification she would be sacked, so she resigned. The EAT said management had been 'gunning for her' to vary her conditions of service; this undermined the relationship of mutual trust and she had been constructively dismissed. (Although the EAT thought the tribunal's decision in favour of the employer was wrong, for technical reasons it was not entitled to substitute its view of the facts and overturn it.) *Woods v W. M. Car Services* 1981 (EAT)

The position was summed up like this:

an employer who persistently attempts to vary an employee's conditions of service (whether contractual or not) with a view to getting rid of the employee or varying the employee's terms of service does act in a manner calculated or likely to destroy the relationship of confidence and trust between employer and employee. Such an employer has therefore breached the implied term. Any breach of that implied term is a fundamental breach amounting to a repudiation since it necessarily goes to the root of the contract.

Constructive dismissal, therefore arises when:

1. Management have broken your contract or made it unambiguously clear that they will do at a specified future time. The breach can be in the form of words, behaviour or acts aimed at destroying your relationship.

2. The breach of contract is so serious that it justifies you in resigning. Or it can be the last straw in a series of individually minor incidents.

3. You leave as a result of the breach of contract and not for some unrelated reason.

4. You leave quickly after the breach. If you wait too long you may be regarded as accepting it, although working under protest. A delay might possibly be justified if you have the good sense not to quit before you have another job to go to.

5. You make it clear that you intend to regard yourself as constructively dismissed – put this in writing to be certain.

Claiming constructive dismissal is very risky. Remember it is *you* who must prove dismissal or constructive dismissal. Only then are management required to show reasons and the tribunal to judge fairness (see below). If you can't stop management taking action against you, try it for a while under protest. Claim unfair dismissal as a last resort.

'Self-dismissal'

Management may try to stop you claiming by saying that, far from being dismissed, you by your own behaviour dismissed yourself. If there is no dismissal, it cannot be unfair. Judges have been swayed by this argument but it is now widely agreed that self-dismissal is really dismissal. If what you have done goes to the root of your contract, management in theory have to decide to accept that you have torn up ('repudiated') the contract. If they accept, they then dismiss you. 'Self-dismissal' occurs only in the very limited number of situations where your misconduct shows you *intend* to bring the relationship to an end. Examples given by Lord Denning are: leaving to get another job; absconding with money from the till; going off indefinitely without saying a word. These show a 'complete and intended withdrawal' of your service:

■ Lanford Clarke, a bus mechanic, asked for unpaid leave for a six-week holiday in his native Jamaica, two years after his previous visit. LT refused because the collective agreement allowed extended leave only once in three years, other employees would demand it, and he had a poor sickness and work record. They said his name would be removed from the books according to procedure, if he went. He still went. When he returned for work (with a Jamaican medical certificate covering the whole of his absence), LT said he had dismissed himself. The Court of Appeal decided that this was not self-dismissal as he never intended to quit. LT had dismissed him, but in the circumstances this was not unfair. *London Transport v Clarke* 1981 (CA)

Employers have also argued in other extended leave cases that failure to return on the agreed date constitutes neither dismissal nor resignation but a joint agreement to end the contract. The number of cases involving West Indian and Asian workers who have been faced with an ultimatum of this sort indicates a total insensitivity by employers to people they employ who have ties abroad. There is clearly a need to negotiate collective agreements to cover extended leave. It might be regarded as the kind of 'cultural and religious need' the CRE 1983 Code recommends management to cater for. Although this is of particular value to ethnic minority workers, it should rather be seen as a negotiated benefit enabling anyone to take additional unpaid leave.

The legal position depends on what was said, and tribunals are very reluctant to acknowledge a mutually agreed termination. A unilateral ultimatum saying that if you do not return on the due date – or for that matter if you commit any other form of industrial 'offence' – the contract will be deemed to be over, is still a dismissal. Even if there *appears* to be mutual consent, it is improbable that someone with a job and some years' service will voluntarily agree to its ending without compensation.

■ John Tracey had been employed as an engineer for 17 years when he heard his father was dying in Jamaica. He asked for three weeks' unpaid leave. As he had previously over-stayed by eight weeks management got him to sign an agreement that if he did not return on the due date 'the company will assume that you have terminated your employment'. He reported back three working days late to be told he had no job but could re-apply as a new starter. When he claimed unfair dismissal the EAT said the contract had not been mutually terminated but he had been dismissed. *Tracey v Zest Equipment* 1982 (EAT)

The EAT also pointed out that EPCA section 140 protects workers from being forced to contract out of their rights. However, if you have been clearly warned and know the consequences of failing to meet requirements it will be easier for management to prove the dismissal was reasonable.

What is not a dismissal?

You are not dismissed if:

- you agree to be suspended
- you resign or leave by mutual agreement
- your employer goes bust, or winds up the company, or either of you dies
- the contract is 'frustrated'.

Suspension

Unless suspension on less than full pay is allowed by your contract, or you consent to it, suspension is dismissal (see page 76). If you do agree to it, suspension is not dismissal, even though you take other work.

■ Andrew Shute refused to pay TGWU dues while employed on lighters on the Thames. Union members refused to work with him. He was suspended on full pay for eight months. At the same time he was working elsewhere. He was not dismissed, but suspended. *Cory Lighterage v TGWU* 1973 (CA)

Resignation

Forced resignation is dismissal. An apparently voluntary agreement to quit can be a dismissal if the facts show management forced you into resigning. In the absence of pressure, you may not be able to prove dismissal. An exception is when, in a redundancy situation, you volunteer to resign and take redundancy pay (see page 253).

Insolvency, winding-up and death

Management's insolvency, or the company's decision to close, count as dismissal only for redundancy purposes. You can't claim unfair dismissal if you are sacked as a result, but you *can* claim redundancy pay.

You are not sacked if a receiver is appointed to run the business till debts are paid. But if the receiver sacks you, you can claim unfair dismissal.

You employer's death terminates your contract unless you are employed by a company. It does not entitle you to claim unfair dismissal. If your employer dies *after* you have been given notice, you can claim unfair dismissal against his/her personal representative. If you die, your representative or estate can still claim. With commendable realism the EPCA 1978 says that in this event the provisions relating to reinstatement and re-engagement 'shall not apply'! (Schedule 12 para 10.)

Frustration of the contract

Some events automatically bring the employment relationship to an end without any need for there to be an actual dismissal or resignation. Lawyers call it 'frustration' of the contract of employment. It occurs where some unforeseen event occurs, which is neither your nor management's fault. It must make carrying on the job either impossible or **something radically different from what was originally intended.** This rule operates in favour of employers because it is up to you to prove that you were dismissed. If you can't, and your employer argues that the contract had come to an end automatically, the tribunal has no jurisdiction even to consider whether there was any fairness or unfairness about it.

The kinds of events that are most likely to cause an automatic termination are:

- death

- serious illness or injury
- imprisonment
- legal impossibility – for example, a driving ban if you are employed only as a driver.

Genuine 'frustration' cases are rare, and the application of the rules is in many ways similar to the rules on fairness and reasonableness. For this reason, frustration due to illness and imprisonment are dealt with below with examples of sickness, misconduct and legal bans.

Although these rules often work against you it is possible to use them to *your* advantage. For example, even if you have to some extent caused the unforeseen event, it can still 'frustrate' the contract. So you won't be liable to any penalty for failing to carry it out. Your employer cannot sue you for breach of contract if you go out without a coat, catch a sore throat and so are prevented from appearing as a professional singer; or if you are prevented by injury from carrying out your duties as a bus driver because you carelessly crashed your car. The intervening act itself (sore throat or injury) has ended (frustrated) the contract.

Unfair dismissal and wrongful dismissal

Protection against unfair dismissal is a right given by an Act of Parliament. Wrongful dismissal is quite different. It means, simply, dismissal without notice – 'summary dismissal' – or without the notice (or wages in lieu) that you are entitled to by virtue of your contract or the EPCA 1978.

Since the introduction of unfair dismissal rights, claims for **wrongful dismissal** based on the **common law of contract** have become very rare. The right exists, though, and could be useful in certain circumstances. For example if you are:

- not entitled to claim unfair dismissal (see below);
- earning so much that the upper limit on compensation for unfair dismissal is below what you could get for wrongful dismissal. This might arise if you are sacked during a long fixed-term contract;
- hoping to get a court order providing for your contract to be continued (see *Hill v Parsons* pages 61, 99).

Claims for wrongful dismissal have to be made in the county

courts (for less than £5,000) or in the High Court. Power has been given to the Lord Chancellor and the Scottish Secretary to transfer this jurisdiction to industrial tribunals (EPCA 1978 section 131), but they have not exercised it.

Legal representation paid for by the state Legal Aid Fund (see page 487 below) is available in courts but not tribunals. So if you need a lawyer, can't afford one, and are eligible for Legal Aid you might consider bringing a wrongful dismissal claim in the courts in order to get free legal representation.

Except for the right to a written statement of reasons for dismissal, the rest of this chapter is concerned only with unfair dismissals.

Who can claim?

Table 4 on page 208 shows the groups of employees who can make claims for unfair dismissal and redundancy pay. A full explanation of the rules on part-timers and working abroad is given on pages 466–74. Something needs to be said about the exclusion of small businesses.

Small firms

Small businesses come in for lavish attention in the Tory psyche, and the Employment Act 1980 contained its share of cosseting for this very vocal, ill-defined species. Employers with fewer than six staff are protected against most claims under the Sex Discrimination Act, and for maternity leave (see page 117), and now small firms are protected against unfair dismissal claims. This is despite official findings that only one small business in 1,000 is likely to face a compensation award in any year.

The protection comes in two forms – specific exclusion for firms with 20 or fewer employees, and a general injunction to tribunals to consider the size of businesses.In both cases, the government is perversely missing the point that it is precisely because small firms have unsophisticated personnel procedures, are unlikely to be organised by unions, and are more prone to domination by personalities, that workers need more not less protection.

If you work for an employer who has 20 or fewer employees **you must have worked for two years** in order to bring an unfair dismissal claim. In other words, the qualifying period is double that for other firms. If you are sacked with less than two years'

Table 4

Who can claim?	Unfair dismissal	Redundancy pay
Employees working 16 or more hours a week	Need 1 year's service (unless alleging TU grounds)	Need 2 years' service
Employees working 8–16 hours a week	Need 5 years' service (unless alleging TU grounds)	Need 5 years' service
Employees on fixed-term contracts	Yes unless specific exclusion in contract of 1 year or more	Yes unless specific exclusion in contract of 2 years or more
Young employees	Yes – No lower age limit	Must be 20 or over
Old employees	Must be under 65 (men) or 60 (women) or below the normal retirement age for your grade (unless alleging TU grounds)	Must be under 65 (men) or 60 (women)
Self-employed workers	No	No
Crown employees	Yes	No. Have own agreement
Health Service workers	Yes	Some. Others have own agreement
Employees ordinarily working abroad	No	No. Unless sacked while on business in Britain
Oil rig workers	Most	Most
Merchant seafarers	Yes if working from UK ports	No. Have own agreement
Registered dockers	Yes and have own agreement	No. Have own agreement
Share-fishers	No	No
Employees of foreign governments	No, except nationals of *other* countries	No
Domestic servants	Yes	Yes except close relative
Employees in firms with 20 or fewer employees	Need 2 years' service (unless alleging TU grounds)	Yes

service, the only claim you can make is one based on trade union activities, or discrimination on the grounds of race, sex or marriage.

There are some important features to note in the new section 64A of the EPCA.

1. The maximum of 20 applies to employees – contract labour on site may not be employees but independent contractors.

2. The total employed by your own employer can be added to those employed by any associated employer, such as subsidiary or parent companies. If the group's workforce exceeds 20, none of the companies is exempt.

3. If at any time during your first two years the total has gone over 20, the exemption does not apply, and you can claim in the usual way if you are sacked after one year's service.

4. The employer's 'undertaking' is not defined, so there is scope for employers to argue that although they are part of a large company, or are a subsidiary, they act independently on personnel matters, and so qualify as a small undertaking when the tribunal considers its size and resources. Precedents under previous legislation show that for two different enterprises to be considered as one 'undertaking' there needs to be 'some evidence of organisational unity, e.g. common accounting, management, purchasing arrangements, insurance and so on' (*Kapur v Shields* 1975 (HC)).

■ **Example:** You start work after 1 October 1982. There are 19 employees, including you. You can be dismissed, and have no claim, any time during your first two years. But after you have been there a year, two part-time staff are taken on. You now have a right to claim. Provided they work 16 or more hours per week, the part-timers, and anyone joining or presently employed there, can claim if they are sacked after they have a year's service.

■ **Example:** As above, if two people leave the total is down to 19 again. New starters after that date need two years' service before they can claim, unless the total staff goes over 20.

The government has said that the dismissal laws are a disincentive to recruitment. Yet the effect of this new provision is to discourage businesses from expanding their workforce above a complement of 20, and to provide great scope for increasing use of agency staff.

If your claim goes to a tribunal, the tribunal is now to consider '**the size and administrative resources of the employer's undertaking**' when deciding whether s/he acted reasonably or unreasonably in sacking you. In practice tribunals do look at these factors, but now they must specifically turn their attention to them – see below.

Date of dismissal

The 'effective date of termination' depends on the way you have been dismissed and is important because your length of service is calculated up to the termination date. This affects

- the three months you have to make a claim (or six months for redundancy)
- the one year's service you need for making a claim (or two years' for redundancy)
- the six months' service you need to claim written reasons
- the amount of the basic award of compensation and redundancy pay.

The rules are that the termination date is

1. if you are given notice and work it out, the date it expires;

2. if you are given notice but told you need not work it out, the date it would expire;

3. if you are given money in lieu and told to leave at once, the date you leave;

4. if you are given no notice or lieu money, the date you leave;

5. if you resign under constructive dismissal, the date you leave;

6. if you are under notice, and you give counter-notice to leave earlier, the date you leave;

7. if, following redundancy, you take a trial period on alternative work then leave, the date your original contract ends.

There are two special circumstances that may affect your contract. Firstly, if you are constructively dismissed or given less than your statutory minimum notice entitlement (see page 195) this is added to your length of service (EPCA section 55); so you can stretch your contract to give yourself the minimum qualifying service, to increase the basic award of compensation, and to take advantage of any higher levels of redundancy pay that may take effect in this period. **But this does not stretch the three- (or six- for redundancy) month deadline on submitting a claim,** which runs from the effective date of termination, or the end of the trial period in redundancy cases.

Secondly, it is not safe to count time pursuing an internal appeal against dismissal. In many disciplinary agreements the final result determines whether or not you get paid between the sacking and the hearing. Even if you are paid retrospectively, or if you are regarded as suspended, it is not safe to think the deadline for submitting a tribunal claim or your length of service are extended. Always ensure a claim is made within three months – a hearing can be postponed if an internal procedure is still in operation.

What is fair and unfair?

Mr Justice Phillips summarised the problems any worker faces when challenging a sacking:

> The expression 'unfair dismissal' is in no sense a common sense expression capable of being understood by the man in the street. (*Devis v Atkins* 1977)

What is fair and unfair can be decided only by the tribunal which hears your case. But you can get some idea of your chances by looking at other cases.

The legislation requires employers to prove that they dismissed you for one of the potentially fair reasons specified below, and tribunals must then go on to judge whether it was a **sufficient reason in the circumstances.**

You have the right to require management to put the reasons for your dismissal in writing. See page 248 below. For it to be potentially fair the reason must:

- relate to conduct
- relate to capability: that is, skill, aptitude, health, physical or mental qualities
- relate to qualifications: that is, relevant to the position you hold
- be that you could not continue to work in the position you hold without contravening a legal duty or restriction
- be 'some other substantial reason' which *could* justify the dismissal of someone in your position.

These categories are ludicrously wide and no employers should have any difficulty in fitting their alleged reason for dismissal into one of them. You will normally find it difficult to attack this part of their case. But you can always attack the second part.

EPCA section 57 says:

the determination of the question whether the dismissal was fair or unfair, having regard to the reason shown by the employer, shall depend on whether in the circumstances (including the size and administrative resources of the employer's undertaking) the employer acted reasonably or unreasonably in treating it as a sufficient reason for dismissing the employee and that question shall be determined in accordance with equity and the substantial merits of the case.

Automatically *unfair* are dismissals

- for membership or non-membership of a union
- as a result of a 'spent' conviction
- of a worker because she is pregnant
- following the 'transfer of an undertaking'.

If you have been dismissed because of your race or sex, or because you are married, you can claim under the Race Relations Act 1976 or the Sex Discrimination Act 1975, as appropriate. You can also claim under the EPCA 1978 if you are qualified by length of service, hours worked, etc., to make a claim of unfair dismissal.

The main impact of the instruction to consider an employer's resources is in the procedural aspects of dismissal rather than in the substance and the reasons for it.

■ **Example:**You are sacked for being late four days out of seven. There is no formal disciplinary procedure at your firm, a supermarket which employs only 30 people. You were given three oral warnings but were never told you would be sacked if you were late again. The manager spoke to you in the shop and you had to explain your lateness there and then. You couldn't appeal to the managing director. The tribunal hearing your case decides that because the shop is small and has no personnel manager the normal requirements of written warnings, formal interview and a right of appeal do not apply, and that the lateness was a good enough reason for sacking you.

So section 57 creates a two-tier industrial law with different standards for large and small businesses.

Courts have developed the statutory obligation to come up with the following rules on fairness:

1. Management's knowledge at the time of the dismissal is relevant; events discovered later are not. This includes matters which they believe, and have reasonable grounds for believing.

2. A dismissal for 'some other substantial reason' must be related to something as serious as the other categories such as capability and conduct.

3. Reasonableness and equity require consistent treatment of employees, and uniform enforcement of standards – see *Wilcox v HGS* page 223.

■ A telephonist struck a colleague in the mouth during an argument in the canteen over trade union matters. He pleaded guilty to assault and was fined £100 and bound over. The Post Office sacked him. The Court of Appeal said the dismissal was unfair because in five other cases over the years the employers had not dismissed a worker for assault on a colleague or a supervisor. Employers should be consistent. Changing the disciplinary policy without warning was therefore unfair. *Post Office v Fennell* 1981 (CA)

4. A reasonable procedure should be followed. Failure to do so can make a fair dismissal unfair (*Devis v Atkins*) unless there is no possibility that the decision would be changed had a proper procedure been followed, as in *Dunning v Jacomb* and *Taylor v Alidair* – page 240.

In a case of admitted dishonesty, for example, management's failure to carry out a proper inquiry won't necessarily make the dismissal unfair. Management must show that even if they had held an inquiry and received the information an inquiry would have revealed, they would still have sacked you, and would still have been behaving reasonably (*British Labour Pump v Byrne* 1979 (EAT).

The precise form of procedure is not laid down. At least for disciplinary matters the ACAS Code requires that you be given warnings, an opportunity to explain, and the right of appeal. This has been extended to require *investigation* in illness cases, *opportunities to improve* in capability cases, *consultation* where the job is being reorganised, and *long notice* of redundancy. What is clear is that management must have reasonable grounds for believing the information they are acting on; behave unreasonably if they do not investigate the facts fully before deciding to dismiss; and part of this decision-making requires them to hear your side.

■ Richard Tepper worked for 14 years on a meat stall at Smithfield market. Despite previous warnings he was observed by police giving an irregular receipt and was later asked to visit the police station. Acting on the police report, management told him that because he had let meat go without a ticket he was dismissed for gross misconduct and asked if he had anything to say. He said he had done nothing wrong and was then told to leave. He was subsequently charged and acquitted at the Old Bailey. The Court of Appeal upheld the decision of unfair dismissal because he had not been given a fair opportunity to explain. Making a decision before hearing him out meant that the employers had not carried out as much investigation as was reasonable. Therefore, the decision was not based on reasonable grounds or on information management ought to have had. *W. Weddell v Tepper* 1980 (CA)

Until 1980, in unfair dismissal cases employers had to prove they acted reasonably. The 1980 Act removes that formal burden and requires tribunals to judge on the evidence each side brings. The effect of this dealt with on page 212.

Applying these rules to the cases that have occurred since 1972, it is possible to formulate a number of very broad *factual* situations covering:

- trade union activity
- industrial action
- closed shop
- sickness and injury
- refusal to carry out instructions
- change in conditions
- mobility
- reorganisation
- criminal acts
- misconduct

- job performance and qualifications
- probationary workers
- gay workers
- redundancy
- legal restrictions

What follows, therefore, is a general guide. You should always bear in mind that tribunals are free to make their own decision on any particular set of facts and are bound only by decisions of law of higher courts.

Trade union activity

Dismissal for being a member of or taking part in the activities of an independent trade union is automatically unfair. See page 299.

You can use the **interim procedure** (page 308) if you are alleging you were sacked for trade union reasons.

Industrial action

Tribunals have only limited jurisdiction to hear your case if you are sacked during industrial action. If an employer sacks a worker because of pressure of industrial action, that pressure must be disregarded. In other words, employers must bear the full responsibility and can't quote industrial pressure as a reason for action – EPCA Section 63. They can, of course, 'join' the union as a co-defendant to any claim – see pages 347, 397.

Closed shop

It is not unfair for an employer to sack a worker who refuses to join a union specified in a union membership agreement, but there are major exceptions. See page 336.

Sickness and injury

If you are sacked while you are sick, or because you have suffered an injury, management will have to prove one of two things if they are to escape liability for unfair dismissal. They must prove that the contract is frustrated, *or* that they acted reasonably in sacking you while the contract continued.

Serious or long-term incapacity

Frustration means there is no dismissal. So there is no question of it being 'unfair'. It is therefore an attractive argument for employers to make in tribunals, although it is hard to establish. The EAT said in the *Leibovici* case (below):

> There may be an event (for example, a crippling accident) so dramatic and shattering that everyone concerned will realise immediately that to all intents and purposes the contract must be regarded as at an end.

A postal worker who loses a leg, a lorry driver who goes blind, a labourer who has a heart attack – all of these may have their contracts frustrated. They may be given other work by management but they have had to abandon their original contracts.

If the event is less dramatic and certain, such as a long-term illness, it is possible for management to argue that your contract is frustrated if the time comes when it can be said that **'matters had gone on so long, and the prospects for the future were so poor, that it was no longer practical to regard the contract as still subsisting'**. This is what happened in Israel Leibovici's case:

■ Israel Leibovici had an accident and was off work for five-and-a-half months. He was paid for two of them. When he asked for his job back he was told it had been filled so he claimed unfair dismissal. Management said the contract was frustrated. The London tribunal disagreed and awarded him redundancy pay. The employer appealed, successfully, to the EAT and the case was sent back for a re-hearing. The EAT said the essential question is: **has the time arrived when the employer can no longer reasonably be expected to keep the absent employee's post open for him?** *The Egg Stores v Leibovici* 1976 (EAT)

There is no rule about the length of time that must elapse before frustration occurs – it depends on a complex set of factors that must be considered in each individual case. In Reuben Marshall's case, his absence for 18 months didn't frustrate the contract:

■ Reuben Marshall had been employed as a fitter at a London shipyard for 23 years when he went sick with angina. He received no wages and after 18 months was made redundant.

He was shortly to have had an operation and would probably have been able to return after that. He was given no warning and only £50 *ex gratia* payment. The Industrial Court awarded him redundancy pay and rejected the employer's claim that the contract had been automatically terminated by the sickness. *Marshall v Harland & Wolff* 1972 (NIRC)

The EAT said in Leibovici's case that the following matters must be considered when an employer tries to avoid a claim for unfair dismissal or redundancy pay by arguing that **the contract has been frustrated,** or that **the dismissal is fair:**

- the length of the previous employment;
- how long it had been expected that the employment would continue;
- the nature of the job;
- the nature, length and effect of the illness or disabling event;
- the need of the employer for the work to be done, and the need for a replacement to do it;
- the risk to the employer of acquiring obligations in respect of redundancy payments or compensation for unfair dismissal to the replacement employee;
- whether wages have continued to be paid;
- the acts and the statements of the employer in relation to the employment, including the dismissal of, or failure to dismiss, the employee; and
- whether in all the circumstances a reasonable employer could be expected to wait any longer.

Some of these points can be considered in detail – for example **the need for a replacement:**

■ In March 1971 Eric Hebden, a sawyer with 20 years' service, stopped work to have an eye operation. He was fit to work in July 1971 but needed another operation. His employers agreed, since business was slack, that he need not work until the operation was over. He reported in every three weeks. He had the operation and was fit to work in January 1973, but his employers made him redundant. The employers said that he was a key man and so the contract between them had been frustrated. But the court said that in view of his **length of service,** the **period of incapacity, the conduct** of Mr Hebden and the employers during his time off **and the fact that he**

was not replaced, the contract still continued. He was therefore entitled to redundancy pay. *Hebden v Forsey* 1973 (NIRC)

If management give you **sick pay,** whether at SSP minimum levels and duration or above, or continue to pay your wages, it is usually evidence that the contract is not frustrated and is still alive. The courts have sometimes disregarded these factors, though!

- ■ Richard Hart was a night fitter when he went sick with industrial dermatitis in 1974. He was a key worker. Nearly two years later he was certified fit for work. His employers said he had been replaced and refused to take him back. They gave him his P45 and six days' holiday pay. The EAT (with the TUC member dissenting) upheld the Nottingham tribunal's decision that the contract was frustrated by the illness, **even though the employer had paid holiday money.** *Hart v A R Marshall & Sons* 1977 (EAT)

Short-term incapacity
Some tribunals have taken an unfavourable view of *short-term* illness:

- ■ Tony Tan was a cellar-keeper for a London wine-merchants. He had a perfect record for his first year of service, and in the second year was off sick for 16 days. During his third year he was sacked after 50 days' absence during a total of 70 working days. On almost every occasion he brought a medical certificate. The court confirmed that he had been fairly dismissed because **the employer's business requirements were such that they needed someone more reliable.** *Tan v Berry Brothers* 1974 (NIRC)

Industrial injury
If, as in Richard Hart's case, your sickness or injury is industrial, there are strong political and industrial arguments that you can use to insist that your contractual relationship has not been frustrated and that dismissal is doubly unfair. However, in an outrageous decision the Industrial Court decided that a painter who had suffered an industrial injury and was not able to carry out his full duties, even though he had been put on

other duties for 12 years, was not entitled to either compensation or redundancy pay when he was dismissed for 'incapacity' – *Kyte v GLC* 1974 (NIRC).

Timing, consultation, alternative work and medical evidence
The principal question in all illness cases is: **can your employer reasonably be expected to wait any longer for you to return?**

That is not the end of the story because management must consider three other matters before they sack you:

1. They must consult you and discuss the problem with you, except in the rare situation where discussion would be totally fruitless.

2. They must consider whether any alternative work is available for you. But they are under no legal obligation to *create* a new job for you to do.

3. They must take all necessary steps to ensure that they have a balanced view of the problem, and this will often include obtaining medical reports.

These rules have been laid down by the EAT in *Spencer v Paragon Wallpapers* (below), *Patterson v Bracketts* 1977 and *E. Lindsey District Council v Daubney* (below).

■ Kenneth Spencer was a reeler in a paper mill. He had back trouble and was off work for two months. His doctor said he would be fit for work after another four to six weeks. Management sacked him because the plant was very busy and he had to be replaced. The Manchester tribunal and the EAT said this was reasonable as the employer could not be expected to wait till then, there was no suitable alternative work available, and Ken Spencer was consulted. *Spencer v Paragon Wallpapers* 1976 (EAT)

This decision was very harsh but the court did make it clear that every case must be taken on its merits. The short timescale of illness, dismissal and expected recovery date in Ken Spencer's case related only to the facts of that case and can't be taken as a precedent.

When seeking **medical evidence,** employers must do so in neutral terms, being careful not to prejudge the issue. The evidence on which the decision to sack is made must be available *at the time* – facts discovered later are not relevant to 'fairness'.

■ Edward Daubney was a surveyor in a local council. He was

56 when he was sacked. The director of personnel wrote to the council's physician asking whether Edward Daubney should be retired on health grounds. The area physician examined him, and said yes. Edward was sacked without consultation. The EAT upheld the Lincoln tribunal's decision that **the council should have discussed the matter with the man** and given him time to get his own opinion, and should not have solicited a medical report in the prejudged way they did. Employers must regard the decision to dismiss as an industrial rather than a medical one. They must get all the information possible. *E. Lindsey District Council v Daubney* 1977 (EAT)

When medical opinion is divided – your doctor says you are fit, the works doctor says not – management do not necessarily act fairly simply by showing they have a medical opinion on their side. All the circumstances are relevant in what is ultimately an employers' decision. Doctors' notes are generally inviolable and employers cannot look behind them to question your state of health; the *Hutchinson* case is a wholly exceptional situation.

■ A Birmingham electrician went sick with sciatica and handed his employer a doctor's certificate for one week. On the second day he was spotted by a manager picketing the EETPU annual conference in Brighton. After consulting the company doctor, management sacked him on the grounds that if he was fit to travel to Brighton, he was fit to work. The EAT thought that since the employers had evidence he was fit for work they *could* go behind the certificate. (According to the tribunal, though, Mr. Hutchinson was considered a troublemaker, had had four warnings, had contempt for his employer and the tribunal and had been protesting in Brighton about 'the anti-working-class policies of the union leadership'.) *Hutchinson v Enfield Rolling Mills* 1981 (EAT)

Protecting your job during incapacity
Many of the cases dealing with **long-term** sickness show a readiness by employers to treat workers as a form of commodity which, when it begins to perish, they can discard. Tribunals have modified this approach only for long-serving employees. They have not attacked the general principle that employers can dismiss for 'lack of capability' workers who become sick.

That employers can continue to do this, especially in cases of industrial injury or disease, is a classic example of the way the law is stacked against you. Clearly, it is unrealistic to rely on the law in these situations. You must use collective agreements and industrial pressure to protect the jobs of workers who are sick and therefore unable to exercise any industrial pressure themselves. Employers will always try to pick off those workers least able to defend their jobs. **So . . . if you think you are going to be sacked because of illness or disability, remember:**

1. Some events terminate your contract automatically because they make it impossible for you to carry out the original contract.

2. If the contract still continues, use the list of factors on page 217 to tell management they are acting unreasonably in attempting to sack you.

3. If they are thinking about sacking you, you have the right to be consulted, to discuss the problem, to get your own medical advice and to be considered for any alternative work there may be.

4. Management can act fairly only if they take the decision to sack you on the fullest information available at the time.

5. Keep in touch with management – send medical certificates, make visits, impress on them that you are still an employee.

6. Keep in touch with your workmates so you know what jobs are available, whether redundancy is threatened, and whether your job is still open.

Refusal to carry out instructions

You are obliged to carry out all lawful and reasonable instructions that your employer or supervisor gives you. See page 57.

You are *not* required to do anything that is not in your contract (however that is put together) or which is not reasonable. Characteristically, the judges tend to take the employer's view of what is reasonable:

> It is important that the operation of the legislation in relation to unfair dismissal should not impede employers unreasonably in the efficient management of their business, which must be in the public interest. – *Dean v Eastbourne Fisherman's Club* 1977 (EAT)

They frequently overlook matters of crucial importance in workplace relationships such as long-established custom and practice, demarcation, and procedures for negotiation. Workers are often cast as bloody-minded if they fail to carry out instructions given to them by their employer. However, there are a few basic rules.

1. Criminal instructions

If you are required to do something criminal you can refuse to do it. If you are sacked it will be unfair.

■ Leonard Morrish, a stores driver, was told by his manager to record in his book that he had been supplied with more petrol than he had actually taken. He was told that this was the normal way of making up deficiencies in the records, and he was told to falsify his entry. He was dismissed for failing to obey orders, and successfully claimed that he had been unfairly treated, although he was awarded only £100 compensation. *Morrish v Henlys* 1973 (NIRC)

2. Health and safety instructions

Specific instructions and sensible standards of behaviour in connection with health and safety must be observed. Failure to do so means you might be in breach of the Health and Safety at Work Act or specific regulations dealing with a particular hazard or particular premises, and you lay yourself open to a fair dismissal.

■ Bowaters issued all workers with protective goggles for use while operating grinding machines. Mr Taylor refused to wear them. The company turned off his machine, because it could not be used without the operative wearing goggles (it is mandatory on employers to issue, and on workers to wear, goggles in such conditions – Protection of Eyes Regulations 1974). He was sacked. The Industrial Court upheld a tribunal's finding that Bowaters behaved fairly, because Mr Taylor had refused, and said he would continue to refuse, to comply. *Taylor v Bowater Flexible Packing* 1973 (NIRC)

If a safety instruction has not been observed for some time, or if management have known that people have not observed it *and* have taken no action, it is unfair suddenly to sack a worker for non-observance.

■ John Wilcox was a gas fitter, employed on conversion to North Sea gas. It was a company safety rule that pressures must be tested before work started. He was sacked when one day management found that he had failed to carry out the test. He claimed that no one else did, that the company knew this and took no action, and that he should have had a warning. The High Court upheld the Middlesbrough tribunal's finding that the dismissal was *fair:* It had been proved that the employer had never 'condoned or acquiesced in that practice'. *Wilcox v Humphreys and Glasgow* 1975 (HC)

As Mr Justice Phillips said in John Wilcox's case:

If this requirement had been ignored for ages to everybody's knowledge, it would not be right, without some kind of warning, to dismiss the first person to break it after the employers took it into their heads to enforce it.

If management give you an instruction to do something contrary to a statute, they are breaking your contract, and you can refuse – compare *Gregory v Ford* (page 54 above).

3. Instructions outside the scope of your contract
You can refuse to obey instructions which are **criminally** unlawful, and also those which are **unlawful simply because they are outside the scope of your contract. If you are forced to do something which you know you are not required to do you can refuse.** Subsequent dismissal *may* be unfair.

■ Charles Wallace, a sheet metal worker, occasionally did pipe-bending, but only after a special rate had been agreed on each occasion. He was asked to do this work without prior agreement on the rate. He refused and was dismissed instantly. He applied unsuccessfully to a tribunal and then appealed to the Industrial Court. There Mr Justice Brightman said 'if pipe-bending were outside his contract of employment, there could be no possible answer to his claim to have been unfairly dismissed because on any reading of the facts and evidence he would merely have been declining to carry out work which he had not contractually bound himself to perform'. The court in fact found that the job was within his contract, but the mere fact that there had been no prior negotiations according to custom and practice was sufficient to make the instruction unlawful, and he got compensation. *Wallace v Guy* 1973 (NIRC)

Because a custom or practice can become a term of a contract, if an adverse practice is developing which is not expressly agreed by yourself or your union you should take steps to stop it, or agree on a set procedure.

Remember, when refusing unlawful instructions, that employers may claim the instructions are covered by your general duty to co-operate (see page 56).

4. Reasonable and lawful instructions

Occasionally you might act reasonably in refusing to accept a reasonable and lawful instruction, so that subsequent dismissal is unfair. Your employer has to ask: could the employee be acting reasonably in refusing to obey my instruction? In this sense your employer must consider the impact of the instruction on you, and any advice you have taken on it.

■ Garry Brain was UCATT's publications officer, responsible for the administrative side of the union's journal. A colleague was instructed by the General Secretary to write an article, which was found to libel the employers' journal *Construction News*. Settlement terms were arranged which included a written undertaking from Garry Brain. On the advice of the NUJ's legal officer he refused to sign as he had nothing to do with the article or the settlement negotiations and had no power over union officials for whom he was also asked to sign. After warnings he was sacked. The Court of Appeal agreed the dismissal was unfair. Although the union's instruction might be reasonable and lawful, in view of his objection it was nevertheless unreasonable to sack him. *UCATT v Brain* 1981 (CA)

What is the effect of an unlawful or unreasonable instruction?
The alternatives are stark but you can

1. refuse to comply. Management would then have to take the initiative, warn you and sack you. You would claim the dismissal is unfair.

2. refuse to comply and tell management that you regard the instruction as so unreasonable that you are going to treat it as a sacking. You would claim constructive unfair dismissal.

3. comply under protest and take management to the county court. You would claim damages for losses you suffer as a result of the unlawful instruction (compare *Gregory v Ford* page 54 above).

4. refuse, or comply under protest, and take the matter up in formal negotiations, or industrial action.

Apart from **4.**, none of these is satisfactory. As the law stands, a dispute about the scope and meaning of a contract can be taken to a tribunal only if it accompanies a complaint about a sacking or relates to the written particulars that must be given under the EPCA.

Change in conditions

A change that radically affects your conditions of work can be unreasonable, and will entitle you to claim unfair dismissal if your employer sacks you for refusing to go along with the change. In times of high unemployment and in industries with weak trade union organisation changes may be difficult to resist. The alternative of claiming constructive dismissal is hopelessly unrealistic. Remember that **employers can't unilaterally rearrange work patterns, reduce transport facilities, introduce shift-working** or **make any other major change.**

■ Mr Blakely was a foreman on day shifts in a foundry for five years. He was requested to go on nights. He refused and was sacked. He had no written contract specifying either day shift or night shift. The Industrial Court said that the employer had **no right unilaterally to vary the terms of his contract of employment,** even though these were not in writing. However, his claim for redundancy pay was rejected for other reasons. *Blakely v Chemetron* 1972 (NIRC)

If you don't object at once to a change in conditions management may argue later that this was a **variation agreed by both sides.** If you are offered alternative work in a redundancy situation, you are automatically given a right to a four-week trial period so you can see if you want to agree to the new conditions. This doesn't apply to changes made by employers where there is no redundancy. So if you want to try the changed conditions for a bit you must carry on working and specifically state that you are doing it under protest, or for a limited period.

In the *Goff* case (page 200), for example, the NIRC considered whether an order to work at another plant had been accepted by L.H. Goff and his son. The court said:

> What is an employee expected to do in these circumstances? He does not want to be out of a job. Nor, if he is a conscientious workman, does he want to let his employer down if this can be avoided. In most cases, therefore, he goes for the new job. He goes with an open mind. There is a period when he is uncommitted. During that period he makes up his mind whether he will accept the new employment, in which case he is not entitled to a redundancy payment; or whether he will leave.

In a subsequent case the court held that toolmakers who were instructed to move to another site, and worked there for two months, had not agreed with their employers that their terms and conditions were voluntarily varied. They got their redundancy pay and the court said:

> The courts have rightly been slow to find that there has been a consensual [that is, agreed] variation where an employee has been faced with the alternative of dismissal and where the variation has been adverse to his interests . . . the court has to decide the question, 'did the employee freely and voluntarily agree to vary the contract of employment?' *Sheet Metal Components v Plumridge* 1974 (NIRC)

A change in *emphasis* in your duties can also be a breach of contract amounting to constructive dismissal.

■ D.S. Pedersen worked as a catering assistant for two years before successfully applying for promotion to a job advertised as 'bar steward/catering assistant' on better money running assembly room bars. After four years, bookings dried up and he was given many menial catering-assistant duties. He did these under protest for eight months then claimed constructive dismissal. The Court of Appeal upheld his claim, saying that the forced *change in emphasis* to the secondary aspect of the job duties he saw advertised and accepted was a fundamental breach of his contractual terms. *Pedersen v London Borough of Camden* 1981 (CA)

Reorganisation

During 1979–80 the courts significantly strengthened management prerogatives. In a string of cases, the Court of Appeal and
the EAT supported the sacking of workers who resisted major
changes to their conditions of employment. Job-security was
diminished and the established expectation of union consultation was substantially downgraded. As a result, employers
may be supported if they have to reorganise their business in
the interests of efficiency, and workers who refuse to go along
with the changes *may* not win unfair dismissal claims.

The first example of the courts' readiness to uphold management's authority was given when a co-operative society worker
refused to accept the consequences of a reorganisation, and was
sacked. The High Court judge said:

> Where there has been a properly consulted-upon reorganisa-
> tion, which, if it is not done, is going to bring the whole busi-
> ness to a standstill, a failure to go along with the new
> arrangements may well – it is not bound to but it may well –
> constitute 'some other substantial reason [for dismissal]'.
> *Ellis v Brighton Co-op* 1976 (HC)

Three years later Lord Denning included not only situations
where the business would come to a standstill, but also where

> there was some sound, good business reason for the reorga-
> nisation . . . It must depend in all the circumstances whether
> the reorganisation was such that the only sensible thing to do
> was to terminate the employee's contract unless he would
> agree to the new contract. *Hollister v NFU* 1979 (CA)

In that case an official refused to accept major changes in his
conditions of employment, including a worsening of his pension
rights. The EAT said that this was made more serious because
there were no negotiations. But the Court of Appeal overruled
them and said that the requirement on employers to do all they
reasonably can does not *necessarily* require negotiation and
consultation. So the employer's ultimatum, without any prior
negotiation, was supported.

This alarming decision started a trend which included support
for an employer who clearly broke a contract of employment.

■ In 1970 Mr McCormack, a supervisor at Bowater's Ellesmere

Port factory, got an agreement that he would not be required to take on any additional duties, or to move departments. In 1979 he was sacked, after 14 years' service, when he refused to accept additional duties as a result of 'reorganisation arrangements which obviously were beneficial to the running of the company'. *Bowater Containers v McCormack* 1980 (EAT)

The EAT overturned the industrial tribunal which had found against Bowaters partly because the reorganisation had been agreed with the union. (As it turned out the plant was closed anyway in 1980.)

Then the EAT said that the head of a hospital supplies department was fairly dismissed when he refused to accept major job changes. Following a reorganisation, he was required to swallow a change in location and duties which added up to a *'fundamental breach of contract . . . quite outside the terms of his appointment'*. Yet when he claimed constructive dismissal, the EAT supported the tribunal's view that this was fair. In other words, the change was so serious it entitled him to resign, but the employers acted reasonably in foisting this change on him (*Genower v Ealing AHA* 1980 (EAT)). This was because he had known about the change for two years, an internal inquiry as a result of prosecutions had recommended staff should rotate, there were no other opportunities for newly trained staff, he had not consulted his union and he had not used the grievance procedure.

Generally, though, there is an obligation to consult before a reorganisation takes place which may affect contractual or non-contractual conditions of employment. Failure to consult *may* amount to constructive dismissal. If, as in the *Bowater* case, a union has been consulted and negotiations on saving jobs have been completed, tribunals may be reluctant to put individuals' rights above a collective settlement of a major reorganisation. Management have escaped the duties to consult individuals, and to refrain from imposing unilateral conditions, only when they have proved that the interests and efficiency of the business required major reorganisation.

Mobility

Many workers are forced to accept conditions in their contracts that require them to be mobile, and to accept flexible working arrangements. Employers are able to take advantage of their superior bargaining power, and introduce inducements such as travelling and subsistence allowances, in order to get the necessary agreement. If it is a part of your contract that you must be mobile, and you refuse to accept an instruction to move, you are liable to be dismissed and you may have no remedy.

■ Kenneth Sutcliffe, an aircraft technician stationed in Norfolk, was requested to move to Scotland. His contract said that he could work at any RAF station in the UK, and he had already worked at several stations. This time, however, he objected to moving because he had bought a house and for other personal reasons. He claimed unfair dismissal and redundancy pay. The court gave him neither, saying that it was a term of his contract that he should be mobile. There was no unfairness about the order to move, and as work existed in Scotland he could not claim redundancy pay. *Sutcliffe v Hawker Siddeley* 1973 (NIRC)

Sometimes, national or local agreements or works rules may class you as a mobile worker. An exceptionally wide agreement will be struck down by the courts but this power should not be relied on too much.

■ An ICI works rule required workers to accept the right of management to transfer workers to another job with a higher or lower rate of pay 'whether day work, night work or shift work'. The company tried to move Mr Briggs, a process worker, to another site. They quoted the works rule. In fact, they succeeded, but the court said that if a works rule or national agreement is unreasonably wide the courts can interpret it narrowly. The court said that on the face of it the rule enabled management to transfer a man from one plant to another plant miles away and to transfer a carpenter to a plumber's job. So they said that the rule really only enabled the company to transfer a process worker to another process job. *Briggs v ICI* 1968 (HC)

If there is no specific term in your contract, and no reference to mobility or flexibility in a collective agreement, the courts may still find ways of giving your employer the right to move you around. Agreement can be *implied*, they have said, by custom and practice and by the conduct of workers and employers in the trade:

■ At the time he was taken on as a steel erector, Edward Stevenson agreed to accept work away from his home in Leyland. When he was asked to transfer to Blyth, Wales or Manchester he refused because the money wasn't right. He said that he was not obliged to move. There was nothing in his written contract, nor in the national agreement, although this did refer to subsistence and travel allowances. The High Court said that there was an obligation for him to undertake travelling work because **all the facts surrounding his employment pointed to this conclusion.** The court approved an earlier judge's statement: 'I have come to the conclusion, though with some regret, that this appeal ought to be allowed. I say "with some regret" because . . . one cannot help feeling that in many of these cases . . . it might have been possible to show that the employees themselves must be taken to have known at the time when they were engaged that they were liable to be sent anywhere in the country.' *Stevenson v Tees-side Bridge* 1971 (HC)

Mobility is important when considering redundancy pay, because you will get your redundancy money only if there is no work offered to you in *any* of the places that you are required to work. See page 265.

Criminal acts

The circumstances that constitute 'conduct' or 'some other substantial reason' sufficient to make a dismissal fair vary enormously.

The cases show five areas where problems have arisen:

- criminal acts in the course of employment
- criminal acts which may affect your job
- criminal acts unconnected with your work
- conviction prior to starting the job
- acquittal following dismissal.

Criminal acts in the course of employment
The legal basis for allowing an employer to dismiss you instantly after a criminal act in the course of employment is that you

have, by your conduct, shown that you are not prepared to abide by your side of the contract of employment. It is incompatible with the fidelity and mutual trust that the courts say must exist between employers and employees for him/her to keep you on. In a sense it is the mirror image of a constructive dismissal. The employer's prerogative exists despite the introduction of unfair dismissal remedies.

The kinds of conduct that generally deprive you of your right to claim are theft, fraud, violence, threats, and 'industrial espionage'. There need be no criminal conviction, and there is no need for the police to be called in. Even in a situation which no one would consider heinous, instant dismissal has been upheld because the judges have accepted employers' views on the rectitude of workers' day-to-day conduct.

■ A betting-shop manager borrowed £15 from the till in order to place a bet. He intended to replace it the next day and did so. This was technically a crime and he was dismissed at once. The Court of Appeal said what he did was 'incompatible and inconsistent with his duty'. *Sinclair v Neighbour* 1967 (CA)

Although there is not much scope for a legal remedy against your employer if you commit crimes while at work, there are four modifications to the employers' prerogative with which you might still win an unfair dismissal claim.

Firstly, management must be acting on information that is available to them at the time they fire you. The Industrial Court said:

> If an employer thinks that his accountant may be taking the firm's money, but has no real grounds for so thinking and dismisses him for this reason, he acts wholly unreasonably and commits . . . unfair dismissal, notwithstanding that it is later proved that the accountant has been guilty of embezzlement. Proof of embezzlement affects the amount of compensation, but not the issue of fair or unfair dismissal. *Earl v Slater & Wheeler* 1972 (NIRC)

In other words, management must be acting reasonably when they deal with information that leads to a sacking. Information justifying dismissal but discovered after it can't make the dismissal fair. The microscope of reasonableness is focused on the time at which the employer makes the decision to dismiss.

■ Rowland Atkins was dismissed as manager of an abattoir in 1974. His employers offered him £6,000 compensation and six weeks' notice money. Six weeks later they discovered he had been guilty of misconduct at work and withdrew the offer. He successfuly claimed unfair dismissal. The company appealed to the House of Lords. They confirmed that evidence obtained after a dismissal cannot make reasonable otherwise unreasonable conduct by an employer. It might affect compensation or reinstatement, but it could not make Rowland Atkins's dismissal fair. *Devis v Atkins* 1977 (HL)

This also applies when information in *your* favour comes to light after the dismissal, such as when you are acquitted in a criminal court (see below).

In all cases of misconduct management must show that they believed on reasonable grounds and following reasonable investigation that you were guilty. It does not matter that a tribunal or anyone else would have come to a different conclusion; as long as management met these requirements they can dismiss fairly (*BHS v Burchell* 1978 (EAT)).

Secondly, they must follow a reasonable procedure and give you a chance to explain your conduct, show that you have previously been well-behaved, and so on.

The court said in *Earl v Slater & Wheeler* (above) that you have to be given the opportunity to state your case, unless there could be no explanation which could possibly prevent management from sacking you. If you are distressed, you must be given this opportunity at a time when you are in a fit state – *Tesco v Hill* 1977 (EAT).

This rule was whittled down by the EAT. Warnings and an opportunity to state your case must 'as a formal practice' be given. But exceptions are permitted if following this procedure would have made **no difference at all** – *British Labour Pump v Byrne* 1979 (EAT).

The ACAS Code of Practice on Discipline (see page 92) puts the rule more firmly. Paragraph 11 says:

> Before a decision is made or a penalty imposed the individual should be interviewed and given the opportunity to state his or her case and should be advised of any rights under the procedure, including the right to be accompanied.

Thirdly, there must be no delay. If management take no

action for some time it will be difficult for them to show that what you did was so serious that it struck at the whole basis of 'mutual trust'.

■ Two oil tanker drivers were convicted of theft. It was not connected with their jobs. Their manager decided to fire them but kept them on till their appeal (which failed) was heard 10 weeks later. He then fired them because there was a rigid policy on this and because their 'customers might not like it'. But the Sheffield tribunal said they were unfairly dismissed, as a policy like this did not take account of personal qualities. If they wanted to protect themselves and their customers it was 'inconsistent, even if lenient' to keep them on. *Donson v Conoco* 1973 (IT)

A delay can also lull you into thinking the matter has been dropped. Subsequent sacking by management might be unfair – *Refund Rentals v McDermott* 1977 (EAT).

Fourthly, sudden unannounced enforcement of a rule can lead to unfair dismissal if an abuse has been condoned in the past, or allowed by custom and practice to develop – see John Wilcox's case, page 223 above.

Criminal acts which may affect your job
The ACAS Code on discipline makes it clear that criminal offences outside employment should not automatically be treated as reasons for dismissal (para 15).

Some criminal acts committed outside the course of employment may affect your job because you are actually prevented from doing it, or because there is a connection with your work. A sentence of imprisonment for 12 months might, for example, make it impossible for you to carry out your duties and your contract could therefore be frustrated.

■ William Hare had been employed by Murphy's for 25 years, 15 of them as a foreman. He got into a fight outside working hours and was sent to prison for 12 months. The employers said they would take him back if he was given any sentence other than imprisonment. He was released after eight months and applied for his job again. But the employers refused. The Court of Appeal rejected his claim of unfair dismissal, saying that the effect of the imprisonment was that it was impossible for him to carry out his job. Therefore the employment had automatically terminated (frustrated). The length of time away from his job and his key position were major factors in deciding this. *Hare v Murphy Brothers* 1974 (CA)

In other cases, conviction might not make it impossible for you to work, but could **change the basis of your employment.** A used vehicle supervisor who was disqualified from driving for a year was held by the Dundee tribunal to be fairly dismissed. 40 per cent of his work was driving and the tribunal said it was unreasonable to expect management to reorganise work arrangements for him as a result of the ban – *Fearn v Tayford Motor Co* 1975 (IT).

More controversially, sackings have been approved where the conviction has been held to have little bearing on the job. A London tribunal has said:

> It would be quite wrong as a generalisation to say that an employer is entitled to dismiss an employee simply because he has been convicted of a criminal offence. This dismissal can only be justified where there is some reason why the conviction for the particular offence makes the employee an unsuitable person to retain as an employee. *Creffield v BBC* 1975 (IT)

In that case a camera operator was sacked after he received a nine-month suspended sentence for indecent assault on a 13-year-old girl. The BBC said he travelled abroad a lot and could not now be relied on to uphold the BBC's reputation. And they could not send him on filming jobs involving children. The latter is probably a valid consideration, since the conviction **directly affected his ability to do the job.** But to justify a person's dismissal on the basis of a possible slur on a company's reputation is wholly unacceptable, and probably would not, as the sole reason, be accepted by tribunals.

Similarly vulnerable to the sack for crimes that might affect their work are: teachers convicted of assault on children, bank clerks and security guards convicted of theft, pharmacists convicted of unlawfully possessing hard drugs, and social workers convicted of breaking and entering. In all these examples the apparent grounds for dismissal under the EPCA would be 'conduct'. This has been defined in broad terms by the EAT:

Conduct does not have to be something which occurs in the

course of the actual work, or at the actual place of work, or even to be connected with the work, so long as in some respect or other it affects the employee, or could be thought likely to affect the employee, when he is doing his work. *Singh v London Country Bus Services* 1976 (EAT)

The facts were that Harbhajan Singh, a bus driver/conductor, was sacked following his conviction for theft and deception. It was his first offence and he was given a suspended sentence. Nevertheless, Mr Justice Phillips agreed that the bus company acted fairly, as the conviction affected Mr Singh's 'trustworthiness'. A similar view was taken when a section leader with 20 years' service at *C and A*'s store in Peckham, South London, admitted shoplifting from *Woolworth*'s in the same street and was told to resign or be sacked (*Moore v C and A Modes* 1981 (EAT)). Each case must be taken on its merits, and if what you have done does not impinge on your work you should not be sacked:

■ Oliver Bernard, a drama teacher, pleaded guilty to possessing and cultivating cannabis. In accordance with his conditions he informed Shirley Williams, the Education Secretary, who decided that he should be given a warning. His employers, however, sacked him for being an unsuitable person. The EAT upheld the tribunal's decision that he should be reinstated. saying that offences like this and sexual offences do not automatically make the sacking fair. *Norfolk C.C. v Bernard* 1979 (EAT)

Criminal acts unconnected with your work
Except when you are physically or legally unable to do your original job – as happened to William Hare (page 233 above) – dismissal following a conviction not connected with or affecting your work is unfair.

Convictions prior to starting your job
The Rehabilitation of Offenders Act 1974 (ROA 1974) gives you the right to refuse to disclose 'spent' convictions (see page 35). If you are sacked for this reason, it is unfair.

■ Mr and Mrs Hendry managed the Scottish Liberal Club. Complaints were made and it came to light that Mr Hendry had been convicted of possessing cannabis. The conviction had become 'spent'. Both he and his wife were instantly dismissed. Both successfully claimed unfair dismissal on the grounds that the sacking infringed the ROA 1974. They got £576 compensation between them. *Hendry v Scottish Liberal Club* 1977 (IT)

■ Two security guards had convictions for minor dishonesty which had become spent. When they applied for jobs they were asked to sign that neither they nor any member of their families had 'ever been convicted of a criminal or civil offence'. Two to three years later management were tipped off about the convictions and sacked them. The EAT upheld the finding of unfair dismissal, making no exceptions for the occupation of security guards. *Property Guards v Taylor and Kershaw* 1982 (EAT)

Other convictions are not protected by the Rehabilitation Act, and non-disclosure has given employers the right to sack.

■ Geoffrey Torr was sacked after working as a guard on British Rail for 15 months. On joining he had denied that he had ever had a conviction. In fact, 16 years earlier he had been given three years for larceny. This sentence is not protected by the ROA 1974 – two-and-a-half years is the maximum. British Rail successfully prosecuted him for 'obtaining a pecuniary advantage by deception', that is getting a job, despite the fact that he actually worked for the money he received and had a good work record. BR then sacked him. The EAT upheld the tribunal's decision that this was fair. Concealment of a record affected the relationship of confidence between Mr Torr and BR, said Lord Justice Cumming-Bruce. *Torr v British Rail* 1977 (EAT)

So . . . if you have a record that is not 'spent', you run the risk of fair dismissal if you deliberately answer **no** to questions about it.

Acquittal following dismissal

It follows from the rule that only information available at the time of dismissal is relevant that your subsequent acquittal at a criminal trial does not affect the fairness of your sacking. This is to many people very hard to swallow, particularly as your character will be damaged by the sacking. The legal (but not moral) justification is that at the criminal trial the key question is whether **beyond all reasonable doubt** you committed the offence. Management, and an industrial tribunal, have to ask whether they are behaving reasonably in treating the information they have as sufficient grounds for sacking you. They and the tribunal need only to be convinced that **on balance** you did it.

Facing a prosecution, you could ask the tribunal to postpone your unfair dismissal hearing until after the court case. If you are convicted, you have little hope of getting your job back, but nor do you stand a much better chance if you are found not guilty. The result technically is irrelevant to a tribunal, but you will naturally try to sway them by telling them of your acquittal and by using it to show that there was insufficient evidence of the alleged offence to justify management sacking you.

Misconduct

'Gross misconduct' is one of the most frequently abused terms in industrial relations. There is no finite list of industrial offences, but if a court or tribunal does find that what you did amounted to gross misconduct it entitles management to dismiss you without notice, and you may not win an unfair dismissal claim.

This is only one aspect of the matter, because if there is *any* form of misconduct you may be disqualified for unemployment benefit for the first six weeks you are out of work (see page 285). You may not get wages in lieu of notice or a reference. So the term 'gross misconduct' is a very powerful and convenient weapon for employers.

It is much harder to analyse conduct which is not criminal but which may justify a sacking. Again, employers may describe as 'gross industrial misconduct' comparatively trivial things. As a broad rule of thumb you can say that if an employer wants to treat a certain act as gross misconduct s/he must give you formal notice of it. Smoking in a food factory or a mine, or clocking someone else's card, may give your employer the right to fire you instantly but only if there is a clear and well-policed rule on this (see also *Wilcox v Humphreys & Glasgow* page 223 above).

■ Hugh Dalton clocked a friend's card. There were prominent notices above the clock, and also in the employees' handbook, saying that this would justify instant dismissal. Even though he had 22 years' service Hugh was fired on the spot. The Industrial Court found no dishonest motive but said it was still fair to dismiss him. The Code of Practice need not be followed in cases of gross misconduct where ample warning had already been given. In a statement reeking of the nineteenth century, the court said the company acted reasonably in view of 'the pernicious effect which laxity in enforcing these warnings may have upon practices which could develop all too quickly under factory conditions'. *Dalton v Burton's Gold Medal Biscuits* 1974 (NIRC)

The ACAS Code of Practice says that there should be an oral and a written warning before dismissal. See page 93 above. Tribunals have to take this into account, and failure to follow the recommended procedure can itself make the dismissal unfair (see *Earl v Slater & Wheeler* page 231 above).

Offensive language has occasionally been held to justify a dismissal. But tribunals, in an effort to keep in touch with industrial reality, have accepted that shop floor relationships generate language as a matter of course which would offend middle-class ears.

■ Philip Wilson was head gardener at Tolethorpe Hall, an 80-acre private estate. The owner was in the garden with his family one Sunday afternoon. He started shouting at Philip, and criticising his work, especially his failure to trim a hedge. Phil said, 'if you remember it was pissing with rain on Friday. Do you expect me to get fucking wet?' After more provocation he said, 'Get stuffed. Go and shit yourself'. Only the two men heard this. The judge found that Phil had a clear conscience and 'did reply somewhat robustly . . . I think he felt a certain amount of grievance . . . ' He said he had not terminated his own contract by the language and had in fact been *wrongfully* dismissed. *Wilson v Racher* 1974 (CA)

Fighting can cause dismissals. Striking a supervisor or manager, because it affects the authority of employer over worker, will usually be found to be grounds for fair, and indeed instant, dismissal. If there is no evidence that the dispute affected the whole employment relationship, dismissal may be unfair.

■ Bill McDougall, a supervisor, went for a lunch-time break to celebrate a colleague's retirement. Back at work, he reprimanded a person for bad work, who then threatened him, or possibly hit him. He hit back. He was sacked, his two internal appeals were turned down, and he claimed unfair dismissal. The NIRC confirmed that this was unfair but that he contributed to it to the extent of 30 per cent. **His action had not gone to the root of his employment relationship.** Although serious, it did not show that he had 'repudiated' his contract. He got £760 in compensation. *Forgings and Presswork v McDougall* 1974 (NIRC)

Evidence of aggression, provocation, self-defence and over-reaction are all factors that can affect the reasonableness of management's action.

Absenteeism and lateness are types of misconduct that depend for their gravity on their extent, and the reasons for them. For other forms of misconduct, too numerous to deal with here, the main question is: **did management act reasonably in all the circumstances in treating the misconduct as sufficient grounds for dismissal?**

Job performance and qualifications

Poor performance, or inadequate qualifications for doing the work you are employed to do, are reasons frequently used to disguise the real reason for dismissal. If your employer is going to sack you on these grounds s/he must have given you warning, and an opportunity to improve your performance.

■ Frances Wiggins ran a boutique in Southend. She was warned several times about her standards and, having failed to respond, was sacked. The court found that 'the whole atmosphere was seedy and lethargic' and that the dismissal was fair because **she had had many opportunities to improve.** Management had to abide by 'general principles of fair play' and the court said they had. *Lewis Shops v Wiggins* 1973 (NIRC)

Most of the cases have concerned white-collar workers, and tribunals have said that the warning need not be absolutely explicit in the case of supervisors and middle management – sometimes you can be given 'the red light' informally. So the contract manager of a shopfitting firm who did not get on with clients was held to be fairly dismissed as his attitude had been referred to on several occasions, even though no specific warning had been given – *Dunning v Jacomb* 1973 (NIRC). If you aren't given some form of indication, you are likely to win a case of unfair dismissal. T.M. Gibson, a farm manager sacked for giving an inaccurate reference on an employee, got compensation because management should have told him they were thinking of sacking him – *McPhail v Gibson* 1976 (EAT).

Manual workers, too, are entitled to warnings and a sacking has been held to be unfair even though it was unlikely that the employee would have improved if he'd had the chance:

■ M. Bromley was a boiler service fitter. He received an oral and a written warning about his lack of enthusiasm for the job. Things came to a head when he couldn't fix the boiler, and production was lost. He got the sack and complained to a tribunal. The EAT confirmed that management should have pointed out his shortcomings, and given him more supervision and encouragement so he could improve. **Even though he probably wouldn't have improved, he should have been given the chance.** *Mansfield Hosiery Mills v Bromley* 1977 (EAT)

Rarely, a sacking can be fair without any prior warning if your performance is extremely bad:

■ An airline pilot made **a single but very serious error of judgment** when landing in his passenger plane. The plane was badly damaged. His employer, who was also on board, suspended him. Following a board of inquiry, the pilot was sacked. His claim for unfair dismissal was rejected, as his mistake was so serious as to justify dismissal. *Taylor v Alidair* 1978 (CA)

Probationary workers

Many employers, particularly local authorities, require you to work a probationary period. Once you have worked for a year you are entitled to protection against unfair dismissal. It doesn't matter what you are called – probationary, casual, temporary – provided you work the one year you are protected. But in practice tribunals often apply a double standard and say that dismissal of a probationary worker is fair in circumstances where a regular employee would be *unfairly* dismissed. Your employer may therefore find it easier to justify your dismissal on the grounds of capability in your early days. **So organised workers should resist pressure to include a special category of 'probationary worker' in collective agreements.**

The EAT laid down the following rule which tribunals should observe in considering whether an employer acted reasonably in sacking a probationary worker:

> Has the employer shown that he took reasonable steps to maintain appraisal of the probationer throughout the period of probation, giving guidance by advice or warning when such is likely to be useful or fair; and that an appropriate officer made an honest attempt to determine whether the probationer came up to the required standard, having informed himself of the appraisals made by supervisory officers and any facts recorded about the probationer? If this procedure is followed, it is only if the officer responsible for deciding upon selection of probationers then arrives at a decision which no reasonable assessment could dictate that an Industrial Tribunal should hold the dismissal to be unfair. *Post Office v Murghal* 1977 (EAT)

If you are on probation, challenge any warning or criticism that you consider unfair. Don't wait till the end of your trial period, as by then an adverse dossier might have been built up, and your job may be jeopardised.

Gay workers

You are entitled to protection, under the general principles of EPCA 1978 section 57, if management dismiss you because you are gay. Nevertheless, tribunals have upheld the sacking of homosexual men and women when broader reasons have been given. A clerk in contact with the public who, against management's instructions, continued to wear a badge saying 'Lesbians Ignite', was held to be fairly dismissed because management said the badge was offensive to customers and colleagues (*Boychuck v H.J. Symonds* 1977 (EAT)). And an odd-jobber whose work at a school camp did not require him to be in contact with children was dismissed because he 'indulged in homosexuality' even though there was no evidence of his involvement with children or that homosexuality made this more likely (*Saunders v Scottish National Camps Assoc.* 1980 (EAT)).

Since employers have been able to convince tribunals that a

worker's sexual orientation is 'some other substantial reason' justifying dismissal, gay workers should rely on trade union organisation to fight management prejudice, and to press for collective agreements to promote equal opportunity regardless of sexual orientation (see page 156).

Unfair redundancy

Redundancy is a potentially fair reason for dismissal under EPCA section 57. It is not sufficient, however, for management to rely on this, since the Act still requires tribunals to look at whether in all the circumstances they acted reasonably in sacking you for redundancy. The courts have developed this duty, and in the leading case *Williams v Compair Maxam* 1982 (EAT) four principles were laid down for employers to follow where a union is recognised, which also have a general application irrespective of union recognition. Breach of any one of the principles does not automatically make your dismissal unfair, but it may do.

1. Advance warning

Management are required to give 'as much warning as possible' of redundancies so that 'individuals and union representatives can know the facts, find alternative solutions and look for other work both in the same firm or elsewhere'. There is a statutory duty to consult recognised unions (see page 449) and it was held that failure to do so made any dismissal unfair when an Amesbury furniture factory was closed without warning – *Kelly v Upholstery & Cabinet Works* 1977 (EAT). The 1971 industrial Relations Code of Practice (para 46) requires: advance warning; voluntary schemes; a phased rundown; a programme of named dismissals; and help in finding other work. If no union is recognised, management would still have to show some special reason existed for not consulting and warning you – *Freud v Bentalls* 1982 (EAT).

2. Consultation with unions

This is aimed at establishing the fairest ways of achieving management's desired result with 'as little hardship as possible'. Fairness means jointly establishing criteria for selecting who is to go, applying the criteria to those individuals and hearing representations from them or their union. In broad terms the target of the redundancies should be agreed, and employers are acting unfairly if the axe falls on the 'wrong' group. For example, they are not entitled to look exclusively at the group doing the work which is drying up. Some of these workers may be moved to work being done by other workers not directly affected by redundancy. Only if management's need for work of a particular kind diminishes or dries up can you or management say you are redundant. In *Haden Carrier v Cowen* (1982), the Court of Appeal approved the concept of 'bumping', whereby a long-serving employee whose work dries up displaces a junior whose work has not; see page 264. It is also unreasonable to select all workers from one production unit while not touching workers doing similar work in another.

3. Objective criteria
The EAT said the criteria should be objective and not be based on one manager's judgment alone. The criteria should pay attention to attendance records, efficiency, experience and length of service. The courts have acknowledged that 'other things being equal', it is fair to operate the last-in first-out principle – see the *Watling* case, page 244, for example.

4. Alternative work
Your employer must look for alternative work for you in the same business or with associated employers before making you redundant.

■ Dennis Bear, a £4,000-a-year works manager, was made redundant. His company was one of 300 in the Tilling group. He got redundancy money, three months' salary, three months' use of his company house and two months' use of the company car. He was given no prior warning and no time off to look for new work. He complained that he had been shabbily treated. The court said his employer should have looked at all the circumstances and **tried to find him a job elsewhere in the group.** He received an additonal £321 compensation. *Vokes v Bear* 1974 (NIRC)

The IR Code of Practice (para 46) says that in redundancy situations management should 'offer help to employees in finding other work'. **If you are offered alternative work, you must be given enough information about it to enable you to make a 'realistic decision whether to take the new job'** – *Modern Injection Moulds v Price* 1976 (EAT).

There are two other situations where selection for redundancy is unfair dismissal:

a. **You are selected because of your membership (or non-membership) of the union** or for taking part at an appropriate time in its activities – EPCA 1978 section 59. See page 300 for an explanation of what this means.

b. **There is a procedure, or established custom and practice, for dealing with redundancies,** for example, last-in-first-out, **which has not been followed** in your case and there are no special reasons for departing from the procedure – EPCA 1978 section 59. If the procedure is followed but is itself unreasonable, management's action can be challenged under the general test for unfairness in section 57.

■ An electrician worked for nearly seven months on site A. In the last week of the job two new electricians were taken on first at site A then transferred to site B. It was custom and practice that the end of a contract means dismissal. Nevertheless the EAT said it was unreasonable to follow this practice when two men with only one week's service were kept on at site B. *Watling v Richardson* 1978 (EAT)

Legal restrictions

A dismissal is potentially fair if it is because 'the employee could not continue to work in the position which he held without contravention (either on his part or on that of his employer) of a duty or restriction imposed by or under an enactment'. A disqualified driver cannot continue to hold the position of driver and drive without breaking the law. Dismissal is potentially fair, although whether it is reasonable to dismiss for this reason depends on the availability of other work, and the length of the ban.

Dismissal of someone who is required to have, but does not have, a work permit is also covered by this potentially fair reason.

■ After a year's employment THF were wrongly advised by the DE that it would be illegal to continue to employ a Tunisian hotel worker, and they sacked him. The Home Office corrected the advice eleven days later and THF offered him an alternative job at the same wage, which he refused. The EAT said the employers had to prove there was a legal ban, not just that they reasonably believed there was, in order to be covered by EPCA section 57. But by a 2:1 majority they said THF sacked him fairly for 'some other substantial reason', i.e. that they had acted on advice from the DE. *Bouchaala v Trust House Forte* 1980 (EAT)

Every case must be dealt with on the basis of reasonableness, and in one case an employer acted unreasonably when he tried to avoid breaking a legal restriction:

■ Robert Pinney worked for a firm dispensing hearing aids. He didn't pass his exams within the five years required. He couldn't legally carry on working without a legal extension of his time. His employer felt he'd never pass the exams and sacked him. The EAT said that the fact that Robert's employer would have broken a statute, and been liable to prosecution, didn't necessarily mean he acted reasonably. He could have got an extension and prosecution was anyway unlikely. *Sutcliffe & Eaton v Pinney* 1977 (EAT)

EPCA schedule 9 gives a government minister, or someone acting on his or her behalf, the power to block your right to claim. If the minister certifies that any action was taken 'for the purpose of safeguarding national security', that is *conclusive*. If it is alleged you were sacked on national security grounds, you can't challenge it in a tribunal.

Not only civil servants are liable to be deprived of their rights. Workers whose employers have government contracts are also particularly vulnerable – especially as they can be subjected to 'positive vetting' by the Special Branch. A certificate by or on behalf of a minister can deprive *any* worker of the right to claim unfair dismissal.

How to claim

Details of how to claim are given on page 490. The time limit is **three months** after your 'effective date of termination'. You can claim if you are under notice.

Remedies for unfair dismissal

If you win your case, the tribunal must consider **all** the remedies in the following order:

- reinstatement
- re-engagement

- compensation.

Reinstatement

An order for reinstatement means management must treat you **in all respects as if you had never been dismissed.** The tribunal must specify any benefits you should have received, arrears of pay, rights, privileges, seniority and the date by which management must comply with the order. You will get the benefit of any wage increase or other improvements in conditions you would have had if you hadn't been sacked. Continuity of employment for all purposes is preserved during your absence and is added to your actual service. Account is taken of any wages or *ex gratia* payments received from your employer in this period.

The tribunal *must* consider three factors:

- whether you want to be reinstated
- whether it is practical for management to comply
- whether, if you caused or contributed to your dismissal (see page 482 below), it would be 'just' to order reinstatement.

Your wishes

The tribunal must explain its powers and ask you what you want to do. It doesn't matter what remedy you have specified in your written application to the tribunal.

Practicability

The EPCA 1978 does not say what is practicable, but industrial relations, workplace harmony and personal attitudes have all been found relevant.

In only two situations can the tribunal take account of the fact that a permanent replacement for you has been hired. The first is when management show that it was **not practicable for your work to be done without hiring a permanent replacement.** The second is when management show that they hired a replacement after a reasonable period of time without having heard from you that you wanted to be reinstated or re-engaged, *and* that it was no longer reasonable to have the work done except by a permanent replacement.

Because of this second defence, **it is to your advantage to include a claim for reinstatement in your tribunal application.**

Contributory fault

Compensation can be cut down by a tribunal which finds you

contributed to your own dismissal (see page 482). With the remedy of reinstatement there is no sliding scale – either it is ordered or it isn't. It would not be 'just', except following a finding of substantial contributory fault, to deny you your right to reinstatement.

Re-engagement

An order for re-engagement means you go back to work for your employer, or his/her successor or an associated employer. But you are not treated in every respect as though you had never been sacked. The tribunal decides what terms should apply. It must consider the same three factors as in reinstatement and it must put you back in comparable or suitable employment on terms which are, as far as is reasonably practical, as favourable as the original terms (EPCA section 69).

The number of applicants reinstated or re-engaged following a tribunal order is very small – see page 192.

Compensation

If the tribunal does not order reinstatement or re-engagement it must assess compensation (EPCA section 68). If a reinstatement or re-engagement order is made **but not complied with,** the tribunal *must* award compensation. In other words, if management disobey an order neither the tribunal nor the courts have power to enforce it. All you are guaranteed is compensation.

You can enforce an award of compensation by applying to the county court. If your employer doesn't comply with a county court order for compensation, the bailiffs can be sent in to seize property, or the employer's bank can be ordered to hand over funds in order to pay off the debt to you.

Compensation consists of:

1. Basic award – the equivalent of your redundancy pay entitlement with a minimum of £2,000 if you were sacked for your union membership (or non-membership) – EPCA 1978 section 73.

2. Compensatory award – to cover net loss of wages, future loss of wages, expenses, etc.

3. Additional award – if management do not comply with a reinstatement or re-engagement order, between 13 and 26 weeks' pay; (between 26 and 52 weeks' pay if you were sacked on the grounds of discrimination).

4. Special award – if you were sacked for your union membership (or non-membership) you get a minimum of two years' pay or three years' if management refuse to reinstate you – EPCA section 75A.

See page 477 for details of how to work these sums out.

Your right to written reasons

Section 53 of the EPCA gives you the right to demand from management a statement in writing 'giving particulars of the reasons' for your dismissal. The right is separate from the right to claim unfair dismissal and can be exercised whether or not your dismissal was fair. It is designed to give you some written proof of why you were sacked. You could use it as a reference if management refuse to give you one.

Who can claim?

You have a legal right to written reasons if you have *26 weeks'* service and are entitled to bring a claim for unfair dismissal (see page 208). You must have been sacked, or be under notice, or a fixed-term contract must have expired without being renewed. Constructive dismissal is not expressly included but the interpretation given to similar rules under the Industrial Relations Act 1971 means you probably can claim.

You can ask management for written reasons in every case, but it is conceivable that in some situations you may not want the reasons recorded.

You can claim if you have not been given a reason, or if written reasons are inadequate or untrue. A simple statement that your dismissal was on the grounds of 'capability' or 'conduct' is not sufficient since it does not include particulars of the reasons. The particulars requested do not need to be in a specific form. But the EAT said:

> The document must be of such a kind that the employee, or anyone to whom he may wish to show it, can know from reading the document itself why the employee has been dismissed . . . So there is no objection to its referring to other documents as well provided that the document which the

employee receives at least contains a single statement of the essential reasons for the dismissal. (*Horsley, Smith & Sherry v Dutton* 1977)

A reference to reasons given orally in an interview is not sufficient unless the reasons are set out.

How to claim written reasons

If management have not responded to your request within 14 days, you can make a claim to a tribunal that they have 'unreasonably refused' to give the information. The time limit is strict, but the EAT said that an employer's inaction isn't *necessarily* unreasonable. You must argue that refusal to respond does amount to unreasonableness.

Details of how to claim are given on page 490. The time limit is **three months** from your effective date of termination. You can make your claim at the same time as a claim for unfair dismissal if you are pursuing both.

Remedies for failing to give written reasons

At a tribunal hearing *you* must prove you were dismissed and if you are saying a written statement is untrue or inadequate, you must prove that too.

The tribunal can make a declaration as to the real reason. And it *must* award you two weeks' pay (see page 474 for calculations). This is without prejudice to any remedies you may get for unfair dismissal.

Fighting the sack

The first and most important rule about dismissal is: don't take your dismissal to a tribunal. The only quick and effective method of securing the reinstatement of a dismissed colleague when the normal procedures are unsuccessful is industrial action. Unfair dismissal occurs most frequently in small firms, mainly in distribution, catering, construction and agriculture. This suggests that the level of union organisation is a key factor. There are fewer cases from larger firms, the public sector and industries such as mining and shipbuilding.

This is only to say what is obvious: workers *can't* trust the law and *can* solve their industrial disputes by solidarity and organisation. These methods carry a considerably higher success rate, and massively more educational value, than any number of tribunal decisions.

But . . . if you are sacked or under notice use this checklist:

- Tell the union rep and call for support from workmates.
- Has the proper procedure in the Code or your collective agreement been followed?
- Have you been given proper notice? If not, demand it.
- If you are offered wages in lieu, refuse to accept and insist on turning up for work.
- If you think you are sacked because of union activity, contact your full-time official and claim 'interim relief' **within seven days.**
- Demand written particulars of the reasons for your sacking.
- Check that you are entitled to make a claim.
- Before making a claim, get help from your union or Legal Aid. (See page 487.) Watch the three-month time limit.
- If you are denied unemployment benefit, demand to see the employer's reply to the DHSS questionnaire. Lodge an appeal within 21 days.

Summary

1. Most workers with continuous employment are protected against unfair dismissal. You can make a claim to a tribunal if you are sacked or given notice after one year's service.

2. If your sacking is connected with your union membership or activities, the rule doesn't apply. You can also bring a claim under the interim relief procedure to keep your contract alive while your case is pending.

3. Most workers with 26 weeks' continuous employment can demand written particulars of the reasons for their dismissal. If this is refused, you can get two weeks' pay.

4. If you claim unfair dismissal management must give a reason and the tribunal must decide whether management acted reasonably in all the circumstances in treating that reason as sufficient grounds for sacking you.

5. Tribunals can order management to reinstate or re-engage you, or pay you compensation.

6. If you don't get proper notice or wages in lieu, you can bring a claim for wrongful dismissal in the courts, for which you may get representation under Legal Aid. (Tribunals may ultimately be given power to deal with these claims – see page 207.) In practice you will get notice money if you win an unfair dismissal claim.

11. Redundancy pay and insolvency

Who can claim redundancy pay / what redundancy means / your employer closes down / or is taken over / work diminishes / reorganisation / changing conditions / 'unsuitability'/ contractors / bumping / mobility / alternative work / changes in pay, travel, status, domestic arrangements, security / trial periods / misconduct / strikes / time off to look for work / how to claim / how much is due / your rights if your employer goes bust / guaranteed debts / a redundancy checklist / and a summary.

The organised worker's first response to the threat of redundancy should always be to take direct action. The purpose of this chapter is to show what is available if the fight for jobs is lost.

Chapter 18 deals with the right of union representatives to be consulted in advance of proposed redundancies. This chapter looks at the individual side of redundancy, which means payments, time off and guarantees if your employer goes bust.

Because a financial carrot is offered for redundancy, some workers have accepted their unemployment as a foregone conclusion. In less organised and determined sectors of industry the challenge to management's right to sack workers has been subordinated to the task of securing enhanced redundancy pay.

The original Act, one of the 1964 Labour government's first priorities, was intended to increase labour mobility and to give workers compensation for loss of valuable assets. The number and value of payments show this has failed. During the first part of 1983, redundancy payments were being made at the rate of 60,000 a month with an average value of £1,330 – roughly the equivalent of eight weeks' earnings. The legislation is widely regarded in the trade union movement as a Trojan horse, substituting militancy and job-security for inadequate financial compensation. Since the right to claim is restricted to employees with two years' service, many other redundant workers went without.

Where to find the law

The Employment Protection Consolidation Act 1978 (EPCA) deals with redundancy pay (sections 81–102); time off to look for work (section 31) and rights if your employer is insolvent (sections 121–127). The Transfer of Undertakings (Protection of Employment) Regulations 1981 SI No 1794 (TUR) cover some takeovers. See chapter 18 for the obligation to consult and give information to unions before redundancies and transfers; and chapter 5 for redundancy following lay-off or short-time.

Who can claim?

The first condition in any claim for redundancy pay is that you have been dismissed. The meaning of dismissal in its various forms is dealt with on pages 193–204.

In addition, you can volunteer for redundancy and still be classed as dismissed. For example, in a redundancy situation management may call for volunteers before deciding finally on who must go. You can claim redundancy pay even if you are the first to agree.

■ Robert Peck was sick for a year. Management suggested he take redundancy pay but wouldn't sack him while he was on the sick list. One day he turned up for work, was given none, and was sent home. He claimed his redundancy money but management said he had left 'by mutual agreement' and was not entitled to any. The High Court confirmed the tribunal's award of £577, saying 'the first to be made redundant are those who volunteer for it . . . **The fact that the employee agreed to this redundancy is no ground for holding that it was not a dismissal**' (emphasis added). *Burton, Allton & Johnson v Peck* 1975 (HC)

The second condition is that you must be in one of the groups of employees covered by the EPCA 1978. The list on page 208 shows that many workers excluded from the unfair dismissal law are also excluded here – part-timers, the self-employed, people who work abroad, and workers over retirement age.

In addition, civil servants, NHS workers and workers with less than two years' service are left out, effectively excluding 80 per cent of dismissals, according to National Joint Advisory Council estimates in 1967.

Specific exemptions are given to workers in the electric power industry, some fixed-term contract workers, and under certain pension schemes (see page 276).

What is redundancy?

Redundancy is defined in section 81 of the EPCA and can be summarised as any of the following:

- Your employer has ceased, or intends to cease, to carry on the business **a.** at all, or **b.** in the place where you were contracted to work.
- The requirements of the business for employees to carry out work of a particular kind either **a.** at all, or **b.** in the place you were contracted to work, have ceased or diminished, or are expected to.

The practical situations in which redundancy arises are numerous, but they can be split up into those where:

- the business closes
- the business is taken over
- a section of it decreases
- you are asked to move.

These are dealt with separately.

In all of the following situations you should bear in mind three things.

First, the closure, or shrinkage in labour, can be permanent or temporary. Attention is focused on the date you are sacked. If the definition fits the facts there is a redundancy situation, however transient that may turn out to be. Closure and sackings, followed in a week by re-opening and hiring of new workers, may indicate a fraud, and be grounds for other claims. But such a situation might arise quite legitimately, and if it does there is nevertheless a redundancy situation.

Second, it doesn't matter for legal purposes what the *reason* for the closure or cut-back is. Typically, it may be caused by automation, lack of orders, increasing competition, unprofitability, obsolete products, asset-stripping or insolvency. The Act is concerned only with the *fact* of redundancy and not the *reason* for it.

Third, many workers sacked during the first seven years of the original Redundancy Payments Act had their claims turned down by tribunals. They might today have a claim for unfair dismissal. Before 1972 there was no alternative, whereas now you should keep your eye on a possible claim for unfair dismissal if your redundancy claim is unsure.

The business closes down

This is the clearest case. It doesn't matter whether the closure is voluntary or due to insolvency. If your employer can't pay, your money is guaranteed (see page 277). If you work for a single employer who dies, and the estate does not continue the business, this too is a redundancy.

The business is taken over

A feeble attempt to comply with EEC Directive 77/187 on Aquired Rights was made by the Transfer of Undertakings Regulations 1981 SI No 1794 (TUR). The intention was to preserve workers' rights when their business is taken over or transferred. The practical effect is very limited. In short, it gives you the right to maintain your old terms and conditions and continuity of employment with the new job; it requires the old and new managements to inform and consult the union; and it requires recognition and other collective agreements to be continued in operation. Consultation is dealt with in chapter 18.

The practical effect is limited because the TUR do not apply in the most common takeover situations, where you need most protection. Firstly, a movement of the ownership of the shares in a company from one group of owners to another, without the whole company changing hands, is not a 'relevant transfer'.

Secondly, 'hiving off' the profitable parts of a business which has gone bust is excluded. In the classic case a receiver creates a new smaller company which has a chance, fires employees from the failed parent company, and finds a buyer for the new company. The buyer may take on all or none of the employees. This practice, reflecting the 'unacceptable face of capitalism', was severely criticised by the EAT when Lonrho took over a profitable part of the failed Brentford Nylons and escaped all responsibility for the employees (*Pambakian v Brentford Nylons* 1978 (EAT)). The winners in such an operation are the secured creditors like the banks, since the old company's liabilities have diminished, and the new owners of the asset-stripped company, who acquire a clean and unencumbered going concern. The state loses because it has to meet the statutory redundancy pay, and the employees lose jobs and probably wages too. A 'relevant transfer' occurs only at the point when the receiver has a buyer, and the buyer has had all his conditions for the purchase accepted. If you are taken on, the TUR apply.

Thirdly, the TUR apply only to the transfer of a commercial undertaking, which excludes non-profit-making organisations like a transfer from one local authority to another, or to the NHS. Privatisation of local authority services is not mentioned, but it has been argued that at the moment when a local authority hands out its refuse collection to a private contractor the operation becomes a commercial venture. Why else would anyone take it on? The sale of just the *assets* of the business is not a commercial undertaking – see below.

If the TUR apply, you are treated as never having been sacked and the new management are obliged to honour your terms and conditions and collective agreements. Your service is unbroken. If the new or the old management sack you in connection with the transfer they must show that it was for 'technical or organisational reasons', and the reasons must be tested for fairness. Otherwise it is automatically unfair. If there are substantial changes to your detriment you can regard yourself as constructively dismissed. In either case you would claim redundancy pay and unfair dismissal; see diagram 6 on page 258.

If for any of the above reasons the TUR do not apply, EPCA section 94 does. This contains the original Redundancy Payments Act rules on the takeover of a business. An offer of a new job must be suitable and reasonable (see below), otherwise you can regard yourself as redundant. If your employer sells out and sacks you, you get redundancy pay. If the new owners take you on, then sack you, you get redundancy pay from them. If they offer you work, the normal rules on alternative work (see below) apply. Provided the business is taken on as a going concern there is no break in your continuity of employment and you don't get redundancy pay. There are, though, some snags which might jeopardise your future position.

The Act applies only to changes in the **ownership of the business.** If the whole enterprise is taken over and run as before, but under new management, you are not redundant and you join the new management with unbroken service. But if only the assets of the business are taken on, and you are offered work in the same shop, there may not be a transfer of 'the business'.

■ Alfred Woodhouse worked for 40 years as a machine tool setter for Crossley-Premier, who made diesel engines in Derbyshire. In 1965 Crossleys moved production to Manchester and sold the plant to PB Ltd, which finished off five diesels and then made spinning machines and steam turbines. There was no transfer of trade name, customers, or goodwill, and the new product was quite different. All but one of the workers were kept on but in 1971 PB Ltd laid them off, with redundancy pay based only on the six years since the sale. The Court of Appeal said that was all they were entitled to. The business hadn't changed hands, merely the assets. (Woodhouse could have got redundancy pay from Crossleys in 1965 but was too late to claim in 1971.) *Woodhouse v Peter Brotherhood* 1972 (CA)

If, like Alfred Woodhouse, you are faced with a transfer you should obtain an assurance (in writing is best) from the new employers that they will treat you as having no break in your continuity of employment. The date continuous service began must be given (within three months) in your written particulars under the EPCA section 1 (see page 37). This is the easiest way to deal with the problem that you may not know precisely the details of the change in the business until it is too late. If you can't get such an assurance, claim redundancy pay from your old employer within six months of the change.

When the sale consists only of the assets, you get your pay and then start from scratch with the new management. If there *is* a sale of 'the business' as a going concern, you won't get the money but you are regarded as continuing in employment, and your service with the old employer will count if the new employer sacks you sometime in the future.

Diagram 6 Your employer sells up

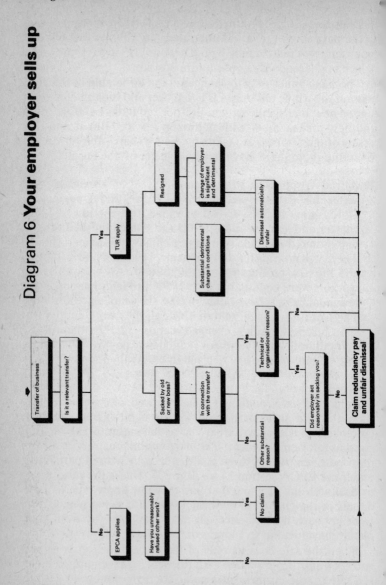

If a proper offer of alternative work (see page 266) isn't made by the new employer before the takeover, you can get redundancy pay, *and* take the job with the new employer.

■ Luigi Camelo worked for a small London company making furniture for 17 years. He was classed by the union as qualified but in fact worked as a labourer (at £26 a week). His employer sold out and Luigi was offered work on new terms by the new employer. There was a transfer of the whole business but a proper offer was not made *before* the takeover. So he got redundancy money from the old employer, and started afresh on a new contract with the new employer. *Camelo v Sheerlyn Productions* 1976 (EAT)

You can also get *severance* pay and retain your continuity of service if the pay is not made according to the obligations of the EPCA. If you are offered suitable work and accept, there is no dismissal. If there is no dismissal any offer of severance pay is not made under the EPCA but under a privately-negotiated scheme, and does not break continuity in the way it would if it were a proper redundancy case.

■ Sylvia Ross had worked for a Walkden, Lancashire food company for four years when her employers decided to sell up. They gave 90 days' notice to the union and the DE. She agreed to redundancy pay and notice money of £500, but agreed to continue to work for another five months until the transfer took place, and then on a new contract with the new employers. Three months later she was downgraded, had her wages cut and claimed constructive dismissal. The tribunal said she had only three months' service so could not claim unfair dismissal. The EAT said the £500 was paid by mistake, and not under the EPCA. As she accepted a new job offer there was no dismissal, so her service was not broken. The money was to be regarded as non-statutory severance pay and did not affect her legal rights. *Ross v Delrosa Caterers* 1981 (EAT)

Your kind of work diminishes

This kind of redundancy is the most fraught with legal difficulties. A typical situation is the reduction of workers employed on a particular kind of work. This can occur even if there is no reduction in *other* kinds of work – process workers can be laid off while white-collar workers are being recruited.

Claims have been made by workers subject to:

- reorganisation
- changes in conditions
- employers' ideas of suitability
- replacement by contract workers
- bumping.

Reorganisation (see also page 227)

The courts have resolutely defended management prerogatives when reorganisation of working conditions is put forward. They have disqualified workers for redundancy pay in circumstances where their employers unilaterally changed established patterns of work. Lord Denning declared in Noreen Johnson's case (below):

> It is settled . . . that an employer is entitled to reorganise his business so as to improve its efficiency and, in so doing, to propose to his staff a change in the terms and conditions of their employment; and to dispense with their services if they do not agree. Such a change does not automatically give the staff a right to redundancy payments. It does so only if the change in the terms and conditions is due to a redundancy situation.

The message is clear. **If you resist changes in hours, shifts and overtime working you are not redundant unless the reason for the change is a need to cut back in the amount of work done.**

■ Noreen Johnson had worked for 20 years at a police station on a five-day week from 9.30 a.m. to 5.30 p.m. To achieve 'greater efficiency' her hours were changed to an alternating shift of 8 a.m. to 3 p.m., 1 p.m. to 8 p.m. on a six-day week. She refused, was sacked, was replaced by a shift-worker, and claimed redundancy pay. The Court of Appeal turned her down, saying, 'If the employers require the same number of employees as before – for the same tasks as before – **but require them at different hours, there is no redundancy situation'** (emphasis added). *Johnson v Notts Police* 1974 (CA)

The threat of unilateral action by employers is very serious.

Indeed, the courts themselves recognise this by saying that claims of unfair dismissal might arise in these circumstances if employers artificially and unilaterally change work practices. Yet at the same time the NIRC and Court of Appeal opened the door to this very threat.

Employers may use this judgment to reduce their workforce, cut overtime and avoid payment. The *possibility* of unfair dismissal claims is a more manageable risk than the *certainty* of redundancy pay, as one company proved:

■ Lesney Products, who made Matchbox Toys in London, had 36 setters employed on days. They reorganised the work pattern to require the same number of men to work double day shifts. The men lost overtime and faced a cut in wages of £14. Six men who refused to accept this claimed redundancy. The court rejected their claims on the grounds that the **amount of work and hours done had not decreased.** *Lesney Products v Nolan* 1977 (CA)

The Court of Appeal asserted that

nothing should be done to impair the ability of employers to reorganise their workforce and their terms and conditions of work so as to improve efficiency. They may reorganise it so as to reduce overtime and thus to save themselves money, but that does not give the man a right to redundancy payment.

If you are faced with this kind of ultimatum, and industrial pressure is ruled out, you should **claim unfair dismissal** (see page 490), and you should investigate whether there is any reduction in management's need for work. If there is, then you may get redundancy pay:

■ Ivan Kykot had worked as a weaver on the night shift for seven years. Management wanted to reorganise the work by introducing rotating day shifts. Ivan's contract did not give management the right to do this. He refused to change and was sacked. Subsequently the night shift was closed down, with only a few workers going on to days. The court said he should get redundancy pay. There was more than a simple reorganisation. The workforce had decreased and so there was a redundancy situation. *Kykot v Smith Hartley* 1975 (HC)

Changing your conditions

The court drew a distinction in Noreen Johnson's case between an alteration in times of work, and alterations which might change the nature of the job done so that **it becomes a different task.** Changes in methods, hours, type of person employed, status, responsibility or remuneration, for example, *might* be redundancy, because the need for the *old* work has diminished.

Some changes are not clear-cut redundancies. There must be a reduction in the particular **kind of work,** not in work done **under particular conditions of employment.**

■ William Chapman and nine other workers in a china clay firm in Cornwall travelled the 30 miles or so to work each day in the firm's bus. Three of the men were made redundant, so the firm said it was inefficient to provide the free bus for the others. There was no public transport so they left, and claimed redundancy pay. Seven men who lived near the works were taken on. The Court of Appeal said the men had a contractual right to transport. Withdrawal of the transport amounted to sacking the men. But the sacking was not due to redundancy because **the amount of work needed was constant.** *Chapman v Goonvean China Clay* 1973 (CA)

So, some changes constitute redundancy if the particular kind of work diminishes. If the work doesn't diminish major changes such as withdrawal of transport constitute dismissal. You could win a claim for unfair dismissal, but not redundancy pay.

You have become unsuitable

Some of the most outrageous court decisions under the EPCA 1978 have involved workers laid off because management feel they have become unfashionable. Since a remedy for unfair dismissal was introduced these cases have withered away, but the ideology represented by employers treating workers like plant is still visible. The rule is that if you are sacked because you have become unsuitable, you are not redundant.

■ Ms Ward worked for 18 years as a bartender at the Star and Garter pub in Blyth. The manager decided to glamorise the pub and to employ 'young blondes and Bunny girls'. Ms

Ward was sacked. She claimed redundancy pay on the grounds that 'her kind of' bartender was no longer required. The lay members on the tribunal in two hearings found in her favour. The High Court said there was still a need for bartenders in general and denied her her money. *Vaux Breweries v Ward* 1970 (HC)

The extent to which the judges say you are supposed to adapt to the whims of your employer, or a new employer, is illustrated by Alexander Butterwick's case.

■ In 1966 the Resolution Garage in Whitby was taken over. Alexander Butterwick had risen to workshop manager after 30 years. He was dismissed because the new owners made demands of him that he couldn't fulfil. Lord Chief Justice Parker and the then Mr Justice Widgery refused to give him redundancy pay. They said, 'an employee who remains in the same kind of work is expected to adapt himself to new methods and techniques and cannot complain if his employer insists on higher standards of efficiency than those previously required.' *North Riding Garages v Butterwick* 1967 (HC)

In that case the Chairman of the tribunal, and this was not disowned by the High Court judges, said, in terms of committed management bias:

Inevitably the new management with new ideas and a natural desire for improved efficiency makes changes. Inevitably **misfits** are found **who have to be dispensed with.** No general rule can be laid down as to whether these misfits come within the scope of the redundancy payments scheme. **The slacker or scrounger who is weeded out** may well not be redundant (emphasis added).

Even if you are a skilled and conscientious worker you are still liable to become 'inefficient' or 'unsuitable', and to be sacked without redundancy pay. A Norfolk boatbuilder was sacked simply because he was 'although an excellent craftsman, such a slow and thorough worker', that his employers found his work unprofitable – *Hindle v Percival Boats* 1969 (CA)

You are replaced by contractors
What happens if management replace direct labour by contract

workers? It is an affront to organised and unorganised workers alike, but Parliament has encouraged the practice by classifying this as redundancy. The needs of management for employees to do the work has diminished, since it is done by contractors. Section 8 of the EPCA 1978 mentions employees only.

This is illustrated by a case that might have come out of Robert Tressell's *Ragged Trousered Philanthropists*.

■ C.A. Evans and A.W. Ball were employed as painters by a small south coast firm of decorators. Management told them one day that with wages, stamps and SET going up they were 'sub-economic'. If they didn't do a fair day's work they would be sacked. They were later sacked and **replaced by Lump labour.** They won redundancy pay, even though their work was still being done, because it was done by fewer 'employees'. *Bromby & Hoare v Evans* 1972 (NIRC)

In the building trades, this encouragement has contributed to the difficulty in stamping out the Lump.

Bumping

Bumping is the system by which a worker who is made redundant in one department is transferred to another, and displaces a worker with less seniority or less skill. For example, an agreement between Pilkingtons and the GMBU for the glassworks in St Helens allows dilutees to do (skilled) cutters' work in certain circumstances. If redundancy arises among the cutters they displace the dilutees, the dilutees displace the labourers, and the labourers are sacked. Although they can see others doing their work, the labourers are still entitled to redundancy pay because their employer's *overall* requirements have diminished.

The last-in-first-out system also survives on the bumping principle. The most junior worker is entitled to redundancy pay, even though it's not his/her own job but a senior worker's which has become redundant.

■ Ann Harding was taken on as a packer in a London plastics factory, then moved to a department making fittings, where the work dried up. She and others were made redundant in 1976, although there was still plenty of work for packers. She claimed unfair dismissal. The Court of Appeal said the employers were obliged to look for work elsewhere in the company and it would have been reasonable to dismiss someone in another department with less service. Failing to do this made the dismissal unfair and the company was ordered to pay £600 compensation. *Thomas & Betts v Harding* 1980 (CA)

You are asked to move

Redundancy occurs when management's need for a particular kind of work diminishes in the place **at which you are employed.** If your contract, either expressly or by implication or custom, requires you to work in a number of different locations you can be sacked for refusing to move. (See page 229.) If there is no such requirement you are not obliged to go. Management might offer you work elsewhere and this might be a suitable alternative. But that is a separate question and arises **only if you can't be required to move.** We are talking here only about a contractual obligation to be mobile.

■ **Example:** you work on a building site in London and you are a travelling operative and can be required to move. You are told to transfer to Brighton. You are not entitled to redundancy pay. It is true that work has diminished in the place you worked, but *in law* this is defined as any place where according to your contract of employment you could be sent. As long as management offer you work on other sites, and you are required to be mobile, you will not get redundancy pay.

So redundancy means . . . a reduction in the needs of an employer for employees to do work of a particular kind and it can occur

- when a business closes down
- when it is taken over as a going concern and you aren't offered work by the new employer. If only the assets are taken over, you can claim redundancy pay and start afresh with the new employer
- when there is a reorganisation of the workforce *provided* there is less work. Rearranged hours alone are not grounds for a claim
- when a change in conditions means that the old job is quite different from the new

- when employees become 'unsuitable' to changing employment conditions
- when contractors are brought in, or you are displaced (bumped) by a redundant employee. In both these cases, the fact that someone is doing your job doesn't mean you are not redundant.

Offers of alternative work

In a redundancy situation, if you are offered work instead of dismissal you may lose your right to redundancy pay if you refuse the work. An offer of other work is therefore management's defence to your claim. The work may be on the same terms and conditions as the old or it may be a new job. This is dealt with below. First **there are four conditions which every employer offering work to a redundant worker must comply with. If any one of these conditions is not considered, you are entitled to your money.**

1. Timing
An offer must be made **before your old contract** or notice runs out. If you don't get the offer until the day after that, the offer is invalid.

The offer of renewal or re-engagement must take effect immediately or within four weeks of the old contract ending. If you finish on a Friday, you must be started by the Monday, four weeks later.

2. Who makes the offer?
Since this is an employer's defence, it is natural to look to your employer for the offer. There are two variations on this. If the company is part of a group of associated employers, an offer from any of them counts as an offer from your own employer. So does an offer from a new employer who is taking over the business.

No other offers are sufficient. **Your employer cannot offer you work with the new employer,** nor with other firms in the area, even if s/he personally makes efforts to place you.

3. What information must be included?
The offer can be made **orally or in writing.** To be sure of what's

being offered, you should insist on the details of the offer being in writing.

Whether the offer is oral or written, it must be *sufficiently* specific for you to know what is involved in the new job. If it does not differ from your old job your employer must say so. But when the employer offers a new job, or different terms s/he must inform you about the 'capacity and place . . . and . . . other terms and conditions of employment' – EPCA 1978 section 82.

You must be given enough information to enable you to reach a decision on whether to accept or reject the offer. If particulars of travel arrangements, rates of pay, duties and so on are missing, the employer hasn't made a proper offer.

4. Failure to make an offer

If there is no proper offer, your employer must pay. Even if s/he makes no offer because s/he knows you will refuse, s/he must still go through the motions.

■ Ms J. Simpson worked in a small sweet shop in Reading. It was taken over by the Thornton's chain. Ms Simpson said she wouldn't work for them, would take two or three months' holiday, then work in a hospital or anywhere but a shop. So Thornton's made no offer to her. She claimed redundancy pay. The NIRC decided that if an employer wants to avoid the duty to pay, there is a strict obligation in the Act to make an offer, even if refusal is likely. So Ms Simpson got her money. *Simpson v Dickinson* 1973 (NIRC)

Offering the same work and conditions

If a proper offer is made to you, you must consider whether there is any change in your conditions. If there is no change and you are offered a renewal of your old job, you can get your money only if you *reasonably* refuse it. You might be acting reasonably if, for example, you were given notice, found another job, made arrangements to move and at the last minute were offered a renewal of your old job (compare *Thomas Wragg v Wood,* page 270 below).

You might get an offer of work which, though strictly within your contract, means you do different work from the work you normally do. This would be an offer of work on the same conditions. If the work is not within your existing conditions, your case is one of 'different conditions' and the work is judged on the grounds of suitability.

Offering different conditions

Your employer may offer you work on different terms from your old contract. You will need to know whether you are jeopardising your redundancy money if you refuse. It is an invidious position to be in because you may have to choose between accepting a poor alternative, and losing your money.

For your employer to avoid payment s/he must show that there was **1.** a proper offer **2.** of suitable work **3.** which you unreasonably turned down. In law suitability and reasonableness are separate issues. Broadly, suitability relates to the job (objective), reasonableness to personal factors of your own (subjective). This can be illustrated by Richard Stratton's case:

■ Richard Stratton was an inspector in an engineering plant. He worked four nights a week. Due to redundancy he was offered five nights, with more money and fewer hours. He refused and claimed his money. The offer was suitable, as it was *substantially equivalent* to his old job, but he personally objected to losing more sleep, having to travel to work once more each week, and spending less time with his family. The NIRC awarded him his redundancy pay. *Universal Fisher Engineering v Stratton* 1972 (NIRC)

In practice the two conditions get mixed up and tribunals don't always make clear the grounds on which they base their decisions. A number of rules of thumb have emerged, though, which show that offers can be safely refused for a variety of reasons. **What follows should not be regarded as an exhaustive list. In every case the test is suitability and reasonableness.**

Pay
If the money you are offered in the new job is substantially lower than in the old you can turn it down. A worker who rejected a drop of 10 per cent was held to be acting reasonably. If there were other unfavourable factors, you could reasonably refuse any drop in wages.

Travel

Two workers told to move to another London factory two-and-a-half miles away were reasonable in refusing (*Shields v Goff* page 200 above). But a Nottingham man offered work 20 miles away in Newark, with travel costs paid for nine months and on flexible shifts, was unreasonable in refusing – *Hitchcock v St Anne's Hosiery* 1971 (HC). Factors you would have to consider – and these should be made clear to you before your old job finishes – are: distance, time, expense, inconvenience, where you live.

Status

A drop in status is something you can reasonably refuse – Mr Marriott did (see page 199). So did a headmaster who was offered a job in a pool of teachers who were obliged to be mobile – *Taylor v Kent* C.C. 1969 (HC). Raymond Harris, a joiner and apprentice trainer, was reasonable in turning down work as a bench joiner without the status that went with teaching apprentices, even though his wages and staff status would have been the same – *Harris v Turner* 1973 (NIRC). But a *chargehand* shipwright unreasonably refused to move to another dock as a shipwright – *Collier v Smiths Docks* 1969 (HC).

Domestic arrangements

Refusal to take a job because it disrupts your family or social life is often a valid reason. A foundry worker who turned down a suitable double-day shift job because his wife was an invalid got his redundancy money – *Allied Ironfounders v Macken* 1971 (HC).

Uncertain future

If you reject a job because it may not last very long, you run the risk of forfeiting your redundancy money. Provided the job offered is of a regular nature, even though it may not be very secure, you should take it. Joan Street turned down a clerical/typist job because it would probably last only 12–18 months (*Morganite Crucible v Street* 1972). Sir John Donaldson, in the NIRC, said she acted unreasonably and refused to award her any redundancy pay. He remarked:

> No employment (with the possible exception of judicial employment) can be said to be almost permanent.

His own judicial employment in that court proved to be no exception!

Combined with *other* factors, though, fears of job security can give reasonable grounds for refusing a job with your present employers.

■ Horace Wood was given notice by the construction company he worked for. He got a job elsewhere, but on his last day at work he was offered suitable alternative work. He refused to take it on the grounds that he was 56, had fears about future redundancy in the industry, had accepted a job outside and anyway the offer came unreasonably late. The EAT upheld his award of £800, saying his grounds were reasonable, when considered all together. *Thomas Wragg v Wood* 1976 (EAT)

Trial periods

When you are offered a job on different terms, section 84 gives you the right to a trial period on the new job. This applies however slight the variation in terms or location or capacity of employment. It lasts for four weeks and gives you the chance to try the new job.

During this period you are free to quit, and claim redundancy pay calculated up to the day the old job ended. If management won't pay, the new job is scrutinised in the usual way, to see if it was suitable and if you were unreasonable. If you are sacked during the trial period – because, say, you are not efficient enough – you are taken to be redundant on the date the old job finished, and are entitled to payment.

If you refuse to take the trial period, management might refuse to pay. A tribunal will test the new job and your refusal for suitability and reasonableness. Theoretically your refusal should not affect these questions, but tribunals may be more ready to consider you unreasonable if you fail to try it out.

Extending the trial period

You can extend the trial period for the purposes of retraining provided you make a written agreement **before you start work** specifying the date the period is to end, and your terms and conditions when it does.

Logically there is no reason why the period should not be extended by agreement to give you a longer trial, or to let you take holidays, but section 84 talks only of retraining. Management might be unable to recoup their rebate if they agree to an extension for other reasons.

It seems that if management give the proper notice to terminate your contract, and offer you new terms, you are stuck with the four-week trial period. If, on the other hand, you are faced with a take-it-or-leave-it ultimatum requiring you to change to new conditions or be made redundant, particularly if you are given less than your proper notice, you have a 'reasonable period' to make up your mind which may be longer than four weeks.

■ Four engineering workers were told their work as polishers would shortly end and were offered work in other departments which under their contracts they could refuse. Instead they agreed to give it a try. More than four weeks later they all left, claiming redundancy pay. The EAT said they were entitled, in view of the employer's repudiation of their original contracts, to a reasonable time to decide whether to carry on working. And if they decided to accept the change they then had the four-week statutory trial period. *Turvey v C.W. Cheney* 1979 (EAT)

Similarly an airline telephonist, who did not like the artificial light and air-conditioning in the basement exchange she had to move into, got redundancy pay after a *two-month* trial – *Air Canada v Lee* 1978 (EAT).

Alternative work – summary

1. An offer must be made by management, or the new management in a takeover, before your notice expires. It must be specific about the main conditions of the new job, which must start within four weeks of the old job.

2. If your contract is renewed without changes, it will usually be unreasonable for you to refuse it.

3. If the work or conditions of the new job are different, you lose redundancy pay if it is *suitable* and you *unreasonably* refuse it.

4. Less pay, lower status, more travel, domestic arrangements and insecurity are all factors to be considered.

5. You are entitled to a four-week trial period in any new job.

Redundancy and misconduct

The 1978 Act deals specifically (sections 82 and 92) with sackings for misconduct in a redundancy situation. These rules can be summarised according to whether you are sacked before or after you have been given notice of redundancy. Employers are keen to invoke these rules because they can use them to avoid redundancy pay. If you lose redundancy pay because of these rules it is almost certain you will also lose any unfair dismissal claim you bring.

Misconduct before notice of redundancy

Suppose a redundancy situation arises but no one has yet been given notice. Management discover you have been stealing from the works. This is grounds for instant dismissal. So they pick you out for redundancy. They can sack you instantly, or with less notice than you are otherwise entitled to. If they let you work out your notice they *must* give you a written statement that they think they are entitled to sack you instantly because of your misconduct but they are letting you work out your notice.

In either case, you don't get your redundancy pay.

Misconduct after notice of redundancy

If you are under notice of redundancy and management then sack you for gross misconduct, you don't automatically lose your redundancy pay. You can apply to a tribunal. It has discretion to pay you all or some or none of your money, according to what it thinks is just and equitable in the circumstances. In other words, it substitutes its judgment for management's.

This right applies only to a sacking while you are working your statutory notice.

■ **Example:** You have been employed for four years. The EPCA entitles you to a minimum of four weeks' notice. Your contract gives you six weeks. If you are sacked for gross misconduct during the first two weeks, you don't get redundancy pay. But if you are sacked in the last four weeks (that is, the statutory notice period) you do.

Redundancy and strikes

Similar rules apply during strikes in a redundancy situation. The risk of losing your rights may affect your decision to resist redundancy by industrial action, so the rules are important.

Striking during notice

The classic case arises when you are given notice of redundancy and decide to strike in protest. If this occurs during your statutory notice period under the EPCA 1978, you do not jeopardise your redundancy money (that is, if the strike does not avert the sackings). But management can require you to make up the days lost through the strike.

The definition of a strike (see page 385) includes a cessation of work, and a refusal to work for an employer. Accordingly a sit-in and a work-in are both covered.

Redundancies declared during a strike

Employers regularly threaten redundancies during a strike. Sometimes it is genuine, sometimes just a scare tactic. You may lose your right to redundancy pay, as W. Simmons did (see page 392). The EAT said Hoovers could refuse to pay because the right to pay is protected only when a strike occurs *after* notice of redundancy has been given.

Since employers are, as we have seen, entitled to sack strikers, they can avoid redundancy payments quite easily. However, the EAT in the *Simmons* case said that a strike in response to deliberate provocation or unreasonable demands by an employer will not prejudice your rights – but see page 395.

If a tribunal says you caused the redundancy yourself – by striking or inefficiency, for example – you are still entitled to redundancy pay. Again, this is because the law applies to the *fact* of redundancy, not the reasons for it.

Time off during notice

If you are under notice of redundancy you might want to start looking for a new job or retraining before you actually sign on as unemployed. Some collective agreements require employers to provide time off with pay, and travelling expenses, for workers under notice.

The EPCA 1978 gives you a legal right to time off. Section 31 applies if, at the date you are due to be sacked, or proper notice would have run out, you have two years' continuous employment. But you still get time off even if, for example by refusing a reasonable offer, you would not be entitled to redundancy pay. This section applies to Crown and National Health Service workers (the other provisions on redundancy don't).

You have two rights:

- to be given a 'reasonable' amount of time off
- to be paid for it.

The purpose of these rights is to enable you **to look for work, or to make arrangements for training** for future employment. You must show that this is how you intend to use your time off.

There is no definition of what is reasonable. This would depend on the difficulty in obtaining work, the time and travel involved, the range of jobs you are looking at, and the requirements of a training agency.

The right to unpaid time off is quite separate from the right to be paid, and is restricted only by what is 'reasonable'. But if management fail to give you time off, or fail to pay you, their liability is limited. This may indirectly impose a restriction on the amount of paid time off you can demand.

If management deny your rights you should claim to a tribunal **within three months** of the day on which you wanted time off. See page 490 for the procedure. The tribunal can order management to pay, but they can't be made to pay more than **two days' pay.** Any pay you get under your contract must be offset against these two days. This means that if management pay you while you work out your notice, but refuse to release you for job hunting, you can't get any more money from them.

Leaving during notice

Supposing you get a job and want to start before you have worked out your notice? You can give notice to finish earlier, and this does not affect your redundancy pay *provided* you take the following steps:

1. You have been given the minimum notice you are entitled to under the EPCA 1978 section 49. If you have been given longer you must wait until you are in the statutory minimum notice period. For example: if you are entitled to four weeks under the Act, but six weeks under your contract, the right to leave earlier applies only during the last four weeks.

2. You give management **in writing** the minimum notice required by your contract.

3. If management don't object, you can leave when your notice to them expires. Redundancy pay is calculated to this earlier date.

Your redundancy pay may be affected as follows:

4. If they do object, they must **in writing** request you to withdraw your notice and warn you that if you don't, they will contest your right to redundancy pay.

5. If you still go ahead and leave, you don't necessarily lose your redundancy money. Tribunals have power to look at all the reasons on both sides, and award you all or part or none of the money.

Lay-off and short-time

Remember that lay-off without pay, and short-time working on half-pay or less, can constitute redundancy and unfair dismissal. See page 86.

How to claim redundancy pay

You must make a claim for redundancy pay **within six months** of your dismissal. If you have worked for a trial period, the six months run from the date your trial period ended. You should make a claim either by writing to your employer (or the receiver/liquidator if s/he has gone bust, or personal representative if s/he has died or the DE if you get not reply), *or* by applying to a tribunal. See page 490 for the procedure.

If you have not received a written statement giving particulars about the reasons for your dismissal, you should demand this in accordance with section 52 of the EPCA (see page 248 above).

Proving it

You must show you were sacked. If management say you resigned, you have to show you were constructively dismissed or voluntarily accepted dismissal on the grounds of redundancy. The onus then shifts to your employer. There is a presumption that if you were sacked, it was because of redundancy. Management must then try to disprove this.

How much is due?

The method of calculation

Redundancy pay is calculated according to the same formula as the **basic award** in unfair dismissal cases. Use the ready reckoner on page 480 to check the calculations.

Tax and unemployment benefit

Redundancy pay is tax-free. Additional redundancy pay made, for example, because of a collective agreement or as an *ex gratia* payment, is tax-free up to £25,000. Anything over that is taxed.

Redundancy pay does not affect unemployment benefit but may affect supplementary benefits since it is treated as capital and therefore counts towards the limit (of £3,000 in 1983/84). Pay in lieu of notice may be taxed, and will disqualify you for unemployment benefit, so it is advisable to have this tied up as 'severance pay', or additional redundancy pay, to avoid reductions.

Pensions

Employers can offset redundancy pay against an occupational pension scheme in limited circumstances. These are set out in leaflet RPL 1, obtainable from union and DE offices. Briefly, they can't offset repayment of your own contributions, or pensions or lump sums which accrue more than 90 weeks after your dismissal. If your employer does not exercise this limited right to offset, s/he can claim the normal rebate from the state fund (see below).

Statement of calculation

You have the right to a written statement explaining how management work out the payment. If they fail to provide this they can be fined £20 for a first, and £100 for a second, offence.

Who pays?

Management pay you. They are entitled to claim a rebate from the state fund to which all employers contribute. The rebate is 41 per cent of the statutory amount they have paid to you. They can't reclaim higher amounts, for example, sums paid under a collective agreement.

If your employer goes bust, or otherwise refuses to pay, the whole of your statutory payment is guaranteed by the state fund – see below.

Your rights against an insolvent employer

If your employer goes bust owing you wages, holiday pay, redundancy pay and so on you will be able to recoup some of these debts from the state fund. Your rights on insolvency depend on what the debt consists of. There are four different methods of dealing with them under EPCA section 21.

1. Fully guaranteed debts

If your employer goes bust, and you are entitled to **redundancy pay,** the state fund guarantees the full statutory amount. Make a claim to your employer's liquidator/receiver and then apply to your DE office.

All statutory **maternity pay** is refunded to employers so this is guaranteed if your employer goes bust before paying you. In addition the whole of the following debts are guaranteed:

- **basic award** of unfair dismissal compensation
- minimum notice money due to you according to the EPCA
- repayment of an apprenticeship premium.

2. Partly guaranteed debts

If your debts are accrued on a weekly basis, such as arrears of pay, the state fund will guarantee the following debts up to £140 (in 1983/84) each week:

- arrears of pay (including the **priority debts** listed below) for up to *eight* weeks
- holiday pay for up to *six* weeks.

The Employment Secretary can raise the upper limit each year.

3. Priority debts

If you still have money owing to you after the state fund has met fully and partly guaranteed debts, you can claim against the company as a preferential creditor. This would happen if you had **arrears of wages** in excess of eight weeks, or £140 a week (in 1983/84), or were entitled to more than minimum notice. The most you can claim for the *whole* of these debts is £800 (1976 Insolvency Act).

The debts for which you rank as preferential creditor are:

- arrears of pay during the previous four months
- notice pay
- holiday pay
- guaranteed wages
- payment for medical suspension
- pay due to union representatives while carrying out duties or training
- pay while looking for work, or retraining, during notice
- a protective award following redundancies.

Sick pay is not specifically mentioned but it could be classed as arrears.

As a preferential creditor, you get paid before some shareholders and other creditors out of any money or assets the company has left. But you rank equally with the tax, social security and rating authorities, who are also preferential. You might get a percentage of what's due to you.

4. Unsecured debts

For any other money owed you, you have to take your chance with the shareholders and all the other creditors. The kind of debts envisaged are:

- priority debts of over £800 after the state fund has met its obligation to you
- compensation for unfair dismissal (excluding the basic award), victimisation, sex and race discrimination.

How to claim

Claim redundancy pay in the way described above. For loss of notice money use Form IP2, and for other debts Form IP1. Write to your employer's representative, that is, the receiver, liquidator or trustee. S/he should send you Forms IP1 and 2. You complete the relevant form and return to the representative, who then passes it to the DE. The DE arranges for the representative to pay you.

If you don't known who the representative is, or if you don't get paid within six months of applying, write direct to the DE.

For other preferential debts, and unsecured debts, you need a **'proof of debt'** form from the receiver/liquidator handling the company's affairs. Write to the company's registered office. If there are a number of you, your union official can file a form on behalf of all of you.

Who are the losers?

The guarantees in the EPCA 1978 are a substantial advance on the slight protection afforded since 1948. They still don't cover all kinds of debts, nor the whole of those that are protected. Parliament has gone some way to recognising that money owed by employers to workers is in a different category from other debts. It should go further.

Shareholders take a conscious risk when they invest in a company which they hope will increase their capital. Companies trading with each other do so to further their own profits. If their judgment is unsound, or the company is unreliable, it is right that they accept the risk of loss. Workers, on the other hand, because they are not involved in such decisions, can't control the finances of their employer and don't have an effective free choice in seeking jobs, should not be put at risk. They should be fully compensated by the state fund for any collapse or failure to pay. Employers should be required to pay more into the fund to meet this eventuality.

The other gap in the protection is that the rights apply only if your employer is insolvent, that is, s/he can't pay. If s/he simply disappears without trace, as sometimes happens in the textile and building trades, you have no protection.

Redundancy checklist

Collective measures to fight redundancy are listed on page 462. **They are the most effective ways to prevent closures and lay-offs.** If you are made redundant you will be entitled to some or all of the following rights as an *individual*:

- time off with pay for retraining or to seek new work
- notice or wages in lieu
- written statement of reason for dismissal
- redundancy payment and statement of how it is calculated

- a protective award (see page 456) if your employer has not consulted the union
- unfair dismissal if a redundancy procedure has been ignored, or you have been selected unfairly, for example on trade union grounds
- a guarantee from the government of some debts if your employer goes bust
- tax rebate if you are out of work.

Summary

1. You are entitled to redundancy pay if management's need for employees to do work of a particular kind either ceases or diminishes.

2. Management can avoid paying you if they offer suitable alternative employment and you unreasonably refuse to take it.

3. You have a right to a trial period if you are offered work on new conditions.

4. If the business is transferred, your employment contract continues unbroken with the new management.

5. You have a right to take time off with pay for job-hunting or training if you are given notice of redundancy.

6. If you are laid off or put on short-time you might be entitled to claim redundancy pay and unfair dismissal.

7. If your employer is insolvent, some debts owed to you are guaranteed by the government, and you get priority over shareholders for some other debts.

8. Organised workers should regard the existence of these rights as minimum standards on which to negotiate, if direct action to oppose redundancy fails.

12. Social security

Your rights under the social security system / contributory and non-contributory benefits / tax / unemployment, maternity, sickness and invalidity benefits / industrial injury, disease, disablement and death / family income supplement / supplementary benefit / what to do if you are denied your rights / collective action / and a summary.

The social security system consists of a wide range of benefits and services. Within the system, some benefits are entirely free to everyone, such as some health services; some are available only to employees; some only to unemployed or retired people; and some only to workers who have paid a specific number of contributions. This chapter deals only with those rights connected with employment. Of necessity, this account is an outline only. Pensions are omitted entirely. For a full explanation see Sue Ward, *Social Security at Work*, Pluto 1982 and the further reading on page 515.

During the 1980s the government began to dismantle the social insurance framework. Sick pay was privatised, earnings related supplements to the major benefits were cancelled, unemployment and supplementary benefit are taxable and family benefits during a strike were reduced. All of these signalled a new policy of self-reliance and withdrawal from the principles of social security.

Although these payments are described as benefits you have a *right* to them and can claim your rights through legal channels.

Where to find the law

Social security benefits are found in the Social Security Act 1975 and supplementary benefits in the Supplementary Benefits Act 1976 (SBA), both amended by the Social Security and the Social Security (No.2) Act 1980 and the Social Security and Housing Benefits Act 1982. Many of the SB rules are contained in detailed Regulations.

Definitions

Before looking at the benefits, it is important to get some definitions straight:

- **Social security benefit** (as used in this handbook): benefit paid under the Social Security Act 1975, including national insurance benefits.
- **Supplementary benefit:** means-tested benefit paid under the Supplementary Benefits Act 1976.
- **Contribution:** payment made to the DHSS by employed or self-employed workers, employers, and people who make voluntary payments.
- **Dependant:** Wife, husband, children, woman looking after a child.
- **SSP** – statutory sick pay – see page 64.
- **Self-certification** – see page 66.
- **Upper earnings limit:** the weekly earnings up to which you pay contributions.
- **Lower earnings limit:** the weekly earnings at which you begin to be liable to pay contributions.
- **Benefit year:** the year, starting on the first Sunday in January, in which you first claim benefit.
- **Doctor's statement:** doctor's note advising you to stay off work until a given date ('closed' statement) or that you should not work until after a set period ('open' statement). You must get a closed statement before you go back to work.
- **Relevant tax year:** the year ending on 5 April *before* the year in which you claim.
- **Interruption of employment:** days when you are unemployed or incapable of work.

Contributions

There are four classes of contribution for social security benefits:

- **Class 1:** paid mainly by employees and their employers.
- **Class 2:** paid by self-employed 'earners'.
- **Class 3:** paid voluntarily by employees and self-employed people, students, apprentices and prisoners, in order to get benefits they wouldn't otherwise be entitled to, or to make up contributions paid.
- **Class 4:** paid by self-employed people engaged in a trade or profession.

You can be credited with paying some contributions if you are unemployed, or sick, even if you don't actually pay. If you have stayed home to look after a child or invalid you can get credit known as home responsibility protection.

In order to claim full benefits for unemployment, sickness (and invalidity) and maternity, you must have paid sufficient contributions in the relevant tax year. These must add up to 50 times the amount someone would have paid if they were on the 'lower earnings limit'.

You can get reduced benefits if you have paid or been credited with the equivalent of 25 contributions at the lower earnings limit. You can also be credited with some contributions and still qualify. In the 1983/84 tax year employees pay 9 per cent and employers 10.45 per cent of earnings up to the upper earnings limit, with lower payments if they are contracted-out of the state pension scheme. Employers also pay one per cent surcharge. Married women still paying 'the small stamp' pay 3.85 per cent up to the upper earnings level but do not get unemployment, maternity, sickness or invalidity benefits.

What benefits?

The following list shows the main benefits that you and your dependants may be entitled to. The classes of contributions are described in Table 5.

Sex equality has not yet come to the social security system. Some benefits are available only to men. Others are available to

Table 5

Benefit	Contributions needed
Unemployment + dependants	Class 1
Maternity allowance + dependants	Class 1 or 2
Maternity grant	None
Sickness + dependants	Class 1 or 2
Invalidity	Class 1 or 2
Widow's allowance + dependants	Class 1, 2 or 3
Pensions + dependants	Class 1, 2 or 3
Child special allowance	Class 1, 2 or 3
Death grant	Class 1, 2 or 3
Attendance allowance	None
Non-contributory invalidity pension	None
Industrial injury (sickness benefit) ⎤ Disablement ⎬ None, but must usually be employee Industrial death ⎦	
Supplementary benefit	None

women and their dependants on different terms from those applying to men. Official discrimination therefore continues despite EEC Directive 79/7 requiring member states to eliminate it. In partial recognition of this obligation, from November 1983 a woman can claim a dependant's benefit for her husband on the same terms as a man for his wife; and from November 1984 she can claim for her children on like terms.

Tax

In 1982 the Tories started to tax unemployment and supplementary benefits in one of a series of administrative attacks on the unemployed. If you become unemployed you do not receive a rebate of the tax you overpaid. If you get another job before the end of the tax year your earnings and benefits are totalled, and the benefit office issues you a new P45 for your new employer, and a statement of your taxable benefits. If you disagree with the statement, you must object in writing within 60 days. The assessment will then be suspended until the end of the tax year. There is therefore a clear advantage in objecting.

If you are still out of work at the end of the tax year, or if you have objected, an assessment is made. Anything you owe is recouped by an adjustment to your tax code as and when you start work; anything they owe you is paid as a rebate. The same rules apply to supplementary benefits paid to your family if you are involved in a strike. Dependent children's benefits are not taxable. If you get supplementary benefit as a couple (with or without unemployment benefit) you are taxed on not more than the standard weekly unemployment benefit.

Unemployment benefit

You have a right to unemployment benefit if you
   1. have paid the appropriate value of Class 1 contributions.
   2. are unemployed or laid off due to an interruption of work for at least two consecutive days in any period of six (Sundays don't count). Two of these periods of unemployment within eight weeks can be linked together to entitle you to claim. This is particularly relevant when you are put on short-time working.
   3. don't earn more than £2.00 (1983/84) for any day you are out of work, and
   4. are available for full-time employment.
   Benefit is not paid for the first three days ('waiting days') or beyond 312 days, i.e. one calender year. It is taxable.
   You may be disqualified for benefit
   1. for up to six weeks if

- you voluntarily left your job 'without just cause'
- without good cause you refuse to accept or apply for suitable employment notified to you by the DE
- you lost your job due to your 'misconduct', that is, 'such misconduct as would lead a reasonable employer to terminate a claimant's employment'.

   2. throughout an industrial dispute if you are laid off. But you *will* get benefit if you can prove you are not taking part, or directly interested, in the dispute.
   You can get increases for dependants and supplementary benefits in addition to unemployment benefit.
   Claim benefit by 'signing on' on your first day of unemployment at your local unemployment benefit office (DHSS). Take your P45 and your national insurance number.

Maternity benefits

See pages 104 and 106.

Sickness benefit

Sickness benefit is important in two situations. You can claim if you are excluded from SSP, or if your entitlement to SSP has run out; see pages 106, 120. In both cases your employer must notify you on the official forms that you are not entitled to SSP. The following section is therefore about sickness after or instead of SSP.

Diagram 7 (pages 288–89) shows what social security rights you have if you are sick or injured. The social security system provides better benefits for injury or disease caused by employment. The benefits for industrial injuries are dealt with below.

You have a right to sickness benefit if you

1. have paid the appropriate value of Class 1 or Class 2 contributions

2. are incapable of work for two or more consecutive days within any six (Sundays don't count).

Benefit is not paid for the first three waiting days of incapacity. It is paid for 28 weeks. After that you go on to **invalidity benefit** (see below).

You can get an increase for dependants and supplementary benefit in addition to sickness benefit. Claim to your local DHSS **within six days** of becoming unable to work, enclosing a **doctor's statement** or self-certification if you can. If not, make sure you give your name, address, date of birth and national insurance number. The official forms which management use to tell you that you are excluded from, or have run out of, SSP also include a sickness benefit claim form.

The eight weeks of SSP count towards your 28 weeks' entitlement to sickness benefit.

Invalidity benefit

You have a right to invalidity benefit if you are incapable of work after 28 weeks and during all of that time you were entitled to SSP, sickness benefit or maternity allowance. You get invalidity *allowance* if you are under 60 (men) or 55 (women) on the first day of incapacity. This is increased according to how *young* you were when first incapacitated. Otherwise you get invalidity *pension*. If you don't qualify for either of these you can get *non-contributory invalidity benefit*.

You can get an increase for dependants and supplementary benefits in addition to invalidity benefits. The DHSS will automatically pay invalidity benefit once sickness benefit runs out.

Notes to Diagram 7

1. These benefits are not affected by any benefit or sick pay scheme negotiated with your employer. But many schemes take account of social security benefits. This is a matter for negotiation with your employer, not the DHSS.

2. Most benefits can be increased according to the number of your dependants.

3. You can get **supplementary benefit** in addition to social security benefits if you are in need.

4. While receiving benefits, you get credits, that is, you are regarded as paying contributions.

Benefits for industrial injury and disease

The government scrapped industrial injury benefit in April 1983 but some recognition is still accorded to workers suffering injury or disease at work. Most importantly, **sickness benefit is available to all employees regardless of your record of social security contributions.** So people, particularly part-time women, who earn less than the lower earnings limit and do not pay contributions or qualify for SSP can still get sickness benefit for industrial injury or disease.

For many workers paying contributions there may be no financial difference between industrial and non-industrial sickness. **But there are major practical reasons for registering industrial injury or disease:**

1. Benefit is paid regardless of contributions or earnings.

2. It is the key to **disablement benefit** which is paid only if you are disabled as a result of industrial injury or disease. And disablement benefit is itself the key to other benefits (see below).

3. Most industrial injuries and diseases must be reported to the Health and Safety Executive, who may take action, and all

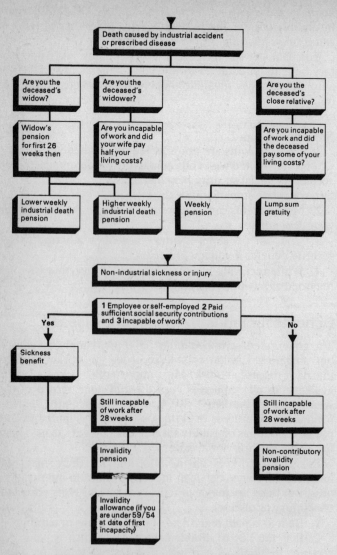

Diagram 7 **Social Security benefits,**
above industrial death
below non-industrial death

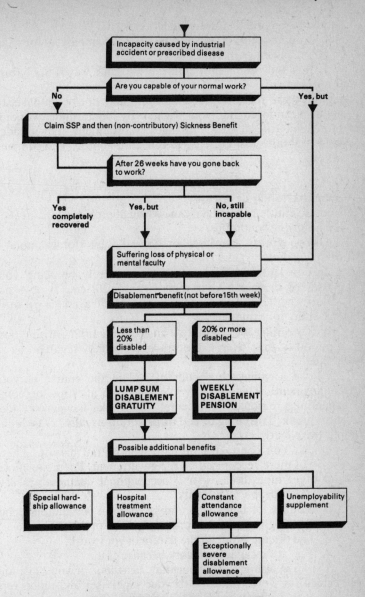

Diagram 7 **Social Security benefits,**
industrial incapacity

should be recorded in the accident book.

4. You may also be advised to sue your employers for causing the accident or disease.

5. Fellow-workers may suffer in the same way if the hazard is not stopped.

For all these reasons your employers may not be enthusiastic about acknowledging your rights. By diminishing workers' protection the 1982/83 changes substantially downgraded industrial injury and disease as cause for concern and compensation.

Industrial injury or disease

You are entitled to **DHSS sickness benefit** provided you meet all the following conditions:

1. You are an employee or office holder (for example, a company director) and *either*

2a. You suffer a personal injury – merely breaking your glasses or damaging your tools is not sufficient. It does not matter whether the injury is immediate or delayed – a cut turning septic, for example.

b. The injury was caused by an accident. Injury arising over a period of time from a process is not usually regarded as an accident.

c. The accident 'arose out of and in the course of your employment'. This means while you were at work, or doing something reasonably incidental to it – like having a rest or meal break. Travelling to and from work is usually *not* included but travel between sites is.

or **3a.** You contract a prescribed industrial disease. There are 50 of these recognised by the government. Pneumoconiosis and other lung diseases, and occupational deafness are also recognised for *special* benefits.

b. You are or have been employed in an occupation recognised by the government as providing a risk of this disease.

c. The disease is due to the nature of your work.

4. You are incapable of work because of it.

You may also get supplementary benefits. If you have any accident at work, report it to your supervisor and union rep, and see that it is recorded in the accident book.

To claim DHSS sickness benefit, get a **doctor's statement** from your doctor or hospital. Fill in the back and send it or self-certification to your local social security office **within six days** of your incapacity (or within 21 days if it is your first ever claim). If you cannot get a doctor's statement, notify the social security office in writing anyway. You may be disqualified if your claim is late.

Disablement due to industrial injury or disease

You are entitled to **disablement benefit** if you meet the following conditions:

1. You have an industrial injury or suffer from a prescribed disease.

2. You suffer a 'loss of physical or mental faculty' as a result. This means that your power to enjoy a normal life is impaired. It is assessed by reference to the condition of a normal healthy person of your age and sex.

Disablement benefit is paid as a weekly pension if, by using this reference point, it is decided that you are 20 per cent or more disabled. If you are less than 20 per cent disabled it is paid as a lump sum gratuity. Your disability can be permanent, like losing an eye, or temporary, like a broken leg.

You receive disablement benefit automatically if your 26 weeks on DHSS sickness benefit expires. Because disablement benefit is designed to compensate for disability not incapacity for work, **you can claim whether or not you are off work.** So you can receive benefit if you never book time off, or when you return to work, or when your industrial benefit runs out after 26 weeks. There is, inexplicably, a waiting period of 15 weeks from the accident or the onset of the disease before you can claim.

Disablement benefit can be increased as follows:

- **Special hardship allowance** if you are unable to go back to your regular work or do work of an equivalent standard.
- **Hospital treatment allowance** if you are in hospital (due to be abolished in April 1984).
- **Constant attendance allowance** if you need someone to look after you during the daytime.
- **Exceptionally severe disablement allowance** if you need permanent constant care.
- **Unemployability supplement** if you are likely to be permanently unable to work or earn more than a limited amount.
- **Supplementary benefit.**

Industrial death

You are entitled to industrial death benefit if you are the widow or dependent child of a man who died as a result of an industrial injury or prescribed industrial disease. Certain dependants and widowers can claim if they are incapable of supporting themselves and were supported by the deceased.

The benefit is paid as a weekly pension. A higher rate is paid to widows with dependent children, and certain others.

To claim, fill in the back of the (free) Registrar's death certificate and send it to your local DHSS office. They will then send you form BW1, on which you claim your rights. This benefit is due to be abolished for claimants after April 1984.

Supplementary benefits

You have a right to supplementary benefits if your 'resources are insufficient to meet your requirements' (Supplementary Benefits Act 1976 section 1).

Your benefit can be reduced by 40 per cent for reasons corresponding to the six-week disqualification for unemployment benefit. You don't have a right to supplementary benefit if you are involved in an industrial dispute, but your dependants can get it. From the benefit will be deducted a figure notionally representing strike pay – £14.50 1983/84. If you get more than this the extra is deducted (Social Security (No.2) Act 1980).

The law is based on two misconceptions: that large sums are paid out; and that £14.50 a week is a reasonable estimate of what unions pay. Firstly, very few strikers' families actually claim benefit – less than £1 million was paid in 1979. Independent research has shown that reliance on benefit during a dispute is minimal, following far behind savings, loans, wages in hand, tax rebates and strike pay (J. Gennard, *Personnel Management*, November 1979). Secondly, many unions pay less than £14.50 a week. And the Act takes no account of whether the strike is official, and therefore likely to attract strike pay, or not.

You can't normally get supplementary benefit if you are in full-time employment. But you can if you have just started and, for example, have to work a week in hand, or if your earning power is reduced because of disability. Anyone can get a one-off payment to meet an 'urgent need'.

Once you are getting supplementary benefit you also get, for example, free prescriptions, dental treatment, school meals.

Claim at your local DHSS office.

Family Income Supplement

You can claim FIS if you work full-time and have a dependent child. 'Full-time' means 30 or more hours a week, or 24 if you are a single parent. It is a weekly payment of half the difference between the 'prescribed amount' for a family with one child and what you actually earn. Up to November 1984 the prescribed amount was £85.50, with a maximum payment of £22 for a one-child family. It lasts for 52 weeks.

If you are denied your rights

You can appeal against decisions made by benefit, insurance and supplement officers, who are all employees of the DHSS or the DE. The letter which rejects your claim, or makes a decision on your benefit, will include details of how to appeal. You also have the right to ask for a *review* of a decision if it was made in ignorance of, or was based on a mistake as to, a material fact, or there has been a change of circumstances.

Some administrative decisions are made on behalf of the Secretary of State and can be appealed only on a point of law to the High Court. Otherwise appeals on social security rights go to Local Tribunals and Medical Tribunals; and on supplementary benefit and FIS to a Supplementary Benefit Appeal Tribunal. Appeals go to a Social Security Commissioner, who has the status of a judge, but you usually need permission ('leave to appeal') from a Commissioner or the tribunal. You can appeal on questions of fact or law except from a medical tribunal, where there must be a question of law.

Legal Aid is not available for any of these appeals but the green form (pink in Scotland) *is* – see page 487.

Collective action

Social security benefits are paid by the state, but this doesn't mean that collective action is inappropriate in this area of workers' rights. If you have good collective agreements on sickness and maternity, or good safety standards so that accidents at work are prevented, or take direct action to prevent sackings, you don't need to resort to social security benefits. Collectively, you can even negotiate to manipulate social security benefits

and wages, for example, in short-time working, in order to max-
imise your money.

Summary

1. You are entitled to the major social security benefits –
unemployment, maternity, sickness, invalidity, widows' allowance and pension – if you have paid sufficient social security
contributions.

2. Some benefits don't depend on your having paid contributions.

3. Benefits are paid for industrial injury, disease, disablement and death without the need for contributions. But you
must usually be an employee at the time of the accident or
disease and it must arise out of and in the course of your
employment.

4. Supplementary benefit is not usually paid to people in
employment. It is payable to anyone whose resources are less
than their requirements.

Part 3:
Union rights

13. Trade union membership

The importance of the right to union membership /
where to find the law / protection against
dismissal and victimisation for union activity / who
is protected / your basic rights / what are union
activities / when is an appropriate time / rights of
union reps / how to claim / proving it / remedies /
recognition of your union by management / the
legal advantages / collective agreements / time off
for union activities / your rights within the union /
inter-union relations / ballots.

Your most basic rights as a worker are the right to be a trade
unionist and to organise the union at your workplace. Only
through exercising these rights can you begin to reduce the
scope of your employer's prerogatives, and to achieve the most
elementary improvement in terms and conditions. Union
organisation is the key to resisting unilateral pressure and to
gaining control over your working environment. The law has
been slow to recognise these basic rights and even now protection is limited. Nevertheless, collective action backed up as
necessary with the threat of legal action can give you some
scope in which to organise.

This chapter deals with three rights:

- to be a union member, and to take part in its activities at
  an appropriate time and, since 1982, the right not to be
- **if your union is recognised**, to make agreements, to be
  consulted and to take time off for union duties and activities

- your rights within the union.

They are expressed as 'protections' rather than as positive rights to organise, as they are in the USA and on the continent. To some extent the first two rights reduce employers' traditional freedom to manage in the way they choose.

Although cast originally (in 1974) in favour of trade unionists, **the Employment Act 1982 now protects equally the right not to be a union member and the right to be one**. But as the Donovan Royal Commission said in 1968:

> the two are not truly comparable. The former condition is designed to frustrate the development of collective bargaining, which it is public policy to promote, whereas no such objection applies to the latter (para 599).

In an attempt to avoid the stigma of providing greater protection to anti-unionists, and in order to promote this spurious balance, the 1982 Employment Act granted the following rights and remedies to trade unionists and to non-unionists too. **This chapter deals only with examples of the positive right but what is said applies to both**, and there is perhaps one situation which is not so clear-cut.

■ Mr Rath, a plasterer, refused to transfer from UCATT to the TGWU when he changed jobs. The TGWU at the new job put pressure on the employers and he was sacked. The employers had no objection to their staff joining *any* union. He was sacked not for being a member of UCATT but for refusing to join the TGWU, and this, before 1982, gave him no claim. After the 1982 Act he could have claimed the negative right not to be a member of a particular union. *Rath v Cruden Construction* 1982 (EAT)

Ironically, as we shall see when looking at union activities in *Crouch's* case (page 302) and the closed shop in *Langston's* case (page 52), the courts' desire to protect reactionary anti-unionists under the Industrial Relations Act has resulted in an *extension* of the rights of trade unionists.

Where to find the law

Unfair dismissal: Employment Protection Consolidation Act (EPCA 1978) sections 58, 72 and Employment Act 1982 (remedies); interim procedure: section 77; victimisation: section 23; time off: sections 77–78 and the Advisory, Conciliation and Arbitration Service (ACAS) Code of Practice. Rights within the union: Trade Union Act 1913, Trade Union (Amalgamations) Act 1964, and the Trade Union and Labour Relations Act (TULRA) section 7; ballots: Employment Act 1980 sections 1 and 2; collective agreements: TULRA 1974 section 29.

Protection against dismissal and victimisation

Who is protected?

All members and people who try to become members of independent trade unions are protected if they are dismissed or victimised **for a reason connected with their membership**. Only share-fishers, the police and workers who ordinarily work outside the UK (because Northern Ireland and Britain have identical protections) are excluded. If your union is recognised by your employer you have the specific right to time off, in some cases with pay (see page 318).

One glaring omission from the rights dealing with union organisation is that they apply only to employees. So *applicants* for jobs are not protected against discrimination at the point of hire, except on racial or sexual grounds. Blacklisting of applicants is by no means uncommon, and evidence of this has been provided.

> At the Old Bailey trial in 1973 of the employees of the Christopher Roberts private detective agency, on charges of conspiracy to obtain confidential information, it was revealed that the firm had been employed to check on workers' political activities. Besides being employed by banks, solicitors, insurance firms and individuals, this and other detective agencies had frequently been engaged by non-unionised companies to investigate the background of prospective employees to make sure that their labour force was not 'infiltrated' by union members. Tony Bunyan, *The Political Police in Britain*, pages 250–51, Julian Friedmann 1976.

There are a number of trade associations, federations and specialist organisations engaged in blacklisting and surveillance of political and industrial activities. Common Cause Ltd, the Economic League, Industrial Research and Information Services, British United Industrialists Ltd, and the former Complete Security Services Ltd, a one-time subsidiary of Securicor Ltd, all collect and disseminate information on individual workers and unions. The National Federation of the Self-Employed in 1978 set up a register of people who claimed unfair dismissal. And the import of American union-busting methods has taken a toll, with consultants advising how to stop or under-mine union recruitment. Yet the EAT has confirmed that there is no redress for a blacklisted worker denied a job because of his union activities.

■ Philip Beyer, a well-known union activist, knew that he was blacklisted as a result of his activity in UCATT. In 1975, in order to get work as a bricklayer with Birmingham Council, he gave a false name. He was discovered within an hour and sacked. In 1976, using his own name, he again got a job with the Council but was again sacked the same day. The reason given was his earlier 'deceit'. The Birmingham tribunal found that he had been sacked because of his union activities and ordered his reinstatement. On appeal, the EAT said the law protected only activities **while an employee**, not **before becoming an employee**. So blacklisted workers have no right to bring a claim. *City of Birmingham District Council v Beyer* 1977 (EAT)

A simple amendment should be made to apply the protection not only to 'employees' but also to 'workers', as this includes persons seeking work (TULRA section 30). Even the Industrial Relations Act (1971) gave this protection.

Your basic rights
You can claim reinstatement and compensation if you have been dismissed unfairly. Your employer must give reasons for sacking you and must show s/he acted reasonably. Dismissal for being a member of an independent trade union or wanting to take part in its activities is automatically unfair. If your employer victimises you to such an extent that you are forced to resign, this counts as dismissal too – 'constructive' dismissal. If you do not give in to pressure and remain at work, you can com-plain of victimisation. You are therefore given the right (EPCA sections 58, 58A) not to be dismissed for:

- being a member of an independent trade union, or pro-posing to join one;

- taking part in its activities 'at an appropriate time';
- refusing to join a trade union.

And you have the right to claim compensation (EPCA section 23) if action short of a dismissal is taken against you – in other words, if you are victimised – and can show that management intended:

- to prevent or deter you from exercising these rights;
- to penalise you for doing so; or
- to compel you to join a union.

The *positive* rights supporting union membership are fundamental and look pretty good on paper. The problem comes in proving your case. To start with, there is the definition of 'union activities' and when is considered to be an 'appropriate time' to engage in them.

To penalise means to 'subject to a disadvantage' and can include even non-contractual matters such as non-allocation of parking spaces. But an agreement with a recognised union which confers benefits on its members even if it creates disadvantages for non-members is lawful unless the *terms* and *intention* of the agreement penalise non-members (*Carlson v Post Office* 1981 (EAT)). **There is therefore no reason why unions should not negotiate members-only agreements on conditions and job-security**.

What are trade union activities?

Section 28 of the EPCA and paras 21–22 of the ACAS Code on time off deal with union activities but this applies only to members of independent unions recognised by their employers who want to take time off for union work (see page 318). They include 'any activities' of your union, and activities in which you are representing your union, for example at trade councils, or local joint committees. If you have been dismissed or victimised because of your union involvement there is no definition of union activities. Since an employer must give time off for these activities when s/he recognises the union, you can argue that it is reasonable to outlaw dismissal and victimisation for taking part in these union activities on the premises during meal-breaks, and after work, even when s/he does not recognise your union.

Some clear rules have arisen as a result of an important case involving the Post Office.

■ On the day the Industrial Relations Act came into force in 1972, several members and officials of the Telecommunications Staff Association claimed the right to take part in the activities of their union, which had registered under the Act. The PO refused, as it recognised only the Union of Post Office Workers. So Walter Crouch and several others appealed to a tribunal and from there all the way to the House of Lords. They won the right to organise at telephone exchanges; a right, in effect, to disrupt stable industrial arrangements and to undermine the unregistered but much larger UPW. The House of Lords recognised and upheld the right of union members to take part in union activities on their employers' premises, **whether or not the union is recognised.** *Post Office v UPW and Crouch* 1974 (HL)

Judgments made under the Industrial Relations Act 1971 are still effective, and the right to take part in union activities is preserved in substantially the same form in subsequent legislation. The *Crouch* judgment is the source of our definition of union activities and it has been applied with approval by the EAT in the *Carlson* and *Zucker* cases (below). Lord Reid in the House of Lords said:

> Men carrying on activities of their union on their employer's premises must do so in a manner which does not cause substantial inconvenience either to their employer or to fellow workers who are not members of their trade union – and employers must tolerate minor infringements of their strict legal rights which do them no real harm.

So **you have the right on your employer's premises and at 'an appropriate time', whether the union is recognised or not, to**

- recruit members
- collect subscriptions
- distribute literature
- leave literature lying about
- have a table in the canteen for union affairs
- occasionally hold meetings (provided you arrange this with your employer)
- meet lay officials of the union who are also employees of your firm (provided you arrange this with your employer).

This obviously falls short of what you should demand and put in your agreements, as it omits such basic needs as provision of a notice board, internal mail facilities, notification of new employees and the right to bring in a union official or other adviser (for instance, on health and safety). And the court's decision excludes the following rights:

- to be recognised and to negotiate
- to take part in any activities that require your employer's active assistance
- to take part in any union activities that involve 'substantial inconvenience' to your employer or other workers.

Still, the positive rights provided are a useful start to organising. Since that time the EAT has agreed that 'the activities of an independent trade union' are to be interpreted widely to mean 'activities of a fairly varied kind', even if you are acting for your own benefit.

■ Two Hull joiners complained to a UCATT official that they were required to cut asbestos on site without protective equipment. The official and a Health and Safety Inspector visited the site, unannounced, and were involved in 'a fairly considerable dust-up' with the employers, which justified the joiners claiming constructive dismissal. Although the men could not prove that contact with the union was the real reason for dismissal, the EAT said that complaining to a lay or full-time official about terms and conditions, and applying approved union practice, are protected activities. *Dixon v West Ella Developments* 1978 (EAT)

You do not have to be acting in compliance with union rules or policy to be engaged in union activities, which might include attending workplace meetings not provided for in a collective agreement and against management instructions (*Rasool*'s case, below) and even meetings **to complain about the union**.

■ Doreen Francis, an AUEW steward, called a lunch-time meeting of her members to discuss the union's lack of progress in getting equal pay for women at BA's Treforest workshops. The members asked her to make a statement in the

Western Mail. She was reprimanded by management. The EAT held that she was penalised for her *union* activities. *British Airways Engine Overhaul v Francis* 1981 (EAT)

Nevertheless, the same broad view of union activities was not taken by the Appeal Court, led by Lord Donaldson, who openly defied the spirit and purpose of the Act by finding in favour of a blatant anti-union employer.

■ Therm-A-Stor opened in Peterborough in 1979 and within a few months more than 60 of its shop floor workers joined the TGWU. The full-time union official wrote asking for recognition. Immediately the 'strongly anti-union' managing director told the chargehands to sack 20 workers. Four union members who did not have the one year's service necessary for unfair dismissal claimed they were sacked for their membership and activities in the union. The Appeal Court criticised the management's 'indefensible reaction to a simple request for union recognition' but refused to condemn them for unfair dismissal. The action was not taken because of each *individual*'s union activity, but because of their *collective* involvement. This, said the court, was not protected by the Act. The Law Lords refused to hear the TUC-supported appeal. *Therm-A-Stor v Atkins* 1983 (CA)

This outrageous refusal to provide protection under the Act means that in a recognition issue you will have to show you are each individually seeking to exercise your union rights, thus making it easy for management to know who is a member. The activities of your full-time officer do not count as yours for the purpose of the EPCA protection.

What is an appropriate time?
You have the right to take part in union activities in three broad situations which are:

- outside working hours
- during working hours if you have management's consent
- during working hours if there is an arrangement or agreement with management.

'Outside working hours' means during meal-breaks, tea

breaks and rest periods, and before and after work. Even if there is no formal meal-break, or if you are paid during meal-breaks, you are still entitled to carry on union activities. Nor does it matter that management have forbidden you to exercise your right. They cannot overrule the EPCA 1978.

The Act does not specifically restrict the right to times when you are supposed to be on the premises, but there is a risk that if you come back to a shift on your rest day you may be a trespasser. Several judges in *Crouch*'s case were very conscious of the employer's property rights, and of the threat to them of workers organising to the fullest extent, so they restricted the times during which you can organise, even though you are organising outside working hours. Lord Justice Scarman said:

> An employer may determine by the contract of employment or workshop practice, when and where a worker may lawfully be on his premises outside working hours; if a worker is there within the ambit of such permission, he may take part in trade union activities provided nothing is required of his employer other than permission to be there.

So permission is still required if you plan a recruitment drive on an unorganised shift, or on premises of your employer other than those where you are entitled to be.

If permission is given either for a specific occasion, or for union purposes in general, or by custom and practice, you are safeguarded. But not otherwise:

■ Leonard Robb worked for a bus company. He joined the TGWU and was appointed shop steward. **During working hours** he tried to persuade others to join. Management moved him to other work 'in order to isolate him'. The tribunal and the EAT agreed that Leonard had been victimised because of his union activities. But as these activities took place in working hours without permission he was not protected by the law. *Robb v Leon Motors Services* 1977 (EAT)

Permission can be *implied* from the arrangements which exist at work. A woman who talked to her colleagues about the union while working, without disrupting production, was protected. Since the employers allowed them to talk, they could not complain if they talked about the union (*Zucker v Astrid Jewels* 1978 (EAT)). However, silence by management when your unaccredited steward telephones the full-time official and

calls a stoppage of members to discuss wages does not necessarily mean permission can be similarly implied (*Marley Tile Co
v Shaw* 1980 (CA)).

So the appropriate time for activities in a non-recognised
union is always subject to your employer's permission – slightly
less restricted outside working hours than in, but still restricted.
This means you must use your industrial strength rather than
the law to enforce your basic worker's rights.

Is industrial action a union activity?

Industrial action is the most notable activity of trade unions, yet
it carries no protection for trade unionists who take part in it.
As we shall see (page 392), workers sacked *during* a dispute
cannot claim unfair dismissal unless management have discriminated by sacking selectively. Victimisation or dismissal of trade
unionists *after* a dispute also seems to be unprotected. Faced
with a clear decision of principle, the courts refused to recognise industrial action as a trade union activity protected by the
EPCA 1978. The EAT, by a majority, held that in selecting
people for redundancy it was reasonable for a Newmarket
trainer to sack five TGWU members (*Cruickshank v Hobbs*
1977). Having taken part in a 12-week official strike in 1975,
five out of six TGWU members were not taken back. Management said this was due to redundancy. The EAT said that in
choosing who was to go it was reasonable for an employer to
select people who had been on strike.

In another case, the EAT said that you cannot claim protection for a union activity which is itself industrial action. The two
are mutually exclusive.

■ A local authority gardener made many complaints about
health and safety and was sacked. He did not have the
necessary length of service (now one year) to bring a claim
of unfair dismissal, but he claimed these were union activities. The EAT said they were not the union's but his own
(therefore unprotected) activities. He then said that the complaints had been part of NUPE's national go-slow in pursuit
of a wage claim. The EAT said that if this were so, he had
been dismissed while taking part in industrial action and
therefore could not claim. *Drew v St Edmundsbury Borough
Council* 1980 (EAT)

It is clear that the EPCA 1978 protection applies only if you have taken part in activities at an *appropriate* time. Since the time requires management agreement or consent, you are not likely to get it. But you could argue that industrial action which follows the exhaustion of procedure, or the giving of proper notice, could well be an appropriate time, and that subsequent victimisation is unlawful.

Since the EPCA 1978 allows management to dismiss strikers only while the dispute is on, it seems wrong in principle and in law to allow trade unionists who took part in an official dispute to be victimised at a later date.

Rights of union officials

Union **lay officials** (for example, shop stewards, collectors, branch secretaries), can probably make the definition of union activities include those of an organiser. In the *Post Office* case, Lord Denning said Walter Crouch was entitled 'to carry on all such reasonable activities as are **normally carried on by a branch organiser**' and Lord Reid said he could in his own time **visit his members at other sites when they weren't working**. Union activities must include elections and activities of branch officials. The Code of Practice on discipline (see page 92) says **no action should be taken against a union rep until the matter has been discussed with a full-time official or senior rep**.

The intention is to avoid industrial action, to stop attacks on stewards who are carrying out their duties, and to give an opportunity for negotiations, rather than to give preferential treatment to stewards facing discipline. But this 'even-handedness' can often lead to unfairness.

■ Stewards organised a mass meeting during working hours to discuss the progress of wage negotiations. They and all who attended were warned in advance that they would be sacked. When they were, the failure to involve the TGWU district officer did not make stewards' sacking unfair; they were treated as ringleaders rather than representatives, and there-fore even more culpable. *Rasool v Hepworth Pipe* 1980 (EAT)

One of the country's leading lay activists, Derek Robinson, was sacked in 1979 for his activities in organising against BL's redundancy plans. Spontaneous mass support was called off in favour of an unsuccessful union inquiry, but his activities would have been protected by the Act had he claimed in time.

Non-employee officials and organisers have no special rights.

They are not allowed to enter factories or even company car parks to give out literature or collect forms. All this must be done outside the gates. In the USA, non-employees have the right to enter premises if 'no other channels of communications' are available for getting the union message across. This applies where workers live in, such as on ships or farms, in holiday camps, hotels, company towns, and in shopping centres. Also in the USA, officials can enter any premises if the employer discriminates about the distribution of literature – giving staff associations the right to recruit but not an independent union, for instance.

So far the only step towards this kind of right in the UK is that taken in the North Sea oil industry, where access of union officials to oil rigs is now a condition in the licence granted to operators.

How to claim
If someone has been sacked or victimised for trade union activity the best way to put it right is by direct action. In a tribunal the claim must be made in the form of an individual grievance, there are massive difficulties in proving it, and the remedies are weak. As in almost every other area of labour legislation it is the individual, not the union, who must complain even though the issue is a collective one.

If you decide the only way to enforce your right is by going to law you must claim (see page 490) **within three months** of the victimisation or sacking, or **within seven days** if you invoke the **interim relief procedure** (below) to stop a sacking.

Using the interim procedure
The 'interim relief procedure' applies in respect of dismissal for union membership and activities. Section 77 of the EPCA 1978 says that if you are dismissed a claim can be submitted up to seven days after the date of dismissal. If you are given notice you can claim as soon as you get it. The form must be accompanied by a letter from a union official (who has been given specific authority by the union to make these statements) saying that s/he thinks you were dismissed for a reason connected with the union. Management will be given seven days' notice and a quick (interim) hearing will be held in front of a tribunal Chairman. S/he has power to declare that wages should still be paid and that your contract should exist pending a full hearing of your case. S/he would do this if the employer fails to turn up or

refuses to take you back, or cannot disprove your allegations.

The procedure is designed to prevent strikes. It might also stop employers buying out union activists by sacking them and willingly paying compensation. If legal action is taken quickly the job might be saved. The threat of instant legal action by a dismissed activist may sometimes be as effective as a walk-out, and to this extent the interim procedure can be very useful. But if management genuinely want to be rid of a union activist there is still no legal way that this can be prevented – they may be forced to pay substantial compensation for refusing reinstatement but it may be worth it to their business.

If you are using the interim procedure there are four points to watch.

1. The application is separate from, and additional to, the claim for unfair dismissal, although you can claim both at the same time.

2. If you have asked for and been given no reason for dismissal, make a separate claim for 'refusal to give a written reason' on your form (see page 248).

3. The claim for an interim hearing must be accompanied by a statement that your union is independent, and that your official is specifically authorised to make this kind of statement – at least one early application by a full-time official in Leeds was turned down because he could not show a specific authorisation, the tribunal showing no sympathy for the purpose of the procedure.

4. The procedure applies only to dismissals where your official thinks the principal reason for dismissal was your union membership or activity. One way in which employers can obscure their bias is by taking advantage of a redundancy to sack activists. If there are genuine redundancies the principal reason for your dismissal could well be redundancy, but your selection for dismissal might be motivated by your union activity. Strictly speaking, you cannot claim on the interim procedure unless the *main* reason for dismissal was union membership or activity. So make sure your claim is expressed in terms of the *main* reason for dismissal being union activity, and redundancy only secondarily.

How do you prove it?
1. Dismissal
Dismissal for union membership or activity is automatically

unfair. But proving it is very difficult. Every management will dress up their dismissal in terms of some other reason such as redundancy, absence or bad time-keeping. They have to *prove* this reason as the basis for their dismissal, but you will have to show it was really because of your trade union membership or activities. The burden of proof is on you, and between 1979 and 1982 your average chance of winning was one in six. Tribunals are rarely prepared to say that an unfair dismissal is related to trade union membership. Nevertheless, occasionally they do:

■ Wages at a small toolmakers in Tamworth were paid well below the national rate. Ten workers decided to join the GMWU and their official sent a letter to the manager. As soon as he read it he entered the workshop and told them 'Piss off, cobblers to all you. I won't have any unions in my factory'. Three hours later he gave them their wages and a letter saying that they were being made redundant. The tribunal refused to accept any of the employer's evidence and said that all the workers had been dismissed because they had joined the union. Six of them shared compensation of over £1,000. *Asson v Brampton Toolmakers* 1975 (IT)

2. Victimisation

Proving victimisation can be even harder. At least when a dismissal occurs there is no disputing that fact, but if you have to show that some subtle pressure was brought to bear on you, and then go on to allege that the reason for it was your union membership, the problems are almost insuperable. Victimisation in the form of a failure to distribute overtime fairly can be proved, but surveillance, general harassment, exaggerated enforcement of works rules, frequent allocation of dirty jobs or strict supervision are things every worker can spot but are difficult to make stick in a tribunal. Threats can be difficult to prove, but they are illegal and cases have been won – *Brassington v Cauldon Wholesale* 1977 (EAT) (employer, during ACAS inquiry, threatened to close down rather than recognise the TGWU). Parliament has not given you the right to send written questions to management as a preliminary step to get their statement before bringing a claim. This is available if you allege sex or racial discrimination.

If you succeed in showing that action of a particular kind took place, the EPCA 1978 says management must then show why they did it. You will have to bring evidence about their attitude to unions, and be prepared to make your own case. There are still two problems. If the tribunal agrees you were victimised, but not because of your union activity, you will lose your case. But the reason for taking the action – as a punishment, for example – or its consequences, may not be within management's power under your contract of employment. So you can challenge them on those grounds. This can't be done while you are in a tribunal – breach of contract is a common law matter for the county court (at least until the Lord Chancellor decides to give power to tribunals to deal with it).

Secondly, management may persuade the tribunal that they did not *intend* to be anti-union, even though the practical effect of their action could still mean that you and other workers were intimidated from joining a union. The EPCA outlaws only action that is **intentionally** discriminatory, not action that in fact is – compare *Carlson*'s case, page 301.

Remedies
1. Dismissal
If you have been unfairly dismissed a tribunal can order your reinstatement in the same job and on the same conditions; or re-engagement in the same firm in a different job; or compensation. Reinstatement is the only effective remedy for a sacked activist because otherwise the trade union organisation he or she built up will suffer, and other workers will be intimidated by the employer's apparent success in the sacking. Compensation is no substitute for a job in any case and it is meaningless in anti-union sackings.

Compensation was massively increased in 1982, when the government extended protection to workers sacked or victimised for refusing to join a union. Compensation up to a total of £7,000 for any losses suffered can be awarded, together with £2,000 or your equivalent of a redundancy payment, whichever is greater (see page 477). If an order is sought for reinstatement or re-engagement, you can be awarded a new special award (see page 483) worth over £20,000. But nothing is available to compensate fellow-workers for the loss of a union activist or the benefits that can flow from organisation.

2. Victimisation
For victimisation, **no maximum amount of compensation is specified**. You can get compensation for your actual losses

(denial of fair overtime, for instance) and expenses (cleaning of clothing if you constantly get the dirty jobs), and you can also get an amount to take account of the extent to which your rights have been infringed (EPCA 1978 section 26). This might include non-financial losses such as stress, frustration or the loss of potential benefits if management threaten closure rather than deal with the union (*Brassington v Cauldon* 1978 (EAT)). Amazingly, the one remedy that you would expect to be given and the one that could be most effective is omitted: an employer cannot be ordered to stop victimising a worker. So if management do it again you must start a whole new legal claim. While workers can be required by injunction to stop picketing or occupying a factory if the courts consider it unlawful, employers systematically carrying on victimisation cannot be ordered to stop. For an action as serious as intimidation of a trade unionist there is no reason why a tribunal should not award amounts in excess of the maximum available for unfair dismissal in these circumstances.

Recognition

Workers can guarantee all their rights by means of trade union organisation, but to be effective a union needs to be recognised as the workers' negotiating body.

Recognition of your union is the essential first step towards attacking management's right to decide everything. The traditional ways of achieving recognition are through organisation, agitation and industrial action. The legal machinery for obtaining recognition under the EPA 1975, rendered unworkable by the courts and its own limitations, was abolished in 1980. All that remain are sections 1 and 2 of the 1975 Act. These require ACAS to promote the extension of collective bargaining and to offer conciliation in industrial disputes 'at the request of one or more of the parties or otherwise'.

Recognition is not an end in itself. It is a way of ensuring you get the benefits you can negotiate through collective bargaining. Fighting for recognition is also an education in building an organisation and in learning what trade unionism is about. It often helps to strengthen the union.

What does recognition mean?

The EPA 1975 section 126 talks about recognition 'to any extent' by an employer or associated employers 'for the purposes of collective bargaining'. This is defined as **negotiations related to** or **connected with** any of the matters listed in section 29 of the Trade Union and Labour Relations Act 1974.

These are:

a. terms and conditions of employment, or the physical conditions in which any workers are required to work
b. engagement or non-engagement, or termination or suspension of employment or the duties of employment, of one or more workers
c. allocation of work or the duties of employment as between workers or groups of workers
d. matters of discipline
e. the membership or non-membership of a trade union on the part of a worker
f. facilities for officials of trade unions; and
g. machinery for negotiation or consultation, and other procedures, relating to any of the foregoing matters, including the recognition by employers or employers' associations of the right of a trade union to represent workers in any such negotiation or consultation or in the carrying out of such procedures.

This list is important because it defines the scope of **collective agreements, disclosure of information and industrial action** over a 'trade dispute'. Rights on takeovers, investment and marketing are becoming collective bargaining issues and are anyway 'related to' terms and conditions of workers in that they affect job-security. While terms of employment means contractual terms, conditions has 'a very wide meaning'. Lord Denning said, in *BBC v Hearn* (see page 402), that it includes **everything understood and applied by the parties in practice**, or habitually or by common consent, without ever being incorporated into the contract.

The EPA 1975 says that collective bargaining involves negotiations (section 126), so if your union is only consulted on certain issues, or given representational rights within a procedure (see *BTP Dioxide* case, page 368), it can claim negotiating rights.

Consultation requires employers to give the union full details of their proposals, to consider union representations and to reply to them giving any reasons for rejecting them (see chapter 18 on redundancies). In negotiations the union is much less passive.

The law does not define negotiations. American unions' experience can give a useful indication of what is required. Some sort of duty to negotiate was first imposed in the USA in 1917 in order to prevent disruption of arms manufacture. Now it is embodied in statute as a 'duty to bargain in good faith'. The following broad principles have been adopted. US employers must:

- genuinely be seeking an agreement
- give any information requested that is in accordance with good industrial relations and which the union needs for bargaining (compare chapter 15)
- not undermine the union's representative by dealing directly with individual members or failing to give notice of proposed changes, redundancies etc.
- not act unilaterally by, for example, giving a wage increase or changing conditions during negotiations
- negotiate reasonably, not simply 'go through the motions' – that is, your employer must be prepared to compromise, put counter-proposals, give reasons, act promptly
- give negotiators authority to settle
- not impose conditions at the start of negotiations, for example that the union drop outstanding grievances
- not pre-empt the union's claim by putting forward their own offer based on research and what they consider is 'best' for you. This illegal strategy was adopted at General Electric after it suffered a crippling strike in 1946.

The legal advantages of recognition

In law an independent trade union which is recognised, and its members, gain a number of important advantages. Only a recognised independent union can demand:

- Disclosure of information under the EPA 1975 (see page 367).

- To be consulted over proposed redundancies (see chapter 18).
- Time off for its representatives and members (see page 318).
- Consultation on occupational pension schemes.
- The right to appoint safety representatives under the Health and Safety at Work Act and Regulations, and for them to exercise their statutory functions (see page 318).
- To be consulted on a proposed takeover of the company where it is recognised, and to demand that recognition and conditions of employment are also taken over (see chapter 18).
- To challenge discriminatory collective agreements under the Equal Pay Act section 3 (see page 183).

Many employers in the public sector are required to recognise appropriate trade unions by law. All nationalised industries do, as does the government itself. Government contractors are required by contractual terms analogous to the Fair Wages Resolution (FWR) to allow their workers the freedom to join unions (although there is no obligation to recognise them when they do), but this has no effect after September 1983.

Collective agreements

Collective agreements between unions and employers cover two-thirds of the working population, although only 50 per cent of workers are trade unionists. This is because agreements are almost invariably made to cover *all* workers in a plant or district or industry. Agreements and custom and practice accepted by management and unions are the basis of industrial relations. They are the vehicle for union organisation and pressure.

Collective agreements are defined by section 30 of TULRA 1974 as agreements *or arrangements* made between unions and employers which relate to any of the issues listed on page 313, and in connection with which a trade dispute can arise. The courts say these must be given a 'very wide meaning' so they cover almost all the matters that unions want to bargain about. Only agreements made by or on behalf of a trade union are within the definition. The agreement can be in writing or can exist as an informal 'arrangement'. The legal definition is important if the question of enforcement arises.

Legal enforcement

There are two questions about legal enforcement:

1. Can the agreement be enforced in the courts by the employer or the union which made it?

2. Can parts of the agreement become enforceable in the courts by individual workers covered by it?

Enforcement by the employer or union

An agreement made today between an employer or federation on the one hand and a union or workers acting on behalf of the union on the other is not legally binding and (according to the Court of Appeal in *Monterosso v ITF* (1982)) is not a contract at all. This means your union or shop stewards' committee cannot be sued if it breaks an agreement by, say, calling a strike in breach of procedure or making a claim for higher wages before the appointed settlement date.

There are three types of agreement:

a. Agreements made before December 1971 and after 16 September 1974, that is, outside the period covered by the Industrial Relations Act. These are not legally binding unless they are **in writing** and specifically say they *are* legally binding.

b. Agreements made between the above dates. These *are* legally binding unless they contain a clause saying they aren't.

c. Agreements which don't count as collective agreements, for example because they deal with things outside the list on page 313, or because they are not made on behalf of a union. These *may* be legally binding, so the union should always insert a clause saying they are not intended to be.

The protection of people and unions against legal action for acts done in contemplation or furtherance of a trade dispute, for example, for recommending a strike or boycotting (see page 398) does not apply to breach of contract. A legally enforceable collective agreement is a contract, so the union can be sued for damages if, for example, it calls a strike in breach of an agreed procedure in a legally enforceable agreement.

Enforcement by individual workers

Some parts of collective agreements can be binding on individual workers covered by them – see page 42. An agreement for wages or hours negotiated between your union and management is not enforceable by either against the other, but usually *you* can sue management if they do not follow it. This is because the agreement has changed your individual contract, and you as an individual (or your employer) can go to court to enforce it.

No-strike clauses

Any particular part of an agreement can be made legally binding. Usually clauses dealing, for example, with wages, hours or holidays, will be binding on individual workers and their employer, even though the collective agreement itself is not legally binding between the union and the employer. If the agreement contains a clause which restricts (*or has the effect* of restricting) industrial action, or restricts it until procedure is exhausted or notice given, section 18 of TULRA 1974 steps in. This part of a collective agreement cannot be binding on individual workers unless:

- it is in writing;
- it specifically says that this restriction is part of every worker's own contract;
- it is reasonably accessible to every worker;
- it is signed by *independent* trade unions; and
- each worker's own contract incorporates this restriction (either expressly or by implication).

This is to protect every worker's right to strike, and any workers who may be tied down by an employer-dominated staff association which attempts to stop them striking.

National and local agreements

As far as the law is concerned it does not matter whether agreements are made at national, local, company or plant level. Nor does it matter whether bargaining is done in a joint council with decisions made 'jointly', or in direct negotiations between, for example, the Confederation of Shipbuilding and Engineering Unions and the Engineering Employers' Federation. Generally, a local agreement will override an existing national agreement. This almost always happens in engineering, construction and many other industries, so local modifications should be given precedence. However, the courts are erratic on this question and have denied workers the right to have an effective local agreement.

■ John Mercer, a gas conversion fitter, worked 54 hours a week and this was provided for in a local agreement for the North East. The national agreement signed by the GMWU and the employers' association provided for a 40-hour week. He subsequently received a written statement of his contract, which followed the national rather than the local agreement. He signed a receipt for 'the new contract of employment . . . which sets out the terms and conditions of my employment'. (See page 40 for the legal effect of this.) When John Mercer claimed redundancy pay based on his 54-hour week, the Court of Appeal said the national agreement was the one to be followed. The court said John had to work the 14 hours' overtime if required, but management weren't legally bound to provide more than 40 hours. Only if overtime is guaranteed does it count for statutory purposes. *Gascol v Mercer* 1974 (CA)

It is not too cynical to say that when there has been a clash between a national and a local agreement the courts have generally said that **the agreement less favourable to the worker is the one that is binding. In order to avoid problems, write into your local agreement 'Insofar as this agreement is more favourable than any national agreement, this local agreement is to take precedence'**, or vice versa if appropriate.

Conditions agreed at Wages Councils and Statutory JICs are dealt with on page 43.

Time off for activities of recognised unions

A necessary feature of collective agreements is the right of union representatives to carry out their duties without loss of pay, and to receive union training. The EPCA gives legal rights and these are clarified by the ACAS Code of Practice on time off. The Code positively supports collective bargaining and strongly urges unions and management to negotiate agreements on all aspects of time off covered by the Code.

The Health and Safety at Work Act 1974 gives safety representatives of recognised independent trade unions the right to time off. Your rights under this Act are not specifically dealt with in this book but they include the right to investigate potential hazards and complaints; to demand facilities and access for carrying out regular workplace inspections; to receive information and records relating to health and safety; and to undergo training. Since many shop stewards are also safety representatives, they can take advantage of the Health and Safety at Work Act or the EPCA, whichever gives better rights. Safety representatives also fit the description of 'official' for the EPCA for many of the duties they carry out.

The EPCA gives three sets of rights. In the circumstances described below you can take time off:

- with pay for union duties connected with industrial relations
- with pay for training in industrial relations
- without pay for certain union activities.

The right to paid time off for union training is very important. The TUC provides material for day-release training courses throughout the country in association with local colleges and the Workers' Educational Association. Some unions have their own training colleges providing short residential courses – ASTMS, EETPU, NUR and TGWU. GMBATU has two colleges. Most unions offer training in-company, or day-release, or at weekend schools. In 1983–84 the TUC was granted £1.5 million (plus a further £200,000 with strings) to support union training, and the TUC planned in 1984 to open its own residential training centre in north London.

Who gets time off?

You have the right to time off if you are an official of an independent trade union recognised by your employer. Recognition means recognised for collective bargaining (see page 313).

'Official' means an employee elected or appointed in accordance with the union's rules to be a representative of employees at a particular workplace. It includes shop stewards, convenors, staff representatives, collecting stewards, chapel officers (in printing), and safety representatives. Branch secretaries are included if they represent members in the procedure at the particular workplace.

As an official your right is to time off for union duties and training.

Members have the right to time off for union activities.

Who pays?
Officials must be paid when carrying out union duties and training. If your pay does not vary according to the amount of work you do, management must pay you as if you had been working. If your pay varies – for example because you are on piece-work or bonus – you are entitled to average hourly earnings.

The general principle is that you are entitled to be paid according to your contract.

■ A senior operator worked shifts in abnormal conditions in a chemical plant. When he was elected as full-time convenor he transferred to day work. He agreed to lose his abnormal conditions money but not his senior-operator or shift pay, amounting to £97 p.w. The company said he should go on to day rates of £79 p.w. The Manchester tribunal said he was entitled to his contractual pay before his election, i.e. £97. *McCormack v Shell Chemicals* 1979 (IT)

This means, however, that you might not get any overtime you would have earned unless it is contractual. If the duties or training last longer than a normal working day, it is arguable that premium rates are payable since EPCA section 27(3) gives a worker the right to pay 'as if he had worked . . . for the whole of that time'.

The Code says nothing about pay for members who take time off for union activities. In many workplaces, management have agreed to time off with pay during working hours to attend mass meetings. You will have to negotiate your own arrangements for paid time off either *ad hoc* or on a regular basis.

How much time off is reasonable?
You are entitled to a 'reasonable' amount of time off. There is no definition of what is reasonable in the Code, which urges unions and management to come to local agreements. Agreements normally allow as much time off as is necessary for *officials* to carry out their duties. You should ask for enough time off for *members* to take part in all union activities.

The Code does, however, give some general factors which would influence what is reasonable. Management need to ensure that the operational requirements of the enterprise are fulfilled. So services to customers and to the public, safety, the needs of continuous process industries and particular problems of small firms are all relevant factors.

You will have special requirements for time off if you work shifts or have spread hours, or work part-time or in isolated locations, or have domestic commitments. Officials have problems of communication and members have problems in attending branch meetings in all these situations.

The Code says you should try to arrange union meetings at times that are least inconvenient from the management's point of view – towards the end of a shift or just before or after a meal-break. If you require time off as an official for training or to attend meetings you should give as much notice as you can, giving the reasons for needing time off and saying where the meeting is taking place and how long it will last. The Code does *not* give management the right to veto your decision if they think the meeting is unreasonable.

A very restrictive, and probably incorrect, view of what is reasonable was given when the EAT decided that an employer behaves reasonably if the denial of paid time off falls within a 'range of possible reasonable responses' to the claim. In doing so the EAT ignored the fact that the right is determined *by the unions* and the ACAS Code.

■ Two stewards applied for a TUC 10-day course on new technology. The employers paid only basic rates, not average earnings, as the course did not relate to any of the stewards' duties. The EAT agreed and went on to say that the *employers*' attitude to the time off is crucial in testing what is reasonable. *Ministry of Defence v Crook* 1982 (EAT)

Management have to provide cover for you when you are gone, but you should ensure that this is done by agreement.

The existence of a procedure agreement covering matters for which you are seeking time off may be relevant in deciding whether it is reasonable to give paid release for what are clearly union duties.

■ ASTMS held a one-day conference on job security for Pye members in Cambridge. A new agreement had just been negotiated. Pye said the matters could be raised there and refusal payment. The EAT allowed time off, but without pay. *Deepledge v Pye Telecommunications* 1980 (EAT)

This decision overlooked the argument that in order to prepare for discussions under the agreement the union reps would need to have their own meeting, which could also be eligible for paid release.

Trade union duties

An official has the right to paid time off to carry out 'those duties of his as such an official which are concerned with industrial relations between his employer and any associated employer, and their employees' (EPCA 1978 section 27). The primary purpose of this definition is to restrict the right to occasions when you are carrying out a role envisaged by a jointly agreed procedure.

This does not mean that the purpose of the meeting for which you are requesting paid release must conform precisely to the contours of the recognition agreement. Preparatory and explanatory work are covered and the courts say a wide interpretation has to be given to 'duties concerned with industrial relations'. While a meeting merely to exchange information between union lay officials would not be included, making a union policy in relation to an employer would, even if the particular union grouping had no status in negotiations (*Beal v Beecham Group* 1982 (CA) – meeting of representatives who within Beechams had different degrees of recognition).

As an official, you must be given time off to carry out duties for such purposes as:

- collective bargaining with management, for example, at negotiations and on joint committees
- informing members about negotiations and consultation, for example, at mass meetings
- meeting lay or full-time officials to discuss industrial issues connected with your employer, for example, at the trade union side of a joint negotiating committee, or prior to raising a grievance in procedure
- interviewing members on grievances and disciplinary matters
- appearing on behalf of members at an outside official body, for example, at an industrial tribunal
- explaining the industrial relations structure to new employees whom you will represent, for example, at induction training or interviews with new starters.

In order to carry out your duties the Code says management

should provide basic facilities such as accommodation for meetings, a phone, a notice board and 'if justified' office facilities. These are not defined but would include a desk, filing cabinets, secretarial help, and access to a photocopier.

All union lay officials should take advantage of the above facilities if you have not already negotiated them in your agreements. Certainly the right to interview new starters and to demand basic office equipment are important extensions in the Code.

Trade union training

The Code says that officials *should* undertake training. You have the right to paid time off to attend courses which are:

1. relevant to your duties concerned with industrial relations between your employer and employees, and

2. approved by your own union or the TUC (or the Northern Ireland Committee of the Irish Congress of Trade Unions).

No syllabus is laid down, but management are entitled to see the programme for any course you propose to go on. You need initial basic training in shop stewards' duties, and further training if you have special responsibilities, or if you are involved in new areas of collective bargaining. For example, you might be a trustee on your company's pension board or management might want to introduce work study or job evaluation. You can get paid release even if the subject-matter of the course is non-negotiable at the time.

■ Daphine Young sought paid release to attend the GMBA-TU's college for a one-week course on pensions and participation. The EAT said she was entitled. Advising members, negotiating, and making representations on the structure and administration of the pension scheme were all industrial relations matters, even though the scheme at the time was run by an insurance company with no employee trustees. (*Young v Carr Fasteners* 1979 (EAT)

You will need union training in order to represent your members effectively. You can also go on training courses if your knowledge gets out of date – training in labour law, for example.

Trade union activities

You have the right as a member of a recognised independent

union to reasonable *unpaid* time off to take part in any activities of your union, or in which you are representing your union. This means that during working hours you can:

- vote in union elections
- attend meetings
- attend meetings of your union or branch executive committee, or annual or special conferences
- represent your union on external official bodies, e.g. Trades Councils.

The Code rightly points out that management have an interest in allowing time off for members to attend meetings during working hours. For example, a meeting may be necessary to discuss an urgent industrial issue. It is in the interests of management and union that decisions are made at representative meetings of members. In many cases, holding a meeting in working hours may not adversely affect production or services.

Industrial action

The Code deals specifically with time off in connection with industrial action. The guidelines laid down are:

1. There is no obligation to permit workers to take time off to carry out union activities which consist of industrial action.

2. When members are directly affected by industrial action by another group of workers, they and their officials may need to hold an emergency meeting.

3. If industrial action has not occurred, management should not alter existing time off agreements.

4. If an official is taking part with members in industrial action, there is no right to time off.

5. But, if you are not yourself taking action, but represent members who are, say, taking unofficial action, 'normal arrangements for time off with pay should apply'.

It is interesting to note that in the Code and this part of the EPCA 1978 industrial action is regarded as a trade union activity. This is in contrast to the approach of the EAT in applying other sections. See page 306.

If management refuse time off

If you don't get time off when you want it, or if you are an official and don't get paid properly, you can claim to an industrial tribunal **within three months** of the date management refused your claim. See page 490 for the procedure.

If the claim is not settled with the help of ACAS the tribunal has power to award any compensation it considers is just, bearing in mind

- management's 'default' in failing to allow time off; and
- any loss you suffered as a result.

There is scope for compensation for non-financial losses (see *Brassington*'s case, page 312).

If management allow you time off as an official, but do not pay you properly, the tribunal can order them to pay up.

In proceedings before a tribunal, the Code must be taken into consideration.

Negotiating time off

The Act and the Code give progressive rights to union officials and members. Of course, arrangements for time off are best negotiated between management and unions as basic parts of a recognition and procedure agreement. Failure to allow time off is ideally dealt with at workplace level as a breach of agreement.

Your rights within the union

In 1980 the Tory government intervened in internal union affairs to give additional statutory rights to members and applicants working in jobs or industries **where a closed shop exists**. These are dealt with on pages 350–59. This section describes the law applying generally to all union members.

Internal activities in your union are affected by the rule-book, by statute and by the rules judges have made. When you join you enter into a contract with the union, the terms of which are found in the rule-book. Like any other contract, it can be interpreted and enforced by the courts. Unlike a contract of employment, though, where only damages can be ordered, it can actually be imposed on the parties, who can be ordered to carry out its terms.

Rules covering eligibility, discipline, elections and other matters can all be enforced by individual members. It is interesting to note that while unions want the law to recognise collective rights, rule-books don't usually give rights to groups within unions. Claims (for breach of contract or for a declaration of your rights) have to be brought in the civil courts. Legal representation under the Legal Aid scheme is available in appropriate cases (see page 487).

The effect of the rule-book and statute can be summarised as follows:

1. The rule-book, and custom and practice which is well known and not inconsistent with it, are the basis of your relationship with the union.

2. You have the right not to be discriminated against on the grounds of sex, marriage, race or Common Market nationality.

3. The rule-book is subject to the 'rules of natural justice' so that if you are liable to discipline you must be given

- notice of the charge against you
- time to prepare your case
- an opportunity to state your case
- a fair hearing before an impartial body.

Rules providing for automatic termination without the above are not enforceable.

4. Procedures laid down in the rule-book must be followed by the union. Although there is no requirement that you must exhaust the internal procedures before complaining to a court, you will in practice have to justify yourself if you have not followed procedure.

5. A union decision said to be final and binding cannot deprive you of your right to go to court, but if the union behaved fairly and followed procedure the courts have no authority to interfere.

6. You have the right to complain to the Independent Review Committee (IRC) of the TUC – see below.

7. You have the right to leave the union at any time provided you give reasonable notice and comply with any reasonable conditions (TULRA 1974 section 7). A condition that you pay arrears, or do not join another TUC-affiliated union contrary to the Bridlington Agreement (see below) might be reasonable.

8. You have the right under the Trade Union Act 1913 to refuse to contribute to the union's political fund, if it has one, and you must not be prejudiced if you do opt out. You can make a complaint to the Certification Officer who has ruled that even a temporary contribution followed by a refund of the political levy is illegal. Unions operating a check-off system which does not permit a reduced contribution each time it is deducted from wages must refund the political levy *in advance* (*Reeves v TGWU* 1979 (EAT). N. Ireland members are entitled to *opt in*.

In 1983 the government put forward proposals for changes in the way in which political contributions are collected, and political activities are funded, by unions.

9. You have rights if your union amalgamates with another, including the right to be balloted.

Independent Review Committee (IRC)

The IRC considers appeals by individual workers who have been *sacked* as a result of being expelled from, or of having been refused admission to, a union in a situation where trade union membership is a condition of employment. Although the IRC was set up under the auspices of the TUC, its three members were appointed after consultation with the Employment Secretary. The procedure is on page 354.

Inter-union relations

The TUC has drawn up a set of rules, known as the Bridlington Principles, concerning inter-union relations. They require every union to ask all applicants for membership if they are or have recently been a union member. The new union must then ask the old union if the member resigned, is clear on the books, is under discipline or should not be accepted. If the old union objects, the matter can be resolved by using a TUC Disputes Committee, any decision of which is 'morally binding' on the unions.

Dual membership is usually permitted only if both unions agree.

A union should not accept any member who is in arrears or involved in an industrial dispute, nor should it start organising workers at any establishment in grades where another union has a majority of the employees *and* negotiates for them.

Most unions have rules which allow them to expel a member in accordance with a decision of the Disputes Committee, and the courts have upheld these rules.

■ Ernest Cheall was ACTSS branch secretary at Vauxhall's

Dunstable plant until he became dissatisfied, resigned and with four others joined APEX. Although the question on the application form about previous union memberships was left blank, APEX knew his background and accepted him without sending the proper inquiry to ACTSS. A TUC Disputes Committee instructed APEX to return the members to ACTSS, and APEX terminated their membership according to APEX rules. Cheall complained that he had not had a hearing at the TUC or at the APEX Executive, and that the TUC agreement was contrary to public policy. The Law Lords unanimously held that individuals had no standing in the TUC agreement, and APEX Executive would not have been able to avoid its obligation to comply with the Disputes Committee even if it had given him a hearing. The Law Lords could not intervene in the decision of the APEX Executive to expel him in accordance with APEX and TUC rules. *Cheall v APEX* 1983 (HL)

Union ballots

The Employment Act 1980, and the detailed Scheme that goes with it (SI 1980 No 1252 and 1982 No 953), entitle independent trade unions to reclaim the cost of postal ballots held for specified purposes. The Certification Officer approves the conduct of the ballot and the award of costs.

The TUC advised unions not to apply for funds, recognising the 'implications for the autonomy of unions' involved in the scheme, and said:

> It is clear that public funds cannot be handed over to unions without the acceptance by unions of some degree of public accountability. *TUC commentary para 3*

Rigid postal ballot procedures reduce tactical flexibility in bargaining, promote individual rather than collective decision making and discourage attendance at meetings. While the government was making savage cuts in public spending its intention to spend £2 million a year in 'assisting' trade unions was sinister.

To qualify for payment, unions must show that the **purpose** and **conduct** of the ballot accord with the Act and strict guidelines. They are described here to illustrate the dangers of accepting funds.

The purpose of the ballot

Section 1 (3) stipulates the purpose for which a funded ballot can be held. Where several questions are asked, each must satisfy the purposes, or relate to them. These purposes are:

1. Calling and ending industrial action. Both the Industrial Relations Act and Labour's 1969 plans for union reform (*In Place of Strife*) sought ways of imposing a ballot on workers before a strike was called. Ironically, North American experience showed that in compulsory ballots the membership usually support the union leadership. So a 'voluntary' approach was adopted instead by the Tories (later reversed by their 1983 plans). The Scheme requires that 'all members likely to be instructed or advised to participate in the strike or other industrial action should be entitled to vote'. It seems that a general ballot would qualify even if selective action is planned.

■ **Example**: In a dispute over redundancies, white-collar civil servants vote for action. The union pulls out key workers on the computer and the switchboard. Provided these members have been entitled to vote, a ballot of all the members would qualify for funding.

Nothing is said about multi-union bargaining, where one union might want to ballot members and apply for funds, and another might consult members through a delegate conference. Presumably the first union could get financial support if it balloted all its own members. But then do all sections of the union who might be affected have to be balloted?

■ The NUJ wanted to discipline members who did not take part in the 1978 provincial newpaper strike. Some members claimed the strike was called contrary to the rules, which require all members of the union to be balloted if a strike 'affects' a majority of them. While provincial journalists are not a majority of the union, other members, particularly freelances and journalists on other publications, were instructed to boycott copy to and from provincial papers. The Law Lords rejected the view that this was merely normal trade union solidarity, and held that the provincial strike 'affected' a majority of NUJ members, even though they were not on strike. So all the members should have been balloted on a strike which directly involved only a minority. *Porter v NUJ* 1980 (HL)

Clearly, the government hope to restrict strike action by requiring a very wide constituency, including people only marginally affected, to vote on the issue.

There are also problems about a vote among constituencies of the same union which consult members in different ways.

■ **Example**: Some regions of a union conduct written ballots of members. Other have workplace or branch meeting votes. Funding would be refused to the former, since not all those 'likely to be advised to participate' in a strike had been balloted within the criteria of the Act.

2. **Elections**. Funds can be obtained for carrying out any election of full-time and principal lay officials, but the Scheme does not provide for electing shop stewards.

3. **Rule amendments**.

4. **Amalgamations**. The Trade Union (Amalgamations) Act 1964 already requires balloting in these circumstances. Funds can now be obtained to obtain a balloted decision.

5. **Rejecting or accepting** employers' offers relating to pay, hours, holidays, pensions and job performance.

6. **Other purposes**. The Employment Secretary has power to add to these approved purposes.

Conditions

The conditions which must be fulfilled before money is given are very strict. They are laid down in the 1980 Act and the Scheme, and the Certification Officer has considerable authority over the form, conduct and expenses of the ballot.

To qualify, the ballot must be cast on secret voting papers, comply with the union's rules, give all entitled a fair opportunity to vote without any interference, be returned **by post** (not internal mail) and be fairly counted. There is no obligation to go to independent counters, as long as the Certification Officer is satisfied that the count is fair.

Workplace ballots

Ancillary to these provisions is the right in section 2 of the 1980 Act which entitles a union to demand facilities for a workplace ballot. This Labour Peers' amendment applies to any union recognised by an employer for collective bargaining, provided there are more than 20 people employed by that and any associated employer.

The ballot must contain a question on one of the approved purposes listed above and it must be in secret. But otherwise the conduct of the ballot is not regulated in the same way as when funding is sought. Your employer must, so far as is reasonably practicable, comply with the union's request to permit the use of the premises to give members 'a convenient opportunity of voting'. If this is refused, the union can (within three months) apply to a tribunal for a declaration that it is entitled to use the premises. And the tribunal can award whatever compensation it considers just and equitable 'having regard to the employer's default . . . and any expenses incurred by the union' as a result.

The principled objections that exist to accepting state aid for union business do not apply to this new union right. In practice it is unlikely that a recognised union will need to enforce the right. Employers are generally ready to co-operate on wage offers and shop steward elections. Besides, the right was already recognised indirectly in the ACAS Code on time off, paragraph 22 of which says: 'Members should be given reasonable time off during working hours to vote in a union election'.

What expenses are paid?

The Certification Officer has to make a payment to a union which applies for reimbursement for a ballot which satisfies the conditions of the Act and the Scheme. The payment consists of:

- a reasonable sum to cover stationery, and printing of voting papers and literature explaining the issue
- the cost of posting and returning the papers by second class post (or more expensive means if the Certification Officer says this is reasonable) or prepaid letter.

Within the package, therefore, campaign literature can be included and subsidised.

Payment will not be made until six weeks after the Certification Officer has received the application, details of expenses and the result of the ballot. If a ballot is arranged but shelved before any voting papers are given out there will be no payment.

The trade union response

The TUC advised unions to refuse to take up state funds for ballots. Taking funds is a step towards acceptance of the Tory laws, and compulsory ballots. Even the new right to workplace ballots is at best unnecessary for well organised workers and at worst an invitation to corporatism and employer suggestion.

There is a role for union ballots. But union decision making and democracy can survive without funding from employers or a Conservative government. **The government made proposals in its 1983 Green Paper 'Democracy in Trade Unions' for ballots before strikes, and the electing of lay and full-time officials.**

Summary

1. You have the right not to be sacked or victimised for being a union member, taking part in its activities, or for refusing to be a member.

2. Activities include recruitment, canvassing, collecting dues and making complaints on management's premises, outside working time or during working time with express or implied permission.

3. A quick 'interim' procedure can be used to continue your contract if you are sacked on union grounds. Compensation for unfair dismissal is increased to substantial *minimum* levels.

4. If your employer recognises the union for negotiations, s/he is also obliged to recognise safety representatives, to consult on pensions, takeovers and redundancies, and to give reasonable paid time off for union duties and training.

5. Collective agreements are not legally binding but parts of them may be incorporated into individual contracts of employment.

6. You have rights within the union based on the rule-book and concepts of natural justice. Inter-union relationships are covered by the TUC's Bridlington Agreement.

7. Government funds are available for union postal ballots on elections and wage offers, and a recognised union can demand workplace facilities and time off for them.

14. Union organisation and the closed shop

Attacks on union organisation / the extent of closed shop agreements / their effect / membership level / genuine objections / the effect on agreements / the Code / pressure to maintain union organisation / union labour only contracts / admission and expulsion of members in closed shops / the role of tribunals / how to stay organised / and a summary.

The Tory march on working-class living standards at some stage had to confront trade unions. Essential for the fulfilment of Conservative policies is the weakening of union organisation. Several routes were chosen for this purpose – high unemployment, lower real wages and Employment Acts 1980 and 1982. In particular, the closed shop was made a prime target because it represents trade union organisation at its most developed and effective level. So the Tories hoped that closed shops – or union membership agreements (UMAs) – would be dismantled or fall apart as a result of the Acts.

The attack on union organisation took the following forms:

1. The grounds for objection to union membership were expanded to an extent that would make virtually meaningless any UMA which incorporated them.

2. Objectors sacked or victimised can complain to industrial tribunals.

3. A new UMA protects employers from individual claims only if a ballot in the specified form is carried out.

4. Unions or individuals can be ordered to contribute to compensation awarded by a tribunal if they put pressure on employers to sack or victimise a non-member.

5. New rights are given to workers expelled or refused admission to a union in employment where a UMA exists.

6. Union officers and members are liable if they put pressure on employers to use only union-made products or materials.

Where to find the law

Union membership agreements are defined in the Trade Union and Labour Relations Act 1974 (TULRA), section 30. Dismissal and victimisation for non-membership is dealt with in the amendments by the 1980 and 1982 Employment Acts to the Employment Protection Consolidation Act 1978 (EPCA) sections 58, 58a and 23; compensation in sections 72–77; special compensation for dismissals between 1974 and 1980 in the Employment Act 1982, section 1 and schedule 1; unreasonable exclusion and explusion of union members in the 1980 Act sections 4 and 5; action to require union recognition in commercial contracts, in the 1982 Act sections 12–14. The DE Code of Practice on Closed Shop Agreements and Arrangements (revised 1983) gives 'practical guidance'.

How important are Union Membership Agreements?

There has been extensive public debate, and much collective bargaining, about closed shop agreements since 1970. But research done for the Department of Employment by the London School of Economics concluded that despite four pieces of legislation public knowledge of the extent and operation of closed shop practice was based on 15-year-old data 'supplemented by piecemeal evidence from coverage given to the plight of individuals adversely affected by the closed shop'.

According to the survey (*Employment Gazette*, November 1979, January 1980 and *Industrial Relations Review and Report* No 289, February 1983), 4.5 million workers, or 23 per cent of the working population, are covered by some form of closed shop. In other words they are in a 'situation in which employees come to realise that a particular job is only to be obtained or retained if they become and remain members of one of a specified number of trade unions'. Among manual workers, 30 per cent are covered by a closed shop, and this affects 43 per cent of members of TUC-affiliated unions.

Traditional areas of 100 per cent union membership such as mining and shipbuilding have declined in absolute numbers, but closed shops have spread into public utilities, local authorities and the food and clothing industries, together with further penetration in transport, oil, engineering and printing. This development began in the late 1960s with moves towards greater formalisation of workplace procedures. According to the LSE/DE survey, the move was already under way before the attempt to outlaw closed shops in the Industrial Relations Act 1971, and its subsequent repeal in 1974.

The trend has been towards ratification in written agreements of existing practices, and the negotiation of new UMAs. Only 16 per cent are in pre-entry closed shops, where you must be a union member in order to get a job, and this figure is declining rapidly with a run-down in traditional industries. The remainder require you to join after you have been employed, and most provide for exceptions.

These trends caused indignation and apprehension in right-wing political (but not necessarily industrial) circles and led to the amendments contained in the Employment Acts. History has shown, though, that legislative constraints in 1971–74 had very little impact on the development of 100 per cent trade union organisation although, as with the 1980 Act, they inhibited new UMAs. The LSE/DE study shows that further expansion on any large scale would have been unlikely even without the 1980 Act, since those sections without UMAs were either weakly organised, or the employers had ideological or political objections to them. Exploitation by the Freedom Association of the loopholes in the 1974–76 legislation had little practical significance despite massive national and local publicity. There were, however, examples of political decisions to rescind existing UMAs. The 1978 bread strike led to the cancellation by the Bakers' Federation of an industry-wide UMA. And some local authority employers in the Midlands and west London pulled out of existing agreements for party political reasons.

The LSE/DE research into formal agreements affecting almost half of the workers covered by closed shops has shown that **exemption clauses** are common. Only 8 per cent provide no formal let-out, the vast majority acknowledging religious objection (as covered by the law between 1974 and 1980) and some conscientious objection. 63 per cent exclude existing non-members at the time of the agreement, and excuse part-timers, temporaries, trainees and specific job holders (e.g. directors' secretaries, and personnel staff). More than half the workers are covered by separate procedures, usually including independent arbitration, for testing non-members' claims to be exempted.

The effect of a Union Membership Agreement

The 1980 and 1982 Employment Acts amended sections 23 and 58 of the EPCA to give workers dismissed or victimised for refusing to join a union where a UMA exists substantial new rights. The complex provisions can be summarised in this way:

1. Dismissal or victimisation for not being a union member is unfair.

2. But where a UMA exists dismissal or victimisation for non-membership is fair.

3. However, the UMA must be *valid*, that is:

- it was in operation before 15 August 1980 and the dismissal or victimisation occurred before 1 November 1984; or
- it was in operation before 15 August 1980, **the dismissal or victimisation occurred after 1 November 1984 and the UMA has been approved in a ballot** (see **5.** below); or
- it took effect on or after 15 August 1980 and was approved in a ballot.

4. In any case, action is still unfair if

- the worker genuinely objects on grounds of conscience or other deeply held personal conviction to being a member of any trade union whatsoever or of a particular trade union – the **'personal objector'**; or
- the worker was there before the UMA took effect and since it took effect has never been a member of a union specified in the UMA – the **'existing non'**; or
- (for UMAs taking effect on or after 15 August 1980) the worker has not since the date of the ballot been a member – the **'new non'**; or
- the worker has a claim pending or got a tribunal decision

that s/he has been unreasonably excluded or expelled from the union, unless s/he is at fault in not applying for, or accepting an offer of, membership – the **'unwilling non'**; or

- the worker is neither personal objector nor existing non *and* holds relevant qualifications *and* is covered by a professional code precluding industrial action *and* has refused to take part in action in breach of the code and has therefore been excluded or expelled from membership – the **'professional non'**.

5. A ballot is approved only if

- for pre-1980 UMAs, either 80 per cent of those entitled to vote, or 85 per cent of those voting, agree to it;
- for post-1980 UMAs, 80 per cent of those entitled to vote agree to it;
- for any UMA which is coming up for a second ballot (presumably as part of a 'periodic review') either 80 or 85 per cent as above agree to it.

6. The ballot must

- be secret;
- give a vote to all those within the class of employees to be covered;
- not define the class by reference to union membership, or objection to it.

7. Dismissal or victimisation for refusing to make some payment instead of being in the union is unfair.

8. Tribunals cannot reduce compensation on the grounds that the worker was in breach of contract by not being in the union.

9. Anyone, or any union, bringing pressure through industrial action on employers to dismiss or victimise a non-member can be ordered to pay compensation.

These grounds are dealt with in detail below. The most important fact to note is that **they don't make closed shops illegal. They simply give sacked or victimised workers a right to sue their employers in industrial tribunals. Existing agreements can continue and there is no legal bar on your negotiating a new UMA which does not have a conscience clause or comply with the ballot requirements set out below**.

A UMA gives an employer a defence against claims for unfair

dismissal and victimisation short of dismissal by workers sacked or disciplined because they did not comply with the agreement. Where there is not a valid UMA or where a worker proves s/he has an acceptable objection, a tribunal can order reinstatement, re-engagement or compensation.

In practice, tribunals must consider whether it is practicable for the employer to comply, so the principal remedy is the very high award of compensation and, in the case of victimisation, a declaration of the victim's rights (not, incidentally, an order for the victimisation to be stopped or that certain ameliorative action be taken – EPCA section 24).

Membership level

A UMA can be a formal written document or a well-known arrangement. It can cover employees in one section of a plant, or the whole manual workforce of a local authority. Provided it is made by one or more independent unions and employers or employer's associations, relates to an identifiable group of workers, and is uniformly enforced, it is a UMA. Certain restrictions have also been created by tribunals on the introduction and maintenance of closed shops. For example, notice of the change in contracts of employment must be given in writing. No particular percentage is required but it should be 'usual' for the relevant employees to be in the union – *Taylor v Co-op Retail Services* 1982 (CA) (90 per cent membership established a 'practice').

Once you have defined your boundaries, **it is crucial that the agreement is enforced uniformly**, as the case involving Ferry-bridge C power station in Yorkshire shows.

■ Six employees of the CEGB refused to join any of the four unions which had signed the Electricity Supply NJIC agreements. They were members of the Electricity Supply Union (ESU), which had for some time been demanding recognition, and canvassing support against the TUC unions, on the ostensible basis of wanting a single union for electricity supply. The ESU is affiliated to a Confederation of Employee Organisations and both bodies are actively supported by Conservative Central Office. The men were told they would be sacked if they did not join one of the TUC unions which had signed the agreement, or apply for exemption on religious grounds. They refused, were sacked and claimed unfair dismissal. Following a 14-day hearing, the Leeds tribunal accepted their arguments. The NIJC agreement was valid, the tribunal said, but because there were members of the Boilermakers' Society in another plant, and possibly other non-unionists elsewhere, the CEGB could not say that they had established the *practice* of rigorous enforcement of the agreement. The tribunal said the Ferrybridge six were being picked on because they were active in the ESU. They got substantial compensation. *Sarvent v CEGB* 1976 (IT)

Although the law has now changed slightly, the lesson of *Ferrybridge* is that **if you have a closed shop you must secure 100 per cent compliance with it**. Stewards must regularly have card checks of members, and if warnings to non-members are not immediately effective, they must report breaches of the agreement to management. Stewards should not turn a blind eye to non-compliance in individual cases as this will affect the 'practice' of the agreement and could, as at Ferrybridge, jeopardise any action taken under it.

Any agreed procedures and 'really essential' conditions laid down in the UMA, for example giving individuals the opportunity to make their case or to appeal, must be followed meticulously – *Curry v Harlow District Council* 1979 (EAT).

Genuine objections

Sections 23 and 58 of the EPCA were amended to provide that victimisation or dismissal of an employee is unfair if a UMA exists and s/he 'genuinely objects on grounds of conscience or other deeply held personal conviction to being a member of any trade union whatsoever or of a particular trade union'. The clause applies to all UMAs. If managements allow workers to exploit such a wide conscience clause, or insist on its inclusion in agreements, many satisfactory UMAs become inoperable.

No guidance is given in the Act on the meaning of conscience or personal conviction. The 1974 Act protected religious objectors and, until 1976, people with reasonable grounds for objecting to any particular union (see below). At the time, the TUC made representations against the special treatment of religious objectors. Clearly in a secular society the elevation of religion is inappropriate, and a general conscientious objection clause in agreements was felt to be unworkable and unprovable. Now, the latter is specially provided for but without further guidance on how it should be interpreted.

In Parliament, the Employment Minister said that to win a case of unfair dismissal the belief must be genuinely held but it need not be reasonable. If you can prove you have a strong conviction – even if it is irrational – you will be protected.

All religious belief, whether personally held or as part of an organised faith, is protected. But 'trivial, superficial or transitory objections to union membership' isn't. The Minister, Patrick Mayhew, also discounted objectors who are temporarily disaffected towards the union leadership or who on grounds of expediency object, say, to an increase in contributions.

He said that personal conviction was distinguished from conscience in the case, for example, of people who resist union membership because they see a clash with their occupational, professional or vocational commitment. A sacked nurse could claim protection if his or her objection were based on the possibility that a nursing union might take industrial action and interfere with the duty to patients. Just in case this exemption is not wide enough, the Act allows people in these circumstances – the 'professional nons' – who are expelled from, or refuse to join, a union to claim – see also page 357. Major unions in the health service – COHSE for instance – have recognised the professional and humanitarian commitments of their members and have given specific guidance on the conduct of disputes, pointing out and respecting members' duties to patients. Despite these reassurances, tribunals can allow objections to union membership on occupational grounds from workers in health, education and other public services.

Objections based on political belief are not mentioned in the Act, but the government confirmed that political objectors will be exempt. And examples were given of workers objecting to the political views or affiliation of union leaders. You could even opt out – as Lord Hailsham specifically confirmed – if you object to a union's affiliation to the Labour Party, notwithstanding that you already have the right to refuse to contribute to a union's political fund. The influence of right-wing organisations, particularly on existing UMAs in the public sector, has spread since the permitted grounds for objection to union membership were extended.

As well as blowing open the grounds for objection to unions

in principle, the Act protects objections to **'a particular union'**. This clause was law between 1974 and 1976, although then you had to prove you had 'reasonable grounds'; 15 successful challenges were reported. But with the extended conscience clause many opportunists may attempt to avoid union membership by citing, for example, the union's failure to take up a grievance, or to handle it successfully, or a particular rule or aspect of union policy. It is possible for people to challenge a UMA on the grounds that they would not wish to join any union which had entered into or enforced a closed shop!

Pre-1980 agreements

'Personal objectors' can object to membership under any agreement. Workers covered by an agreement existing before 15 August 1980 are given limited protection against dismissal and victimisation for non-membership. This applies only to people who

1. were in the class of employees covered by the UMA 'since before' the agreement required them to join, and

2. have never since then been a member of a union specified in the UMA.

■ **Example**: Under a UMA agreed before the Act had effect, all new employees must join the union. Existing employees have two months to join. Mr A joins on the last day but resigns in September 1980. Ms B refuses to join at all. Both are given notice and sacked. Mr A can't claim the benefit of this exemption clause as the UMA was in effect before the Employment Act and he had been a member at some time after the UMA took effect. Ms B is protected since she had never joined.

Although most closed shop agreements are now in writing, there are workplaces where it would be impossible to say when an ancient arrangement, or unspoken understanding, or unilateral union practice first 'had the effect' of requiring union membership.

New employees coming into an area covered by an existing UMA cannot claim this exemption and must join.

It is important to recognise the limited scope of this exception. **If they have been members, workers cannot use this section** to win unfair dismissal claims. Nor are they likely to prove they have 'genuine objections' to union membership.

Although not protected under the EPCA until 1980, existing non-members at the date a UMA took effect were and are protected under Article 11 of the European Convention of Human Rights, to which the UK subscribes.

■ When a UMA was introduced in British Rail in 1975 three workers refused to join and were sacked. They complained that under Article 11 they had the right to 'form and join trade unions' and that in BR they effectively had no choice but to join the NUR or TSSA or be sacked. Although the Convention does not guarantee the right *not* to be a member in the same way as it guarantees the positive right to join, every situation had to be treated separately and the introduction of a UMA which did not provide for 'existing nons' was an infringement. The UK government was ordered in 1982 to pay £18,000, £46,000 and £10,000 respectively to the men covering financial loss and non-financial damage such as harassment, humiliation, stress, anxiety and difficulty finding other work, plus £65,000 legal costs and interest. *Young, James and Webster v UK* 1983 (European Court of Human Rights)

Clearly the money involved in a claim like this is vast, but the claim did not establish that closed shops are a violation of human rights. After the 1980–82 Acts, claims for protection by 'existing nons' are unlikely to be taken to Strasbourg.

In an unprecedented exercise of retrospective legislation, the Tory government provided up to £2 million to compensate non-unionists dismissed from closed shops between 1974 and 1980, when dismissal was lawful. The first award made by Employment Secretary Norman Tebbit was of £10,500 to a 65-year-old engineer and Freedom Association member. Despite a massive advertising campaign, fewer than 200 valid applications were received in the first six months. The average payout to claimants was £5,170. 1 November 1983 was fixed as the latest date for applications.

Dismissal or victimisation of *anyone* after 1 November 1984 is unfair if the UMA has not during the previous five years been approved in a ballot by 80 per cent of those entitled to vote, or 85 per cent of those voting. The TUC advised unions not to get involved in these ballots, but in any event the practical problems involved are enormous, particularly in multi-plant or industry-wide UMAs.

Post-1980 agreements

UMAs which take effect on or after 15 August 1980 are affected by the above exemptions for genuine objectors and existing non-members. If your employer wants to escape liability for sacking or victimising a worker who refuses to comply with a new UMA, s/he must show that a ballot has been carried out. The only relevance of the ballot is in providing management with a defence. **Otherwise an 'approved UMA' has no legal effect, and a non-approved UMA is not in itself in any way unlawful. There is no legal obligation to follow the new ballot rules, and UMAs can be negotiated freely**. The following paragraphs on ballots are given for reference, and should therefore be read in that context.

If you decide to follow the provisions of section 58 of the EPCA as amended, a secret ballot for an 'approved' UMA must be conducted among those employees who are to be covered by it. The ballot must show that **'80 per cent of those entitled to vote'** voted in favour of the UMA. This means all employees in the class to be covered by the UMA who are employed on the date of the ballot.

The 80 per cent requirement is far tougher than similar provisions for an agency shop under the Industrial Relations Act 1971, and the effect on individuals of a successful ballot is less onerous, since in 1971 there was no escape for existing non-members or for free-riders.

An important lesson from the practice of Labour's 1974 legislation was that you could choose your constituency for the UMA to exclude likely areas of contention. If you know there are groups of employees or individuals who will refuse to join, you could define your UMA to leave them out. Now, however, if you decide to put your new UMA to a ballot, the Act says that 'any restriction of the class by reference to membership (or objection to membership) of a trade union shall be disregarded'. This gloss was purely political. Why should people who will anyway be exempt be included in the vote? Presumably the reference has to be explicit. So if you don't expressly refer to union membership, and choose some other identification, these excluded people might not form part of the class eligible to vote and you will not therefore dilute your majority with certain anti votes.

Again, no guidance is given in the Act on what the constituency should be, or what form the secret ballot should take. Industrial tribunals have to deal with questions arising out of dismissal and victimisation cases, although the High Court could be involved in challenges to the form or conduct of ballots.

If your employer changes, as a result of a takeover or merger for example, there is no requirement to conduct a ballot, or a new ballot, if you already have a UMA.

Scope for opting out is even given to employees who are covered by an approved UMA. EPCA section 58, says that an employee will be protected against dismissal and victimisation if:

1. s/he was entitled to vote in a ballot,

2. the ballot produced an approved UMA, i.e. 80 per cent or more of those entitled voted for it, and

3. s/he has not been a member of a union specified in the UMA 'since the day the ballot was held'.

In some cases this could work against a person resigning from a union, but the blanket protection of section 58 would then apply:

■ **Example**: X is a member of the union who voted against the UMA in a ballot on 1 November 1983. The result was announced on 3 November 1983. He resigned. The UMA took effect on 1 December and he is sacked after that. His dismissal is unfair. He was a member after the day the ballot was held so he can't be protected by section 58, but he was not a member when the agreement **took effect**.

Implications

The implications for collective bargaining are very serious. Non-members among existing employees who have been quietly left alone on the introduction of UMAs may take the new laws as a licence to advertise their non-membership. Present members might find reasons for resigning based on 'personal conviction' against their union, possibly digging up old grievances and grudges. Union representatives, particularly at workplace level, could be put under pressure to conduct ballots to ratify existing long-standing UMAs.

Most seriously, the law attempts to affect collective agreements which have been reached voluntarily by unions and managements according to their own special needs and wishes. Stable negotiating arrangements are threatened with fragmentation if members withdraw from their own unions and start to organise in other, non-recognised, unions. Scope is given for anti-unionists to weaken established bargaining either by dropping union membership or by joining other unions.

■ **Example**: Ten of your members resign, saying that the union does not adequately represent people with their skills, and that they therefore share a genuine personal conviction against joining your union. They join a craft union. They are entitled to claim against management if they are sacked or victimised (EPCA section 58). Their right to be members of the craft union and take part in its activities on your employer's premises is also protected (EPCA section 23). So trade union organisation is fragmented and collective bargaining made unstable.

Further complications could occur if the craft union refused to admit these people on the grounds that the TUC Bridlington Agreement precludes such a transfer – see page 327.

Encouragement is also given for the formation of breakaway unions whose independence from management control would be questionable. In the electricity supply industry, for example, and the Post Office, there are small organisations which have long sought to usurp the existing trade union structure. The loosening of UMAs as a result of the Employment Act adds further scope to the activities of these groups.

The European Court of Human Rights' views (page 342), although not binding, are likely to influence tribunals and courts in Britain.

The Code of Practice

The 1983 Code of Practice on the closed shop contains additional restrictions on the introduction, content and operation of UMAs. Like other codes it creates no legal obligations, but can be cited in tribunals and courts. It is, however, of very limited value there. Tribunals have jurisdiction on unfair dismissal and determine whether a UMA exists and whether an objection to union membership is genuine. If it finds the objection is genuine, the dismissal is unfair. If it is not genuine, it is fair – the tribunal is not looking for 'reasonableness', as in other dismissal cases. Apart from encouraging unions and management to agree UMAs only when membership is 'very high', and to review them periodically, there is little in the Code that is relevant to testing the major issues that arise. No firm guidance is given on constituencies, or genuineness of beliefs, for example. But see page 353 for its effect on union rules.

The Code gives management grounds to object to and to delay negotiation of UMAs. And, of course, it makes it appear that new UMAs *must* be approved by ballot. As a prescription for collective bargaining, its effect is very limited.

Proving it

The existence of a UMA is an employer's defence to a claim for unfair dismissal by a worker who is not in the union. If the worker claims the UMA is not valid, or that s/he has genuine objections to joining, s/he must prove them. If the objection is proved to be genuine, the dismissal is unfair

Extending union organisation

Three main avenues for extending union organisation were blocked by the 1980 and 1982 Acts. It is unlawful:

- to use industrial action to pressurise employers to dismiss a non-unionist;
- to include union labour only (ULO) clauses in commercial contracts or tenders; and
- to use industrial action to pressurise employers to include union labour only clauses.

These are dealt with separately.

Pressure to sack non-unionists

From the time unfair dismissal rights were introduced, employers have been precluded from citing industrial action by other employees as a justification for sacking someone. Section 63 of the EPCA says that a tribunal can take no account of any pressure, through industrial action or threats of it, exercised on management to dismiss a worker. They cannot pass the buck and must take the consequences of the business decision they have made. If they can give no other reason for the sacking, they will lose in an unfair dismissal case since the tribunal must disregard this reason.

Under new sections 26A and 76A of EPCA, however, a further dimension is added to these cases. The employer or the workers can bring in, or 'join', a trade union, as a co-defendant, which will be liable to pay compensation if the tribunal considers it to be 'just and equitable'.

This liability arises when:

1. management say they were induced to dismiss or victimise the employee by pressure;

2. the pressure came through a strike, or other industrial action, or threats of it; and

3. the reason for the pressure was that the dismissed employee was not a member of any union, or of a particular union.

The liability extends to a union or any other person. If the dispute is official the employer would presumably join the union as a party to the proceedings at the tribunal. But whether it is official or not, anyone can be 'joined' as a co-defendant, if s/he has 'called, organised, procured or financed' industrial action. This means shop stewards, branch officials, staff representatives and individual employees of the same firm.

The employer has to 'join' you before the hearing of the dismissal claim, although the tribunal has discretion to allow late claims, and, as a party, you are entitled to argue your case. If the tribunal awards compensation (no action is taken if it awards reinstatement or re-engagement) and agrees that the employer *was* under pressure, it can order you to pay all or some of the compensation. In a case like this, compensation can be over £30,000.

Faced with this legal scenario, union representatives could try to get employers to indemnify them against having to pay a contribution, but this, too, could be illegal.

■ **Example**: By long standing custom and practice all maintenance fitters must belong to the AUEW. One member refused to take part in an official overtime ban and dropped out of the union. The other members refused to work with him and threatened a strike if, following several warnings, he was not sacked. The employer dismissed him, he went to a tribunal and the employer 'joined' the union in the proceedings. The tribunal upheld the man's 'deeply held personal conviction' against the union. It awarded compensation and ordered the union to pay half the employer's liability. The union refused and called a strike. This might be using 'unlawful means' and could be stopped by the employer seeking an injunction in the courts. The debt itself is also recoverable through the civil courts.

In practice, it is unlikely that in an organised workplace employers would so inflame the situation by bringing action against their own employees. **But section 76A can be used whether or not a UMA exists.** So if there is no union membership agreement, and management are resisting one, it is quite conceivable that they would 'join' the union in proceedings. And of course the dismissed worker can also 'join' the union as a co-defendant.

■ **Example**: You are a shop steward at a firm when redundancies are announced. You don't have a UMA and insist that non-members go first, threatening a strike if they don't. Management sack them, and they complain they have been unfairly selected for redundancy. Management 'join' you as a party to the hearing, and the tribunal awards compensation against you for threatening to call a strike to get non-unionists sacked.

Union labour only contracts

Trade unionists have traditionally attempted to extend union organisation by working only with trade unionists and demanding that all products used are union-made. A requirement that all products or services supplied at your workplace should come from unionised workplaces is a safeguard against exploitation, it preserves negotiated terms and conditions, it ensures better standards of skill and health and safety, and it provides additional pressures during disputes. For all these reasons the Conservative government took steps to prevent the constraints on 'competitiveness' arising out of union solidarity.

Sections 12 and 13 of the 1982 Employment Act proscribe in a variety of ways any insistence that contractors use union labour only (ULO) or, for purely cosmetic and formal even-handedness, non-union labour. The ban applies to indirect methods of enforcement such as requiring contractors to recognise or consult with a union. Firstly, a ULO condition in a contract for goods or services is not enforceable. Secondly, terminating a contract because the contractor uses non-unionists is unlawful. Thirdly, it is unlawful to keep contractors off a list of approved suppliers, or to stop them tendering or to decide not to give them the buisness, if one of the grounds is that the work is likely to be done by non-unionists.

No new offences are created by the Act, but it is enforced by saying that employers have a statutory duty to suppliers and 'anyone who may be adversely affected' by a ULO requirement. So if contractors fail to win in a tender bid because of their anti-union practices, not only can they sue, but so can any sub-contractor of theirs who suffers a loss as a result, and any employee of theirs who may be made redundant through lack of work.

Pressure in support of union labour

Contracts and tenders are placed as a result of business decisions by your employer. The extent to which you can legally influence the decision is seriously restricted by section 14 of the 1982 Act, which withdraws the normal legal immunities from union action in ULO claims. You can be sued if you induce your employers to include a ULO requirement in any of their contracts or to exclude any contractor on ULO grounds. Industrial action, and possibly simple persuasion, would amount to inducement if management acted upon it.

Secondly, legal immunity is withdrawn and you can be sued on ULO grounds if you indirectly interfere with the supply of goods or services by inducing workers to break their contracts. If you ask colleagues not to handle products from a particular non-union supplier you are indirectly interfering with the supply. If by refusing management instructions they break their contracts, you would be liable to be sued by your employer, or more likely by the supplier.

Avoiding liability

For nearly 20 years after the General Strike there was a ban on union membership conditions in public sector jobs, and in contracts with the public sector. In relation to contractors, the 1982 Employment Act restored this position and extended it to *all* contracts. Taken with the repeal of comparability claims under Schedule 11 of the EPA 1975 and the Fair Wages Resolution, the intention was to reduce wages and to weaken union organisation. The impact of the Act can, however, be minimised.

There is nothing unlawful about a condition requiring contractors to observe minimum terms and conditions. For example, the national building workers' agreement requires all sub-contractors to pay collectively agreed national minimum rates. Employers cannot specify union membership but can specify adherence to union-negotiated rates. Pressure to include a requirement like this, and to exclude contractors who do not observe it, is quite lawful. Although the Fair Wages Resolution was repealed in 1983, it never did apply directly to local authorities and nationalised industries but was incorporated voluntarily into their contractors' conditions. In some local authorities similar terms form part of their standing orders. In so far as they require contractors to observe the going rate, therefore, they are unaffected by the repeal of the FWR or by sections 12–13 of the 1982 Act.

In any event, you can ensure your pressure is directed against contractors not observing proper health and safety standards, skill levels, equal opportunities, apprentice ratios, pay and other conditions arising out of union organisation.

If a union is recognised by a contractor, but it has complained about redundancies or health and safety, you *can* refuse to deal with the product or services. The Act says discrimination against a contractor who does not consult with a union is illegal, but since there is a legal obligation to consult recognised unions on takeovers, redundancies, health and safety and pensions, your refusal to deal with contractors who did not or do not consult on these matters is due to *their* refusal to observe the law, rather than *yours*.

Admission and expulsion of members in closed shops

Members' rights within the union are laid down by the rulebook and the 'rules of natural justice' (see page 326). You also have the right, on giving notice and complying with any reasonable conditions, to resign (TULRA section 7).

Applicants for membership, however, had no right (except during 1971–74) to join or to be fairly considered, despite a contrary view expressed by Lord Denning in 1966.

Sections 4 and 5 of the Employment Act 1980 now give substantial new grounds on which individuals can challenge unions. **If you work, or are seeking work in a job where there is a union membership agreement (UMA) you have the right:**

1. not to have your application for membership of the union unreasonably refused; and

2. not to be unreasonably expelled from the union.

You can claim compensation if the union infringes these rights. Union rules or collective agreements cannot exclude these rights, which are additional to any you have under common law or the rule-book. A Code of Practice contains the government's view of trade union practice which tribunals can use when assessing 'unreasonableness'. Although not binding, this Code is very influential – see page 345.

Who can claim?

The new rights apply only to 'employment by an employer with respect to which it is the practice in accordance with a union membership agreement, for the employee to belong to a specified trade union or one of a number of specified trade unions'. So there must be evidence of such a UMA in practice.

■ **Example:** If you are working in a company where a UMA is in force, or if you have applied for a job there, you can bring a claim if the union does not admit you.

There is no requirement, though, that you must have been dismissed or refused a job by any particular employer. While it is possible for you to claim against a union without showing you have suffered any direct loss, problems of proof are likely to arise.

If you can't show some connection with 'employment with an employer' who operates a closed shop your claim should fail. Some industries are exclusively unionised – the merchant navy and West End theatres – so you can easily say that any employment in them will be covered by a UMA. But it is possible to get a job in journalism, for instance, without being in the NUJ. Unless you can demonstrate the practice of a UMA at some particular newspaper which you have applied to, it is difficult to say that you are covered by section 4.

In many cases a claim against the union is the only remedy,

with no right of action against any employer. This is so when loss of union membership results in dismissal from a job in a long-standing closed shop. The employer has a defence against an unfair dismissal claim (see page 336) but this does not preclude a claim against the union for unreasonable explusion. Nor is there any claim on an employer who **refuses to hire** an expelled member.

■ **Example**: X has been expelled from the union. At a job interview he tells this to a prospective employer who then refuses to hire him. X may have a claim against the union, but no claim is possible against the prospective employer.

In some circumstances a claim could succeed against both an employer and the union.

■ **Example**: A new UMA is concluded between the union and the management. Y applies to join the union and is refused. Y is dismissed because of non-membership. She can sue the employer for unfair dismissal because existing employees are exempt (see page 336). If she thinks the union's grounds for refusing membership are unreasonable, she can sue the union. And if the union put pressure on the employer to sack her, the employer can 'join' the union as a co-defendant and require it to pay some or all of the compensation awarded for unfair dismissal.

What is unreasonable?

No definition has been provided in the Act of what constitutes unreasonableness. The Code is therefore of direct relevance. Government ministers glibly said that tribunals are already experienced in dealing with the concept in unfair dismissal cases so need no further assistance. Yet the issues involved in union membership cases are likely to be economic and political, making it impossible for tribunals to judge what a 'reasonable union' would be. Wide discretion is given in section 4 (5) of the Act, which says that decisions are to be based on

equity and the substantial merits of the case, and in particular a union shall not be regarded as having acted reasonably only because it acted in accordance with the requirements of its rules, or unreasonably only because it has acted in contravention of them.

Policies and rules determined by democratic organisations are therefore pushed into second place to value-judgments of industrial tribunals. Members already have the legal right to require adherence to rules. If individuals find the rules offensive, they ought to challenge them through the democratic procedures of the union and not through the law.

The government has not only given the tribunals power to override the rules, but has also stipulated the kind of rules unions ought to have. The Code of Practice gives a list of matters that should guide unions in making rules, or making decisions, on admission and expulsion.

1. Qualifications

The Code says that unions should have a clear definition of who is qualified to join. Unions define this in many ways. Some demand that you should be in a specific occupation, such as a government scientist, or work in a specified industry, such as the railways. Some require craft status by virtue of having served an apprenticeship. Some require a qualification – a pilot's licence, or a deputy's certificate in mining. Some deliberately restrict entry in order to control labour supply.

Now all of these qualifying rules can be challenged by a person refused entry. It is unlikely that tribunals will override clear occupational, industrial or professional stipulations. But those based broadly on economic grounds could be opened up by tribunals asking whether an applicant 'has the appropriate qualifications for the type of work done by members of the union'.

2. Internal procedures

Individuals are not required to pursue or exhaust any internal appeal procedure before going to a tribunal. But the Code says that unions should not take action which would mean individuals losing their jobs until all internal procedures, including the Independent Review Committee (see below), have been exhausted. The TUC recommend that no penalty should be imposed before the appeal process has been completed. According to an official study, 75 out of 79 unions studied, representing 11.6 million members, had procedures for appeals against disciplinary action (*Employment Gazette*, June 1980). Yet the Code encourages individuals to ignore these:

Since an individual may face considerable loss or adverse social consequences as a result of exclusion or expulsion from a union, it would be unreasonable to expect him to defer his application to a tribunal.

Tribunals might, however, develop the Code's procedural rules and require individual workers to use internal appeal procedures which 'are to be preferred to legal action' (para 53).

Any rule prohibiting legal action against the union, or until procedure has been exhausted, is of no effect (1980 Act, section 4 (11)), and the courts have not been slow to step into internal union affairs:

■ As part of its campaign for increased London allowances, NALGO asked its members not to volunteer to assist in the 1974 London borough elections. Louise Esterman refused and was summoned to a disciplinary branch meeting. She got an injunction to stop the meeting on the grounds that she **doubted whether NALGO acted within its rules** in calling for this action **and** because she considered NALGO's decision was 'insupportable and objectionable'. She **did not pursue internal appeals**, or even wait for the branch's decision. *Esterman v NALGO* 1974 (HC)

3. Independent Review Committee

The TUC's Independent Review Committee (IRC) hears complaints by individuals who have been sacked from a closed shop as a result of being expelled from, or refused admission to, a union. Its constitution requires individuals to have exhausted their union's internal appeal procedures. In its first four years, 30 cases within its terms of reference were registered. None of its recommendations has been rejected by affiliated unions. Reference to the IRC is now envisaged in many closed shop agreements negotiated after 1976, and in rules of several unions. Specific mention was made of its functions in the TUC Guide on Union Organisation, published in February 1979, following the short-lived agreement with the Labour government. The Code also envisages reference to the IRC as a step in internal appeals. Although it enjoins unions to use it before refusing or excluding membership, the Code does not place such a duty on the complainant.

The Committee's procedure is:

1. You complain to the Secretary at Congress House, Great Russell Street, London WC1.

2. The Committee must be satisfied, before considering an

appeal, that you have been dismissed and have exhausted all internal union procedures.

3. The Committee will discuss the case with the union and you, and will try to resolve the matter by agreement.

4. If agreement cannot be reached the Committee will make a recommendation about whether or not you should be admitted to the union, or, if you have been expelled, whether or not you should be taken back into the union, and, if so, upon what conditions. There is then a 'clear responsibility' on the part of the union concerned to act upon such a recommendation.

4. Inter-union procedures

The TUC stipulates model rules on the handling of applications for membership from members of other unions (see page 327). The Employment Acts say nothing about these. Only the Code mentions that unions can reasonably have regard to TUC principles and Disputes Committee findings in rejecting members.

TUC rules preclude unions from organising workers in an establishment where another has a majority of the employees in membership and negotiates for them, as is the case wherever a UMA exists.

■ **Example**: New starters at XYZ food factory must join the GMBATU within four weeks. A is taken on and says he was a member of USDAW. In response to an enquiry it appears that A is three months in arrears, so the GMBATU refuse to admit him. A is sacked for not being in compliance with the UMA. He claims the GMBATU has unreasonably refused membership. The tribunal could ignore the TUC rules, and decide that a matter of only three months' arrears was insufficient reason for rejecting a member and causing his dismissal.

Established demarcation and bargaining unit boundaries could be overturned by impulsive exercise of tribunals' powers.

■ **Example**: A closed shop exists in a local authority requiring emplyees to be members of the TGWU, NUPE or GMBATU. Spheres of influence have been agreed by the unions, so that refuse collectors are in the TGWU and street cleaners in NUPE. The TGWU refuses to accept a new starter in street cleaning who objects to joining NUPE. When s/he is sacked for not being a member, s/he claims unfair dismissal against the council. The tribunal says his/her reasons for objecting to NUPE aren't genuine. But it says s/he has the right to join either GMBATU or TGWU, rejecting the latter's argument that it was precluded by the spheres of influence agreement from taking in street sweepers.

In the above example, if the tribunal's award were followed, an inter-union row could arise which could be settled only by a TUC Disputes Committee ruling, consistent with the Bridlington principles but inconsistent with the tribunal's (see *Cheall*'s case, page 327, however).

5. Lapsed members

Many union rule-books say that members in arrears automatically cease to be members, and have no rights of appeal. Almost all unions place responsibility for payment of dues on the members. Section 4 (9) of the 1980 Act treats this as expulsion, so tribunals have jurisdiction to hear whether or not a particular union's rules on lapsed members are reasonable.

6. Maintaining job-security and working conditions

Some unions operate in industries where, without closed shop agreements, job-security and working conditions would deteriorate rapidly. So control is exercised over those entering the industry by controlling union admission. Some crafts, for example, and the entertainment industry, control labour supply in order to resist dilution and unemployment of members. In assessing whether an applicant has been unreasonably refused admission tribunals are forced to make judgments about unions' labour market policies.

The Code, at least, recognises that unions can act reasonably in refusing membership if,

> because of the nature of the work concerned, for example, acting, the number of applicants or potential applicants is so great as to pose a serious threat of undermining negotiated terms and conditions of employment.

7. Industrial action

More explicit is the guidance given in the Code in cases where members are expelled for reasons connected with their failure to participate in industrial action. These owe more to bogeymen created by the media – particularly during the 1979 lorry drivers' strike – than to practice. Nevertheless feelings run high against members who don't observe union solidarity in a dispute, and subsequently get the benefits members have fought for.

■ In 1967 James Goad refused to take part in an unofficial
strike by AUEW members at CAV's Sudbury, Suffolk plant.
He allowed his membership to lapse and was refused
readmission in 1971. He got a ruling under the 1971 Act that
he was entitled to be a member. The Industrial Court
ordered the union to allow him to attend branch meetings,
but it refused to comply. The AUEW's assets were seized
and it was fined £55,00. *Goad v AUEW* 1972 (NIRC)

The Code therefore says that action should not be taken
against a member who refused to take part in industrial action
which would involve breach of a statutory duty, the criminal
law, a procedure agreement or professional ethics, or cause
serious risk to public safety, health or property, or which had
not been affirmed by secret ballot!

The 1982 Act introduced an amendment for workers who
hold qualifications which subject them to a code of conduct (see
page 337). If you are expelled from a union for refusing to take
part in industrial action or refuse to join a union because industrial action is in breach of the Code, you can claim compensation should you be sacked for non-membership. The provision,
designed to promote non-militant professional bodies to the
exclusion of the bona fide trade unions, applies mainly to medical, para-medical and nursing professions, where, for example,
the General Nursing Council decreed that striking was inconsistent with nurses' duties.

■ NALGO called a strike in Scottish Gas in support of sacked
members. The UMA in the gas industry acknowledges that
safety cover needs to be maintained and that in a dispute discussions will ensue between the unions and the employer to
agree cover. No agreement was made, since NALGO felt
that this provision would be and was being abused to break
the strike. An engineer who was told to return to work was
expelled by the union branch. Before appealing to the
national executive he went to court. The court said that the
NALGO rule requiring members to follow instructions to
strike, although generally valid, was overridden by the specific clause in the UMA which was part of their contracts of
employment. The union was therefore acting beyond its rules
and could not expel him. *Partington v NALGO* 1981 (Court
of Session Outer House)

The Code also says it is unreasonable to take action against people who cross a picket line 'which the union had not authorised or which was not at the member's place of work'. There is, though, no statutory protection for members who face disciplinary action by their employers as a result of refusing to cross a picket line.

All these conditions are aimed at cutting down the ability of union members to enforce their own rules. The list of excuses in the Code is used as a general test of the acceptability of industrial action. In fact it is difficult to envisage any action which does not run foul of one or another of them.

■ In 1963 a Bradford textile firm locked out its unionised workers. The dispute lasted two years. The National Union of Dyers and Bleachers has ever since boycotted the firm and anyone who subsequently worked there. J. Thompson worked there in 1965 for three months, when he was 19. Thirteen years later his union card was removed and as a result he was sacked from the firm where he had been working for three-and-a-half years. He appealed to the IRC, which said the union had not followed its own expulsion rules and anyway that he could not have been acting contrary to union policy 13 years earlier as he was not then a member. The IRC gave him back his card and asked the union to help him find work in another section of the industry covered by the union. If did not, however, say that the boycotting of the firm was unreasonable. *Thompson and NUDB & TW* 1979 (IRC)

Most unions contain rules providing for expulsion of members who act contrary to the interests or policies of the union, and these are the grounds on which expulsion connected with industrial action occurs – see, for example, *Porter v NUJ* (page 329). Some unions explicitly define anti-union activity. The NGA makes it an offence, for example, for members to handle work from an 'unrecognised source', a rule which may cause further liability under section 14 of the Employment Act 1982 (see page 348). And the sheet metal workers' union prohibits members from adopting certain forms of work measurement.

8. Political reasons
Workers refused admission, or expelled, because of their political views are not precluded from alleging that this is unreason-

able if they work in a closed shop. Unions have repudiated members of the National Front and there is certainly scope within most rule-books for expulsion of racists for acting against the interests of the union. Several unions, and the TUC, have policies to prevent racists holding office or using the union as a platform.

■ The NUJ refused to admit a National Front member, working on a National Front publication. He claimed that this was unreasonable and arbitrary under section 5 of the TULRA, which was repealed in 1976. The tribunal and the EAT upheld the NUJ mainly on procedural grounds – he had not pursued an internal appeal. But they added that he would not, in any event, be able to comply with the union's standards as he stood for much that was against the subsequently adopted NUJ Code of Conduct. *McCalden v NUJ* 1977 (EAT)

Claims

A claim under section 4 of the Employment Act 1980 must be presented to a tribunal within six months of the date of expulsion or refusal. The tribunal has power to extend this period if it was not reasonably practicable to present the claim in time.

There may be some difficulty in deciding the date on which the action took place, so two further definitions are given in the Act.

If the application for membership has not been granted or rejected within a reasonable period, the union is taken to have refused admission on the last day of this notional period. If the rules say that you lose membership on the happening of some specified event – such as beng so many weeks in arrears, or moving outside the industry – the Act treats this as expulsion.

As we have seen, the Act places no obligation on the individual to follow any appeals procedure within the union before bringing a claim to a tribunal, but under the 1974–76 law the EAT said that, in determining reasonableness and the grant of remedies, it is 'relevant' to ask whether internal rights of appeal have been pursued. By analogy with unfair dismissal cases, tribunals will look less favourably on an individual who rushes to a hearing before exhausting the union's own internal procedures. This might even include exercising the right of appeal to the IRC, especially when the union, or the collective agreement setting up the UMA, specifically refers to such a right (see page 354).

Powers

If the tribunal finds that the union acted unreasonably in refusing admission or in expelling the claimant, it must make a declaration to that effect. The tribunal does not have power to order the union to admit the individual but s/he can apply for compensation.

This application can be made as soon as four weeks or up to six months, after the date of the declaration. This effectively leaves only four weeks for negotiations before permitting individuals to seek legal sanctions.

There are two routes to compensation, depending on whether or not the union has acted on the declaration. In both cases the amounts can be enormous.

1. If the union complies: The applicant can still claim compensation even if the union admits or readmits him/her. The claim is made to an industrial tribunal which has the power to award what it considers appropriate for the purpose of compensating the applicant for the loss sustained by him/her in consequence of the refusal or expulsion.

This is subject to the same upper limits as those applying in unfair dismissal cases – £11,700 in 1983/84, see pages 477–83. Compensation in unfair dismissal cases partly depends on age and service, but no such limitations apply in union exclusion cases. As with unfair dismissal, the amount can be cut down if the applicant caused or contributed to the exclusion, or failed to mitigate his/her loss.

In reality, assessing compensation is made difficult by imponderable factors, particularly in refusal-to-admit cases.

■ **Example**: X, an HGV driver, is refused admission to a local branch of the TGWU in an area where many drivers are out of work. He applies for a job where there is a UMA requiring employees to join the TGWU within 21 days. He doesn't get the job and management give no reasons. He claims this was due to his not holding a TGWU card. But to get compensation he would have to prove the connection. Would he have got the job? Would he have been refused admission again? Could he have got a job anywhere else?

Similar problems have faced workers' claims under the sex

and race discrimination laws. Losses are even more difficult to calculate if there has been no job refusal. For instance, not holding a TGWU card may not be fatal to a professional driver's career. Many employers have no UMA or no union at all. Other unions – URTU and GMBATU – organise in the industry and their cards would suffice. It is only in cases of dismissal from existing jobs that compensation is likely to be directly attributable to loss of union membership, and here compensation can be very high.

Nor are the losses limited to those arising between the date of expulsion and readmission. Theoretically any loss in consequence of the original decision attracts compensation, and readmission to the union does not halt the union's liability.

2. If the union doesn't comply: A complainant who has been given a declaration can apply to the EAT, if s/he has not been admitted or readmitted to the union. In assessing compensation, the EAT must consider whether the complainant has caused or contributed to the expulsion or refusal, or has failed to do everything to reduce the losses suffered as a result. But the basis of compensation is now quite different from that used in cases where the union has admitted or readmitted the member. Instead of calculating the member's losses, the EAT can award whatever money it considers just and equitable in all the circumstances up to the maximum available in unfair dismissal cases (£18,980 in 1983/84).

Appeals

Union exclusion receives preferential treatment over all other cases. You can appeal to the EAT **on a question of law** against a tribunal decision relating to any of your individual employment law rights. But you can also appeal **on a question of fact** in cases of union exclusion or expulsion. This facility **should** be available in other cases, but the only justification for elevating union exclusion cases above all the other individual employment rights is to encourage attacks on union organisation.

An appeal on **facts** can be brought only against the intitial hearing by a tribunal. An appeal against compensation – the second hearing – must be on **law**.

The role of tribunals

Industrial tribunals have the task of judging workers' claims

about exclusion or expulsion from the union, and of victimisation and dismissal, in relation to closed shops. They now decide
not only questions of fact and law but the political and
economic issues involved in individual objections to union
membership. They assess the genuineness of a personal conviction, or the strength of a conscientious belief. They determine
the substance of grievances against any particular union which
may be the grounds for a refusal to join, and they are required
to judge democratically-made union policies and rule-books.
The scope for endless litigation and individualistic value-
judgments is enormous.

Problems can also be raised about any ballots conducted
under the new requirements. For example, a worker sacked for
non-compliance with a UMA could challenge in a claim for
unfair dismissal the employer's defence that the UMA was
approved in a proper ballot. The tribunal therefore would
decide whether the constituency of the bargaining group balloting for a UMA was correct or reasonable, and whether a fair
procedure was adopted. There is no escaping the fact that such
claims are subject to economic and political considerations
which tribunals are not competent to deal with. In particular,
they are empowered to apportion compensation where a union
or individuals put pressure on an employer to dismiss someone.

It is inevitable that the High Court will also have a role in
UMAs. Actions by individuals claiming that a ballot was
improperly conducted, or that certain groups were left out of
the constituency, can be brought in the High Court. Again no
criteria are given in the Act for settling such questions of industrial relations and economics. Furthermore, unions have no role
in disputes over union membership unless 'joined' as a party by
the employer or worker – see above. **The TUC therefore advised
all its nominees on tribunal panels not to take part in hearings
involving disputes over union membership**.

How to stay organised

Many strong trade union workplaces are threatened by the
Employment Acts. Workplace representatives are under pressure to change agreements and to test them by ballot. You can
withstand attacks on your agreements by strengthening union
membership and tightening up on procedures negotiated with

management. For example, 100 per cent membership can be maintained if you:

1. Make regular checks of members' cards, or agree check-off facilities, i.e. deduction of union dues from wages.

2. Ensure immediate contact is made with new starters.

3. Ask management to screen job applicants for possible objections to union membership. There is no remedy for someone refused a job on these grounds.

4. Refuse to renegotiate existing agreements and insist on rigorous adherence to them.

5. Resist calls to conduct ballots of the Employment Act type.

6. Refuse inter-union transfers except in accordance with the TUC Bridlington Agreement.

7. Educate and re-educate your members to counteract pressure to dismantle existing closed shops.

8. Get your employer to maintain a **fair list** of contractors who observe proper standards and procedures for pay, conditions, health and safety, equal opportunities, training and skill. These are all going to be better in organised workplaces.

Summary

1. A valid UMA gives employers a defence to dismissal and victimisation claims.

2. There is no legal ban on UMAs and no general requirement that they be approved by an Employment Act ballot.

3. People employed before the UMA, or who have a personal conviction against unions in general or any particular union, are protected against dismissal and victimisation.

4. Union labour only requirements in contracts are unlawful, as is pressure to impose them or to exclude people from tendering; but it is legitimate to require adherence to specified minimum labour standards and to union-negotiated national or local rates.

5. Workers unreasonably expelled or excluded from a union in an industry where a closed shop operates can claim to a tribunal.

6. In this, and in dismissal and victimisation cases, the union can be 'joined' as defendant and ordered to pay some or all of the substantial compensation which can be awarded.

7. After 1 November 1984 any dismissal is unfair if the UMA was not approved by ballot during the previous five years.

15. Disclosure of information

Your right to get information from your employer / financial information companies must give under company law / information for tribunal proceedings / information employers must give for bargaining under the Employment Protection Act 1975 / who can claim / what kind of information / the exceptions / the procedures / and their effectiveness / information relevant to health, safety and welfare / trade union demands.

Disclosure of information to trade unions is often confused with discussions on workers' participation and industrial democracy. In fact these are entirely separate issues. Disclosure of information is an integral part of collective bargaining between unions and employers, and does not necessarily erode the conflict between them. Indeed information discovered about the company has always been an essential weapon for trade unionists in any struggle. Employers' reluctance to divulge information is an admission of conflict. This chapter looks at disclosure of information, and not at any proposals for industrial democracy.

Disclosure is not an end in itself. It is a step towards giving the unions power to discuss issues from the same background of knowledge as management, and thereby to spot management's half-truths, concealment and deceit. The right to know what's going on at work is a basic demand. The law recognises this right only to a limited degree.

For this reason unions need to demand information, and

force management to agree to regular disclosure. Targets for union demands are dealt with at the end of the chapter.

Where to find the law

The law requires information to be made available in the following ways:

Financial information	Companies Acts 1948–81
Information on employee involvement	Companies Act 1967 Section 16 as amended by Employment Act 1982
Information for bargaining	Employment Protection Act 1975 (EPA) sections 17–21
Information for tribunal proceedings	Industrial Tribunal Regulations 1980 (SI 1980 No 884)
Information for health, safety and welfare	Health and Safety at Work Act 1974 (HSWA) sections 2, 3, 28, 79
Consultation about redundancies and business transfers	EPA 1975 section 99; Transfer of Undertakings Regulations 1981 (see chapter 18)
Particulars of your contract of employment	Employment Protection Consolidation Act 1978 section 1 (see page 37)

Diagram 8 on page 375 sets out the various procedures that you have to follow in order to get the data you want.

Financial information

A full list of what every limited company is obliged to disclose annually under the Companies Acts 1948–81 is given in the detailed legislation itself. The annual balance sheet and profit and loss account must be prepared by independent auditors *for the shareholders* and this is open to inspection by the public at Companies House (addresses on page 512).

The Registrar does not, however, keep the records up to date. At any one time about one-third of the 800,000 or so registered companies are in default, yet there are fewer than 1,000 prosecutions a year.

Local authorities, nationalised industries and charities are required to render annual accounts too.

Ironically, despite a Royal Commission under Lord Bullock, a government White Paper and years of debate, the only formal advance of workers' interests through greater control of public companies came with the Tories' 1980 Companies Act, section 46 of which says:

> Duty in relation to employees: the matters to which the directors of a company are to have regard in the performance of their functions shall include the interests of the company's employees in general as well as the interests of its members [i.e. the shareholders].

For over 200 years the directors of companies had no duty to consider the interest of employees. Indeed, if they did they acted illegally and could be challenged by the shareholders. This happened in 1962 when a shareholder sued the directors of the *News Chronicle* who wanted to pay compensation – redundancy pay – to their employees who were sacked on the spot one night when it 'merged' with the Daily Mail (*Parke v Daily News* 1962 (HC)).

Even with the new duty, it is only the shareholders and not the employees who can complain if the interests of employees are not considered. Nor are the directors obliged to *act* in the employees' interests – only to *consider* them. In section 74 companies are given power to make payments to present and former employees. But the exercise of this power will continue to be controlled by the shareholders unless the company's constitution is amended to empower the directors. The 1982 Employment Act, which amends section 16 of the Companies Act 1967, requires companies employing on average 250 people a week in the UK to provide a statement in the annual accounts describing action that has been taken to introduce, maintain or develop arrangements aimed at:

- providing employees systematically with information on matters of concern to them as employees,
- consulting employees or their representatives on a regular basis so that the views of employees can be taken into

account in making decisions which are likely to affect their interests,

- encouraging the involvement of employees in the company's performance through an employees' share scheme or by some other means,
- achieving a common awareness on the part of all employees of the financial and economic factors affecting the performance of the company.

Information for tribunal proceedings

You can demand disclosure of the documents you need for industrial tribunal proceedings on the same grounds as are allowed for county court cases – IT Regulations 1980 rule 4. Broadly, these cover all papers except those which the tribunal considers 'are not necessary either for disposing fairly of the proceedings or for saving costs'. Failure to provide sight of the documents carries a £100 fine and the case can be dismissed.

Questionnaires are available in sex and race discrimination cases to probe employers on their practice and procedures – see page 490.

Information for bargaining

Section 17 of the EPA 1975 imposes a duty on employers to provide unions they recognise with information for bargaining. The Advisory, Conciliation and Arbitration Service (ACAS) has published a Code of Practice giving guidelines on what should, and should not, be disclosed.

Who can demand disclosure?:
An independent trade union recognised by an employer can request information. The information must be given to representatives who are **authorised to carry on collective bargaining**, such as full-time officials or shop stewards. The union must be recognised for the group of workers which is making the request and the recognition must be for *negotiations*.

- ASTMS was recognised for negotiating a range of conditions including salary scales at BTP's five factories and labs in north-east England. It also had the right to make representations on behalf of members within the procedure for challenging job evaluation. The union sought information about the scheme which the CAC said was relevant to its dual role – negotiating and making representations. On appeal, the High Court said that ASTMS could use the EPA only for matters on which it had recognition for *negotiating* rights and not for making representations within the job evaluation procedure. *R v CAC, BTP Dioxide* 1981 (HC)

Employers have to disclose information only if requested to. Your employer can get you to put your request in writing, and it is always best to do this anyway.

The Crown and the NHS are covered by the same duty, and can be told by the Central Arbitration Committee (CAC) to disclose information, but there is no way of enforcing this.

What information?
Under section 17 of the EPA 1975 your employer must disclose information which satisfies all the following four conditions:

1. The information is needed for any stage of negotiations.

2. Without it the union representatives would be seriously impeded in negotiating.

3. Good industrial relations practice requires the employer to give this sort of information to the union to help in its negotiations.

4. The information must be in his/her or an associated employer's possession.

The information is to be made available **for all the stages of collective bargaining.** As preparing for negotiations is part of collective bargaining you can start collecting and preparing data long before the negotiations begin.

■ Three universities refused to respond to a NALGO questionnaire on the grounds that no claim was currently being made. The CAC ordered them to reply. The union would be impeded in collective bargaining if it could not get information which would influence the formulation of a claim. *Universities of Birmingham, Warwick and Aston v NALGO* 1979 (CAC)

A claim for information can also be pressed even if the negotiations it relates to are over or never got off the ground as long as the subject matter remains relevant.

■ BL wanted to increase production at Cowley. The TGWU objected and when the issue was put into the disputes procedure, requested specific information. BL then dropped the proposal and refused the information. The CAC said that since the issue related to staffing levels it was recurring and therefore information on it was within the scope of the EPA. For other reasons, however, the CAC turned down the claim. *Pressed Steel Fisher v TGWU* 1979 (CAC)

The legal scope of bargaining issues is given on page 313. Employers may argue that mergers, pricing, marketing, investment, research and developement are not covered by the legal definition. But 'conditions of employment' is probably wide enough to include these subjects.

The CAC (or the Northern Ireland Industrial Court) judges what constitutes *serious impediment*, but no criteria are laid down. It also judges *good industrial relations practice*, for which the Code of Practice sets guidelines. (See page 17 for the effect of Codes).

The Code lists the following data that should be given.

Pay and benefits: principles and structure of payment systems; job evaluation systems and grading criteria; earnings and hours analysed according to work-group, grade, plant, sex, outworkers and homeworkers, department or division, giving – where appropriate – distributions and make-up of pay, showing any additions to basic rate or salary; total pay bill; details of fringe benefits and non-wage labour costs.

Conditions of service: policies on recruitment, redeployment, redundancy, training, equal opportunity and promotion; appraisal systems; health, welfare and safety matters.

Manpower: numbers employed analysed according to grade, department, location, age and sex; labour turnover; absenteeism; overtime and short time; manning standards; planned changes in work methods, materials, equipment or organisation; available manpower plans; investment plans.

Performance: productivity and efficiency data; savings from increased productivity and output; return on capital invested; sales and state of order book.

Financial: cost structures; gross and net profits; sources of earnings; assets; liabilities; allocation of profits; details of government financial assistance; transfer prices; loans to parent companies and interest charged.

This list is *not exhaustive*, nor is it mandatory. It is useful as a checklist when drawing up your basic demands. The TUC has also drawn up a checklist – see page 379.

You can use the EPA 1975 to get financial information from organisations not covered by the Companies Acts, such as associated and subsidiary companies, local authorities, charities and private companies.

■ ASTMS wanted information about the performance of Sweda, part of a US-owned conglomerate which had pleaded poverty in response to a wage claim. The CAC said that as a general rule a UK subsidiary of a multinational company should disclose to the unions the accounts which would be required of a UK company. *Sweda International v ASTMS* 1981 (CAC)

What are the exceptions?
The Act and the Code are riddled with exceptions. Obstructive employers with sharp advisers will be anxious to exploit them. There are six specific situations (section 19) where there is **no obligation to disclose.** These cover information which:

1. it would be against the interest of national security to disclose;

2. your employer is under a statutory obligation to keep secret;

3. 'has been communicated to the employer in confidence';

4. relates to a specific individual who does not want it disclosed;

5. 'would cause substantial injury to the employer's undertaking for reasons other than its effect on collective bargaining';

6. is obtained for the purpose of legal proceedings.

National security can be pleaded by any employer. If it is backed up with a certificate from a government ministry, it cannot be challenged in any way. People who work for the Crown, the NHS and government contractors are most vulnerable.

The confidentiality and substantial injury exceptions are full of difficulty for unions. Information about takeovers, expansion, capital spending, investment, and research and development might be wrapped up in these two exclusions. These are not, however, mentioned in the Code. The examples given in it are the cost of individual products, *detailed* analysis of proposed investment, marketing and pricing policies, price quotas, and the make-up of tender prices.

In practice, employers have used a combination of the above exceptions, together with restrictive views of recognition, 'serious impediment' and 'good industrial relations practice', as arguments to refuse disclosure. Some illustrations may be useful in making claims.

The most important limitation is the concept that a union is entitled only to information relevant to the workers it represents, and the matters for which it is recognised. The CAC said this 'limits the trade union to the parameters of its own bargaining table'.

■ The non-TUC Institute of Journalists sought information about pay in a range of non-journalist grades. The CAC said a union had to show the information was not only relevant but also important for its members, so that pay in other bargaining units should be disclosed only if it was closely relevant and good practice required it. This included employee numbers, pay structures, wage bill and rate changes of broadly similar earnings groups including journalists, managers and skilled production workers. *Daily Telegraph v IoJ* 1978 (CAC)

These limitations denied claims for information about directors' pensions when staff employees were faced with apparently less advantageous arrangements (*Ingall v APEX* 1979 (CAC)) and knowledge of the profits of a three-site company in which the AUEW had members at only one, since the union would not be impeded in its *local* negotiations (*Airwork v AUEW* 1978 (CAC)). Clearly, if you can show national factors are relevant in local bargaining, you can demand the national information.

Information relating to other bargaining units is often important and should ideally be exchanged between the TUC unions. If·this does not happen you can't expect the CAC to order it.

■ Four unions negotiated separately. In order to prepare a claim for semi-skilled workers the TGWU sought information about skilled workers' bonus. The CAC said the union was not impeded in *its* negotiations and, since the unions defended separate bargaining, it was not good practice to disclose it. *Fairfield-Mabey v TGWU* 1980 (CAC)

Similarly BSC refused to give details of a plant-wide productivity scheme applying to 4,000 workers when asked by UCATT, which represented 100 others. It got only the information relating to building workers (*BSC, Stanton and Staveley v UCATT* 1979 (CAC). Nevertheless, you can always argue that pay arrangements for other workers do affect your claims and that you cannot negotiate realistically without hearing of all the pay and bonus schemes on site.

If one group's scheme *directly affects* yours, the information can be ordered.

■ ASTMS negotiated for junior staff grades 1–6, who wanted a productivity scheme. It sought details of the schemes used for senior staff above grade 6. The CAC ordered disclosure of the scheme's details because there was an overlap of work done by junior and senior staff, and the union was entitled to assess the validity of management's view that extension of the scheme was impracticable. *TI Tube Division v ASTMS* 1980 (CAC)

Unions have been refused information relating to privatisation of public services. Despite the fact that unions are often forced to negotiate blind against undisclosed feasibility study savings or tender returns, the CAC has upheld employers' refusal to disclose vitally relevant price information.

■ The Ministry of Defence at Bath said cleaning was cheaper under contractors and the CSU asked for information about the contractors' conditions. The Ministry said the contractors gave the information in confidence, and since they resisted disclosure to the union the CAC 'reluctantly' did not order it. *CSU v CAC* 1980 (HC)

You could argue that as employees of the public authority you are not in the same arm's-length position as firms submitting tenders, should not be covered by the same strict rules on tendering, and should as part of the collective bargaining process be entitled to see the lowest bid before a decision is made. Nor would the confidentiality exception seem to prevent your obtaining sight of the tender bids so long as the contractors' names are kept secret.

The substance of reports made to councils can be demanded under section 17.

■ The Tory-controlled GLC considered a report on the future of its housing construction branch. It routinely gave council and committee reports to the unions but in this case gave only the factual information and not the opinions. The CAC said existing practice should not be changed and the substance of the opinions should be disclosed. *GLC v GLC Staff Association and UCATT* 1979 (CAC)

If the information you are seeking is copyright, the CAC cannot order its disclosure but it does have the power to inspect it itself.

■ The Access credit card consortium and the union agreed to salary reviews based on a survey conducted by an independent company. Access agreed to give the relevant information but not to hand over the actual report. The CAC said the information had been obtained from survey subscribers in confidence and was copyright material. As the substance had been disclosed, the actual report need not be. *Joint Credit Card Co v NUBE* 1978 (CAC)

Information from which individual employees' data can be gleaned can sometimes be the subject of a CAC order even though this information in itself could be regarded as confidential.

■ APEX thought the company operated the criteria for progression through grades either incorrectly or discriminatorily, so it asked for minimum and maximum salaries, and the spread of pay rates according to sex and hours worked. The company said if it gave these, individuals' salaries could be identified. The CAC nevertheless felt that collective bargaining required the data to be given. *British Aerospace Dynamics v APEX* 1980 (CAC)

The Code says that management must explain their reasons in detail and they must be able to substantiate them at an

enquiry by ACAS or the CAC. The burden of proof is on management, who will not be allowed to get away with ticking 'confidential' labels on all their documents, or with over-reacting to
the prospect of injury to their business. The Act excludes information which *would* cause substantial injury, not that which
could possibly cause it.

Packaging the information

You can ask management to disclose information, or to confirm
it, in writing. But you have no right to have the data audited
either by independent examiners, or by union-appointed auditors. Nor is your employer required to allow you to inspect any
document, or to make a copy – see the *GLC* and *Joint Credit
Card* cases above. So you may have to accept management's
written assurance as to what a document contains. There is no
obligation on your employer to disclose matters which are relevant, but merely *incidental* to the data requested. For
example, you may be given raw figures from a management
consultant's report, without the consultant's comments and
opinions.

Management can get out of providing information if this
'would involve an amount of work or expenditure out of reasonable proportion to the value of the information in the conduct
of collective bargaining'.

The law treats shareholders much more seriously than it
treats unions. Shareholders' information is packaged according
to the Companies Acts and it must be prepared and certified by
independent accountants.

How to claim

Diagram 8 on page 375 shows the procedure for making a legal
claim for information. The Northern Ireland Industrial Court and
Labour Relations Agency correspond to the CAC and ACAS.

Step 1: Complaint

The union complains in writing to the CAC if, following a written request, management
  1. refuse to provide information, quoting one of the
defences, for instance 'substantial injury'; or
  2. provide inadequate information; or
  3. provide information which the union thinks incorrect.

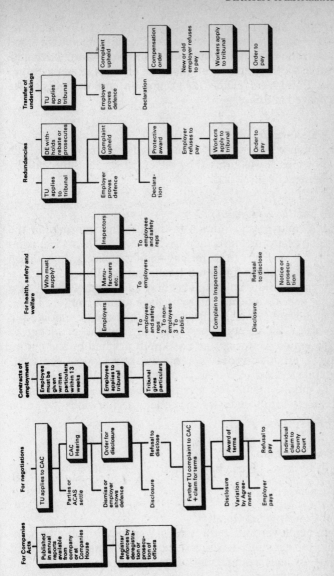

Diagram 8 **Procedures for obtaining information**

The CAC may (but is not obliged to) ask ACAS to conciliate. If there is no conciliation, or if there is no settlement, the CAC must hear the complaint. Any person or organisation having an interest in the complaint is entitled to a say – for example, other unions. Employers' claims for exemption, and defences, have to be proved at this stage.

Step 2: Declaration
If the union wins, the CAC must specify the information, the date on which it was refused by the employer, and the date by which it must be disclosed.

Step 3: Further complaint
If your employer still refuses to disclose the information the union complains *again* to the CAC. The CAC hears the complaint and gives its reasons for any finding it makes. In addition the union can **claim improved terms and conditions** for a particular group of employees. This may be a money claim, **or a claim for specific information to be given to each worker.** This is most important because if it is accepted, it can be enforced in the courts (see below). The CAC may tell the employer to observe either the terms and conditions claimed by the union, or any terms it considers appropriate. Any award the CAC makes takes effect as a term of every individual worker's contract of employment. The award can be made only for those workers and for those terms and conditions for which the union is recognised.

Step 3A: Variation
Awards of the CAC can be varied by agreement or by the CAC itself.

Step 4: County court claim
If your employer still refuses to pay money or observe conditions (for example, to disclose certain information) awarded by the CAC each individual worker can present a claim in a county court for breach of contract.

How effective are these rights?
Even after going through all these steps, management can still

get away with refusing to give you the information. It is left to the individual worker, and not the union, to take the final steps of enforcement.

The Act preserves managerial secrecy. Only information in the possession of your company or group need be given. You do not get to see the original sources and cannot verify the facts by independent audit. You must know the data exists in order to request it, so you cannot rummage for it; and management can say it will cost too much to prepare. The Act and Code give unions no effective right to challenge traditional management prerogatives.

But the Act and Code are not entirely worthless; a little knowledge is better than none. Your union does have rights and, weak as they are, they should be used to obtain maximum disclosure and publicity. The TUC has advised unions to negotiate 'information agreements' with employers. These would provide for regular disclosure about changing aspects of the company. In a well-organised firm this will be better than resort to law. The objectives of these agreements are set out on page 379.

Health, safety and welfare

The Health and Safety at Work Act 1974 (HSWA 1974) imposes obligations on employers and others to disclose information on health, safety and welfare. The Health and Safety Commission has published Regulations, a Code of Practice and guidance notes. Only the disclosure provisions are dealt with here.

Disclosure by employers

Management are meant to provide whatever information is necessary to ensure, as far as is reasonably practicable, your health and safety while at work. If you are a union **safety representative** the Commission's Code requires management to give the information you need to carry out your work, including information about: plans, performance and changes affecting health and safety; hazards from plant including information provided by manufacturers and suppliers; precautions; accidents, diseases and near-misses; measurements and samples.

You can inspect documents which the law requires employers to keep – about accidents, dangerous near-misses and hours of women workers. Employers must give information **to the public** who may be affected by their business (section 3), but for this the business must be 'prescribed'. None has been – pressure from people living close to a noxious plant could lead to information under this section.

Employers must also give information to the **Health and Safety Inspectors,** who have power to order disclosure.

Section 79 of the HSWA 1974 changes the Companies Acts. When the change takes effect companies must include information on health and safety in annual reports.

Disclosure by manufacturers and others

Under section 6, manufactures, designers, importers and suppliers of any product used at work must make available adequate information 'about the use for which it is designed and has been tested, and about any conditions necessary to ensure that, when put to that use, it will be safe and without risks to health'.

This information is usually given to employers, not to the workers who are exposed to the risks. But the section says that the information must be available 'in connection with the use of the article at work' so workers and safety representatives can get their employers to disclose this data to them.

Disclosure by inspectors

Inspectors are required to contact workers' representatives at every workplace they visit. Inspectors must keep workers and safety representatives informed about health, safety and welfare matters affecting them. This means factual information (not opinions) about the premises and activities going on there, and action they have taken (section 28).

Trade union demands

The ACAS Code favours the negotiation of information agreements, which would ensure that specific or general information is made available on a regular basis to recognised unions, and in an agreed form. Although the Code follows the narrow contours of the EPA 1975 the principle of bargaining for information could be adopted. Failure to agree should be dealt with in the same way as any other failure to agree under your procedures.

So what demands should a union make?
There is no point in asking for information you don't need or can't cope with. The important thing is to fight for the **right** to any information, in any form, whenever you want it.

The TUC set out a shopping list in its negotiator's guide *Good Industrial Relations* (1971) under the following headings:

Manpower: Numbers of employees by job description; rates of turnover, short-time, absenteeism, sickness and accidents; details of existing provisions for security, sickness, accidents, recruitment, training, redeployment, promotion and redundancy.

Financial: Sales turnover, by main activities; home and export sales; non-trading income including income from investments and overseas earnings; pricing policy.

Costs: Distribution and sales; production costs; administrative and overhead costs; costs of materials and machinery; labour costs including social security payments; costs of management and supervision.

Incomes: Directors' remuneration; wages and salaries; make-up of pay – negotiated rates, payment-by-results, overtime and bonuses.

Profits: Before and after tax and taking into account government allowances, grants and subsidies; distribution and retentions.

Performance indicators: Unit costs, output per worker, return on capital employed, value added etc.

Worth of company: Details of growth and up-to-date value of fixed assets and stocks; growth and realisable value of trade investments.

Prospects and plans: Details of new enterprises and locations; prospective close-downs; mergers and takeovers.

Trading and sales plans: Investment plans including research and development.

Manpower plans: Plans for recruitment, selection and training; promotion, regrading and redeployment; short-time and redundancy provisions.

A description of the company's activities and structure: Details of holding companies and subsidiaries; organisational and managerial structure; outside contracts.

Details of ownership: Directors and shareholders in the company and in holding companies; beneficial control of nominee shareholdings.

To these can be added details of overseas associates and subsidiaries (particularly important as company law does not require complete data about subsidiaries of a group); labour costs such as a breakdown of all wages by grade and number of employees; names and formulas of all products that might be harmful at work; nature and worth of all investments; sources and uses of all funds; injuries and disease statistics.

Crucial to these demands is the target of independent audit for all the information given. Many unions have facilities in their research departments for analysing technical financial data, and the Labour Research Department also provides expert analysis and information.

Conclusion

Beyond the workplace level, an immediate demand is for changes in company law to widen the scope of information which public authorities and companies must give (see page 365) and to ensure rigid adherence to reporting obligations. Independent audit of all information for unions must be provided.

These proposals will be strongly resisted. **So the fight for the right to know must go on at individual workplaces and throughout multi-plant companies.**

Summary

1. An independent union recognised by management is entitled to demand information relevant to collective bargaining, health, safety and welfare, proposed redundancies, and business transfers. Legal procedures exist to enforce disclosure or, if resisted, acceptance of union claims for improved conditions.

2. Management are required to give individuals written particulars of their main conditions of employment.

3. Financial information is required to be given to the Registrar of Companies under the Companies Acts. Companies with 250 or more employees must include in their annual report a statement about steps taken to increase 'employee involvement'.

16. Industrial action

The 'right to strike' / workers who have no right / government emergency powers in disputes / what industrial action means / strikes, work-to-rule, go-slow, boycotting, work-in / the purposes of industrial action / whether action is official or unofficial / how it affects your contract / discipline, sacking / legal action against your union, and strike leaders / injunctions / lock-outs / how a strike affects redundancy pay, social security benefits, and continuity of employment / a summary / and the demand for a legal right to strike.

The right to strike

There is no positive right to strike. There are merely some defences and immunities workers and workers' leaders can use if employers try to take offensive action in the courts as a result of a strike. From 1871, many acts and agreements which are likely to occur during a strike, and which would normally be illegal, have been blessed with a legal immunity.

Many attempts have been made by Parliament *and the judges* to abolish these immunities and to make strike activity unlawful. Following a strike in 1900 over victimisation of a union activist, the Taff Vale Railway Company successfully sued the Amalgamated Society of Railway Servants for £23,000 and £12,000 in legal costs. The 1906 Liberal government, pressurised by new Labour MPs, overruled this by the Trade Disputes Act 1906, which became the basis on which unions and workers were relatively free to conduct industrial action.

After the General Strike, the Tories tried to curtail so-called 'political' strikes and union activities by the Trade Disputes and Trade Unions Act 1927, which was not repealed until 1946. During the two world wars, there was a ban on strikes and lock-outs with compulsory arbitration as the alternative final step. Elements of the wartime orders continued until 1959.

During the 1960s, with unemployment low and profits booming, employers were unable to resist many demands from unions for better terms and conditions. But occasionally they fought back and, with the help of the judges, restrained the ability of workers to conduct industrial action. Disputes over a closed shop at Heathrow Airport and recognition on the London waterfront and in Torquay hotels gave the judges the opportunity to create laws that jeopardised strike activity throughout industry. No dispute could be conducted without the threat of legal action hanging over the strikers.

In 1968 the Labour Cabinet introduced its White Paper *In Place of Strife*, which contained proposals for plugging judicial loopholes, but which also sought compulsory ballots and cooling-off periods before strikes. It was opposed and defeated by the trade union movement.

In 1971, the 'right to strike' was reduced still further by the Tories' Industrial Relations Act. Unions were ordered to pay compensation and fines, ballots were ordered, strikes postponed and workers imprisoned. Even after the Act was repealed, litigation against the TGWU continued until 1976 and the Tory and Liberal amendments to the repealing Act of 1974 were not deleted until 1976.

The Employment Acts 1980 and 1982 severely circumscribed the boundaries of legal industrial action and, having dug deeply into internal union affairs, exposed them to legal action for the first time since 1906. Government Green Papers on union immunities (1980) and union democracy (1983) foreshadowed further inroads. What we have now can in *no* sense be regarded as a right to strike, and employers are still able to sack all workers engaged in any dispute. In 80 years no real advance has been made to guarantee the most fundamental of workers' rights.

Where to find the law

The Trade Union and Labour Relations Act 1974 (TULRA) section 29 contains the definition of a trade dispute. The Employment Protection Consolidation Act 1978 (EPCA), as amended by the 1980 and 1982 Employment Acts, deals with dismissal of strikers (section 62). TULRA as amended also contains the immunities from legal action, union liability and secondary action. The Emergency Powers Act 1920 provides for government action.

Workers denied 'the right to strike'

Although the right to strike exists only in the form of defences against some forms of legal action, some workers are specifically denied access to these. They are:

Merchant seafarers. Many workers can be sued in the civil courts by their employers for breach of contract, but seafarers are liable to **criminal** prosecution if they disobey orders at sea, or, by their absence, prevent a ship from sailing. The 1970 Merchant Shipping Act allows strikes only when your ship is safely moored in a UK port and you have then given 48 hours' notice of your intention to terminate your contract. In other words, you can strike if you no longer work for your employer!

The police. Since the 1919 police strike was broken, the police have been denied the right to join a trade union – the Police Federation is not affiliated to the TUC and is not a trade union as such. It is a criminal offence to 'cause disaffection' or to induce police officers to withhold their services or breach discipline. Governments play down the political implications of police being considered as workers (they are 'office-holders') and behaving as trade unionists. This makes it easy for employers and government to use them against other workers.

The armed forces. You can retain your union membership if you join the services but you must not be active. You cannot join a union while in service and it is a criminal offence to organise. The requirement of obedience effectively denies the freedom to strike. Again, the implications of a unionised soldiery are too much for the establishment to contemplate.

Communications workers. The Post Office Act 1953 makes it a criminal offence for postal workers wilfully to delay or detain a letter or parcel. They can get two years in gaol or a fine or both. Anyone (including a union) who tries to get postal workers to delay or detain letters or parcels also commits an offence. The Telegraph Act 1863 makes it an offence for British Telecom workers to fail to deliver or transmit a message (for instance by phone or teleprint) or to delay it. The penalty is up to a £20 fine.

These Acts can be enforced by a prosecution by the police or a complaint to the civil courts for an injunction to prevent a threatened offence. Only the Attorney-General or someone acting with his/her consent can do this.

■ In 1977 the TUC called for a week of action against South Africa. The Post Office unions threatened to advise members to boycott communications to and from South Africa. John Gouriet, leader of the right-wing National Association for Freedom, asked the Attorney-General to stop the threatened boycott. When this was refused, Gouriet got an injunction in the Court of Appeal and the boycott was stopped. Months later, the House of Lords unanimously overturned this judgment, saying that a private citizen could not, without the Attorney-General, intervene to stop a *threat* of action by postal workers. Nor could the Attorney-General's reason for refusing to intervene be questioned. Even if Gouriet had suffered *personally* (for example, by losing business) from the boycott, *he* could not sue the Post Office or the unions. They are exempt from civil liability. But if an offence was actually committed, the police could prosecute. *Gouriet v UPW* 1977 (HL)

The 1983 Bill to privatise British Telecom placed the same restrictions on employees of contractors in the private communications industry.

Apprentices. Some indentures preclude apprentices from striking. Others which contain no bar require apprentices who take part in a strike to make up the lost time by adding it to their service.

The professions. Workers belonging to certain professional and vocational bodies are precluded by their own rules or codes from taking industrial action. The General Nursing Council has threatened disciplinary action against nurses involved in industrial action which may affect their obligations to care for patients – see page 357.

Emergency powers

The government can intervene in any industrial dispute. Under the Emergency Powers Act 1920, the Queen can proclaim an emergency if there are events of such a nature 'as to be calculated, by interfering with the supply and distribution of food, water, fuel, or light, or with the means of locomotion, to deprive the community, or any substantial portion of the community of the essentials of life'. Use of the Act must be approved by Parliament and renewed monthly. The Act gives almost unlimited powers to the government to make orders, but it cannot ban strikes and picketing or introduce military and industrial conscription. Since troops can be and usually are moved in, the effectiveness of a strike can be substantially undermined.

An emergency has been proclaimed 12 times since 1920, including three times by Labour governments and five times by the Heath government.

What is industrial action?

You need to know what constitutes industrial action because it affects your contract, management's power to sack you, and your immunity from legal action during a dispute.

Strikes
There is no all-purpose definition of industrial action. A *strike* is defined for the purposes of working out how long you have been continuously employed if you are claiming, say, redundancy pay, since a week does not count if during any part of it you have been on strike. The definition has been accepted by the courts as having a wider use and is contained in the EPCA (Schedule 13 para 24):

> the cessation of work by a body of persons employed acting in combination, or a concerted refusal or a refusal under a common understanding of any number of persons employed to continue to work for an employer in consequence of a dispute, done as a means of compelling their employer or any person or body of persons employed, to accept or not accept terms or conditions of or affecting their employment.

The judges have gone further than the EPCA definition. Lord Denning, for example, in a commercial case about shipping delays, said that there could be a strike even though there was no breach of contract. Dockers who quite lawfully refused to change to a 24-hour three-shift system and stuck to normal day work were held to be on strike – *Tramp Shipping Corp. v Greenwich Marine Inc.* 1975 (CA).

A strike is still a strike even if all the strikers have been dismissed, and it is a strike whether or not notice has been given. The timing of people joining a strike, or going back to work, is important in cases of selective dismissal during industrial action. Examples are given on page 393.

Other industrial action

Problems of definition are even harder when looking at industrial action short of a strike. You can escape liability for going on strike if you give proper notice to terminate your contracts, but nothing can validate other industrial action. In a case following a refusal by clerical workers in the TGWU to do additional work connected with handling cargo for Iberia Airlines, Sir John Donaldson said:

> almost all forms of industrial pressure short of a strike fall within the definition . . . and a safe working rule is that there is no alternative to either striking or doing the full job which the employees are employed to do . . . . Any concerted form of working without enthusiasm, or prolonged tea-breaks, or departure for the relief of natural pressures – the forms of industrial action are limited only by the ingenuity of mankind – all of them constitute . . . industrial action . . . and are prohibited with or without notice. *Seaboard World Airlines v TGWU* 1973 (NIRC)

A **ban on voluntary overtime** and a **withdrawal of goodwill** *may* count as industrial action even though you have not 'sold' these as part of your contract and cannot be said to be breaking it. This was confirmed by a decision which is outrageously partisan and unjust.

■ During wage negotiations three workers refused to do overtime when asked – nor did their contracts require them to. They were sacked. The Appeal Court confirmed that *motive* and actions are important. As the workers had banned overtime as a form of 'weapon', it amounted to industrial action. *Power Packing Containers v Faust* 1983 (CA)

In 1972, a **work-to-rule** by the three rail unions was declared unlawful under the now-repealed Industrial Relations Act, and a cooling-off period was ordered followed by a ballot (which went, predictably, against the employers and the Tory Employment Secretary).

Why should mere adherence to your employer's own rules be considered illegal? – a tricky problem for judges who insist on observance of rules. But they were undeterred and found that there is more to your contract than you think. Lord Denning said that the rule-book constituted lawful instructions which every worker had to obey and that it was a breach of contract to 'construe the rules unreasonably'. He said if any worker:

> with the others, takes steps wilfully to disrupt the undertaking to produce chaos so that it will not run as it should, then each one who is a party to those steps is guilty of a breach of his contract . . . what makes it wrong is the object with which it is done . . . it is the wilful disruption that is the breach. *Secretary of State for Employment v ASLEF* 1972 (CA)

Lord Justice Buckley went even further and revealed that 'the employee must serve the employer faithfully with a view to promoting those commercial interests for which he was employed'.

Lord Denning was prepared to say that whatever you do, whatever your contract says, you can be acting unlawfully in taking industrial action if you have a 'wilful' state of mind, including working only your contractual week. This is certainly wrong but, as they stand, the breadth of the implied terms – not wilfully to disrupt the undertaking and to promote its commercial interests – could possibly be used to justify mass sackings.

Workers who left their work-benches and gathered round two machines to **stop them physically from being tested** were considered to have taken industrial action and were sacked – *Thompson v Eaton* – see page 395.

A **go-slow** is a refusal to perform your contract efficiently and constitutes industrial action. See *Drew v St Edmundsbury*, page 306.

Boycotting and **refusal to work with non-union labour** have been declared to be breaches of contract and unlawful industrial action. At a time of mass redundancy, TASS members at C.A. Parsons Ltd refused to handle work done by UKAPE members or to work with them. The NIRC ordered them to stop – *UKAPE v AUEW (TASS)* 1972 (NIRC). Inducing people to boycott goods coming from an employer who has a dispute with his/her employees can sometimes be unlawful secondary action (page 403) or quite lawful union activity, as in the *Hadmor* case (page 399). Inducing people to refuse to work with non-union labour is also unprotected (page 348).

Refusing to cross a picket line can also be industrial action if you refuse because of union instructions or obligations, or as an individual making a voluntary decision, but not if you did so out of fear (see also page 432):

■ Boilermakers and engineers had separate wage agreements with a firm of power station contractors. The engineers failed to agree and went on strike. An engineer's mate, on holiday when the strike started, refused to cross the picket line and advised management. He did not say he was on strike, did not receive strike pay and did not refuse out of fear. His action was the voluntary decision of an individual. He may not have been part of the same strike but he did take industrial action. *McCormick v Horsepower* 1981 (CA)

At first sight there is no reason why a **work-in** should be unlawful – you are, after all, merely doing without supervision what you are employed to do and probably more efficiently. But if in a work-in or occupation you refuse to leave the plant or office, you will be disobeying lawful instructions.

That means you might be sacked, but in order to get you off the site management will have to start a claim for trespass. The grounds on which they can do this are set out on page 446.

Picketing is dealt with in chapter 17.

The purposes of industrial action

It doesn't matter why you are taking industrial action – for industrial, social, political or sympathetic reasons – the rules on breach of contract and mass sackings are the same. When shop stewards, union officials and others call on workers to take industrial action, they are protected from most legal action only if there is a trade dispute. This is defined on page 399 and may exclude some strikes.

As we have see (page 348) you have no immunity from civil law if you call for industrial action in pursuit of a union labour only claim.

Official or unofficial?

Strikes in breach of procedure – that is, before the disputes machinery has been exhausted – are more likely to have legal consequences for the workers involved. These strikes will usually be unofficial. Whether a strike is regarded by the union as official or not is a crucial question to workers involved in it, and other workers affected by it. The law, however, is concerned in two situations. Firstly, official action makes the union liable to the same civil law claims as individuals and the union can be sued – page 397.

Secondly, in any official strike most unions pay strike benefit. This is relevant in assessing your family's right to supplementary benefit, which is discounted by the flat-rate deduction (£14.50 in 1983/84) or any higher amount of strike pay – see page 292.

How does industrial action affect your contract?

The law on strikes has been turbulent since the mid-1960s, with decisions of the courts creating confusion and danger. It is still unclear, but the prevailing view might be summarised in this way:

1. Your contract of employment is not suspended during a strike. It continues unless and until you give and work the required notice to terminate the contract, which is the only way a strike can be entirely lawful.

2. This means that you usually commit a breach of contract when you strike or take other industrial action.

3. Usually, but not always, this breach will be so serious that your employer can discipline you for it. This means withholding wages, suing for breach of contract or giving you the sack.

4. During industrial action there is nothing to stop your employer sacking all those taking part.

5. If only some are sacked or not taken back after the dispute, they can claim unfair dismissal.

Now, these rules are very complicated and depend on an interpretation of several important cases. The following questons usually arise in connection with strikes and other industrial action.

Is striking a breach of contract?

Contracts are not usually suspended during a strike – it is assumed that the obligations under them continue to be operative and if you do not turn up for work, you are breaking your contract in the most fundamental sense. **It's important to find some suspension if you are going to say that the normal contractual obligations do not apply**.

If there is a procedure agreement providing that no industrial action will be taken until the procedure is exhausted and some notice given, the courts *might* say that the workers' contracts are suspended until the strike is over. But they do that only if the agreement is incorporated into every worker's contract – see page 316.

Usually when you go on strike the contract does continue. This means that you are breaking it, but not in a way which terminates it, for the EAT has said:

> . . . the whole point of men withholding their labour is so that the existing contract can be put right, so that grievances can be remedied, so that after a period in which they are on strike, management will agree to their demands . . . It would be a disaster in our view if the going on strike were to be regarded as a termination of the contract. Indeed the law makes it perfectly plain that it is not so. *Wilkins v Cantrell and Cochrane* 1978

However, although you do not intend to terminate your contract, your employer can use your breach of contract as grounds for sacking you. You are then entitled neither to notice money under your contract, nor to claim unfair dismissal – see below.

What disciplinary action can be taken against strikers?

Because most strikes involve a breach of contract, employers often want to take action against strikers. They might withhold wages, sue for breach of contract or dismiss you.

Withholding wages

If you are on strike you will not get paid. Some agreements have made management pay up after the strike is settled. The attraction of less dramatic forms of industrial action, such as a work-to-rule or go-slow, is that you continue to be at work and to receive pay. But if the judgments in the 1972 rail work-to-rule case (page 387) were taken literally, there is no right to pay. If you 'wilfully disrupt' management's business – and the judges will be quick to classify all industrial action in this way – you are behaving in a way that is inconsistent with *your* contract, so their obligations under it are offset. In practice, though, most employers do not reduce or refuse to pay wages during an industrial action short of a strike unless the action has a direct effect on bonus or commission.

Suing for breach of contract

This was a favourite with the mine-owners and the National Coal Board. Any breach of any contract entitles the injured party to go to court to obtain damages to put him/her in the same position as if the contract had been properly carried out. The same applies to a contract of employment. A major difference is that the courts cannot directly order you or management to carry out the terms of the contract, that is, actually to force you to go back to work or management to employ you (TULRA 1974 section 16).

As your employer can sue for damages only, it will not be worthwhile. This form of legal action has been so discredited and the value of the damages, even if they are obtainable, is so small that employers have not used this remedy in any important dispute since 1956.

Sacking

The EAT confirmed the old common law right of an employer to sack an employee without notice (or wages in lieu) when 'there was a settled, confirmed and continued intention on the part of the employee not to do any of the work which under his contract he had engaged to do':

■ Bill Simmons had worked for Hoover in Perivale for 10 years when a strike occurred in 1974. He was off sick at the time. When he recovered he notified Hoover but did not return to work because of the strike. Just after Christmas he was given one week's notice of dismissal. He quickly found a new job and on the day he started it, the strike was settled. He claimed redundancy pay, but Hoover said that the law (now EPCA 1978 section 82) allowed them to refuse a payment to any worker whose contract entitled them to dismiss him instantly. And the strike amounted to such conduct. The EAT agreed. *Simmons v Hoover* 1976 (EAT)

The right to claim reinstatement or compensation under the unfair dismissal law is limited – see below.

Can all strikers be sacked?

There is nothing to stop an employer sacking *all* workers taking part in a strike or other industrial action.

Provided *all* are sacked, none of them can claim unfair dismissal. The tribunal cannot even hear the claim (EPCA 1978 section 62). The position of workers *locked-out* is the same and is dealt with on page 413.

Employers frequently threaten, or actually carry out, mass sacking of strikers. Grunwicks sacked all APEX strikers, then sacked the TGWU drivers who much later came out in support. Tribunals turned away the sacked workers' claims. Even though the motive for sacking was clearly anti-union, the tribunals had no jurisdiction to hear the merits of the cases.

The reason advanced for allowing employers to get away with this is that Parliament never intended industrial disputes to be assessed for reasonableness by courts and tribunals. But by giving *no* support to strikers whose employer has carried out mass sackings, the law supports the employer.

The lesson is clear to every employer. In any strike s/he can stop union activists by sacking all the workers. **This difficulty can be overcome only by ensuring absolute solidarity** and by keeping strike breakers out. Until we get a right to strike and suspension of contracts, this is the only way to tackle this employers' offensive.

The judges' justification for allowing employers to escape unfair dismissal claims, adopted by the EAT, is:

> to give a measure of protection to an employer if his business is faced with ruin by a strike. It enables him in those circumstances, if he cannot carry on the business without a labour force, to dismiss the labour force on strike; to take on another labour force without the stigma of its being unfair dismissal. *Heath v J F Longman* 1973 (NIRC)

In other words, mass sacking followed by the employment of scab labour is not unlawful. The purpose of the strike is quite irrelevant. The only question is: did the employer sack all the workers participating in the industrial action and has s/he refused to re-engage all of them?

The following rules are important if you are considering industrial action and suspect management may threaten sackings:

1. The sacking must take place while the action is continuing. Once it is over, or management have been told it is over, you can claim unfair dismissal (*Heath v Longman*, above).

2. Similarly, if you give notice of industrial action and are sacked before the notice runs out you can claim unfair dismissal.

■ TGWU members at a plastics factory gave notice to management that if their claims were not met by 11 a.m. they would take industrial action. Management sacked the negotiating committee before 10 a.m. and claimed immunity from unfair dismissal claims. The EAT said notice of industrial action does not mean the action has begun or that it will begin. It is a common step in negotiations. Any dismissal during the notice period can be challenged. *Midland Plastics v Till* 1983 (EAT)

3. If you clearly indicate that you are going to join colleagues *already on* strike, you will be considered as being on strike even if the shift you are due to work has not started.

■ A TGWU shop steward and four other coach drivers held a meeting after work and told management they would not come to work the next day. Three were sacked. The steward was held to have been on strike at the time of his dismissal since although not at work, he had clearly stated that when he was next contractually bound to work, he would not. *Winnett v Seamarks Bros* 1978 (EAT)

4. Workers absent sick or on holiday at the *start* of the action are not considered to be taking part in it (Lord Dilhorne in *Frank Jones (Tipton) v Stock* 1978 (HL)).

5. But workers sick during the dispute are taking part in it unless they indicate differently.

■ In support of sacked NUJ members, journalists at a sister

newspaper took industrial action. They strictly observed tea-breaks, did not work during lunch-time, refused to handle non-union copy and called a one-day strike. They were all told that if they did not undertake to work normally the day after the strike they would be sacked. A sub-editor took the industrial action but went sick on the day after the strike. Like the others he was sacked. The EAT by a majority said he was taking part in the action even though at the time of his dismissal he was not at work and therefore could not ban lunch-time working, etc. He had given no indication that he intended to drop the action so was considered still to be involved. *Williams v Western Mail* 1980 (EAT)

6. The reason for dismissal is irrelevant, so management can use the dispute to disguise redundancy or unfair dismissal.

What if only some strikers are sacked?
If only some of the strikers are sacked or if only some are taken back after the dispute, the rest can claim unfair dismissal. Management must say why they chose *you* for dimissal and must justify it. You cannot win your case just by showing you were picked out – management may go on to show that they sacked you for reasons not connected with the strike.

In an attempt to make it easier for employers to break strikes, changes were brought in by the Employment Act 1982 to put a time limit on this right. You can complain about selective dismissals or selective refusals to re-engage *only if this occurs within the first three months of your sacking*. After that management are free to offer re-engagement to selected strikers.

What if the return-to-work terms are different?
Suppose you are offered a return to work on conditions which do not apply to others. EPCA section 62 says you must go back to the job you had before the dispute or in a different job which is reasonably suitable. This means the capacity and place in which you were previously employed, and on the same work. However, discrimination not involving changes in these conditions was held to be lawful when some strikers were taken back unconditionally while others got written warnings.

■ National Theatre stage-hands were sacked during a strike

and then offered their jobs back. Some had no conditions attached, but 30 were told they would be treated as having had a second warning within the disciplinary procedure. They claimed unfair dismissal on the grounds of selective re-engagement. The EAT said the warnings did not affect their employment capacity or the job they did, and disallowed their claims. *Williams v National Theatre* 1981 (EAT)

Legitimate self-defensive reaction to employers' unreasonable demands is still a strike. Take, for instance, the action of Bill Thompson and five fellow-engineering workers in Bolton, who objected to the introduction of new machines into their shop without agreement – *Thompson v Eaton* 1976 (EAT). A dispute arose, management would not put the matter into procedure, so six of the workers left their benches and physically obstructed access to the machines until the manning and testing arrangements had been agreed. The men were warned, then sacked. They claimed unfair dismissal, but were turned down because at the time of the dismissal they were all taking part in industrial action. The EAT recognised that management behaved 'obtusely' but agreed with this decision.

If your employer's action amounts to breaking your contract in a fundamental way you are entitled to regard yourself as being dismissed. This means you can claim unfair dismissal. It follows from what was said above, about contracts continuing during a strike, that if you strike in response to management's action you are not treating the contract as ending, but trying to improve it. If however, management's action unambiguously terminates the contract (see page 60), your dismissal during a subsequent strike is irrelevant. In other words your dismissal took place *before* the strike. The EAT has said that you can challenge management action in these circumstances.

■ Twelve lorry drivers went on strike after repeatedly complaining without success that their vehicles were overloaded, dangerous and in breach of the Road Traffic Acts, and that by forcing them to drive management were breaking their contracts. They were all sacked. The EAT accepted the employers' line that the overloading was not deliberate or persistent and did not amount to a serious breach of contract. If it had been, the men could have regarded it as a dismissal. Far from being excluded from bringing a claim because they were on strike, they would have a claim arising *before then* out of management's illegal instructions. *Wilkins v Cantrell and Cochrane* 1978 (EAT)

Since employers know they can sack you in a dispute they may try to provoke you into taking action in order to get rid of activists or to escape redundancy pay. If you are concerned that dismissals are practicable and the threat is real, you are faced with the dilemma of *either* striking and risking dismissal without the right to claim, *or* treating management's action itself as a dismissal and taking a chance on winning at a tribunal. In the first case you still have a job, albeit at risk while you are on strike; in the second you decide to quit and hope for reinstatement at a tribunal.

Does it make any difference if you give strike notice?
Giving strike notice can be regarded only as a tactic. Use it if you think it is worthwhile for industrial reasons, but in general it confers no legal benefit or immunity. From the courts' point of view, you are usually outlawed if you take industrial action of any sort.

This is because strike notice means that you are going either to break, to terminate or to suspend your contract. A breach of contract is still a breach even if you give management advance warning – see *Winnett v Seamarks*, page 393, where the strike started when the employers were told there would be no work on the next shift.

If you give the amount of notice necessary to terminate your contract and in fact terminate it, you are doing nothing unlawful. But it is totally unrealistic to do this, as it means that the workforce is split according to length of service and status (staff or hourly-paid), as different notice periods are required of different workers. It also means that you are jeopardising your continuity of employment and your right to claim unfair dismissal and redundancy pay, and you are disqualified from receiving unemployment benefit for six weeks following a resignation 'without just cause'. So **don't give strike notice in the form of notice to terminate your contract of employment.**

Suspension of contracts is not possible unless there is some form of agreement allowing for it.

The only way you can be sure that notice will not prejudice

you contract is to provide in your collective agreements that a strike after due notice (whatever you agree) will be treated as suspension of each worker's contract, so the failure to work does not give your employer the right to sack.

Legal action against the union

A union can commit crimes – as, for example, the UPW was alleged to have done when it threatened to boycott South African mail (see page 384). It can also be liable for breach of contract – for example, to its own employees or to printers, builders, cleaners and solicitors who do business with the union.

From 1906 to 1982 a trade union could not, however, be sued in its own name for most civil wrongs (torts). It can be sued for civil wrongs involving personal injury or involving the use of its property. So it can be sued by people libelled in union literature or injured on union premises. **But** if the civil wrong was done 'in contemplation or furtherance of a trade dispute' the union before 1982 could not be sued at all. The Employment Act 1982 made the most radical and serious attack on trade union organisation for over a century by exposing union funds to legal action. It repealed the immunity contained in TULRA 1974 and made unions liable in the same way as individuals. A union is liable under normal legal principles for acts done by its officials and members on behalf of the union. For acts done *in a dispute*, there are special rules for determining whether the union can be held responsible.

The legislation aims to stop calls for action. The position is dealt with in detail below and can be summarised as;

1. Individuals taking part in a dispute are usually breaking their own contracts of employment, but in practice do not risk being sued. They can all be sacked without the right to claim unfair dismissal.

2. Calls for action are lawful if they are 'in contemplation or furtherance of a trade dispute', which is narrowly defined.

3. If these calls fall outside this definition, or add up to *unlawful* secondary action, individuals are liable for inducing breaches of, or interfering with, contracts or threatening to do so, intimidation and conspiracy. They can be ordered to stop by an injunction, or to pay damages.

4. A union is liable in the same way if the calls have been authorised or endorsed by a 'responsible person' in the union.

5. The union is liable to pay damages on *each* claim up to limits determined by the size of its membership. (There is no limit on legal costs, or fines for contempt of court).

Number of members	Limit on damages
Fewer than 5,000	£10,000
5,000–24,999	£50,000
25,000–99,999	£125,000
100,000 or more	£250,000

6. Money in the political fund, or a separate fund for provident benefits, cannot be touched.

Acts are taken to have been authorised if they were endorsed by the national executive committee, the president or the general secretary, or by a full-time official or the committee s/he regularly reports to as long as they are not prevented by the union's rules from authorising this kind of action. Even then, the union can escape liability if the official's or committee's action is 'repudiated' by the national executive or general secretary, who must then be seen to act consistently with this repudiation. A 'responsible person' also includes someone who is empowered by the rules to endorse the action. Rules include the rule-book and any other *written* provisions affecting the relationship between members and the union. This means that shop stewards without *written* authority to authorise industrial action cannot make the union liable if they have obtained their authority by custom or implication.

In 1972, disputes over container transport were initiated and conducted by Merseyside and Hull dock workers' shop stewards' committees. The Law Lords said they had *implied* authority to commit the TGWU to industrial action in support of union policy (*Heatons Transport v TGWU* 1972 (HL)). Although the union was liable under the Industrial Relations Act, it would not be liable under the 1982 Act unless it had given written authority or endorsement to the stewards.

Legal action against 'strike leaders'

It is usually assumed by the media and politicians that strikes are 'led' and that there are 'ringleaders', the majority of workers being unwilling to take industrial action. In legal terms, this is translated into a search for those who ask others to break their contracts by taking industrial action, or by not fulfilling their commercial commitments. These include union executive committees, local officials, shop stewards and individual workers, for example on picket duty.

Protection in civil law is given to workers and unions for all acts likely to arise in connection with industrial action, provided they are done **'in contemplation or furtherance of a trade dispute'** and do not constitute **'unlawful secondary action'** against an employer who is not party to the dispute. These terms are crucial and are explained below. The protection applies to all persons, whether or not they are employees, so union officials and workers in other industries are covered. The protection, which is found in section 13 of TULRA 1974, means you can:

1. induce someone to break any contract, or interfere with it, or induce someone to interfere with it;

2. threaten that any contract will be broken, or interfered with, or threaten to induce someone to break or interfere with any contract;

3. conspire to injure someone (non-physically) in a way which does not involve committing a tort;

4. conspire to do something which is not a crime if only one person does it (Conspiracy and Protection of Property Act 1875 section 3).

What all this means is that you can **post pickets, persuade fellow-workers not to work, ask drivers not to deliver, contact the supplying companies, ask customers and customers' workers to boycott goods and encourage sympathetic action. All provided you are 'acting in contemplation or furtherance of a trade dispute'.** There are many loopholes here, so the definition is important.

Trade dispute

Problems have arisen as to what 'contemplating or furthering' a dispute means. It has five elements.

1. The dispute is real

It must exist or be imminent. If you *think* a dispute may occur, you must wait until there is some real likelihood of it. Action over fears about job-security or future redundancy can be a trade dispute.

■ Following union policy and a branch decision, ACTT officials instructed technicians at Thames TV to stop the transmission of a series of *Unforgettable* rock music programmes which had been made by contractors and sold to

Thames. The contractors sued. The Law Lords said this was 'a classic instance of a trade dispute arising out of fears for job-security in a period of high unemployment', since the union was protecting its members from outside competition. Telling members to disobey management instructions did not deprive the officials of their TULRA protection. Although members acted unlawfully in breaking their employment contracts on union instructions, this kind of illegality did not expose officials to claims of furthering a dispute by 'unlawful means'. Otherwise *every* call for action would be unlawful. *Hadmor Productions v Hamilton* 1982 (HL)

Similarly, a NALGO instruction to NHS members not to co-operate with a firm seeking contracts to privatise computer maintenance in the NHS was held to be 'in contemplation of a dispute' which would exist if the NHS did hand over a contract and thereby deprive NALGO members of jobs – *Health Computing v Meek* 1980 (HC).

2. Between workers and their employer

Somewhere there must exist a dispute between workers and their own employer. A union cannot take action in dispute with an employer if his/her own employees are not in dispute – for example over his/her refusal to pay the going rate of wages.

■ The International Transport Workers' Federation (ITF) seeks to maintain employment standards in the shipping industry. It operates a policy of boycotting ships which don't observe ITF conditions, and in particular those which fly flags of convenience, enabling the owners to hire cheap labour. The *Nawala* was sold by its Norwegian owners, whose crew had ITF conditions, to a Hong Kong company which hired a Chinese crew at sub-ITF rates. When the ship reached Redcar, the ITF got TGWU dockers to boycott it. The owners got an injunction on the grounds that the dispute was about the flag not the conditions, therefore political not industrial. On appeal, the courts held that since the ITF's claim was **connected with** industrial conditions, they were covered by section 13, and the injunction was lifted. *NWL v Woods* 1979 (HL)

This kind of campaign has been unlawful since 1982 because it does not involve a dispute between workers and their own employer, is about conditions outside the UK and might be considered to be mainly political (see below).

A dispute between a union or unions and an employers' association, for example the parties to a joint industrial council, is not a dispute between workers and *their* employer. Nor is a dispute between workers and workers, for example over demarcation. Most demarcation disputes can, however, be reduced to a dispute with your employer over allocation of work.

If you have been sacked you can, nevertheless, be in dispute with your former employer provided you were sacked during the dispute, or your sacking was one of the causes of the dispute. Disputes with the government are covered if government workers are in dispute, or if a minister is represented on a Joint Council, or if s/he has to be involved in settling any matter.

3. In the UK

A dispute relating only to matters outside the UK is excluded. You cannot legally take action in support of workers abroad, even though you may be working for the same transnational company, *unless* your conditions are likely to be affected by the outcome of the dispute. So you could mount an international campaign against a common employer over job-security or investment or health hazards, and you could support striking workers abroad if their jobs affect yours.

4. Wholly or mainly about conditions

The dispute must 'relate wholly or mainly' to one or more of the matters specified on page 313. A casual connection with working conditions is not sufficient to establish a dispute. But conditions are interpreted freely to include custom and practice and much more than simply contractual terms and conditions (*Hadmor v Hamilton,* above). After 1982, the union in *NWL v Woods* would be held liable for its actions.

A personal grudge, or the judges' perception of a vendetta, does not amount to a trade dispute:

■ T. Bailey Forman Limited owns the *Nottingham Evening Post,* which refused to recognise the NGA. In pursuit of its claim the NGA and SLADE asked advertisers in the *Post* to desist. 180 did but 16 continued to advertise and the unions boycotted their ads nationally. The advertisers, and major national news companies, all sued the unions. The court granted the injunction, saying the unions were not covered by TULRA because there was no trade dispute. The action was taken to punish the *Post's* owner, Pole-Carew, for his active part in the 1978 provincial journalists' dispute. It was also illegal, said the judges, **to interfere with the freedom of the press,** and to stop public adverts. *Associated Newspapers v Wade* 1979 (CA)

Purely political disputes, or at least those which the courts don't regard as industrial disputes, are not protected. So when a union at the BBC refused to beam the 1977 FA Cup Final to South Africa, its general secretary was outside the protection of the Act. He was said to be involved in a political issue, not connected with terms and conditions of employment – *BBC v Hearn*.

The TUC's Day of Action on 14 May 1980 against the Conservative government's industrial policies, and the Employment Act, was also the target of an injunction by Express Newspapers (*Express Newspapers v Keys* 1980 (HC)). They tried to stop the three printing unions and the NUJ calling on their members in the Express Group to support the one-day stoppage. The High Court held that it was a political strike, unprotected by section 13. It was irrelevant that the unions' general secretaries had said there was a free choice among members as to whether they followed the call, and that there would be no disciplinary action against them if they worked. In the event, **one union** (Natsopa) **refused to lift its call for action**, probably the first occasion this has happened under the 1906 or 1974 Acts.

The courts are likely to see through any attempt to translate a political demand or statement into an industrial one by attaching a claim for changes in conditions. The dispute must be wholly or mainly industrial – see page 410.

5. You are contemplating or furthering it

The test for finding out whether you acted in contemplation or furtherance of the dispute is subjective. The only people to ask are those doing it. It is irrelevant that your contribution does not, and is not likely to, further the dispute as long as you believe it does. In two disputes, the Law Lords wisely refused to substitute their judgment about the effectiveness of industrial action for that of union organisers. They accepted that provincial journalists calling on Press Association journalists, and British Steel Workers calling on private steel workers, were aiming to further their disputes (*Express Newspapers v MacShane* 1979; *Duport Steels v Sirs* 1980 (HL)).

Secondary action

'Secondary action' and 'secondary picketing' are terms invented by the media, the latter during the lorry drivers' strike of 1979. It had never been used in any British or American legislation. To many people the term 'secondary action' has become pejorative and associated with illegality. To trade unionists it describes solidarity, sympathetic action, boycotting, support and assistance. The term 'secondary action' is used here simply because it is now in the statute.

The 1980 Act is really about **commercial contracts.** Secondary action is action taken by workers against an employer who is not a party to the original dispute. Section 17 aims to protect commercial contracts from action by workers not immediately in dispute supporting those who are. Under the Act **unlawful secondary action** means interference with commercial contracts caused by interference with the employment contracts of people working for any **employer who is not a party** to the dispute. The only exceptions are action at **direct suppliers and customers** or **at associated employers**, and **lawful picketing.**

So section 17 applies in the following circumstances:

1. There has been secondary action 'relating to' a dispute, meaning that you:

- induced workers to break their contracts with their employer who was not a party to the dispute – e.g., called for a sympathy strike; or
- interfered with the performance of it – e.g., called for product to be boycotted; or
- induced someone to interfere with it – e.g., asked the workers' own union official to interfere; or
- threatened to do any of these – e.g., threats to either of the employers in question; or
- threatened to break your own contract if you do not work for an employer who is a party to the dispute.

2. As a result, a party to a commercial contract has been induced to break it; or the performance of it has been interfered with; or there have been threats of either of these.

Generally speaking then, 'secondary action' has three stages: you persuade someone else to break their employment contract, and as a result their employer's commercial contract is broken. But when you threaten to break your own contract, there are only two stages, and in a very real sense this adds a further burden to anyone taking supportive action.

In conducting a dispute and calling for trade union support, a factor you might be forced to consider is the possibility of legal action by management or their contractors. Because the law is so stacked against you, your first consideraton should be the ways to win your dispute by calling on support from other trade unionists. It is impossible to give definitive advice on how to escape liability. The degree to which you need it, and get bogged down in legal wrangling, reflects the degree of organisation and determination among your members. If you are looking for legal excuses for not taking action, the Employment Acts are full of them. Guidance is given here in case you are forced to contemplate the legal consequences of solidarity. Diagram 9 on page 408 is intended to cover most problems you may have.

1. The inner circle
A call to workers who are not themselves in dispute is not always unlawful. **There is an inner circle of customers and suppliers who deal with your employer whose employees you can legally call on.** Solidarity action can be summoned if section 17 is complied with:

> a) the **purpose** or the **principal purpose** of the secondary action was **directly** to **prevent or disrupt** the supply **during the dispute** of goods or services between an **employer who is a party to the dispute** and the **employer under the contract of employment** to which the secondary action relates; and
> b) the **secondary action** (together with any corresponding action relating to other contracts of employment with the same employer) was **likely** to achieve the purpose. (emphasis added)

Very few of the phrases used in this defence have been defined and there is much scope for the judges to restrict its application. Some guidance can, however, be given.

2. The purpose of the action
The purpose of the call for action must be clear. If there are several purposes, the **major one must be to disrupt supplies.** You will lose your defence if the court says your purpose was to

'punish' an employer for his/her anti-union attitudes (the *Wade* case, page 402) or to further a purely political aim (the *Day of Action* case, page 402).

The target is directly to disrupt supply lines. This is defined in section 17 of the Employment Act 1980 as excluding an indirect attack, by means of action against, say, suppliers' suppliers.

The Act talks of goods and services, but does not specifically mention the utilities, and statutory undertakings such as the mail and telephone services. It would be hard to argue that these are not services. However, the supply line must be in pursuance of a contract, between the party to the dispute and the supplier or customer, which is **subsisting at the time of the secondary action.** How are strikers to know the exact state of the relationship at any given time? The contract may exist at the time you call for support, but not when the support is given. It may be terminated during the dispute because management can't carry it out, or because their customer knows it will be boycotted and therefore refuses delivery.

The contract may be with a holding company, different from the manufacturing side, which could be a separate entity. Or the supplies could come through a third party carrier, or broker, who forms a new link in the contractual chain. The ITF's campaign against low wages on flag-of-convenience ships foundered when a ship-owner far up the contractual chain had a Liverpool tug workers' boycott stopped – *Merkur Island Shipping v Laughton* 1983 (HL). If management get wind of your intention to approach suppliers' unions, they may suspend the contract, or get the supplies 'laundered' through a third party. As soon as the contract ceases between management and the supplier or customer, your action is unprotected, and anyone affected can sue you.

Finally, the action must be in furtherance of a trade dispute.

3. Achieving the purpose
The second part of the defence depends on an objective assessment of whether the 'secondary action' was **likely to achieve** the disruption.

Yet the job of evaluating a union's intentions is exactly what one judge, Lord Scarman, was relieved to escape from.

It would be a strange and embarrassing task for a judge to be called upon to review the tactics of a party to a trade dispute and to determine whether in the view of the court the tactic employed was likely to further, or advance, that party's side of the dispute. And the difficulties . . . are a persuasive argument for keeping this act of judgment in the industrial arena and out of the judicial forum . . . . It would need very clear statutory language to persuade me that Parliament intended to allow the courts to act as some sort of backseat driver in trade disputes. *MacShane* case, page 402

Now since the Employment Acts the judges are in the driving seat, deciding the feasibility of union action, at least as far as secondary action is concerned.

Summary
If you call for support from people who work for the employer in dispute, you are protected if you genuinely believe you are furthering the dispute. But a call to workers **who don't work for the employer in dispute** is unprotected if it does not fit into section 17. The call must be likely to achieve the disruption of direct supplies to management.

'Associated employers'
The second defence under the Act is available where your firm is controlled by another, or where both are controlled by the same person or company. They are associated employers. Now if the associate supplies or receives goods and services in substitution for your firm's during the dispute, you can call on workers of either the supplier or the associated employer.

■ **Example:** Your firm is associated with B. During your dispute no product gets to customer C. The contract is broken. But B makes the same product as your firm and delivers substitutes to C. You can call on workers at B *and* C not to handle the product.

The rules about purpose and likely effect are the same as in the first defence.

In some industries, disputes are carried on with all the firms in an employers' association. The Act now says that a firm is a party to a dispute between unions and its association only if it is 'represented in the dispute by the association'. Individual firms seeking to settle the dispute on their own therefore cease to be parties.

Picketing .
'Secondary action' arising out of lawful picketing is also protected. So you need not know the exact contractual relationship between management and anyone who arrives at the picket line outside your workplace. Employees of companies seeking contracts, for instance, can be persuaded not to carry out their employment contracts.

If employees of a customer of your firm picket their own workplace in support of your dispute, they are also protected. Suppose a product from your firm is still getting through, and members of another union at the customer's warehouse refuse to handle it. They set up pickets in protest against their firm's continued trading with yours. Their picketing is not unlawful. But if they cause breaches of commercial contracts between their firm and *any other but yours*, they are unprotected by TULRA 1974 section 13 (see page 399).

Notes to Diagram 9 on page 408
You are a shop steward representing members on official strike at BL Cars, Birmingham. You·want to make the action effective so you make normal solidarity appeals to workers in related industries to boycott BL Birmingham. You therefore:

1. Call on **Lucas** workers not to make or pack lamps for BL Birminhám. PROTECTED.

2. Call on **BRS** workers not to handle any lamps destined for you which have been despatched by Lucas supervisors. NOT PROTECTED. No contract between BL and BRS.

3. Call on **Rolls-Royce** workers, in view of Lucas's continued delivery to BL, to boycott all Lucas products. NOT PROTECTED. As above.

4. Call on **Glass Ltd** workers not to supply Lucas with headlamp glass. NOT PROTECTED. Although your firm has a subsisting contract to buy other forms of glass, the headlamp glass is not supplied directly.

5. Call on **Glass Ltd** workers not to supply BL. PROTECTED, as in **1.** above.

6. Call on workers at **UK Dealers**, **US Dealers** and **Transport Ltd** to boycott cars. PROTECTED, as in **1.** above.

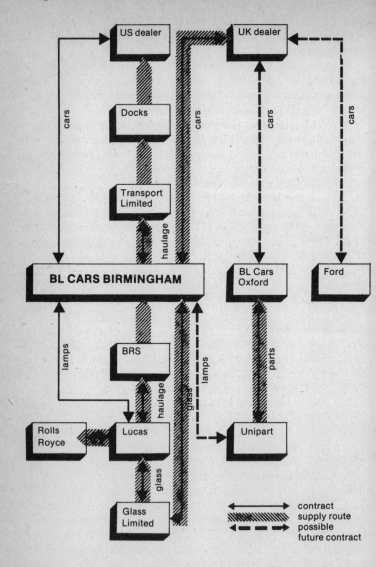

Diagram 9 **Secondary action**

7. Call on **dockers** not to handle the cars. NOT PRO-TECTED if the freightage contract is between the port and shipping authorities and **Transport Ltd.**

8. Call on **Unipart** workers not to handle any order for lamps that BL might place. PROBABLY PROTECTED. Although no existing contract, interference with any contract actually placed would be protected as in **1.** above.

9. Call on **BL Cars, Oxford** workers not to make cars trans-ferred from you. PROTECTED. Both are the same, or at least associated, companies.

10. Call on **Ford** workers not to supply UK Dealers with cars of similar specification to BL's. NOT PROTECTED. As **2.** above.

Avoiding trouble

If you have been forced to consider the possibility of legal action, you can take steps in a dispute to avoid liability for 'unlawful secondary action' in the following ways:

1. Go directly to secondary employers.

2. Bring employees of secondary employers into dispute.

3. Make what American unions call 'hot cargo agreements' so you can lawfully boycott dispute-ridden product.

4. Don't induce, merely inform.

5. Get to likely alternative suppliers and customers before contracts can be placed.

None of these is guaranteed, but they might raise sufficient doubts and risks to put employers off the idea of taking legal action against you.

Direct approaches

If you approach a supplier or a suppliers' supplier, and ask him/her to break his/her commercial contract, you are not carrying out secondary action under the Act. You are directly inducing, or interfering with, commercial contracts and as long as you genuinely believe this furthers the dispute, you are protected by TULRA section 13.

This may be the only choice open to you if the suppliers' workers are not organised. But it can also work in very well organised industries, as the NGA proved (page 402). Employers may prefer to end a commercial contract rather than be seen to be trading with an employer in dispute.

Extending the dispute
You could ask a secondary employer not to require his/her employees to work on products destined for your factory, or to handle goods coming from it. If s/he refused, you could have a new dispute about the terms and conditions on which his/her staff were employed. This would obviously be more justifiable if both groups of workers were in the same union, but in theory there is no reason why a new trade dispute could not exist further down the line from the main dispute. However, the Law Lords, by a 3–2 majority, attempted to stop this logic by distinguishing between 'legitimate' union demands, which since 1982 would be those relating *wholly or mainly* to terms and conditions of employment, and 'illegitimate' ones, where the connection is artificial or tenuous:

> A trade union cannot turn a dispute which in reality has no connection with terms and conditions of employment into a dispute connected with terms and conditions of employment by insisting that the employer inserts appropriate terms into the contracts of employment into which he enters. *Universe Tankships v ITF* 1982 (HL)

'Hot cargo agreements'
Before you are asked to boycott supplies or deliveries from employers in dispute with a TUC union you could negotiate an agreement that you would not be called on to handle a product in circumstances where it is 'hot cargo' – as unions in the US put it. Some unions – the NGA for instance – already include in their rules instructions that members should not handle copy from employers 'antagonistic' to the union, and many employers accept this in practice. If no employment contract is broken, there is no 'secondary action' and section 17 does not apply.

Information
To be liable for causing suppliers to break a commercial contract as a result of action by their workers, you need to know of the contract and intend it to be broken. The courts have widened the scope of both these elements:

> Even if they did not know of the actual terms of the contract, but had the means of knowledge – which they deliberately disregarded – that would be enough . . . . For it is unlawful

for a third person to produce a breach of contract knowingly, or recklessly, indifferent whether it is a breach or not. *Emerald v Lowthian* 1966 (CA)

'Inducement' under TULRA must 'involve some pressure, persuasion or procuration' (*Camellia Tanker v ITF*). In that case a flag-of-convenience ship was unable to leave Manchester because of a dispute about the crew's conditions. The company could not prove that an NUS official had **induced** breaches of contracts even though he: desired that tugmen and dock-workers would refuse to help the ship to leave Manchester; passed information to the TGWU hoping and believing that this would achieve his desire; asserted that in his view the ship would not leave Manchester, partly because of the probable action of TGWU members; and 'hoped for and expected support from members of affiliated unions without the need for incitement or threats'.

Mere advice and information to union members is therefore not an inducement since otherwise 'trade union officials could not open their mouths without being told that they were making an inducement or making a threat which was actionable if they were supported by fellow trade unionists not in dispute' (*Camellia* case).

So if you distribute leaflets or make speeches pointing out that there is a dispute, and members of their own accord offer to boycott a supplier, you have not induced them to break their contracts.

Cut off alternative suppliers

If you know management can get supplies from another source, you will want to try to stop this by approaching the workers at the alternative suppliers. It is doubtful that this is secondary action as defined in the Act, since you have not yet induced a breach of the workers' contracts of employment. In one case, though, the courts ordered a union official to stop such a pre-emptive approach to suppliers since there was an intention to disrupt the supplies if a contract were made (*Torquay Hotel v Cousins* 1969 (CA)). Now, even after 1980, if a contract were made for alternative supplies you could quite lawfully persuade the supplier's workers, and no injunction could be granted to stop you. So, logically, there should be no injunction to stop a pre-emptive appeal to them.

Duties to the public

Lord Denning has suggested that action taken in furtherance of a trade dispute *could* be illegal because it interferes with some duty to the public. TULRA protects you if you induce people to break contracts, or cause commercial contracts to be broken. But there is no protection in the Act for acts which cause someone to break a duty imposed on them by the law.

■ GMWU and NUPE lay officials advised London's Haringey Council that school caretakers were going on official strike in support of the 1978/79 pay claim, and all schools would be closed. The Labour-controlled authority blamed the action on the government's pay policy, supported the unions' claim and instructed staff not to do the strikers' jobs. Special schools and safety cover were not affected. A parent sought an injunction to get Haringey to open the schools as it was in breach of its duty under the Education Act 1944 to provide primary and secondary education. The six-week strike ended on the day of the trial so the judge refused the injunction. The parent appealed. *Meade v Haringey Council* 1979 (CA)

Although the Court of Appeal did not grant the injunction, and was called on to pass only a preliminary view, two judges said (a) that Haringey had unlawfully conspired with the unions, and (b) the unions, by inducing someone to break a statutory duty, were not protected by section 13 of TULRA.

All action by public sector workers would be threatened if this view were adopted.

Injunctions

An injunction (or an interdict in Scotland) is an order of a court requiring someone to do or not to do something. It is normally intended to preserve the *status quo* pending a full legal trial and can be issued very quickly, often without the person against whom it is issued having a chance to be present. This is an *ex parte* injunction. It is a favourite tactic of employers in stopping union officials and shop stewards calling for industrial action on behalf of their members. They are often successful.

If anyone can show a judge that **1.** they have a serious issue that they want to bring to court, and **2.** the 'balance of convenience' in preserving the *status quo* is in their favour, the judge may order an injunction to stop a particular event ocurring until the 'serious issue' has been decided finally. Because of the speed at which strikes progress, it is a powerful tool for employers. But in trade disputes it is now restricted by statute.

Strike leaders and, since 1982, unions, are the main targets for injunctions. Employers cannot get an injunction to stop individual workers from breaking their contracts by striking (see page 61). Section 17 of TULRA says that if it looks as though you are likely to claim you are 'acting in contemplation of or furtherance of a trade dispute', the court must give you every opportunity to attend. If an injunction is to be granted, the court (except in Scotland) must consider whether it is *likely* that you will succeed in showing you have the defence of acting in a trade dispute.

Lock-outs

Management's crudest weapon is the lock-out. Because they control the plant, premises and pay, their opportunities for exerting pressure are unlimited; they rarely need a full lockout. A lock-out is defined in Schedule 13 of the EPCA as the closing of a workplace, or suspension of work, or refusal to continue employing people because of a dispute, done with a view to *either* compelling workers to accept terms and conditions *or* to helping another employer. Unless the employer gives the notice necessary to terminate every worker's contract of employment, or there is a provision in a collective agreement, a lock-out is a breach of contract but **not necessarily equivalent to a sacking.**

■ Ten lorry drivers, members of the TGWU, held a one-day strike for better wages in August. The next day management refused to give them any work until they signed an agreement that effectively reduced the wages of eight of them by substituting the bonus scheme for a percentage increase. They refused and were locked out. Seven weeks later in October they were given their cards. The NIRC said they were dismissed *in October* because of redundancy and were entitled to payment. The lock-out in August did not amount to a sacking. *Davis Transport v Chattaway* 1972 (NIRC)

Dismissal of *all* workers by means of a lock-out and refusal to re-engage *any* of them means that tribunals cannot even *consider* a claim of unfair dismissal (page 392). But if there is no real dispute – if, for example, management close the gates one day – the lock-out constitutes unfair dismissal.

A lock-out without notices equivalent to every worker's appropriate entitlement is a breach of contract and wages in lieu can be claimed.

Strikes and redundancy

If you are given notice that you are being made redundant and decide to strike to oppose the plan, you will not prejudice your right to a redundancy payment if the strike fails to stop the redundancies (EPCA 1978 section 110). Management can require you to return to work after the strike to work out the balance of your notice. The same is probably true if you sit-in, as the definition of a strike (see page 385) seems to include a sit-in. It may not include a work-in or other industrial action. In this case, section 110 gives a tribunal discretion to order management to make a redundancy payment or part of one.

A frequent ploy used by employers is to threaten redundancy during the course of a strike, saying that the strike has caused a reduction in the need for particular kinds of work. They may have lost customers, for example. If this happens, you are in trouble. All they have to do is spread a few rumours, wait for a strike and then sack all the workforce. There is no need to pay redundancy. And as all the workers are sacked, none can claim unfair dismissal. Since gross misconduct entitles the employer to dismiss instantly, you do not get your notice or wages in lieu.

If you are made redundant *after* the strike is over, you can claim redundancy pay. For example, if management lose customers during the strike and have to make people redundant, the fact that you have been on strike does not prejudice your right to pay.

Strikes and social security

Social security benefits can be denied to workers involved in strikes and lock-outs. Supplementary benefit can be made to their dependants.

You cannot get unemployment or social security benefits if you are on strike or are laid off because of a stoppage due to a trade dispute at your place of employment in which you are participating or directly interested. See page 292.

Strikes and pensions

Many pension schemes disallow the time spent on strike in calculating pensionable service. Certainly, some employers are quick to remind you that if you go or stay on strike your pension will be affected. In practice, discounting the time spent on strike will have only a minimal effect on the occupational pension you have been paying into during your working life. But it may affect you if your pension scheme provides benefits according to *whole* pensionable years of service. For example, a two-week strike could stop you getting credit for a full year if you retire close to an anniversary.

Strikes and continuity of employment

The basic rule is that a day when you were on strike does not count in adding up your total continuous service, but it does not break it either. How you calculate your length of continuous employment for redundancy, maternity, compensation and other purposes is dealt with in chapter 19.

Summary

As we have seen, strike activity is surrounded by legal restrictions. The initiative to take legal action lies almost exclusively with employers and it is up to them to decide what to do. There is no guarantee that strikers will be in the clear legally, whatever they do. **The extent to which employers launch legal offensives depends on their financial strength, the availability of substitute labour, the political climate, public feeling and the solidarity of the strikers and their supporters.** The following broad rules sum up the position of workers in dispute:

1. Most strikes involve breaches of contract. The only exceptions are:

- strikes where you have given proper notice and resign
- strikes which have been deliberately provoked when the employers have seriously broken their contracts with you
- strikes in which contracts of employment are regarded as suspended.

2. Almost all other industrial action involves breaches of contract.

3. Breach of contract in these circumstances usually, but not always, entitles your employer to sack you without notice or wages in lieu.

4. S/he can, alternatively, sue you for breach of contract but in practice never will.

5. Provided *all* the workers who at the time of the dismissal were taking part in the industrial action are sacked, no one can make a claim. But if there is some discrimination, the victims can claim unfair dismissal.

6. Anyone, whether fellow-workers, shop stewards or union officials, can ask people to break contracts during a trade dispute. So sympathetic action and boycotts can be encouraged among workers whose employer is a party to the dispute or is a direct customer or supplier.

7. There are restrictions on employers getting injunctions during a trade dispute.

8. Unions can be sued for civil wrongs committed in a dispute in the same way as individuals, provided the action has been authorised.

The need for a right to strike

The right to terminate your contract in the way the contract stipulates can in no sense be described as a right to strike. Workers' rights are undermined by: the courts regarding almost all forms of industrial action as breaches of contract, employers' rights to dismiss strikers for 'misconduct', employers' freedom to carry out mass sackings. There is no point in the law giving workers the right to notice, maternity leave, time off and so on if it does not give them the right to withdraw their labour to get these rights.

The following legal requirements are minimum demands:

1. A legal right to strike.

2. In any strike contracts of employment should automatically be suspended, to be resumed after the dispute is settled. This is what both sides intend anyway.

3. EPCA 1978 section 62, which permits mass sackings, should be repealed.

4. Government changes on union liability, and liability for secondary action, should be repealed.

17. Picketing, occupations and public meetings

The absence of legal rights / legal actions that can be brought against you if you picket or occupy or demonstrate / criminal and civil liability / how to organise industrial picketing / non-industrial picketing / what to do in an occupation / police powers in public meetings and demonstrations / and a summary.

There is no positive legal right to freedom of speech, to demonstrate, to picket or to hold public meetings in the UK. There is no written constitution guaranteeing these freedoms, so, in exercising what should be your rights, you are at the mercy of the police and the judges. The police have very wide powers to 'execute their duty' in preventing what they see as potential disturbances. In addition, employers, landlords and their agents, local authorities and embassies, when confronted by a well-organised picket, may rush to the courts and will be treated sympathetically by the judges. Lord Chief Justice Hewart said in 1936:

> English law does not recognise any special right of public meeting either for a political or any other purpose. The right of assembly . . . is nothing more than a view taken by the courts.

Still, if you know your rights on a picket-line or a demonstration, you may be able to put the police on their best behaviour or even get a police officer to reverse a decision.

Pickets in an industrial dispute are given a very limited protection against some legal threats. But in practice non-prosecution of pickets is due to police toleration of them, rather than the existence of a 'right to picket'.

If newspaper headlines and TV coverage were the sole guide to what happens in industrial relations, picketing would be seen as the most pressing industrial issue. The Tories gave the highest priority to restricting the already illusory rights of pickets. The reasons for taking the steps contained in the Employment Act 1980 and the Code of Practice were purely political. The public had been whipped into antagonism towards all disputes which involve picketing, yet the Tories created this out of misinformation and deceit.

There was certainly no lack of law to throw at pickets. Civil actions by employers have long been possible against workers who do anything other than just 'attend', communicate and try to persuade. In the criminal law, the Tory Attorney-General saw no gaps, and acknowledged that the inadequacy was in respect of public knowledge rather than criminal sanctions.

The newspapers often express the view of the public and if one reads them it appears, for example, that lorries may be stopped by the pickets from entering works. They express a view that an excesssive number of pickets is not contrary to the law and cannot be interfered with by the police. Those are two typical examples of the way in which the law is misinterpreted. **The criminal law is sufficient to cover the various offences that have been demonstrated by the pickets over a number of years.** (emphasis added)

The issue was law enforcement rather than law enactment. But the government had to be seen to strengthen the law. Picketing by workers in dispute, and supporters, represents working-class militancy and solidarity in its most visible grassroots form, and it is frequently effective.

Picketing is one aspect of industrial relations and trade union organisation where members are directly and personally involved and where the risk of legal action is very high. Unlike civil injunctions, which are usually granted against general secretaries and executive committees, legal action arising out of picketing is most likely to be in the criminal courts against individual members and shop stewards. With one or two notable exceptions full-time officials do not often bear the brunt of picket-line activity and prosecution.

Where to find the law

The main statutes the police can use against you are: Highways
Act 1980 section 137 (obstruction); Police Act 1964 section 51
(obstructing the police); Conspiracy and Protection of Property
Act 1875 section 7 (intimidation); Public Order Act 1936
(offensive or racist language); Prevention of Crime Act 1953
section 1 (offensive weapon); Criminal Law Act 1977 sections
1–11 (conspiracy, entering property, obstructing court officers).
See also Trade Union and Labour Relations Act 1974
(TULRA) Section 15, the Employment Act 1980, the Code of
Practice on Picketing 1980, the Criminal Justice (Scotland) Act
1980, the Burgh Police (Scotland) Acts 1892 and 1903, the Trespass (Scotland) Act 1865 and the Prevention of Incitement to
Hatred (N. Ireland) Act.

Civil and criminal law

Former Employment Secretary James Prior frequently asserted
that the changes he introduced would affect only civil liability
and not create new criminal offences. This is pure deception.
**The effect of the changes in the civil law is that many more pick-
ets are exposed to criminal prosecution** and these changes have
inevitably altered police behaviour and magistrates' attitudes
when faced with industrial picketing. The 1980 Employment
Act has practical consequences on picket-lines but the legal position is that **the criminal law is not changed by the Act, or by the
Code (see page 421), which cannot of itself create new offences.**
Indeed, the Code asserts that 'the police have **no** responsibility
for enforcing the civil law'. The 1980 Act and TULRA are civil
statutes. But they undoubtedly influence the police and the criminal courts. The standards set by the civil law must have a
bearing on many offences where the courts have to decide questions of degree – wilful obstruction, conduct likely to cause a
breach of the peace, threatening behaviour. Furthermore, the
criminal law can influence civil actions, since a conviction for an
offence arising out of picketing can be quoted in a subsequent
application for an injunction.

The civil law was available to employers long before the 1980
Act. With the police ready to make arrests and courts ready to
convict, civil action was usually an unnecessary expense. Yet if
you exceeded the limited bounds of TULRA section 15,

'attending' in order to make your persuasion effective, an injunction was and is available. Under the Industrial Relations Act 1971, employers got the Industrial Court to order dockers' shop stewards picketing Midland Cold Store in East London in 1972 to desist. When they refused, the 'Pentonville Five' were gaoled until spontaneous trade union action forced the courts to adopt a face-saving method of freeing them. And in the 1979 lorry drivers' dispute, an employer got an injunction preventing a TGWU shop steward not only from picketing unlawfully, but from picketing at all (*United Biscuits v Fall* 1979 (HC)).

So why did the Tories decide to extend civil liability? From an employer's point of view, an application for an injunction can provide a very useful distraction from the real subject of the dispute. As was seen in the steel workers' case (page 402), a temporary injunction, wrongly granted, succeeded in confusing the strikers and misleading the public for just enough time for it to be effective in stopping supportive strikes. Injunctions can be obtained more quickly than convictions, especially on charges where pickets have the right to elect trial by jury.

By amendment to TULRA, the Employment Act 1980 restricts the picketing that you can do at your own place of work, stops supporters joining you, stops your tactical movement of pickets to other places, and stops other workers supporting you by picketing their own place of work.

All these latter three forms of solidarity action have been labelled as 'secondary picketing' by the press (see page 403).

Industrial picketing

The only time the law gives you a written right to engage in protest activities in a public place is when you are picketing in connection with a trade dispute. Since 1906 there has been a clear right, on paper at least, to picket. **It is severely restricted by the criminal law and by the judges.** What protection we now have is given by section 15 of TULRA as amended by the Employment Act 1980, which says:

> It shall be lawful for a person in contemplation or furtherance of a trade dispute to attend at or near his own place of work . . . , for the purpose only of peacefully obtaining or communicating information, or peacefully persuading any person to work or abstain from working.

While this looks like a fairly broad right, there are many restraints. It still says that 'it shall be lawful' for you to do certain things in the course of a trade dispute. Already downgraded by the failure of the courts to give it precedence over any part of the criminal law, it permits very limited forms of action so long as these do not interfere in any real way with ancient civil law provisions such as nuisance and obstruction. The Tory Attorney-General said that the 'immunity' in section 15

> does not extend to any wrongful act such as violence, threats of violence or similar intimidation – whether by excessive numbers of pickets or otherwise or molestation amounting to a civil wrong.

In practice, the right to picket is illusory, providing the semblance of a positive right yet omitting to give this any teeth. There are exceptions for union officials, and sacked and mobile workers, which are dealt with below. The effect of section 15 on the civil law, and on management's willingness to take action, can be summed up as:

1. If you picket in any way other than peacefully, you can lose the immunity of section 15 and all immunities against civil actions for inducing breach of contract, etc.

2. If you picket anywhere other than at your own workplace you are a secondary picket and lose all the above immunities.

3. If you picket your own workplace *and* your employer is a party to the dispute you are furthering, you are immune under section 15, and immune from civil actions for inducing breach of contract, etc.

4. If you picket your own workplace but your employer is not a party to the dispute – that is, you are picketing in support of workers in dispute with their employer somewhere else – you are immune under section 15, and immune from civil legal actions for inducing breaches of employment contracts. But if, as is almost inevitable, you cause a *commercial* contract to be broken, *you are liable*.

The Code of Practice
Having discredited the TUC's guide on the conduct of disputes, the government published its Code of Practice on Picketing in 1980. It contains some of the advice and control mechanisms of the TUC guide, and goes considerably further. **The Code is not**

law, and does not lay down inflexible rules. It deals with several major problems for pickets, and its provisions are considered separately below.

What is picketing?

Picketing is not defined. It involves attendance to pursue the permitted purposes by prescribed methods. Section 15 of TULRA 1974 covers action taken **in contemplation of further-ance of a trade dispute.** So picketing and leafleting in further-ance of purely political objectives is not given the limited protection of the Act, nor is picketing in pursuit, for example, of a factory-gate union recruitment campaign. Mere peaceful attendance in these situations is in strict law a trespass to the highway and an obstruction.

The methods you can use to further the dispute are confined to 'peacefully obtaining or communicating information, or peacefully persuading any person to work or abstain from work-ing'. The Code affirms the right of people to ignore you. The difference between communication and persuasion is important if your picketing is outside the scope of section 15. Mere pro-vision of information about a dispute should not give rise to a civil action for inducing breach of contract, whereas persuasion could. You can persuade people not to work (and to work!). You are *not* covered as a picket if you try to persuade con-sumers not to use a product or workers to boycott a product.

The right to attend to communicate information, and to per-suade someone not to work, does not extend to stopping vehicles and people who do not want to stop.

■ During the 1972 building workers' strike John Broome, a union official, held up a placard and stood in front of a lorry which was trying to enter a site. The lorry driver stopped and listened and then tried to manoeuvre round the picket. A police officer arrived and Broome was arrested for obstruct-ing the highway. The magistrates found that the whole oper-ation took only nine minutes, that this was a reasonable period of time and that otherwise the right to picket was meaningless. The House of Lords overturned the decision, saying that he lost the protection of the Act when he tried to do more than 'peacefully persuade', that is, when he stopped the vehicle. *Broome v DPP* 1974 (HL)

The judges in this case were divided about the scope of the

right to persuade. Lord Reid, for instance, said that you have the right to stand about and try to persuade people, and even to walk along with them, but if they decide they have heard enough, or do not want to listen at all, you have no right to detain them. Nor can you stand in the road and halt a vehicle.

Once you go beyond peaceful communication or persuasion you lose the section 15 immunity from **general civil law complaints**, and also your immunities under section 13 against specific civil law claims for **inducing breaches of contract**.

■ With over 1,000 container-lorry drivers unemployed, the TGWU organised a preference system for union members serving Liverpool docks and attempted to enforce this against 'cowboy' haulage operators undercutting wage rates and taking business. A peaceful picket stopped all container work and the dock company got an injunction against four pickets on the grounds that they created a civil law *nuisance* in obstructing vehicles. By going beyond mere communication of information and, it was said, intending to compel ship-owners to use TGWU drivers, they lost their pickets' protection and were liable for civil nuisance. The judge agreed with Lord Denning in *Hubbard v Pitt* (page 435) that non-violent picketing (as here) is not a nuisance, but went on to outlaw it if the pickets' intentions went beyond communication. Incidentally, the court did not say the pickets, who sometimes trucked out of the terminal but were also unemployed or working elsewhere, were 'secondary'. *Mersey Dock and Harbour Co v Verrinder* 1982 (HC)

Similarly, you are liable to civil action if you trespass on management's premises, and intimidate while you are picketing. In a major legal assault, a court trying a case in full, not just for a temporary injunction, awarded massive damages against a union official.

■ Workers at a pharmaceutical company in Newry joined the Irish TGWU and arranged to meet at the union office. That day, seven members were sacked. Martin King, the ITGWU branch secretary, asked the owner to reinstate them and when he refused he went inside the factory and called a strike involving 30 of the 50 process workers who started picketing. The owners went for an injunction. The court said King's entry was a *trespass*, in the course of which he *induced breaches* of employment contracts. His picketing went beyond peaceful communication into *intimidation* and *obstruction*, and therefore became a *civil nuisance*. The unlawful picketing *interfered* with the owner's commercial contracts and since this was done by agreement, it was a *conspiracy* to damage the owner. These were all outside the immunity given in trade disputes, but in any event the judge held that, as King did not give evidence saying he was pursuing a trade dispute, he accepted the owner's statement that King was pursuing unprotected personal hostility towards the owner. He was ordered to pay £7,500 damages. *Norbrook Laboratories v King* 1982 (HC)

If the police **prevent you from communicating** with people, there is nothing you can do to exercise your right to persuade:

■ Peter Kavanagh, a former TGWU official, was outside St Thomas's Hospital building site in 1973 during an electricians' strike. Scab labour was being used and when a caoch-load of blacklegs left the site, the police formed a cordon and **refused to allow even the four offical pickets to speak to them.** Kavanagh tried to push through and when stopped, punched a policeman. He was fined £20 for assaulting and obstructing a police officer, who was **executing his duty to prevent a breach of the peace.** *Kavanagh v Hiscock* 1974 (HC)

Identical tactics were used daily by the police in 1977 at Grunwicks (see pages 7–8).

So, by trying to stop a vehicle and by trying simply to speak to blackleg workers when the police deny you access to them, you lose the limited protection of the Act. You are liable to some or all of the civil and criminal actions described in this chapter.

Moving pickets

As the highway is to be used for travelling along, you might think it would be lawful to do this carrying placards. This idea occurred to the leader of a technicians' strike committee during an official dispute at English Electric in 1964.

■ Harold Tynan was leading about forty pickets in a circle outside the directors' and visitors' entrance on the East Lancs

Road, Liverpool. He was told to stop the circling and, when he refused, he was arrested for obstructing a police officer in the execution of his duty (and also for intimidation, but this was not proved). The full-time ('stipendiary') magistrate, the Liverpool Recorder and the High Court all upheld the police decision. It was an obstruction of the highway, and so the police were entitled to break the picket up. The pickets had intended to seal off the entrance so **their purposes exceeded those of information and peaceful persuasion.** *Tynan v Balmer* 1966 (HC)

So moving pickets have no special advantage.

Who can picket?
Although it is only the Code which attempts to restrict numbers of pickets, the Act defines who can make up the numbers. Simply, the Act says that you can picket only your own workplace for the permitted purposes. There are exceptions for union officials, people with changing or inaccessible workplaces, and former employees (below).

Your own place of work
Your 'own place of work' is the location where you actually work. If you have a number of locations you might be considered to work 'otherwise than at any one place' and so be caught by the more restrictive section on mobile workers. If your contract gives management the right to move you to other sites it is clearly arguable that your place of work covers all of them. The courts have taken this line to deny redundancy pay to workers covered by a wide contract who refuse to transfer. Logically, these same courts should recognise that if management have the right to move you, you should be able to picket all the 'places of work' embraced by the contract.

You can picket 'at or near' your place of work. The Code says this 'means the entrance or entrances to (or any exit from) the factory, site or office at which the picket works'. This creates two problems. The police could move you away from your spot *at* the main gates to a place across the street which is *near* them. Your right is not denied but hopelessly enfeebled. Secondly, if you picket at the entrance to the road which serves your workplace, rather than the gates themselves, you may not be near enough to your own place of work.

■ **Example:** You work in a supermarket in a large privately owned shopping mall, and are on strike for recognition. The security staff won't let you picket inside the mall by the shop entrance so you have to stand at the main entrance in the High Street. The police could argue that you were not 'at or near' the place you work, and therefore not covered by section 15. You would say this was as near as you could get and you were therefore protected.

The Employment Act 1980 aims to stop you picketing

- the head office, or town hall, of your employer;
- other sites of the same employer, which are perhaps more sensitive to effective picketing;
- other companies trading with yours;
- other companies trading with a supplier who continues to supply your employer;
- associated companies who do work transferred from your company.

In the last case secondary production by an employer in dispute is lawful, but following the work and picketing the new site is not. Some industrial problems are unresolved:

■ **Example (i): A large single-employer complex.**
The example frequently cited is Ford's Dagenham complex covering hundreds of acres, any part of which could be a 'place of work' to anyone working anywhere in the complex.

■ **Example (ii): A large multi-employer complex.**
Many companies operate within the Heathrow Airport perimeter. The 40,000 workers there could all say they worked on the airport, and picket the main entrances, even if they work for a small freight company in a remote corner.

■ **Example (iii): A large factory with different buildings.**
You are a computer programmer at a large engineering plant. The computer is in a separate building, served by its own entrance from the street. In a dispute you want to picket the gates used by the manual workers. The whole

factory should count as your place of work.

■ **Example (iv): Contractors on the same site.**
You work for a chemical manufacturer which has a fleet of
vehicles owned and operated by a transport contractor whose
trucks bear your firm's livery and name. Your workplace
should cover the whole site, including the transport yards run
by the separate company.

■ **Example (v): Workers not in dispute.**
Other employees of the same employer, who are not in dispute, picket the gates in support of you. They are at their
own workplace and therefore covered by section 15. But
people who don't work for the employer in dispute are
unprotected, and they might even make the lawful picketing
unlawful if they join in.

Picketing suppliers and customers
Picketing of direct suppliers and customers **by their own
employees** is lawful provided the picketing is targeted at the supplies going to or from the employer in dispute – 1980 Act section 17(5). A general picket aimed at all incoming goods is
unprotected.

If you picket suppliers or customers as 'flying pickets' you are
not covered by TULRA section 15. No matter how essential to
the effective conduct of your dispute, flying picketing is unlawful, except in the limited case of workers who are mobile or
whose picketing is 'impracticable'.

Mobile workers
If you work or normally work 'otherwise than at any one place',
your workplace then becomes any premises of your employer
from which you work, or from which **your work is administered.**
Refuse collectors and gas fitters would work from their depots,
transport drivers from their factories if they work for own-
account employers. In some cases, though, you could be denied
the right to picket.

■ **Example:** You are a construction worker employed in a
finishing trade, so you move from site to site. If you are in
dispute, section 15 does not allow you to picket the site on

which you are presently working. Since you normally work in different locations, your workplace for picketing purposes is the head office or sub-office where the paperwork for your jobs is done.

In the above examples, you could argue that ultimate control of the administration of your work rests at the company's head office, or the local authority's town hall. So picketing there could be permissible for employees without any fixed workplace. In some circumstances – for publicity purposes – such a move could be useful, but it would be more effective if you stopped the job by picketing the site you work at rather than appealing to clerical workers in a remote office block.

Where picketing is impracticable

A similar exception is made if you work 'at a place the location of which is such that attendance there . . . is impracticable' for the purposes of picketing. In this case you can picket at the depot or administrative centre. Probably envisaged by this exception are offshore oil rig workers and merchant seafarers, but workers on private trading estates or shopping precincts, as in the example on page 426, could qualify here. That, of course, would be a disadvantage if it removed you even further from the shop or factory you were aiming to close.

Union officials

Section 15 of TULRA 1974 says that if you are a union official, you can picket in furtherance of a trade dispute provided you are at or near the workplace of a member whom you are accompanying, and you represent. The Tories put it in the Act apparently in response to union demands. In this way, they got the unions to acknowledge the legitimacy of restrictions on picketing, and incorporated officials into a policing role.

A union official is widely defined in TULRA section 30 and includes full-time and lay officers, and shop stewards, safety and staff representatives. If you are a shop steward you can picket your own workplace without your members even being in dispute. Otherwise officials must accompany at least one member.

The Act says a union official can accompany only those members s/he is elected or appointed to represent. A branch secretary of one branch would not 'represent' members of another. But 'otherwise an official of a trade union shall be regarded . . . as representing all its members.'

■ **Example:** You are a district officer for west London within the Home Counties region, appointed by the region and available by your contract to be moved at the regional committee's discretion. You could therefore 'represent' any member in the region.

■ **Example:** Jack Dromey was secretary of Brent Trades Council during the Grunwick dispute. APEX, the union whose members were on strike for recognition, affiliated to the Trades Council. Under the Act, a federation of unions is a trade union, so officials of it could arguably accompany APEX members on the Grunwick picket-line if the 1980 Act had been in force then.

■ **Example:** All lay members elected to a district or regional committee are officers of the union. They can therefore accompany members, not only of the branch which elected them to the committee, but of any branch within the district or region.

■ **Example:** The union appoints all its full-time officers as 'organisers' or 'picketing officers' specifically required to represent union members on picket-lines whenever they occur, or even only for the duration of a particular strike. They are probably union officials within the Act and can picket anywhere their members can.

■ **Example:** An official arrives on the picket-line and stays there while the members go to a nearby café. Temporarily at least, he is not accompanying any members. Is a short absence of the members permitted?

Where you have **multi-union representation,** an official of one union can equally represent members of other unions which are party to a joint agreement, and is arguably a lawful picket in these two examples:

■ **Example:** Three unions form the staff side of a local authority's joint works committee. The unions' lay officers and delegates are officers of a trade union (the staff side) and represent all the workers in the borough.

■ **Example:** Three unions are represented on the Food Manufacturing JIC. Officers on that body are appointed by their respective unions, but come together as officers of the trade union side of the JIC, so represent all the trade union members in the industry.

Sacked workers

Picketing by **sacked workers** is permitted by TULRA. You are entitled to picket your last place of work if you do not have a job anywhere now, and your last job was 'terminated in connection with a trade dispute' or your termination 'was one of the circumstances giving rise to' the dispute (Employment Act 1982 Schedule 3). This implicitly refers to the fact that workers cannot get a tribunal hearing if they are all unfairly dismissed during industrial action, and none is taken back (EPCA 1978 section 62).

All the strikers in the *Grunwick* dispute (pages 7–8) were sacked because they were on strike. Today, as then, nothing would prevent them picketing after they were sacked.

Number of pickets

The law does not stipulate how many pickets are lawful, but the police have the power to limit the size of a picket if they anticipate an obstruction or that a breach of the peace will occur. Police, judges and employers know that the larger the picket-line, the more effective it will be in furthering industrial action. The Liverpool Recorder in *Tynan v Balmer* said:

> I can quite see the value, from the point of view of advertising the strike and underlining the number of people involved and demonstrating their solidarity, of having a substantial number of people near the prestige entrance, but forty seems to me to be a number far in excess of what was reasonably required.

He wanted to see only two or three, so he allowed the leader to be fined.

In *Piddington v Bates* 1960 (HC) a policeman restricted the number of pickets at a plant on strike to two on each entrance. When a worker tried to join the line, he was arrested for obstructing the policeman in the execution of his duty. The courts upheld this decision but refused to make a ruling that two pickets are sufficient in *any* situation. Lord Chief Justice Parker said it was up to the discretion of local police in every case. This means that a local police force can't make a general ruling about the number of pickets *in advance*.

Mass picketing, such as was seen at Saltley coke-works in 1972, at Shrewsbury during the 1972 national building strike and at Grunwicks, has been very successful. The law does not expressly say how many pickets you can have, but nor does it allow an unlimited number. Lord Reid said in John Broome's case (above):

> The section (now section 15) does not limit the number of pickets and no limitation of numbers can be implied . . . But . . . it would not be difficult to infer as a matter of fact that pickets who assemble in unreasonably large numbers do have the purpose of preventing free passage.

In other words there comes a time when the mere size of the picket deprives it of its limited protection. However, it is at this stage that mass arrests become impracticable. For this reason and because it is a demonstration of solidarity, **mass picketing is usually the most effective method.**

The Code says 'the law does not impose a specific limit on the number of people who may picket at any one place; nor does this Code affect in any way the discretion of the police to limit the number of people on a particular picket-line'. The Code does, however, go on to give this guidance: 'pickets and their organisers should ensure that in general the number of pickets does not exceed six at any entrance to a workplace; frequently a smaller number will be appropriate'. This is advice to pickets, **not** to the police.

Organisation of picket-lines

The Code gives much attention to the orderly organisation of picketing. It suggests that pickets should have an organiser who would police the picket-line, distribute armbands, receive instructions from the police, and turn back supporters from other workplaces!

Essential supplies

According to the Code, there is no activity that could not qualify as an essential supply or service which should be allowed through a picket-line. The lorry drivers' dispute of 1979 led to a vast array of essential services being included in the Code.

Then, shop stewards' committees issued passes to firms qualifying as essential. But that did not prevent abuses – an anti-union manufacturer of medical supplies in Norfolk got dispensation to move essential products to a specific location. Having been given a TGWU pass, the vehicle went in the opposite direction.

No attempt is made here to list the Code's provisions. Trade unionists are capable of exercising their own judgment about the essential needs of a business or the community. The Code is merely a strikebreakers' charter.

Crossing a picket-line

This theme is continued in the Code's positive statement that you have no obligation to stop at a picket-line, and that action to deter you is unlawful – an allusion to the reported but unproven threats to lorry drivers of loss of union membership in the 1979 dispute. Yet nowhere in the Code or the Act is a statement that if you do refuse to cross a picket-line you will not be subject to disciplinary action by your employer. In the USA, for example, such solidarity is declared to be lawful – page 388.

Police consent

As we have seen, the police have substantial control over pickets. Often small numbers of officially accredited pickets are left alone. But even if you escape interference by the police, civil injunctions are still possible, as happened in *Hubbard v Pitt*, where a tenants' group mounted a picket with the full knowledge of the police, who did not intervene at all (see below). And an orderly picket can become the source of individual prosecutions if one police officer decides to exercise authority at any particular time – see *Tynan v Balmer* (pages 424–25).

Civil claims

Pickets who are not covered by section 15 might be challenged in the civil courts. The extended scope for legal action, and the unlimited range of potential plaintiffs, make the possibility of injunctions, and even damages, against pickets quite real.

The grounds for claiming

The main civil liabilities that you are exposed to as an unprotected picket are interference with contracts, intimidation and conspiracy. These arise out of your inability to call on TULRA section 13 to protect acts customarily done in disputes. There are other possibilities, too: nuisance, libel, obstruction, molestation.

One escape route is provided by the fact that picketing to **communicate information** is not actionable in itself (see page 410). So statements, leaflets and placards explaining the issues and advising people that a dispute exists might be safe. Make sure you conduct your picketing as an exercise in information, and you might escape liability.

Who can sue?
Anyone harmed by your unprotected picketing can sue you. Your employer, his/her suppliers and customers, suppliers' suppliers, even scabs who don't go to work because they feel threatened, can sue.

The most likely step is an application for an injunction, the procedure for which is dealt with on page 412.

A practical example
During a strike for recognition by GMBATU members at Chix Confectionery Ltd, Slough in 1979/80 there were many examples of picketing. Diagram 10 on page 434 shows the way in which a dispute can be furthered by picketing. Had the 1980 Act and Code been in effect then, most of the picketing would be illegal, as the following summary shows:

1. Picketing at **Chix** by members and local officials was reinforced by members of trades councils, political organisations, community relations council, the MP, councillors, trade unionists from other areas, Punjabi translators, strikers' families, Asian community leaders, street entertainers. ALL UNPROTECTED.

2. Metrostore and **BS Carriers** were used by Chix as 'secondary' distribution centres, since the manufacturers of main supplies wouldn't deliver to Chix. Picketing there is UNPROTECTED.

3. Tunnel was the sole UK supplier of glucose. It disguised its supplies to Chix by using **XYZ** as a third party, delivering overnight with a police escort. Picketing of **Tunnel** and **XYZ** sites UNPROTECTED.

4. Country Storage hired plant to **Chix.** Picketing there UNPROTECTED.

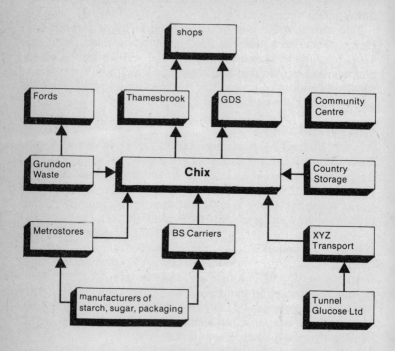

Diagram 10 **Picketing**

5. Grundon picked up waste from Chix and Ford's Langley plant. Boycott by Ford workers caused Grundon to terminate Chix's contract. Picketing at Fords by Ford workers ILLEGAL unless to disrupt supplies between Ford and Chix (not Grundon).

6. Picketing of **Slough Community Centre** for refusal to serve the strikers UNPROTECTED, even though connected with the dispute.

7. Thamesbrook transport and warehouse refused to cross Chix picket line but accepted goods delivered by Chix's hired truck driven by Chix's temporary driver. Picketing at **Thamesbrook** UNPROTECTED.

8. GDS was the wholesale distribution centre in Sheffield. Picketing there UNPROTECTED.

9. Picketing of **shops** to get owners to remove Chix product from their shelves, and to dissuade shoppers, UNPROTECTED.

Non-industrial picketing

If you think your rights to picket in industrial disputes are puny, they are almost non-existent where there is no trade dispute. Consumers protesting against a store, women campaigning against discrimination in banking and insurance, parents protesting against a school's policy, voters complaining of cuts in public expenditure, tenants seeking to expose racketeering – none of these groups has a right to picket under TULRA. Whether or not they have any *other* right is unclear, and depends on an interpretation of one case.

Hubbard v Pitt was heard in 1975 by the Court of Appeal but as it was about an application for a temporary injunction, it was not a full hearing. So the judges were giving only a preliminary view. But, as with most injunctions, the preliminary judgment decided the whole issue.

■ James Pitt and nine others objected to the property speculation going on in London in the early 1970s. In Islington a tenants' group picketed the offices of Prebbles, an estate agent which they claimed had been harassing and winkling out tenants. They were there on Saturday mornings, in numbers of up to eight. The picket was orderly and aimed to give information to passers-by. The firm claimed the picket was a private nuisance and asked for an injunction to stop it. This was granted because a 'serious question' had arisen concerning their property rights. The pickets had no protection under any Act, so they were banned until the serious question could be tried. *Hubbard v Pitt* 1975 (CA)

The Court of Appeal confirmed the injunction by a two-to-one majority. The majority said the presence of the pickets constituted a nuisance because they were 'watching and besetting' the office with a view to compelling people not to do something they had a right to do. In granting the injunction, the judges said that the **interference with free speech was a minimal worry compared with the possible loss to the agent's business.** The judges said the pickets might not be able to pay for any losses Prebbles might suffer, but Prebbles *could* afford to compensate the pickets for any loss *they* might suffer for interference with their free speech if Prebbles lost the case. So the 'balance of convenience' lay with granting an injunction.

But Lord Denning did not agree, and what he said *may* provide the basis of a **common law right to picket** in non-industrial situations. What he said was:

> There was no obstruction, no violence, no intimidation, no molestation, no noise, no smells, nothing except a group of six or seven people standing about with placards outside [Prebbles'] premises all quite orderly and well-behaved. That cannot be said to be a nuisance at common law.

In other words, **orderly picketing** for communication or persuasion is **lawful** under this interpretation, which was subsequently adopted by the judge in *Mersey Dock v Verrinder*, page 423.

Since the Court of Appeal does not operate in Scotland or the six counties of Northern Ireland, and since the law on non-industrial picketing has never been interpreted in the same way as it is in England, non-industrial picketing is probably lawful there.

Occupations

An occupation is not itself illegal. The Criminal Law Act 1977 (page 445) and the procedures in the civil courts make it easy for the police and the courts to support employers against workers who are occupying a plant. The offence of violent entry is committed if someone – a security guard for instance – *believes* violence has been threatened. Sheer numbers of workers might constitute a threat. Entry from one part of a plant to another – for example from the shop floor to the administration offices – might make you a trespasser. You are then guilty of remaining there after being told to leave.

Many items found in a factory could become offensive weapons in the imagination of the police and judges. Lying down in front of your employer's agents, authorised by a court to serve an eviction order, means you are committing an offence. The new powers of the police to intervene on suspicion of any of these offences means that occupations have become a public rather than a private industrial matter.

You can minimise the threat of police intervention in an occupation, or stall it temporarily, if you:

1. stay on the part of the plant where you are entitled to be
2. don't enter residential areas unless the workers who live there agree, for example, in hotels, ships, farms
3. don't carry tools or anything that could remotely be considered 'offensive'
4. gain entry with a key, or by consent of someone inside
5. don't enter in such large numbers, or in such an aggressive way that a charge of threatened violence is credible
6. don't damage any property or plant while the occupation is on

If the bailiffs do get in, demand to see credentials and a court order. Bear in mind that only police **in uniform** can intervene without a warrant, and they must have reasonable suspicion that an offence under the Act has been committed – ask them to specify their grounds.

Public meetings and demonstrations

Many workers talk of the right to free speech. But as it is not a right contained in any Act of Parliament, it is elastic and easily manipulated by the police and judges. There is, for instance, no general right to hold a meeting in a public place. The only time you can demand premises from a local authority is on behalf of a candidate in a parliamentary or local government election (Representation of the People Act 1949).

In some towns the police control the holding of meetings because local by-laws require that police permission must be obtained before a meeting can take place – in many parks, for example. In fact, though, if there is no by-law, public meetings cannot be banned in advance by the police. Demonstrations can. However, some civil liability may be incurred if you use a roadway for a public meeting, because roadways are usually owned by local authorities, who make them available for 'reasonable use', by people, which means for passing to and fro along. If you do anything in excess of this 'privilege', you can be sued by the local authority for **trespass to the highway** (page 446). In practice this power isn't used and it is the police who break up meetings.

On what basis can they do this? It is usually to prevent a breach of the peace, or an obstruction. In one case police who entered private premises and broke up a public meeting acted lawfully. It is not clear whether they can do so if they merely suspect a breach of the peace – they probably can't – or whether there must be a suspicion of sedition, that is, serious anti-government agitation. If a breach of the peace – any disruption – actually occurs, the police can enter premises and put it down. The police can intervene in a meeting wherever a breach of the peace occurs, or where it is expected to occur.

A demonstration is technically a reasonable use of the highway. Each participant is doing what s/he is entitled to do on the highway, that is to walk along it. But the police can intervene on the grounds of obstruction, and if you do not do as you are told you are obstructing the police in the execution of their duty.

In addition, the Public Order Act 1936 (page 444) passed to try to stamp out Fascist marches, allows the police to lay down the route that must be followed by a demonstration if there is a risk of serious disorder. If that is considered inadequate they can ask the appropriate local authority (Home Secretary in the Metropolitan Police area) to ban certain demonstrations for up to three months. The police refused to ban National Front marches in Lewisham and Ladywood in 1977, despite pleas for these Acts to be enforced. However, in order to prevent a National Front march in Manchester in 1977 the police used the Public Order Act 1936, for the first time in recent years, to ban *all* marches for five weeks. Since then it has been used on many occasions to ban all marches in London and other parts of England.

In most of Scotland, all of Northern Ireland and in the by-laws of many places in England and Wales, advance notice or even permission is required for all marches and demonstrations.

A failure to observe directions or a ban would mean prosecution for unlawful assembly, obstructing the police and worse. Forty Right to Work marchers were prosecuted in 1976–77 following contradictory police instructions when they marched through Hendon, north London.

What happens if you meet a counter-demonstration which

tries to disrupt your demo or meeting? The law is unclear. But in 1902 a Liverpool Orangeman was 'bound over to keep the peace' when he led a march into a Catholic area and caused a disturbance. He was found to have known that disruption would be obvious, **because he used insulting language and behaviour** (*Wise v Dunning*). National Front marchers in West Indian areas could be charged with this. If they actually assault people, they can be charged with various offences.

You can distribute leaflets in the street if the printer is identified on the leaflets. You can use a loudspeaker between 9 a.m. and 8 p.m. but there are frequently by-laws regulating what you say through them. You cannot collect money unless you have a licence and you are unlikely to get one if you are not a charity or other similar cause.

Civil rights

The move against pickets forms part of a wider attempt to restrict demonstrations and supportive action. A number of major cities now require advance notice of marches. The government published a Green Paper in April 1980 reviewing the 1936 Public Order Act and related legislation. Among the proposals was:

> whether a requirement of advance notice and the power to lay down conditions and, in the last resort, to ban on public order grounds should apply to assemblies of people in public places in the open air (including the highway) . . . .They might not apply . . . to peaceful picketing, though they could apply to large scale demonstrations in support of pickets. (para 78)

It is clearly envisaged that advance warning would have to be given to the police and local authorities of picketing activities beyond those laid down in the Code of Practice.

In most parts of Scotland it has been obligatory since 1892, and more recently in Northern Ireland, for advance notice to be given of all marches, and compliance with conditions laid down by local authorities in consultation with the police. The Criminal Justice (Scotland) Act 1980 introduced new police powers to require you to identify yourself and give an explanation if you are suspected of committing an offence. You can be detained for questioning for six hours, and fingerprinted, without being arrested if you are suspected of committing an imprisonable offence. You have the right to have word passed to a friend, and to a solicitor if you are detained, without delay but they do not have a right of access to you. There is also power to search you on suspicion of carrying offensive weapons. The evidence since 1980 showed that two-thirds of personal searches failed to produce offensive weapons.

The Northern Ireland (Emergency Powers) Act 1973 gives extensive powers to the security forces there to question, search, arrest and detain for up to 48 hours (72 hours on suspicion of terrorism). The Prevention of Terrorism Act 1976 applies throughout the UK and gives police the power to arrest and detain you for up to 72 hours on suspicion of supporting a banned organisation such as the IRA, or being involved in 'acts of terrorism'.

Summary of main legal threats

Criminal offences
Obstruction
Section 137 of the Highways Act 1980 says that anyone who, without lawful authority or excuse, wilfully obstructs the highway commits an offence and can be arrested without a warrant. There is scope for arguing that you are protected as long as you use the highway reasonably. Lord Chief Justice Parker said in *Nagy v Weston* (1965):

> It depends on all the circumstances, including the length of time the obstruction continues, the place where it occurs, the purpose for which it is done and, of course, whether it does in fact cause an actual as opposed to a potential obstruction.

In practice this approach appears too liberal, since many campaigners have been convicted for doing nothing more than causing a technical breach of section 137. You can argue reasonableness, but the Act makes *any* wilful obstruction illegal unless the obstruction is very slight and purely temporary in nature. The maximum penalty is £50.

In Scotland, the Burgh Police Act 1892 and various local Acts and by-laws contain wide proscriptions on obstruction, such as 'occasioning any kind of obstruction, nuisance or annoyance in any street, public place or doorway' in Glasgow. You can get up to 60 days in gaol or a £25 fine.

Public nuisance

Behaviour that materially affects 'the reasonable comfort and convenience of life of a class of Her Majesty's subjects' is a public nuisance at common law, and a prosecution can be brought. There must be discomfort to a class of persons, such as a group of shopkeepers or residents affected by picketing. An individual can do nothing if s/he is just obstructed by a picket, but if s/he is actually injured, s/he can sue for damages in the civil courts or ask the police to prosecute. Local authorities are given wide powers by the Control of Pollution Act 1974. They could serve a notice on a noisy picket or public meeting and have the noise stopped. Local authorities also have a duty to see that the Highways Act is enforced and may themselves prosecute pickets causing an obstruction or making a nuisance.

Obstructing the police

Section 51 of the Police Act 1964 says that it is an offence to assault a police officer carrying out his/her duty, for which you can get up to two years in gaol and an unlimited fine. If you 'resist or wilfully obstruct', you can get up to one month in gaol and a £200 fine.

The officer must be doing his/her duty – if s/he tells you to move on, it must be because, for instance, you are causing an unreasonable obstruction, or because s/he considers there are reasonable grounds for saying that some disruption (a 'breach of the peace') is genuinely likely to occur if you don't. The scope of the officer's authority is very wide.

■ In 1934, a woman was held to have obstructed the police when she held a meeting of unemployed workers outside a means test centre after being told to hold it elsewhere. It was alleged that a similar meeting 14 months earlier had led to a disturbance, so the police were acting to stop a breach of the peace. The disturbance was that workers had sung 'The Red Flag'. *Duncan v Jones* 1936 (HC)

Outside Scotland, the police have no right to detain you for questioning. If you refuse to stay for further questions you are not interfering with the exercise of the police officer's duty and the officer can detain you only by arresting you. In Scotland, obstruction must take some physical form, whereas in England and Wales it can be oral.

Intimidation, following and watching

Section 7 of the Conspiracy and Protection of Property Act 1875 says that it is an offence if you 'wrongfully and without legal authority' use violence against or intimidate a person or their family, persistently follow them around or 'watch and beset' their house or business premises, with a view to compelling them to do or not do something they have a legal right not to do or do. This section was used extensively in 1926. Charges of intimidation were brought against 12 building workers in Flint following a national strike in 1972. They were all acquitted. The Shrewsbury pickets (see below) were convicted of conspiracy to intimidate, that is, the Act was used as a peg on which to hang the conspiracy charge.

A Scottish union official was convicted for following in his car two members who were collecting and working on mail during the 1981 civil service strikes – *Elsey v Smith* 1983 (HC).

Conspiracy

This offence was created by the judges and added to by them over the years without an Act of Parliament. In other words, it was a common law offence, for which the punishment was unlimited. The Criminal Law Act 1977 makes conspiracy a statutory offence, although some common law conspiracies remain. Much of the Act does not apply in Scotland, where conspiracy is still a common law offence involving an agreement to do something with others which would be criminal if done alone.

Conspiracy is an agreement by two or more people 'that a course of conduct shall be pursued which will necessarily . . . involve the commission of any offence . . . if the agreement is carried out in accordance with their intentions'.

It is the agreement that has always worried the ruling class. Organisations of workers represent a threat – whether or not you carry out your agreed aim, you are guilty of an offence.

If, during an industrial dispute, you agree to do something unlawful at civil law – to break a contract or to cause a nuisance – you cannot be prosecuted for conspiracy. Agreements to do something criminal are unprotected unless the criminal act itself does not carry a penalty of imprisonment. So you can't be charged with **conspiracy to cause an obstruction** if you agree to picket.

Since the 1977 Act you can't get more for *conspiring* to do something illegal that you could get if you were convicted of doing the act itself. If you carry out your agreement, there is nothing to stop the prosecution charging you with conspiracy *and* with the offence itself. During the Tory administration of 1970–74, several outrageous prosecutions were brought – including the trial of the Shrewsbury pickets:

■ Between July and September 1972 there was a national strike of building workers for higher wages. During the strike self-employed Lump labour continued to work. The strike action committee in Chester and North Wales organised coaches to transport strikers to picket building sites where Lump labour and others were still at work. Six shop stewards on the committee were arrested in Shrewsbury while on a flying picket. 13 months later they came before Mr Justice Mais and a jury at Shrewsbury, facing 42 charges. Only three were proceeded with. The others – intimidation, damage to property, threatening behaviour and assault – were 'left on file'. All six workers were convicted of unlawful assault and each got two years' suspended sentence. John Jones, Eric Tomlinson and Dennis Warren were convicted by a majority of 10–2 of conspiracy to intimidate workers to abstain from working, and unanimously of affray. They got a total of nine months, two years and three years respectively. The Court of Appeal quashed the affray convictions but upheld the rest. The three men served their full sentences, despite massive rank-and-file pressure and some corridor lobbying by the TUC for their release. *R v Jones and Others* 1974 (CA)

The following points can be made about the case:

1. The charges were not brought until long after the strike, following instructions by Robert Carr, the then Home Secretary, to get tough in industrial disputes.

2. Charges of actual assault and intimidation were brought in a similar earlier trial in Flint and the men acquitted.. These charges were not pressed at Shrewsbury.

3. Instead, conspiracy charges were used, making the prosecution's job easier. Hearsay evidence and evidence against others can be introduced. The judge could also pass sentences much higher than could be passed for intimidation. (The 1977 Act restricts this right.)

4. By the time the final appeals were heard in March 1974, Labour was already in office. Roy Jenkins, the Home Secretary, thereafter steadfastly refused to free the pickets.

5. Demands by the TUC for a right to picket and to stop vehicles were ignored by the Labour government.

6. Only in 1977 did the Inland Revenue take firm measures to control tax evasion by Lump labour.

7. UCATT and the TGWU, whose members were in gaol, and the TUC, refused demands for official industrial action to free them.

Breach of the peace

The most common charge used against pickets and demonstrators is for breach of the peace. It can take two forms. You can be brought before a magistrates' court without being charged with an offence and be bound over to keep the peace. This is not a conviction but is a court requirement backed up by your recognisance (promise) that if you break the requirement you lose the money. It is in theory designed to *prevent* a conviction.

You could also be bound over if you have been charged with or convicted of a criminal offence, and typically pickets will as a condition of bail be ordered to stay away from the picket line.

Alternatively, under the Public Order Act 1936 it is an offence punishable by magistrates with up to six months in gaol and/or a £1,000 fine (more in race cases) for anyone in a public place or public meeting to use threatening, abusive or insulting words or behaviour, or to distribute or display anything threatening, abusive or insulting, with the intention or likelihood of provoking a breach of the peace or stirring up racial hatred. Colin Jordan and John Tyndall were convicted for saying 'Hitler was right' in Trafalgar Square in 1962, because this led 'hooligans', that is, anti-Fascists, to break up the meeting.

On the directions of Judge McKinnon, John Kingsley Read was acquitted in 1978 of similar charges following a National Party speech when he talked of 'niggers, wogs and coons' and said 'a million to go' following the murder of a young Asian. McKinnon said this wasn't racist!

In Scotland, breach of the peace is covered by common law, by-law and statute, and police powers are more extensive than in England and Wales. There is, however, no power to bind over. Additionally there is a serious common law offence of mobbing and rioting, which is essentially intimidation by numbers or the threat of violence. It was used unsuccessfully against strikers at Longannet power station in 1972.

The Prevention of Incitement to Hatred (Northern Ireland)

Act 1970 outlaws language intended to stir up hatred or fear on the grounds of religious belief, colour, race or ethnic origin in the six counties (where the Race Relations Act does not apply).

Possessing an offensive weapon

Section 1 of the Prevention of Crime Act 1953 creates the offence of carrying an offensive weapon in a public place 'without lawful authority or reasonable excuse'. Unusually in English and Scots law, it is down to the accused to prove s/he had an excuse or had no intention of using it as a weapon. Since 'offensive weapon' would include acid, pepper, workers' tools, placards and even, as was alleged in a 1975 prosecution of Newcastle building workers, a shoe, the scope for police harassment in a demonstration or picket-line is very wide.

Criminal trespass

Trespass has always been a common law *civil* wrong. In certain circumstances it is also a crime – on railways, public utilities and in the vicinity of explosive factories, and if there is an intention to steal, rape or injure. If you squat or sit-in and refuse to leave, or enter premises without permission, you are a trespasser. You need not do any damage or cause any loss to the normal occupier.

In the last few years, as the courts realised how squatting and occupations threaten property rights, they developed special rules of civil procedure (see below). Parliament also passed the Criminal Law Act 1977, which contains serious restrictions on direct action.

This creates the following new criminal offences:

1. Violent entry. It is illegal to use or threaten violence to secure entry to any premises if there is someone present on the premises and you know this. Violence or the threat of it can be directed against people or property. The maximum sentence is two years in gaol after trial by jury.

2. Remaining on property. It is an offence to fail to leave premises when requested to do so by a 'displaced residential occupier' or by a person who has bought the premises, provided you entered the premises as a trespasser. Residential occupation is not defined and might be proved by an owner who doesn't actualy live on the premises, but leaves some furniture and occasionally visits them.

You could get six months in gaol and a £1,000 fine for this offence. You have no right to a jury trial.

3. Trespassing with an offensive weapon. If you have entered any premises as a trespasser and have an 'offensive weapon' with you, you could get two years in gaol and a fine, after a jury trial. Offensive weapon is widely interpreted – see above.

4. Trespassing in embassies. This is designed to prevent direct action against offensive foreign governments and follows protests in the embassies of Iran, Syria, Cuba, Bangladesh and Libya. You could get one year in prison after a jury trial.

5. Resisting bailiffs. If your employer or the owner of the property gets a civil court order to evict you, it must be enforced by a court officer. This is either a full-time bailiff of one **authorised for this occasion** – which could mean an employee or agent of your employer. If you resist or wilfully obstruct them, you could get six months in gaol and a £1,000 fine. You have no right to a jury trial.

A police officer in uniform can arrest you without a warrent if s/he has reasonable grounds for believing you have committed any of these five offences. In order to arrest you for one of these offences s/he can also enter and search any premises without a warrant if s/he suspects that you are there.

The Criminal Law Act sections on trespass do not apply in Scotland, where trespass is a crime under the Trespass (Scotland) Act 1865. You can get up to 14 days in gaol and a £10 fine.

Civil liability
Civil trespass

Procedures in the High Court (Order 113) and the County Court (Order 24) make it easy for property-owners and occupiers to evict you. Civil writs for possession can be served on *unnamed persons*, they need not be given to you *personally* and can be left in a bag at a factory gate. If orders for possession are obtained against a group of workers, they can be used against a completely different group if the composition has changed by the time the bailiffs arrive, even though the order was not made against them and they have had no opportunity to state their case. Alternatively, owners can get an *injunction* against named people to prevent you trespassing and this can be followed up, if you occupy premises, by a possession order.

Trespass to the highway

Committed by anyone who uses the highway in an unreasonable manner, that is, for anything other than travelling along. Industrial pickets are protected from this law. People taking part in unlawful or disorderly public meetings are not. Local authorities usually own the highway and, although they rarely sue, they might resort to suing for trespass if their own offices were continuously picketed.

Nuisance

For private nuisance there must be some interference with someone's enjoyment of their *land*. Smells, smoke, noise, vibration, queues, cars can all be a nuisance, as can a large demonstration or public meeting. Actual damage need not be proved – it is enough for someone to say they object to a particular activity because it diminishes their enjoyment of their land and thereby causes them a 'loss'. Damages and injunctions can be awarded.

Summary

1. You have no positive right to picket, sit-in, demonstrate or hold public meetings.

2. You have a very limited protection from some civil liability if you are picketing in an industrial dispute.

3. Non-industrial picketing is not protected, but it is arguable that there is a limited common law right.

4. Police discretion to intervene, to control the number and location of pickets is very wide. They have total power over pickets.

5. In practice, agreement with the police on numbers has been effective. The most effective picketing method is mass picketing.

6. The Criminal Law Act is a disincentive to workers occupying a workplace and the police have wide powers to intervene on suspicion without a warrant.

7. The civil law is not as quick, but can be used by property owners against pickets, and against workers occupying a workplace.

8. Police powers to ban or re-route a march are extensive.

18. Saving jobs

Direct action to prevent redundancies / using the law if direct action fails / your union's right to be consulted / which employers must consult / what consultation means / when it must begin / how employers can get out of consulting / how to claim a protective award / management's duty to notify the Department of Employment / consultation about takeovers / government measures to hide unemployment / a summary / and what to demand if redundancy is threatened.

Direct action by many workers in the 1960s forced government and managements to acknowledge that their policies meant mass sackings. The White Paper *In Place of Strife* conceded:

> The disparity of power between employee and employer, though much reduced, still persists, particularly in areas where trade unionism is weak. Lock-outs are now almost unknown, but in their place has come the new threat of widespread redundancies as industry is restructured and mergers multiply.

Still, no action was taken to require employers to negotiate with unions or to inform the Department of Employment (DE) about proposed redundancies until 1975. Workers have no right to work and government agencies have no power to veto sackings. Instead the Employment Protection Act 1975 gives workers a right to (limited) monetary compensation and the DE can withhold a fraction of employers' rebates of redundancy pay.

Sometimes workers have done better themselves. **Your first response to all redundancies must be resistance. Only if all your efforts fail do you need to look at the statutory methods of fighting.**

Your rights to notice, redundancy pay, protection against your employer's bankruptcy and unemployment benefit are dealt with in chapters 10, 11 and 12. This chapter deals with action your union can take.

Throughout, the definition of redundancy is the same as that used in chapter 11.

Where to find the law

Sections 99–107 of the Employment Protection Act 1975 (EPA) deal with consultation and notification about redundancies. The Transfer of Undertakings (Protection of Employment) Regulations 1981 SI No 1794 (TUR) give unions rights in a takeover.

The union's right to be consulted

Section 99 of the EPA requires employers to consult recognised independent unions about every proposed redundancy. So long as the union is recognised for workers of the description the employer proposes to sack, union representatives (full-time, or lay if they are recognised for negotiations) must be consulted. It does not matter whether the proposals relate to members of the same or another union, or non-members, or to workers of the same description in another location.

A union is recognised if the employer negotiates with it over any of the list of matters set out on page 313. There doesn't have to be a formal agreement – recognition can be inferred from the conduct of the union and the employer, provided this clearly shows the intention to recognise:

■ A TGWU member was sacked by a Scottish haulage firm. Trade unionists on the docks boycotted the company. A union official offered to lift the boycott if the member was reinstated and this was agreed. Later three union members were made redundant. When the TGWU claimed under section 99 the EAT said the union was not recognised, and recognition could not be inferred from the earlier meeting as

the employer never intended it. *TGWU v Andrew Dyer* 1977 (EAT)

An employer who belongs to an employers' association which negotiates with a union does not *necessarily* recognise the union, according to the EAT. It is an important factor, but the union will need to show that the employer (not just the association) negotiates with the union.

Who is covered?

The Act applies to all workers threatened with redundancy whether or not they are entitled to redundancy pay. **So workers with less than two years' service, and part-timers are covered.**

The Act applies to all employers except the Crown, small parts of the National Health Service, the police and the armed forces, and employers of: self-employed workers, registered dockers, share-fishers, workers who ordinarily work outside Great Britain, merchant seafarers, workers covered by an agreement approved by the Employment Secretary, and short-term workers. This last group is a major escape route for employers.

Short-term workers according to section 119 are: **1.** workers on fixed-term contracts (defined on page 195) of three months or less; **2.** workers taken on to do a specific task which is not expected to last more than three months. If in either of these cases they actually work more than three months they are protected. Clearly many workers will be excluded in jobs with fluctuating prospects such as building, catering, shipbuilding, ship repair and supply teaching.

An employer claiming to be exempt must prove it. This means showing that the duration of the work was fully explained at the point of hire, or that the workers must have known there was a custom and practice of short-term contracts.

■ Swan Hunters took on 17 painters to paint a ship. They were told they would be on 'short-term contracts' but this was not fully explained. Their union was told the job would last only three to four weeks, and the DE was notified. All the painters were sacked within four weeks and UCATT claimed the employers had failed to consult them. The Newcastle tribunal said the union and the DE had been notified of the hiring, and as ship repair is a 'type of "in and out" occupation', the men must have known they were on short-term contracts. *UCATT v Swan Hunters Ship-repairers (Tyne)* 1976 (IT)

Abuses of the Act are common in these vulnerable trades, with employers taking on workers for three months, sacking them, and later re-engaging them. Remember you are considered to have been employed continuously unless you are unemployed for a whole week, Sunday to Saturday. And in any event you might be able to show this was absence due to a 'temporary cessation of work' (see chapter 19).

What is consultation?

The EPA requires consultation not negotiation. But if your union is recognised for collective bargaining, management must by the terms of your agreement negotiate on redundances. Consultation is a lighter responsibility. Section 99 says it means giving in writing to the union:

1. the reasons for the proposals, for instance, lack of orders, automation

2. the numbers and descriptions (that is, what they do) of those affected, for example, by department, skill, shift

3. the *total* number of workers in those descriptions

4. how the employer proposes to select them, for example, last-in-first-out, age

5. how the employer proposes to carry out the sacking, for instance, timing, calling for volunteers, methods of payment.

After this, management *must*

1. consider the points made by the union; and

2. reply to them, giving reasons for any they reject.

When must consultation begin?

Consultation over any redundancy must begin 'at the earliest opportunity'. When mass sackings are proposed the following timetable must be observed as a minimum:

- If 100 or more workers are to be sacked at one establishment over a period of up to 90 days: consult at least **90 days** before the first sacking;
- If 10 or more (but fewer than 100) workers are to be sacked at one establishment over a period of up to 30

days: consult at least **30 days** before the first sacking. This means employers must give information and begin consultation as soon as they propose to make cuts. A Nottingham tribunal said:

> Indeed until that information is supplied there is probably not a great deal of point in entering into consultation because the information is what the trade union needs in order to consult with the employers. *EESA v Ashwell Scott* 1976 (IT)

If management ignore this timetable, all workers sacked can get compensation.

■ **Example:** if the board of XYZ Ltd wants to sack 150 workers during September the following minimum timetable must be followed:

1 July – Board meets and decides in principle on 150 redundancies. Notifies local union official and shop stewards by letter.

3 July – Union receives letter. Demands disclosure of relevant information.

5 July – Employer sends information.

7 July – Union receives it. Makes representations and seeks meeting.

7 October – First dismissal can take effect, that is, 90 days after full information given to union.

Problems
1. The consultation period

The earliest date on which notice of dismissal can be given to each employee is 7 July. Notice can run concurrently with the consultation period, so many employers give notice to employees and union on the same day or a day later. Of this the EAT has said:

> there is nothing to prevent it, but that, if it is done, it may well be the case that . . . there has never been any meaningful consultation by the employer such as is required by section 99, in which case that will be a ground of complaint. *NUT v Avon County Council* 1978 (EAT)

If management have decided who must go and given them their notices *before* the union is informed, they cannot say the sackings are 'proposals'. The earliest opportunity for consultation is the date the decision in principle, as opposed to the final decision, was made. In industries like construction, where eventual redundancy on a site is obvious from the outset, consultation should occur when the workforce is at its peak, hiring has ceased, and shrinkage is inevitable.

■ Four UCATT members worked on a site where, at peak, there were 50 workers. In March 1976, 29 were made redundant. On 14 April the four were told there was no more work, given a week's notice, and their convenor was informed. UCATT claimed they had not been properly consulted. The London tribunal agreed, saying that consultation must begin 'when the tide has turned and the work has actually begun to run out'. But it exercised its 'discretion' not to award the men any money, as the employer was not seriously 'in default'. *UCATT v G. Ellison Carpentry Contractors* 1976 (IT)

In cases where there is only a **remote possibility** of redundancy, consultation is not required until a decision has been made to dismiss. In 1976 NUPE complained because General Cleaning Contractors failed to consult them over the possibility that 96 redundancies might occur if GCC failed to get its contract with Barking Hospital renewed. The London tribunal said consultation was not required until the tender had been turned down by the hospital.

The duty to consult the union would obviously arise earlier if the contract was *likely* to be terminated. Unions should demand full details about all renewable contracts since these might give rise to 'special circumstances' excusing employers for failing to consult (see below).

In short, the duty arises once employers have 'a state of mind directed to a proposed course of events . . . . The employer must have formed some view as to how many are to be dismissed, when this is to take place and how it is to be arranged. This goes beyond the mere contemplation of a possible event.' This judgment excused a major engineering company in Kilmarnock which did not consult while it had a very real prospect of selling out and keeping the business as a going concern (*APAC v Kirvin* 1978 (EAT)).

2. The date of dismissal

Consultation must begin as soon as possible before the first dismissal. This means the date of the first sacking, if you are given

454 Rights at work

no notice. If you are given money in lieu of notice your dismissal takes effect on the day you leave. So management can't claim that the notice period is part of the consultation period unless you are still working. In *NUT v Avon County Council* (above) the EAT said that **consultation must begin 90 (or 30) days before the first dismissal notice is sent.**

3. The definition of establishment

Local authorities, nationalised industries and others proposing cuts across the board in a number of departments may try to escape or reduce their obligations by saying each department is a separate establishment – even though all the departments belong to one enterprise. Geographical separation is not conclusive. A chain of bakery shops, and 20 British Gas depots in the south-east, have been held to be single establishments.

4. Timing

Section 99 states that if management begin consultation, for example, over 50 redundancies and then decide to sack a *further* 50, they do not have to give the 90-day warning that would be required if they had proposed 100 redundancies straight off. If this happens you can claim that the union was not given the full information in the first place, and so the consultation period did not begin until the second series of redundancies was announced.

If 20 redundancies are proposed during a period of **90 days,** management must consult at the earliest opportunity. If any 10 fall during any 30-day period, the legal minimum of 30 days' consultation must begin.

Employers' defences

Employers can get out of the following obligations if they can show (and it is up to *them* to prove it) that there were **'special circumstances'** which made it **'not reasonably practical to comply'.**

- To consult at the earliest possible opportunity.
- To give the specified information.
- To consider and reply to the union's points.

If management prove this, they must still show they took all reasonable steps to keep the rules. So a Scottish business which relied on getting a second loan under the 1972 Industry Act, and went bust on the day in 1977 when this did not materialise, was excused by these special circumstances. But even so, some degree of consultation *could* have been carried out while the application was pending, and the company was liable (*Hamish Armour v ASTMS* 1979 (EAT)).

Circumstances are 'special' only if they are 'exceptional or out of the ordinary to an extent that rendered it not reasonably practicable' to carry out the proper consultation. A gradual business decline is not exceptional, even if the final decision to dismiss workers is sudden and necessary (*Clarks of Hove v Bakers' Union* 1978 (CA)).

The following examples show the way in which employers' claims of 'special circumstances' have been treated:

1. If a Receiver is called in, it is unlikely that section 99 will be applied meticulously. Insolvency is not on its own a reason for escaping consultation, but it *may* be if your employer delays in order to preserve a fraction of the assets, or to avoid liquidation in a genuine (but erroneous) belief that the business can be saved and dismissals avoided.

2. A company failed to apply for government aid to avert redundancy. But the tribunal still said it had done everything practicable to consult.

3. A company can't escape its obligations simply by writing to the head office of the union concerned.

4. An employer can't claim the effect the news would have on the workforce as a reason for not keeping to the timetable.

5. Employers in industries such as construction, where precise advance planning is difficult, cannot necessarily escape by citing bad weather, widespread resignations in the closing months, uncertain delivery of materials and unpredictable contractors (*ASBSBSW v George Wimpey* 1977 (EAT)).

How to claim

A recognised independent union which has not been consulted can complain to an industrial tribunal **within three months** of a dismissal taking place (see page 490). It can also complain about a **threatened** sacking but, as we shall see, there may be a disadvantage in doing this when it comes to getting compensation.

If the tribunal agrees with the union, it will say consultation should take place, or information should be given. It *may* also make a **protective award.**

Compensation

A **protective award** requires management to pay your wages for a 'protected' period of time. The award:

- specifies the workers covered;
- says that management have sacked, or plan to sack, some of these workers on the grounds of redundancy; and
- says that management failed to carry out properly the section 99 procedures for consultation, information or representation on particular sackings or proposed sackings.

The length of the protected period is decided by the tribunal, but it cannot exceed the minimum consultation period. So the maximum you can get is:

- **90 days** if 100 or more workers are to be sacked within 90 days.
- **30 days** if 10 or more workers are to be sacked within 30 days.
- **28 days** in any other case (that is, if fewer than 10 workers are involved).

The actual length of time depends on what the tribunal considers fair after taking account of the seriousness of the employer's failure to comply with any requirement of section 99. **The aim is to penalise your employer for failing to adhere to section 99.** Tribunals and the EAT have, however, taken more notice of the amount of money workers have lost.

You should bear in mind three further points: **1.** The amount of money awarded is based on a 'week's pay', not earnings. (See page 474.) **2.** The date on which the protected period must begin is either the date of the first dismissal, or the date of the award. **3. Earnings and notice money coming from management can be used to offset the obligation to pay during the protected period.**

This means you are better off if your union waits until near the three-month deadline for submitting claims. Although sackings may have taken place, a protective award will actually mean something in money terms. Because you are less likely to be working, or receiving money in lieu of notice, your protective award will not have to be offset.

If you are offered different work, or work on different terms, during the protected period, you are entitled to a trial period of four weeks. If the job turns out to be unsuitable and you leave, or if you turn down the opportunity in the first place, you still get your protective award.

If management fail to pay you as ordered, you have **three months** in which to complain to a tribunal (see page 490). This has to be your claim, not the union's, although the union should represent you.

Redundancy pay and unfair dismissal
Don't forget . . . that you are still entitled to your full redundancy pay if you have two years' continuous service. This is not affected by consultation. And a failure to consult or warn about redundancy will often be grounds in itself for an additional claim of unfair dismissal – see page 242.

Notifying the DE

The Department of Employment must be notified about mass sackings. Section 100 of the EPA 1975 lays down a timetable similar to section 99, with two differences. There is no overriding requirement to notify 'at the earliest opportunity'. And while an employer who sacks fewer than 10 workers without union consultation can be ordered to pay a protective award for 28 days, the obligation to notify the DE arises only when 10 or more redundancies are planned.

Notification must be in writing. Form HR1, which is nowadays required by the DE, asks for the same kind of information as must be given to unions. If a union is recognised, the form must name the union, say when consultation began, and a copy must be given to the union. This notice is in addition to the employer's claim for a rebate for redundancy pay. If you discover that this claim is made at the same time, it will be clear that the dismissals were fixed and proper consultation was not held prior to this decision being made.

Again, employers can escape liability on the grounds of 'special circumstances'. Failure to comply entitles the DE to withhold up to one-tenth of any redundancy rebate, or to prosecute for a fine of up to £400. Neither is particularly onerous, and for workers who have less than two years' service there is no rebate to withhold anyway. The DE is slow to take action. In the first 18 months there were no prosecutions and rebates were withheld on only 169 occasions; the amount withheld averaged £91. Employers, but not unions, can appeal to an industrial tribunal about the amount of any rebate withheld.

Consultation about takeovers

The Transfer of Undertakings Regulations (TUR) apply in the situation described on page 255. Their application to union organisation means that when there is a 'relevant transfer' management must provide information to, and carry out consultations with, a union whose members are affected by the transfer. The new management must give sufficient information to your employer to enable him/her to give the union details of the 'legal, economic and social implications' of the transfer, and the measures both employers are taking which may affect the employees. The information must be given 'long enough before a relevant transfer to enable consultation to take place'.

Again the duty to consult is watered down if special circumstances (see page 454) make it not reasonably practicable for him/her to consult *and* s/he takes whatever steps are reasonably practicable.

All workers have the right to retain their conditions with the new employer, and collective agreements are also carried over.

If management fail to consult, you can claim compensation from them or in some cases from the new employer. The maximum amount a tribunal can award is two weeks' pay and any money coming to you from a protective award, or other payments, is offset against this. The luke-warm remedy for this right makes the TUR more a sop to the Common Market which imposed it than a genuine protection of workers affected by business wheeling and dealing.

Government measures to hide unemployment

With unemployment at its highest level ever, and reported redundancies running at more than 28,000 a month in 1983, the government continued to slash the schemes set up to save or create jobs. The budget of the Manpower Services Commission (MSC), despite a 300 per cent increase in unemployment and protests from both sides of industry, was cut by an average 21 per cent in each of the years 1979–84, with cash limited to below the 1978 level.

The true level of unemployment is much greater than the DE monthly statistics show, since many people, particularly married women, do not register. In addition almost one million people in 1983 were on some form of government scheme of work, training, subsidised make-work or generally under-employed. About a dozen schemes exist in Britain, and many special measures apply in the six counties of Northern Ireland.

Details of the present availability of any of these schemes can be obtained from any DE office, Job Centre or Careers Office. The result is that if you are threatened with redundancy, or out of work, there is a possibility of your getting some subsidised work for some time, particularly if you are under 20. But many workers would say there would be no need for such a panoply of elaborate short-term schemes if the government had put employment as a first priority.

Job Release Scheme
JRS is designed to encourage people close to retirement age to retire and to open up jobs for unemployed workers. Women aged 59 and men aged 62 can utilise the scheme. Retiring people got £55 a week in 1983 if they had a dependent spouse, or £43.50 if not. A special scheme exists for disabled workers, but the allowance is taxable and is available at age 60. You can get half the JRS allowance if you cut down to part-time work and an unemployed worker is taken on. From April 1984 the eligible age is raised to 64 for men but remains at 59 for women and 60 for disabled men.

Temporary Short-Time Working Compensation Scheme
This was introduced by the Labour administration in 1979 and aims to avoid redundancies by encouraging work sharing agreements. Management can get a rebate of 50 per cent of normal wages and national insurance payments for nine months if you adopt short-time working following notice of 10 or more redundancies. (Half of this amount can be obtained if no redundancies are threatened.) Total lay-offs are not eligible – you must work at least one day in eight. Between 1979 and 1982 900,000 workers operated the scheme.

Community Programme
This scheme has 130,000 places aiming to cover 200,000 people

a year. It is designed to get unemployed workers doing socially useful work under the sponsorship, through the MSC, of local authorities and voluntary bodies. Sponsors must pay the going rate locally, with hourly rates of £2.22 and an average of £60 a week (1983/84), and get union approval of the project. It lasts for up to a year for full- or part-time workers. The MSC can pay the supervisors and managers.

Community Industry
This is for 'socially and personally disadvantaged' 16–18-year-olds and provides work in about 7,000 places a year.

Job Split
One of Norman Tebbit's inventions, this scheme pays employers £750 for every full-time worker who is replaced either by two part-timers, or shares his or her job with someone unemployed or who would become unemployed. The money is paid in four instalments and both jobs must continue for a full year.

The scheme was heavily criticised by the TUC. It represented yet another move towards involuntary cuts in working hours and underemployment.

Young Workers Scheme
This scheme also assists employers to pay low wages and exploit the high level of youth unemployment. The MSC pays £15 a week (1983/84) to any employer paying a 16–17-year-old less than £40 a week (or £7.50 if the pay is less than £45). It is not available in public sector employment.

Youth Training Schemes
From September 1983, this scheme aims to give all 16- and some 17-year-olds a training opportunity for a year and to provide nearly 500,000 places a year. Trainees get £25 a week and employers get £550 per trainee. Trainees are not employees (see the *Daley* case, page 32). However, TUC policy is to encourage employers to give trainees employee status, which will occur if they are paid anything above the MSC rate.

In an effort to counter some of the many abuses of the Youth Opportunities Programme scheme, union involvement is encouraged. The criticisms of job-substitution, cheap labour and poor health and safety records remain.

TOPS

The Training Opportunities Programme (TOPS), Direct Training Services and Training for Skills programmes had between them 116,000 takers in 1981/82 on intensive training courses.

European Social Fund

In 1981 the UK got £141 million (of the £600 million available) from the Common Market budget, rising to £257 million in 1982. The fund is available for training and resettlement of workers leaving agriculture or the textile industry, or facing techological change, or in the Assisted Areas, migrants, women over 25 returning to work after family responsibilities, the disabled, and workers under 25 training or in their first jobs. Applications are made to the DE and the fund pays 50 per cent (55 per cent in Northern Ireland) for public sector jobs and will match UK state aid to private sector jobs.

Summary

1. A recognised union must be consulted about every redundancy at the earliest opportunity.

2. If 10 or more workers are to be sacked, the union must be consulted and the DE notified 30 days before the first sacking. If 100 or more workers are to be sacked, the period is 90 days.

3. Information must be disclosed and the union's views considered before any final decision is made.

4. The union can claim **a protective award** for workers when there has been a failure to consult.

5. The DE can prosecute, or part-withhold redundancy rebates, if there has been inadequate notification.

6. If redundancy cannot be attacked by direct action or through the legal procedure, there are a number of government schemes for saving jobs.

7. Recognised unions must be consulted and given information about business takeovers.

What to do if redundancy is threatened

As basic measures to prevent redundancies you should make the following demands to your employer:

1. Discharge sub-contract labour and agency staff on site and withdraw work sent to outside contractors;

2. Consider transfer of workers to other departments and changes in working arrangements;

3. Restrict overtime;

4. Consider short-time working to cover temporary fluctuations;

5. Retrain employees in skills still needed;

6. Stop recruitment;

7. Consider work-sharing by reduction in hours or other means;

8. Retire workers over retirement age;

9. Consider what alternative products could be made.

If these measures fail, resort to:

10. Applying for government assistance;

11. Early retirement with full pension;

12. Ensure that the benefits of job-saving procedures apply to all trade unionists;

13. Voluntary redundancies;

14. An agreed procedure, for instance, last-in, first-out, and the statutory procedure of consultation with recognised unions, and notification to the Department of Employment.

Part 4:

Making a claim

19. Doing the sums

How to work out your claim / part-timers and temporaries / working abroad / the definition of continuous employment / why it's important / the effect of working less than 16 hours a week / and of breaks in your contract / a summary of the basic rules on continuity / calculating 'a week's pay' / why it's important / a summary of the rules for different groups of workers / using the formula for working out compensation for unfair dismissal / redundancy pay and basic awards for unfair dismissal / a ready reckoner / an example of unfair dismissal compensation / and a summary.

Before rushing off to a tribunal to enforce any of the rights mentioned in this handbook you should ensure that you are entitled **in law** to make a claim, and work out what the claim is worth. In any event, knowing the answer to both these questions will give you the basis on which to negotiate with management, ask workmates to support you, and deal with ACAS in conciliation.

The two calculations you must make are:

1. the length of your continuous employment; and
2. the amount of your week's pay.

In everyday industrial relations these sums should not prove difficult to do. But in legal terms they present great complexity, and involve the most convoluted and inaccessible parts of the legislation. As a result, many injustices have occurred. John

Mercer, for example, the gas fitter who always worked 54 hours a week, got redundancy pay on the basis of only 40 (see page 318).

The TUC's request for simplification in this area has been denied. Governments have refused to modify the strictness of the continuity of employment rules, where a break of a week can deprive you of all your statutory rights. And demands for redundancy pay to be based on earnings instead of 'a week's pay' have consistently been turned down.

Where to find the law

The Employment Protection Consolidation Act 1978 (EPCA) deals with: continuous employment (schedule 13); 'a week's pay' (schedule 14); redundancy pay (schedule 4); compensation for unfair dismissal (sections 72–76).

Part-timers, temporaries and new starters

There is no definition of a part-timer but all employment protection rights apply to workers who work 16 or more hours a week, or who have worked eight or more hours for five years. The law therefore protects part-time workers who have the appropriate 'continuous employment', except those below 16, or eight hours.

Nor are temporary or casual workers defined. The only time this is recognised is to exclude workers hired on fixed-term contracts of three months or less, or on jobs not expected to last more than three months, from the right to guarantee, medical suspension and notice pay, and consultation on redundancies. If you in fact work for more than three months you can claim. Dismissal rights may also be excluded in certain one- and two-year contracts – see page 195.

There is no justification for Parliament to exclude these groups of workers. An unfair sacking doesn't cease to be unfair simply because the victim is a part-timer or new starter. The Act is designed to outlaw unreasonable behaviour, yet many workers are unprotected, often at the crucial time when they are learning a new job and most vulnerable. Effectively it gives management a free hand during your first year.

Employees working abroad

Employees who work abroad are excluded. If you work abroad

for only part of your time, you may still be excluded if a tribunal finds you '*ordinarily*' work outside Great Britain or outside the UK.

The rules that the courts have laid down for *unfair dismissal* and *redundancy* are:

1. If under your contract you normally work outside Britain, and only occasionally work here, you can't claim.

2. If you normally work in Britain and on odd occasions go abroad for some special purpose you *can* claim.

3. If you work here and abroad for considerable periods of time in the normal performance of your contract, you can claim *only* if your *base* is in Britain.

4. In deciding this question, tribunals must look at the express and implied terms of your contract at the time it was agreed. So if your contract says you can be sent abroad in the normal course of your duties, a tribunal must look at the expected duration of the contract and decide, as from the start of the contract, where your base is likely to be.

5. If, using this test, your base is in Britain, it doesn't matter that *in fact* you spend more time abroad – *Wilson v Maynard Shipbuilding* 1977 (CA).

Additionally, you get redundancy pay if you ordinarily work outside Britain but are sacked while you are here on your employer's instructions.

You are excluded from all other rights if you ordinarily work outside the UK. Seafarers on UK registered ships are excluded from redundancy pay, time off and insolvency rights, and only a few get notice. If they work wholly outside Britain or are not ordinarily resident here, they have no statutory rights. Offshore oil workers have all the rights except time off for union and public duties. If you work in a business that requires travel – oil company representative, service engineer, commercial traveller – you can preserve your rights by getting an agreement from management that you won't be treated as 'ordinarily' working abroad. Such a deal can't give a tribunal jurisdiction if it finds that in fact you are excluded from claiming. But the deal can give you a contractual (as opposed to a statutory) right against your employer, which you can enforce in the courts.

Continuous employment

When considering a claim to your employer or a tribunal yoi

should first use the **Workers' Rights Checklist** on page 507. Find out whether you need to have worked for a specified period in order to make the claim. Most rights require this – unfair dismissal, redundancy, maternity, notice and guaranteed wages, for example. Others, such as claims of discrimination and dismissal for union activity, and for equal pay and time off, are available to all employees irrespective of length of service.

The rules for calculating **continuous employment** are important for two reasons. Firstly, a break in continuity deprives you of your rights. Once you have continuous employment for the requisite period, you are protected until there is a break. Secondly, the value of some of your rights depends on the length of your continuous employment. Redundancy pay, the basic award in unfair dismissal claims, and notice money all increase with service.

In all the Acts there is a presumption in your favour that employment is continuous. If your employer says that continuity is broken, s/he must overcome this presumption and prove the point. Continuity runs while you are with the **same employer** and also if the **business is taken over,** or you **transfer to an associated employer**. The presumption applies even if you have worked for **several employers** – *Evendon v Guildford Football Club* 1975 (CA). And it applies even if you finish one week and are started the next on a new contract.

Continuous employment depends on your working, or contracting to work, a specified number of hours each week AND on there being no gaps in the period covered by your contract. Sections **1–4** below deal with hours; section **5** with gaps. Many 'part-timers' have full legal rights.

1. Your contract requires you to work 16 or more hours each week

While your contract lasts, your continuity is preserved. It doesn't matter whether you *actually* work 16 hours or not, since you are governed by a contract that normally requires it.

This can mean many things. In some jobs you can count as when you are working beyond the minimum laid down in written contract. A retained fireman, who was on stand-by 02 hours a week, got redundancy pay by saying that he ployed not merely when he was actually called out but hole of the 102 hours – *Bullock v Merseyside County* 77 (EAT).

2. Your contract requires you to work less than 16 hours
Continuity is broken if you don't work 16 hours in any week
(but see section **4** below). However, if you *actually* work 16 or
more hours, you can start to build up continuity.

■ **Example:** you provide school meals five days a week for three
hours a day. But you work half an hour overtime each day.
You have continuous employment because you actually work
at least 16 hours a week.

3. Your contractual hours are reduced below 16 hours a week
If your hours are reduced to **less than eight** you lose all your
rights unless you actually worked 16 or more hours each week.
But if the reduction is to somewhere **between 16 and eight**
hours, you are protected in two ways.
   a. Any periods of up to 26 short weeks you work on this contract count as weeks of 16 hours, even though you are not contracted to work them nor in fact work them.
   b. After that, any rights you have become entitled to by
length of service are preserved. You can count weeks either
**because you were on a contract for 16 or more hours a week, or
because they are part of a 26-week period that counts in a.
above. Once you have become entitled to any right, it is preserved so long as you keep working eight or more hours a week,
or are on a contract to do so.**

■ **Example:** you start work on 1 January 1980 at 40 hours a
week. On 1 March 1982 you ask to work part-time at 15
hours a week because of family commitments. On 1 March
1983 you are made redundant. You have three years'
continuous employment and get three weeks' notice, and
redundancy pay based on three years. This is because you
had **already become entitled to notice and redundancy rights
before the reduction in hours,** that is, after four weeks for
notice, and after two years for redundancy.

4. You work eight hours a week for five years
Long standing part-timers are treated as if they had worked 16
hours or more. If you have worked for less than 16 hours, but
at least eight, **for five years,** you have the same rights as full-
timers.

■ **Example:** you are an office cleaner working for two hours o five nights a week. Until you have done this for five years, you do *not* have 'continuous employment' and can't use any of the rights that depend on it. But after five years you have the full protection of all statutory rights in the Checklist on page 507.

5. There is a temporary gap in your continuity

A week in which **you are not covered by a contract at all** breaks your continuity. If you resign or are sacked and then come back after a week or more you lose all your continuity. The exceptions to this rule are when your contract is terminated because of: **a.** sickness, **b.** pregnancy, **c.** temporary cessation of work, **d.** agreement or custom, **e.** unfair dismissal, or **f.** industrial action.

If you are in doubt about your continuity, an assurance from management, given at any time, is sufficient to preserve your rights. If management say your continuity is intact, they can't deny it if some time later you have cause to claim redundancy pay or other rights (*Evendon v Guildford*, above).

a. Sickness and injury

Provided you are taken back within 26 weeks of your termination, and the reason for the absence was that you were sick or injured, your continuity is not broken. The weeks off are added to the weeks during which your contract exists.

b. Pregnancy

The same is true if the reason is pregnancy. Continuity is anyway preserved for women who are entitled to the full EPCA rights, if they return to work within 29 weeks of the week of confinement. The right here is useful for women who are not entitled to the full EPCA rights – because, for example, they do not have two years' continuous employment.

❧ **Example:** you join the firm as a typist on 1 June 1982 and want to take maternity leave on 1 June 1983. The firm doesn't have an agreement on this, and you don't have the two years necessary for maternity rights under the EPCA. So 1 June 1983 you resign and have your baby in September. 5 November the firm is advertising for a typist and you accepted back. The weeks of absence count and you have continuity as though you had never left.

c. Temporary cessation of work

your contract continues during a temporary lay-off,

even if you are claiming unemployment or social security benefit. When you are laid off and your contract is terminated you
can still claim continuity if you are subsequently taken back.
There must be a cessation, it must be the cause of the absence
and it must be temporary. In looking at these rules you must,
as Mr Justice Phillips said, do so 'as the historian of a completed
chapter of events, and not as a journalist describing events a
they occur from day to day'.

■ Blackburns closed their engineering works in 1963. D.
Crown, who had 15 years' service, found work in one firm,
then another, for two years. S. Miller had 15 years' service
but he was out of work for 21 months. In 1965, both were
offered work with Bentleys. Bentleys and Blackburns were
associated employers. The men were made redundant in
1974 and claimed payments based on unbroken continuity of
employment from their first days at Blackburns. The High
Court said that the periods of two years and 21 months were
absences due to a 'temporary cessation of work'. Important
factors were: length of service, duration of the gap, the
nature of their work and what was said on re-engagement.
Bentley Engineering v Crown 1976 (HC)

A gap between a series of *fixed-term* contracts does not break
continuity provided the gap is temporary in relation to the combined duration of the two contracts on either side of it, and it
is caused by the non-availability of work. This right is crucial to
workers habitually subject to hiring and rehiring, such as
teachers and manual workers in educational services, and seasonal and casual workers.

■ A teacher was employed from 1971 to 1979 on contracts
which subsisted during short holidays but ended at the start
of each summer vacation. In 1979 no new contract was
offered to her. The Law Lords held that she had continuity
of service during every summer. Looking backwards from
1979, she had nine months on, three months off and nine
months on. The gap was in these circumstances merely temporary. It was due to the absence of students and classes t
teach. There was therefore a temporary cessation of wor
which counted in assessing her total period of employmen
Ford v Warwickshire C.C. 1983 (HL)

d. Agreement or custom

In some industries you are by custom and practice regarded as continuing in employment even if your contract is terminated. For instance, you might be 'loaned' by management to another employer. You might, on the other hand, ask for time off during which you may be regarded as still in employment even though no contract exists. In these situations, you don't forfeit your rights if you are regarded as continuing in employment 'for all or any purposes'.

■ Ms Moore worked as a doubler in a Glasgow factory. Her son had a serious accident and she left work for three months in 1968 to look after him. She told her supervisor that she didn't know how long she would be off but she hoped to return. Clarksons kept her cards. In 1970 she was made redundant. The President of the Scottish tribunals said there was no break in her continuity. There was an arrangement that **suspended the contract** until her domestic situation allowed her to return. *Moore v James Clarkson & Co.* 1970 (IT)

If your pension or other benefits continue while you are away or if your 'cards' (nowadays your P45 and contribution record) are kept you can say your contract is continuing. But if there is no formal relationship between you, it will be difficult to establish continuity.

■ A Derbyshire County cricketer played for his club from March to September each year and worked for Pontins travel agency in the winter. Each March he got his cards and P45 from the agency. He got no money from Pontins during the summer, but was re-engaged each autumn. The Derby tribunal said he did not have continuity of employment with Pontins. He was not regarded as employed with them during the cricket season. *Rhodes v Pontins* 1971 (IT)

engagement after unfair dismissal

sacked and reinstated in your old job, or re-engaged employer, or an associated employer, you preserve uity. Provided you make a complaint of unfair dismissal re taken back following conciliation by ACAS or a your period off work counts. But not otherwise, ment agree this.

f. Industrial action

Lock-outs don't break your continuity. All the time during which you are locked-out counts.

Strikes, however, are treated differently. These don't break your continuity. But if you were on strike on any day, *that* day does not count towards your total service.

■ **Example:** you joined the company on 10 March 1980 and were made redundant 10 April 1983. You would expect redundancy pay and notice based on three years' continuous employment. But on 10 May 1982 you took part in a 10-week strike. Your continuity is not broken but your service is reduced by 10 weeks. So you get redundancy pay and notice based on two years and 46 weeks.

Preservation of continuity in a strike is an important right. Without it even short strikes would jeopardise every striker's accrued legal protections.

Remember: in all the above six cases we are talking about a period when you are not covered by a contract, and do not have management's assurance that continuity is unbroken. If you are covered by a contract or have an assurance, continuity is preserved.

Summary of continuous employment rules

1. Every week counts in which you work, or have a contract to work, at least 16 hours.

2. Any week in which you have a contract which requires less than 16 hours breaks continuity unless

    a. you actually worked 16 or more hours;
    b. you have worked eight or more hours for five years; or
    c. you have been reduced *from* 16 or more hours *to* eight or more.

3. Once you have built up enough continuous employment to entitle you to any particular right, that right is preserved so long as you work, or are contracted to work, at least eight hours a week.

4. Any week in which you have *no* contract and you do not work breaks continuity unless you return to work

a. after being sick for 26 or less weeks;
b. after being away for 26 or less weeks because of pregnancy, and you are not entitled to the full EPCA right;
c. after a temporary cessation of work;
d. after a period during which you are regarded by agreement or custom as having continuity;
e. after claiming unfair dismissal;
f. after a strike or lock-out.

5. Your service can be extended if you are given less than your statutory notice – see page 209.

'A week's pay'

The starting point for determining the amount of pay to be given in compensation under many parts of the legislation is Schedule 14 of the EPCA. This lays down an absurdly artificial formula for finding out basic weekly pay. It is used for calculating: **redundancy, notice** and **maternity pay**, wages during **medical suspension** and **while looking for work** in a redundancy situation, the amount of a **protective award** when your employer has not followed the procedure for handling redundancies, and the **'basic award'** made in a finding of unfair dismissal. The amount payable for any of these rights often bears very little resemblance to industrial reality, particularly with regard to overtime. Nevertheless, the rules are rigid. In this handbook 'a week's pay' refers to pay calculated in accordance with this chapter.

Before you can find out what your week's pay is, you must know what the method of calculating your wages is. In other words, **1.** whether you have no normal hours or **2.** whether you work normal hours, and if you work normal hours, whether you are a time-worker, piece-worker, or shift-worker. They all have different rules, which are found in the EPCA.

With no normal hours

A small group of people – union officials, commercial travellers, college lecturers, for example – who work on a fee-paid contract. If they are made redundant their week's pay is determined by reference to the average weekly pay in the last 12 weeks. If they are dismissed for redundancy and are given proper notice, the 12 weeks dates back from the date notice was given. If no notice was given, or if inadequate notice was given, the 12 weeks is taken from the date of termination. For pay during maternity, and medical suspension, the calculation date is the date immediately preceding the date of absence. For notice pay, it is the date preceding the date notice was given.

Workers with normal hours

If you have a set number of hours each week, beyond which you are regarded as working overtime (whether or not you get a premium), you have 'normal hours'. Most workers come into this definition and fall into one of the following categories.

1. Straight time-workers

If you are not on shift-work, and receive wages that do not vary with the amount of work done, that is, you are a straight time-worker, calculate your week's pay by reference to the amount received in the last week before notice was given in cases of redundancy, dismissal, etc., and before absence began in cases of maternity and medical suspension.

2. Piece-workers

If the amount of pay varies according to the amount of work done, that is, because of piece-work or variable bonus or commission, a week's pay is worked out by reference to the 12 weeks preceding the date on which notice of redundancy or dismissal was given, or before the date on which maternity leave or medical suspension began.

Any hours that were worked at overtime rate are included but the overtime premium is disregarded. The average weekly rate can therefore be determined by dividing the 12 weeks' pay by 12. If there are short weeks because, say, of lay-off or sickness, go back further and find 12 full weeks.

3. Shift-workers

If you are on shifts and your pay varies according to the day of the week on which you work, you calculate your week's pay in the same way as **2.** above.

4. New starters

If you are have not worked for 12 weeks you take a figure which fairly represents a week's pay. Look at the amount received and rates paid to similar workers inside and outside the company.

What is included in a week's pay?

Not all forms of payment qualify to be included in a week's pay. The most unjust exception is **non-contractual overtime**. Overtime which is obligatory on both employee *and* employer will count, but no other. So if your normal working hours are 38, with five hours' conditioned overtime, **and the employer is obliged to make payments in respect of these five hours whether or not work is given**, then these 43 hours will be included. However, when there is a stipulation to work overtime 'as and when required by the employer to do so', **you** are obliged to work reasonable overtime, but management are under no obligation to give you any. So even regular overtime of this kind does *not* count towards a week's pay. **There must be a mutual obligation to provide, and to work, overtime if it is to qualify**, as John Mercer found out (page 318).

A bonus will qualify if it is contractual. Tips and payments from people other than your employer cannot be included except in one narrow case. If your employers take a certain percentage off their customers and put it in a kitty, in the hotel trade for example, and this is then paid out amongst the workers concerned, this will qualify as part of a week's pay. However, if it is given by a customer direct to you it will *not* qualify . Lodging allowances do not qualify if, for example, they go with the job. If you live above the shop and get a free flat you cannot include the value of this flat in your week's pay. Expenses qualify only in so far as they represent a profit to you. If they are a genuine estimate of what you are likely to spend, they will not qualify; but if there is an element of profit involved then it can be taken to be part of a week's pay. It will, of course, have tax consequences each week in this case! Payments for travelling time do not qualify, nor do benefits in kind even if they can be assessed in value. Cars, for example, cannot be part of 'a week's pay'. But mobility payments are. Threshold and cost-of-living payments count.

Summary of rules for working out a week's pay

The precise formula is explained in Employment Legislation leaflet 11, 'Rules governing continuous employment and a week's pay', available free at DE offices. The following are offered as reasonable rules-of-thumb which will bring you very close to your actual entitlement:

1. If you have no fixed hours:
   a. Count back the last 12 weeks you actually worked before notice was given.
   b. Add all gross pay.
   c. Divide **b.** by 12 to give average weekly pay. This is a week's pay.
2. If you are a time-worker:
   a. Find gross pay for all hours worked, excluding pay for non-contractual overtime, in the week before notice was given.
   b. This is a week's pay.
3. If you are a shift-worker, or are paid by the piece, commission, bonus:
   a. Count back the last 12 weeks you actually worked before notice was given.
   b. Add all gross pay excluding pay for non-contractual overtime.
   c. Add all hours excluding non-contractual overtime.
   d. Divide **b.** by **c.** to give average hourly rate.
   e. Divide **c.** by 12 to give average weekly hours.
   f. Multiply **d.** by **e.** to give a week's pay.

Why is a week's pay important?

All the rights in the Checklist require a calculation based on a week's pay. The only exception is compensation for victimisation for union activity. Some *also* take account of earnings – unfair dismissal, time off for union representatives, and guarantees when your employer goes bust. Two rights provide automatic compensation based on a combination of length of continuous employment, amount of a week's pay, and age. These are redundancy pay and the basic award in unfair dismissal cases.

Compensation for unfair dismissal

We have seen (page 247) that if you win a case of unfair dismissal and are not reinstated or re-engaged your compensation may consist of

1. basic award
2. compensatory award

3. additional award

4. special award.

Basic award for unfair dismissal and redundancy pay

If you are unfairly dismissed the tribunal must order management to pay you a **basic award.** The calculation for this and for **redundancy pay** is the same except that for redundancy pay no credit is given for work before your 18th birthday.

The formula for deciding how many weeks' pay you get is as in Table 6.

The Ready Reckoner on page 480 shows how this formula works out in practice.

■ **Example:** you were dismissed at 50, having worked for 15 years continuously. You are entitled to 19½ weeks' pay. This is made up of six years at one week (that is, under the age of 41) and nine years at one-and-a-half weeks (for the years over the age of 41).

This formula is subject to some restrictions:

1. If you are 64 (59 for women) your entitlement goes down by 1/12th for each month after your 64th (59th) birthday.

2. Only 20 years can be counted. So working back from the date of dismissal and taking your most valuable years (that is, those when you were 41 or over), the highest number of weeks' pay you can get is 30.

3. The maximum allowable for a week's pay is £140 (1983/4), although the Employment Secretary must review this limit each year (EPCA 1978 section 148). If your week's pay is over £140 only £140 counts.

Table 6

If you were aged	but less than	number of weeks' pay for each year
	22	½
22	41	1
41	65	1½

4. If you get redundancy pay, this is offset against your basic award. So is any compensation you get under the SDA 1975 or RRA 1976 for loss of redundancy rights.

5. Your basic award can be reduced if the tribunal thinks

- you partly contributed to your own dismissal
- you unreasonably refused an offer of complete reinstatement
- things you did before the dismissal, but discovered only after it, make it just and equitable to reduce the compensation (see *Devis v Atkins* page 232 and EPCA section 73).

Compensatory award

EPCA section 74 says tribunals can award as much compensation as is just and equitable for losses attributable to management's action. The maximum a tribunal can award was, from 1 February 1983, £7,500. Higher *settlements* can be reached. The following matters are all relevant in working out compensation for a settlement or a hearing:

1. Notice money. If you are sacked without notice the tribunal should ensure you get at least as much as your proper notice money. This is the 'irreducible minimum' which must be given in accordance with good industrial relations, and the net amount should be paid regardless of earnings received from other sources. The EAT said this in *Vaughan v Weighpack* 1974, and a later decision (*Tradewinds Airways v Fletcher* 1981) casting doubt on it is probably wrong.

2. Losses up to the hearing. These are your *net* losses. Social security payments you receive between the date of sacking and the date of the tribunal's decision can be recovered. The tribunal must go through a complicated process to enable the DHSS to recoup these payments from your employer. In other words, your employer, not the DHSS, must bear the cost of your being out of work, at least up to the date of the decision.

The tribunal must say how much compensation is attributable to the period leading up to the date of its decision, that is, how much your net loss is for this period. It will then notify the DE, who will check with the DHSS on how much you have received. The DE may then deliver a bill to your employer. Your employer must pay the bill, which consists of the amount of your social security pay, to the DE. Only then can s/he pay you

Ready reckoner for redundancy payments and unfair dismissal basic awards

NOTES:

To use the table

Read off employee's age and number of complete years' service. Service before the employee reached the age of 18 does not count. The table will then show HOW MANY WEEKS' PAY the employee is entitled to.

The redundancy payment due is to be reduced by one-twelfth for every complete month by which the age exceeds the 59th birthday for a woman or the 64th birthday for a man. Entitlement ceases entirely at 60 for a woman or 65 for a man.

SERVICE (years)	2	3	4	5	6	7	8	9	10	11	12	13	14	15	16	17	18	19	20
AGE (years) 20	1	1	1	1	—														
21	1	1½	1½	1½	1½	—													
22	1	1½	2	2	2	2	—												
23	1½	2	2½	3	3	3	3	—											
24	2	2½	3	3½	4	4	4	4	—										
25	2	3	3½	4	4½	5	5	5	5	—									
26	2	3	4	4½	5	5½	6	6	6	6	—								
27	2	3	4	5	5½	6	6½	7	7	7	7	—							
28	2	3	4	5	6	6½	7	7½	8	8	8	8	—						
29	2	3	4	5	6	7	7½	8	8½	9	9	9	9	—					
30	2	3	4	5	6	7	8	8½	9	9½	10	10	10	10	—				
31	2	3	4	5	6	7	8	9	9½	10	10½	11	11	11	11	—			
32	2	3	4	5	6	7	8	9	10	10½	11	11½	12	12	12	12	—		
33	2	3	4	5	6	7	8	9	10	11	11½	12	12½	13	13	13	13	—	
34	2	3	4	5	6	7	8	9	10	11	12	12½	13	13½	14	14	14	14	—
35	2	3	4	5	6	7	8	9	10	11	12	13	13½	14	14½	15	15	15	15
36	2	3	4	5	6	7	8	9	10	11	12	13	14	14½	15	15½	16	16	16
37	2	3	4	5	6	7	8	9	10	11	12	13	14	15	15½	16	16½	17	17
38	2	3	4	5	6	7	8	9	10	11	12	13	14	15	16	16½	17	17½	18
39	2	3	4	5	6	7	8	9	10	11	12	13	14	15	16	17	17½	18	18½
40	2	3	4	5	6	7	8	9	10	11	12	13	14	15	16	17	18	18½	19
41	2	3	4	5	6	7	8	9	10	11	12	13	14	15	16	17	18	19	19½
42	2½	3½	4½	5½	6½	7½	8½	9½	10½	11½	12½	13½	14½	15½	16½	17½	18½	19½	20½
43	3	4	5	6	7	8	9	10	11	12	13	14	15	16	17	18	19	20	21
44	3	4½	5½	6½	7½	8½	9½	10½	11½	12½	13½	14½	15½	16½	17½	18½	19½	20½	21½
45	3	4½	6	7	8	9	10	11	12	13	14	15	16	17	18	19	20	21	22
46	3	4½	6	7½	8½	9½	10½	11½	12½	13½	14½	15½	16½	17½	18½	19½	20½	21½	22½
47	3	4½	6	7½	9	10	11	12	13	14	15	16	17	18	19	20	21	22	23
48	3	4½	6	7½	9	10½	11½	12½	13½	14½	15½	16½	17½	18½	19½	20½	21½	22½	23½
49	3	4½	6	7½	9	10½	12	13	14	15	16	17	18	19	20	21	22	23	24
50	3	4½	6	7½	9	10½	12	13½	14½	15½	16½	17½	18½	19½	20½	21½	22½	23½	24½
51	3	4½	6	7½	9	10½	12	13½	15	16	17	18	19	20	21	22	23	24	25
52	3	4½	6	7½	9	10½	12	13½	15	16½	17½	18½	19½	20½	21½	22½	23½	24½	25½
53	3	4½	6	7½	9	10½	12	13½	15	16½	18	19	20	21	22	23	24	25	26
54	3	4½	6	7½	9	10½	12	13½	15	16½	18	19½	20½	21½	22½	23½	24½	25½	26½
55	3	4½	6	7½	9	10½	12	13½	15	16½	18	19½	21	22	23	24	25	26	27
56	3	4½	6	7½	9	10½	12	13½	15	16½	18	19½	21	22½	23½	24½	25½	26½	27½
57	3	4½	6	7½	9	10½	12	13½	15	16½	18	19½	21	22½	24	25	26	27	28
58	3	4½	6	7½	9	10½	12	13½	15	16½	18	19½	21	22½	24	25½	26½	27½	28½
59	3	4½	6	7½	9	10½	12	13½	15	16½	18	19½	21	22½	24	25½	27	28	29
men only 60	3	4½	6	7½	9	10½	12	13½	15	16½	18	19½	21	22½	24	25½	27	28½	29½
61	3	4½	6	7½	9	10½	12	13½	15	16½	18	19½	21	22½	24	25½	27	28½	30
62	3	4½	6	7½	9	10½	12	13½	15	16½	18	19½	21	22½	24	25½	27	28½	30
63	3	4½	6	7½	9	10½	12	13½	15	16½	18	19½	21	22½	24	25½	27	28½	30
64	3	4½	6	7½	9	10½	12	13½	15	16½	18	19½	21	22½	24	25½	27	28½	30
SERVICE (years)	2	3	4	5	6	7	8	9	10	11	12	13	14	15	16	17	18	19	20

the balance. The delays and complications that can arise are formidable!

If you settle the case through ACAS or privately the Recoupment Regulations do not apply, so your employer will save money if s/he settles first.

3. Manner of dismissal. If you are sacked in an abrasive or humiliating way which causes you additional loss, for example if it were adversely publicised and this causes you to be blacklisted, you can claim.

4. Loss of statutory protection. In any new job it will take time to build up rights to claim unfair dismissal and minimum notice. The standard figure is now one half of the statutory minimum notice right you accrued – *Daley v Dorsett* 1981 (EAT).

5. Expenses. i.e. Looking for new work, and even removal costs.

6. Future losses. Tribunals have to estimate how much you will be out of pocket in future. If you have no job they must consider how long it will take to get one and what the pay is likely to be, and make up the difference. If you have a job the assessment is easier. No limit is placed on the number of years which can be taken into account.

In looking at the *net* loss, social security benefits you will get are not relevant. But social security rules disqualify you if you are receiving any compensation for future losses for up to one year from the date of dismissal. Nor does it matter that your compensation may have been reduced by the tribunal, because for example you *contributed* to the dismissal (see below). You lose the whole of your benefit. In these circumstances there are clear advantages in reaching a conciliated settlement which does not itemise future losses rather than have the tribunal do it.

Future losses can include the loss of a company car, tied accommodation, tips and profitable expenses.

7. Pension. This is by far the hardest loss to quantify. You have lost not just your own and your employer's contributions, but the expectation of the future improvements in your pension entitlement which your service would bring. Unless you have less than five years' service you will need to do an elaborate calculation to work out your rights, based on the capitalised value of your pension. You should get from the tribunal office (address page 511) a copy of the Government Actuary's

Department's suggested method for assessing pension losses following unfair dismissal (also published in *New Law Journal*, 19 June 1980).

8. Reductions. Your award can be reduced in three circumstances.

Have you received other payments?

Any payment your employer has made you as notice money or severance pay goes towards reducing his/her liability. If you are claiming unfair redundancy, any statutory payment offsets the *basic* award. Any extra redundancy pay goes to offset the compensatory award.

Did you contribute to your own dismissal?

The tribunal can reduce your compensation by any amount it considers just and equitable if you have to any extent caused or contributed to your own dismissal. If it finds you were as much to blame as your employer, it might reduce your money by 50 per cent. For example, you may have been to blame in failing to repair a machine properly, but your employer may have given you no warnings or taken too drastic action.

The House of Lords has said that there is nothing to stop the tribunal reducing your money by 100 per cent (*Devis v Atkins* page 232). In practice, reductions of over 80 per cent are highly exceptional.

Employers frequently try to reduce their compensation bill by saying you were partly to blame.

Did you try to reduce your losses?

The tribunal can also reduce your compensation if it finds that you failed to 'mitigate your loss'. You can't sit back and do nothing waiting for your case to be heard. You must be seen to be taking all the steps that a reasonable person would if they had no hope of getting the job back. You should register as unemployed and actively look for jobs while your case is pending.

Again, employers will often produce evidence such as newspaper advertisements to show that jobs are plentiful and that you haven't tried hard to reduce your losses. You will have to bring evidence of the jobs you have applied for to combat this.

Additional compensation for unfair dismissal

If the tribunal orders your employer to reinstate or re-engage you, you can complain to the tribunal if the terms of the order aren't carried out to the letter. If the tribunal agrees with you it can order your employer to pay an additional amount of £7,500 (1983/84). If management refuse to have you back, the tribunal must award you an additional amount of *either* between 13 and 26 weeks' pay, *or*, if you have been unfairly dismissed for a reason connected with race or sex discrimination, between 26 and 52 weeks' pay.

Special award

In the 1982 Employment Act a new special award of compensation was made available for workers dismissed for reasons related to union membership. The Tories aimed the law at workers who object to union membership, but EPCA section 72 applies equally to anyone sacked because they joined a union or for taking part in its activities. As we have seen, there is a minimum basic award in all these cases of £2,000 (all figures are from November 1982). In addition the special award is 104 weeks' pay or £10,000, whichever is greater up to the maximum of £20,000. If reinstatement is ordered – the most important remedy for a sacked trade unionist – the award is 156 weeks' pay or £15,000, whichever is greater, with no maximum. A compensatory award of up to £7,500 can be made in every case.

Example of unfair dismissal compensation

The example is based on the following assumptions:
1. You were born 1.2.1927.
2. You started with XYZ Ltd on 30 March 1967.
3. You were sacked without notice on 30 July 1983.
4. You earned £150 a week gross, £15 of which was voluntary overtime. You took home £110 net.
5. You got an *ex gratia* payment of £100.
6. You were disqualified for unemployment benefit for six weeks, but got supplementary benefit at £20 a week.
7. You then got unemployment benefit at £40 a week.
8. Your case was heard on 30 October 1983.
9. The tribunal found that you would not get work until about 1 March 1984. You would probably get only £120 (£90 net) a week because you would not have seniority.

A. Compensatory award

		£
1. Loss of net earnings from 30.7.83 to 30.10.83 13 weeks at £110	=	1,430
Loss of half-yearly bonus payable 1.10.83	=	50
		1,480
Less *ex gratia* payment		−100
		1,380*
2. Loss of earnings from 30.10.84 to 1.3.84 17 weeks at £110	=	1,870
3. Loss of earnings from 1.3.84 for 1 year (say) 52 weeks at £20	=	1,040
4. Expenses looking for work		50
5. Loss of pension rights (say)		2,000
6. Loss of right to 12 weeks' notice (say) 6 weeks at £135 (£150 −£15 overtime)		810
Total 1–6		7,150
7. Less 20 per cent contributory fault		−1,430
Total 1–6 minus 7		5,720

B. Basic award—16 years' service

23½ weeks at £135	=	3,172.50
Less 20 per cent contributory fault		−634.50
Total		2,538.00

C. Additional award

Nil	=	000
Grand Total A + B + C		8,258

Summary

1. Before you negotiate or make a claim for any workers's right, check that you have continuous employment for the requisite period. Most rights require a minimum period of service.

---

* In practice the tribunal will itemise this as the 'prescribed amount'. The DE can recoup from your employer the equivalent social security benefits you have received. Your employer must then pay you be balance. See page 500.

2. To calculate what compensation you need, you usually have to calculate 'a week's pay'.

3. For unfair dismissal you can get compensation for your losses, an additional award if your employer refuses to comply with a tribunal order, and a basic award.

4. The basic award and redundancy pay are based on the same formula. This takes account of your age, length of continuous employment and a week's pay.

20. Going to a tribunal

Bringing a legal claim / preliminary steps / legal advice and representation / costs / documents you need / time limits / test cases / witnesses / conciliation / settlement / hearings / enforcement / reviews and appeals / and a summary.

If you are sacked, made redundant, discriminated against or denied almost any right in Part Two of this handbook, and you can't assert your rights at workplace level, you will have to consider taking legal action.

The procedure described in this chapter relates to an industrial tribunal. If you are exercising your right to social security benefits, disputed claims go to a Local Tribunal or a Medical Appeal Tribunal. Disputed claims for supplementary benefit go to a Supplementary Benefit Appeal Tribunal. If you are claiming that a civil wrong has been done to you, for example, that you have been injured by your employer's negligence, or that you are threatened with eviction from a flat that goes with your job, you go to a county court or the High Court, depending on the amount of money involved.

Where to find the law

Powers of tribunals are found in the Industrial Tribunals (Rules of Procedure) Regulations SI 1980 No 884 and 885 (Scotland), and SI 1976 No 661; and the Employment Appeal Tribunal Rules SI 1976 No 322.

Preliminary steps

There are four preliminary matters that you must check before you start. Using the **Workers' Rights Checklist** on page 507, make sure:

1. that you have worked for the minimum number of weeks required for making a claim;

2. that you have worked, or normally would have worked, for the appropriate number of hours in each of those weeks;

3. that your service is unbroken except by illness, holidays, absence with leave or maternity; and

4. that you are within the time limit for making a complaint.

You may need advice in deciding whether you have met the above conditions.

Advice and representation

Unions

The most obvious source of help is your union. Its officials should provide advice and representation, and will be most able to get your rights without going to a tribunal. Unions have different procedures, but the TUC has recommended that a special internal application form be printed by each union. Ask your union rep or local official how to apply for advice and assistance. Once you apply make sure the application has been received and acted upon.

Some unions require you to send the originating application **form IT1** (see below) to the tribunal yourself. In this case, it is still important to contact your official to get advice on how to fill it in.

Legal Aid

If you are not in a union, your scope is limited.

Legal assistance is available on what is known as the Law Society's **green form** (pink, in Scotland) for general advice. You have the right to £40 worth (sometimes more) of a solicitor's time to be given free, or at a discount, according to your means. Means are assessed by reference to your savings and to your disposable income. Disposable income is what you have left after deductions and rent, and after dependants are taken into account. Generally speaking, you are entitled if you are out of work. Not all solicitors give legal assistance on the green form – ask and make sure before you get an interview. Also ask if they have experience of industrial tribunal matters, as many solicitors are new to this kind of case.

If you don't qualify for free or cheap legal advice and assistance you can usually get half-an-hour's advice for £5 from most solicitors. Ask for a 'fixed fee interview'. The Legal Aid Solicitors' List, available in public libraries and Citizen's Advice Bureaux, gives the names and addresses of solicitors on a local basis, and the subjects they specialise in.

There is no equivalent in Northern Ireland to the green form, but some solicitors offer half-an-hour's advice either free or almost free.

Legal Aid is not available for representation at a tribunal. This is a major denial of rights to many working people. But solicitors can use the green form to:

- give advice
- fill in your tribunal application form
- prepare evidence
- write letters
- tell you how to present your case
- get counsel's opinion on difficult points (the £40 limit can be raised for this).

Law Centres in London and other big cities will help you without charge and will often represent you. Citizen's Advice Bureaux give basic advice but often have no industrial experience. They can advise you where to get more help.

Equality Commissions

You can sometimes get legal assistance from the Commission for Racial Equality or the Equal Opportunities Commission in discrimination cases.

ACAS

You can get advice free from ACAS. Addresses on page 511. See also 'Conciliation' below.

Other representation

At the hearing you can be represented by **anyone you like** – a union official, lawyer, or a friend – or you can present your own case. A 1974 survey showed that in 53 per cent of cases the applicant had no representation, but those who did clearly fared better.

Costs

It is important to mention costs at this stage because they are frequently referred to by employers right from the moment you consider claiming against them. In fact, **there is little chance of a tribunal ordering you to pay your employer's costs**. It has power to do so *only* if it is of the opinion that you acted 'frivolously or vexatiously', or if you have postponed the dates of a hearing (see below).

In these cases the tribunal, or the other side, can requisition a **pre-hearing assessment** (PHA). This is a short preliminary hearing by a different tribunal from the one which may eventually hear your case. If it considers your case is 'unlikely to succeed', or any allegation in it has 'no reasonable prospect of success', it can give its opinion that you may be ordered to pay costs if you 'persist in' taking the case to a full hearing. The second tribunal and the other side see this opinion.

This procedure was introduced in 1980 in response to employers' complaints that they were not winning enough cases, and were put to expense. The results of the first 15 months show that about one case in 20 went to a PHA. Costs warnings were given in half of them, and only one-third of PHA applicants went on to a full hearing. If you do press on after a costs warning you stand a one in ten chance of winning, but only a one in three chance of having costs awarded against you. If you get no warning you stand a one in five chance of winning, with a minimal chance of costs against you (*Employment Gazette*, December 1982).

Costs are awarded as a fixed sum, or on the county court scale of bands up to £1,000.

Costs can, of course, be awarded **against your employer**:

- ■ Eileen Laws was assistant manager at a Ramsgate supermarket, taking home £44 a week. With the full knowledge of her manager, she openly paid staff in goods rather than cash for overtime they did. The employers behaved 'lamentably' when they sacked her without notice or any investigation and treated her as a criminal. They threatened to sue her if she sought legal advice. She claimed unfair dismissal and at the hearing the employers offered no evidence. She was awarded £4,272 compensation and her costs. The EAT agreed the employers had acted 'frivolously' because had they investigated the circumstances they would have realised their case was manifestly futile and, disputing only compensation not liability, the hearing would have been much cheaper and shorter. *Cartiers Superfoods v Laws* 1978 (EAT)

You are entitled to your own costs if you represent yourself and win. The Litigants in Person (Costs and Expenses) Order 1980 applies to compensate you for your time and expenses in preparing and presenting your case if costs are awarded.

A tribunal will not without warning make you pay costs simply because you are bringing a case that turns out to be hopeless. Some employers' solicitors (in particular, one London firm acting for a large leisure group, usually against non-unionists) frequently make the threat of costs.

If you are claiming a right which is not available to you because, say, you have not worked enough weeks, it is just possible to envisage a tribunal making an order of costs. But the tribunal secretary will write to you in confidence and explain the law so you will be aware of the possible threat. An order for costs will not be made unless your employer asks for it.

These are the *only* circumstances in which the possibility of costs can arise. In practice it can be disregarded. If you are extremely unlucky and also not represented by a union (which would bear the costs) you would have to pay all or part of the other side's costs.

Documents

Questionnaire
If you are thinking of pushing a claim of sex or race discrimination you can use a question-and-answer form to get information from an employer before you take action. The answers will form part of the evidence at the hearing. Although employers aren't obliged to answer, their failure to do so can be noted and inferences can be drawn by the tribunal.

Originating application
No formal document is necessary to make a claim. If you write giving the following basic information, your claim is a valid originating application:

1. your name and address
2. the name and address of the person or company you are claiming against

3. the grounds on which you are making a claim and particulars of it.

Most applicants use the official Form IT1.

Originating application – Form IT1

This is the basic document for all industrial tribunal claims. It is available from union and DE offices and a specimen is shown on pages 509–10. If you are getting assistance, fill in the form with the help of your representative. The form is not in duplicate, so ask for two copies and keep one for yourself or your representative.

As a general rule it is better to say little rather than a lot on the form, so that you are not tied down later, or tripped up in fine distinctions such as those in redundancy and unfair dismissal. If you have given too little information, the employer can always ask for further particulars (see below).

Time limits

The form must be sent to the Central Office of the Industrial Tribunals in London, Glasgow or Belfast, according to where the case arose. Addresses on page 511. It can be sent by you or your representative, but should be signed by you. It must be received by the Central Office within the time limit.

■ **Example**: You are sacked without notice on 15 September. You have three months to claim. Your application must reach Central Office on or before 14 December. If 14 December is a weekend or holiday, it must be delivered on or *before* that day.

The tribunal has discretion in most claims to extend the time limit if it is satisfied

1. that it wasn't reasonably practicable for you to make the application within the time limit *and*

2. that when you were able to make the application, you did so within a further reasonable period.

The deadline for most claims can be extended. For redundancy pay it can be extended by six months. For equal pay, there is no power to extend the deadline beyond six months after you leave the employment. In discrimination cases the deadline can be waived indefinitely if the tribunal considers it just and equitable.

The tribunal is unlikely to extend the time limit if the delay is caused by: bad advice or default by your representative, or the fact that you were **pursuing negotiations or going through procedure**, or that you didn't know of your right to claim. It might extend it if you have been ill, or if your employer asked you to hold back pending negotiations.

Do not delay registering your claim. Once you have registered it, you can ask for a hearing to be postponed if you have a good reason. This might be useful if you are pursuing an internal appeal, or if you are waiting for criminal proceedings to be over (see page 237).

Action by the tribunal

The Central Office allocates your claim to a regional office, to whom all further correspondence should be sent. (In Scotland there are no regions but there are local offices of the tribunals.) If the regional secretary considers that the tribunal has no power to deal with your claim, s/he will write to you saying this. For example, s/he would do this if you hadn't worked long enough to claim redundancy pay.

When your claim is registered, the tribunal notifies the other party, who has 14 days in which to file the Respondent's Reply on Form IT3. A copy is sent to you by the tribunal. You are given 14 days' notice of the date set for the hearing. If you have named a representative, that person will receive the reply and notice of hearing and must notify you and all of your witnesses.

Further particulars

Either party can ask for more details about the other's case. You can ask about names, places, written documents, dates, numbers of male and female employees, or anything else that may help your case. If you disbelieve that there is a redundancy situation you can ask to see the accounts, order books and stocklists. If you think you have been selected unfairly for dismissal, ask for a breakdown of all employees by grade and length of service. If you are alleging sex or race discrimination, ask for details of applicants for jobs or for promotion over a period of time.

Of crucial importance in proving a case of discrimination is evidence of the way your employer favours men, and of any special information your employer acts on. Often employers claim as confidential information which is essential to your case if you are trying to show that you were better qualified for promotion than a man who got the job. See, for example, *Perera v Civil Service*, page 126. Yet despite the critical value of information such as the records, qualifications and performance of job applicants, the courts have refused to order employers to hand it over to applicants alleging discrimination.

■ Joan Nassé, a married clerical officer and chair of her CPSA branch, complained that she had not been selected for an interview panel because of union activities and her marital status. She asked for the annual assessment reports of herself and two male colleagues who had gone to the interview. Her employer gave hers, but refused, on the grounds of confidentiality, to give the men's. Without these she had no firm basis for comparison and would probably be unable to prove her case. The House of Lords upheld the employer's refusal, saying that the tribunal Chairman must decide what papers are necessary. *Nassé v Science Research Council* 1979 (HL)

You write direct to your employers or the person representing them. Give them a time limit of, say, seven or 14 days in which to comply with your request. You could even ask for the managing director to bring the order-books to the hearing. If they refuse, or do not reply, write direct to the secretary at the tribunal office which is dealing with the case, enclosing a copy of your original letter to your employers, and ask for an order to be issued. The Chairman of the tribunal may grant this request and if so the order will be sent to you, or your representative. You must then write to the employers or their representative enclosing the order and asking for the information to be provided. Send it by recorded delivery so you know it has been received. The tribunal can itself initiate an order for either side to provide more information.

Sometimes, employers' solicitors will say that the documents you are looking for can be inspected at their offices, and they will produce them at the hearing. You can always ask them if they will send you a photocopy. If they ask you about, say, your attempts to find a new job or your present wages, and you want to stall, you can allow these to be inspected by appointment during certain hours at your union or solicitor's office. Anyone refusing to comply with a tribunal order can be fined up to £100. Their claim or defence can also be struck out.

Amendment

If you want to add or delete something, write to the secretary at the tribunal office, explaining the amendment and asking for 'leave to amend' your application form; and send a copy to the employers' representative.

Documents for the hearing

If a hearing is inevitable, you will be asked by the tribunal to bring with you your wage slips, contract, agreements and other documents relating to your work with your employer, and, if you have been sacked, relating to your present work or the period while you were out of work. This would include details of social security payments, wages earned, and money in lieu of notice. It is a good idea to bring any letters from employers you have applied to, and copies of advertisements you have followed up. These will show you have been trying to get work and will favourably affect the amount of any compensation you may get.

Any documents or collective agreement – for example one which contains a disciplinary procedure, or equal opportunity clause – that you want to use should be photocopied, if possible five times. This means that you have copies for your representative, the employers, your witness and the three tribunal members. Some documents will be uncontroversial and the other side will not object. You can even draw up a jointly agreed 'bundle' of relevant documents. If you are represented, the tribunal's preliminary instructions ask your representative to do this. But if you don't agree to, say, a management report being submitted because you think it was made after your sacking you can object at the hearing.

Test cases

Test cases can be brought in tribunals. If you and a number of other workers have an identical dispute over equal pay or mass sackings you must all file individual claims. If the issue in each case is precisely the same your union may want to try one test case. This can be agreed informally between the union and the employer, with both sides agreeing to follow the result. But it can't prevent you bringing you own claim and, conversely, management can't be forced in law to accept the test case as binding them. Obviously, if you won your test case, it would be foolish for management to resist other cases on the same facts, and costs might even be awarded to them.

In a genuine attempt to save time and expense the union could agree to treat one case as a test case but 'without prejudice to each member's right to bring his or her own claim'. If you are in any doubt about the suitability of the test case chosen – for example if it isn't quite the same as your own – get your union to apply for a hearing for you. You need not proceed with it, and can get the tribunal to wait until the test case is decided before hearing yours. If no claim is registered, you may find you are time-barred, so **all claims should be registered even if a test case is being tried**.

Since 1980 it has been possible for tribunals to order a test case at the request of one of the parties if there is a common question of law or fact, or the same remedy is being claimed, or if 'for some other reason it is desirable'. So a union, or a women's or civil rights group or ethnic association, can bring test cases on behalf of members – provided they all file originating applications.

Third parties

The 1982 amendments to EPCA sections 26A and 76A allow tribunals to order a union or any person to be 'joined' (in Scotland 'sisted') as a party to the case if they have organised industrial pressure to dismiss a non-unionist. A worker dismissed or victimised as a result of this pressure, or the employer, can before the hearing request the tribunal to make an order. And of course any award of compensation can be made either wholly or partially against any of the parties.

Witnesses

You can bring any witnesses you choose, and in any order you choose. You will usually be a witness yourself. If your union official has been involved at workplace level in your dispute, and is also presenting your case, s/he can appear as a witness if you think it helps your case. Get a full statement from each of your witnesses so that you know the basic ingredients of what they are going to say. They can see and sign the statement but can't take it into the witness-box.

Witnesses are paid some travelling expenses, loss of earnings and subsistence by the tribunal. Tell your witnesses this. They must be allowed time off to attend. Victimisation of a fellow-worker who gives evidence for you would amount to criminal interference. Special protection is given in discrimination cases against this sort of victimisation – see page 134.

A witness who is not prepared to attend can be ordered to do so. The procedure is the same as for obtaining an order for further particulars or documents. You should be wary, though, of calling a witness who is unwilling to come, as their evidence may turn out to be different from what you expected. But if their evidence is important to your case, call them.

You are not obliged to tell the tribunal or the other side the names of your witnesses. And even if you do tell them, you can change your mind at any time, even during the hearing. Witnesses can remain throughout the hearing except in Scotland, where they are excluded until they have given evidence.

Conciliation

A feature of almost all individual complaints to an industrial tribunal is the existence of facilities for conciliation. ACAS get a copy of every form except those claiming redundancy pay only. ACAS will act if both parties request, or if the conciliation officer assigned to the case thinks there is a reasonable prospect of settlement. Either party can ask for conciliation after a dismissal has taken place but before a claim is presented (EPCA section 134) and *in practice* either party can ask the conciliation officer to intervene at any stage.

You won't know who has been assigned to the case and you can't find out from the tribunal office. Often the conciliation officer makes contact in person or by phone with you or with your representative if you have nominated one. If you want immediate help, contact the regional office of ACAS (addresses on page 511) quoting the number of your case.

In dismissal cases, ACAS's primary duty is to get you reinstated, preferably using any agreed procedures. Failing that, re-engagement and compensation must be tried.

If you are not represented ACAS can be very useful, as you may find it difficult or be unwilling to talk to the other side. If you are represented by a union official it is less likely that you will need ACAS, as the official can talk direct to management or their representative. If you are represented by a lawyer, ACAS can be a useful intermediary by providing industrial experience in discussions on a settlement.

The ACAS officers responsible for conciliation of individual cases are in a different branch from those who conciliate strikes. They are expected to know the law and in practice help both parties to reach a settlement by suggesting from experience the possible outcome of the case if it goes to a tribunal. They are supposed to be impartial, and to seek simply to get a settlement. In fact, they often go further than this. Although they are not supposed to suggest figures for compensation, they sometimes do.

It is a good idea to give the conciliation officer a detailed breakdown of the money you are claiming (see page 479). It is also useful to ask for your job back, even if you are not keen, because it looks better to the tribunal if management turn you down, rather than vice versa. It may also prevent them taking on a replacement until the hearing is over.

Judging by the statistics for unfair dismissal claims (page 192) you have a reasonable chance of getting some form of conciliation settlement.

Use ACAS if you want to keep talking to your employer. But remember that the conciliation officer is not your representative. Many employers will settle even the most hopeless case against them for a 'nuisance value' figure of anything up to £300 (half the conciliated settlements in 1981 were at or below this figure). It would cost your employer at least that for a day in a tribunal with a lawyer and witnesses, so this is something you can keep in the back of your mind when bargaining.

Settlement

If a settlement is reached with or without conciliation there are two procedures you can follow. You can simply withdraw the case. Technically, the case is dismissed by the tribunal, and you cannot come back if you do not get your money. On the other hand, if you settle the case between yourselves or through ACAS, the agreement can be reported to the tribunal, which will record it as a binding decision. This means that it becomes an order of the tribunal and can be enforced through the county court. You do not need to extract an admission of liability from your employer, and very often it is a condition of the settlement that no liability is admitted, but if you have the tribunal record it, it is tantamount to showing you were unfairly dismissed. This might be useful if you are suspended from unemployment benefit, or in need of a clean sheet when you are looking for a new job. So it is always advisable to get your settlement recorded in writing by the tribunal.

If you use ACAS the usual procedure is that you and your employer sign a form, and once the conciliation officer has the cheque, s/he will get the tribunal to record the settlement. Whether or not you use ACAS, the form of words will depend on the type of agreement you have reached. You should be able to sign something like this.

> I have received the sum of £—— in full and final settlement of all claims arising out of and in connection with my dismissal on (date).

It is important not to sign away '*all* claims against XYZ Ltd' (although this wording is often suggested) because this might preclude you claiming damages for something quite unrelated to the sacking, such as an industrial disease. So make sure you mention only the dismissal. The tribunal then makes a decision following the wording you have agreed.

Dealing with employers

If ACAS is not successful, your representative might find it useful to talk direct to your employers or their representative a few days before the hearing to see if a settlement can be arranged. You are not in any way conceding if you make this approach, and the threat to management of wasting time and money in a hearing can be helpful.

'Without prejudice'

If an offer is made 'without prejudice', it means without prejudice to any subsequent action your employer might take. It can be withdrawn later. It really means that by making it management cannot be taken to admit liability, or to indicate a binding obligation to pay the amount offered. Similarly, in putting forward your figures for the loss you suffered, or stipulating the terms on which you will go back, you should say that this is without prejudice to any claim you may make at the tribunal if your terms are rejected. 'Without prejudice' documents will be respected by solicitors, and the tribunals will refuse to admit them in evidence.

Adjournment

Hearings can be postponed usually by either party writing to the tribunal and giving a reason. You may need more time to prepare, or to conciliate, or your representative may not be free on the appointed day. Some tribunals are more flexible than others, but generally they will allow one postponement by each party. Provided you give some notice you should not run the risk of having to pay the costs of the other side caused by the postponement. But the tribunal may order payment if you cause substantial last-minute inconvenience and the employer asks for costs.

Hearings that can't be finished on the appointed day will be reconvened on another. Unless you have told the tribunal you expect to go on for a second day, the chances are that you will have to wait – in some cases delays of seven or eight weeks have occurred. Always object if this happens.

The hearing

An interim hearing can be held in cases of dismissal for union activity (and for refusing to be a member) – see page 308. If you want to prove a preliminary point, you could go to the tribunal to decide just this point, then adjourn.

This section gives guidance for you, or your representative if you have one, on tribunal procedure.

Administration

You or your representative will receive a letter telling you where and when the hearing will be held. It will usually start at

10 a.m. or at 2 p.m. The clerk will take your name and names of witnesses, and explain the procedure, so you should arrive a few minutes before the start. If you are unemployed the clerk will also ask you a number of questions about social security benefit you have received. This is to enable the DE to recoup this money from your employer if compensation is awarded. If you have a representative you will need to give him/her the up-to-date details about your job prospects, earnings, and social security payments.

Procedure
The chair will usually start by outlining the procedure to be followed. 'Chairman' or 'Madam Chairman' is a proper and non-obsequious form of address. If you want to make any amendment, or to challenge a point of jurisdiction, for instance, that the employer failed to enter a defence in time, you should do it now. Likewise management will raise such issues as whether you have worked a sufficient number of hours and weeks to enable you to bring the particular claim, or whether you claimed too late. The party who has to prove the point goes first, and sums up last. If you are claiming unfair dismissal, and management admit you were sacked but claim it was fair; or if you are claiming victimisation and they admit you were treated in the way you describe but say it had nothing to do with your union activity, the batting order is:

1. employer makes an opening speech

2. calls first witness, who swears or affirms that s/he will tell the truth, and answers questions

3. you cross-examine

4. the tribunal asks questions

5. the employer re-examines

6. calls further witnesses

7. you make an opening speech, call first witness, and follow as **1–6** above

8. you sum up and address the tribunal

9. employer does the same

10. tribunal adjourns.

If management contest the fact that you were sacked (saying you resigned), or if you are claiming equal pay, sex or racial discrimination or other individual rights, then *your* side goes first and brings witnesses.

Opening statement

Your side need not make an opening speech, but if you do your representative should briefly outline the nature of your claim and the kind of evidence your witnesses will be giving. This gives the tribunal an idea of how things will develop, and it is anyway a useful platform for your views.

Your witnesses

You should be clear about the facts that each of your witnesses will testify to. Strict rules of evidence and procedure are not followed but your case will be stronger, and you will be less interfered with by the Chairman, if you do not 'lead' your witnesses. This means you should not put words in their mouth by asking questions that suggest the answer, or by asking them to confirm a long statement of your own.

■ **For example**, don't say: 'Is it correct that you saw the shift manager stagger drunkenly into the workshop and order Mr X to collect his cards when he refused to work on an unguarded machine?' Instead, ask the witness in separate questions to describe the manager's appearance and manner, what was said by each person, how close s/he was to them, and the condition of the machine.

After the other side and the tribunal have cross-examined your witnesses, you can then re-examine them. Here you can clarify statements made in the initial evidence in a way that is favourable to you, but you can't introduce new material at this stage.

Cross-examination

You can lead the other side's witnesses. You are aiming to extract statements that are beneficial to your case, and which show the witness is unreliable because of self-contradiction.

If your side's evidence is different, **you must give the other side a chance to comment on the events or conversations you say took place**. So if you are concentrating on what was said at the time of dismissal you must ask all the people who were there about it. Otherwise the employers will object when your witness raises the matter for the first time.

You should always object to hearsay (second-hand) evidence. Tribunals are not bound by the same rules as courts, which exclude most hearsay evidence. They often override objections to hearsay on the basis that it may be helpful and they will note that it is hearsay. But the damage is already done, particularly as the tribunal lay members may not be experienced in dealing with the relative value of evidence received. Hearsay statements cannot be admitted in a court to ascertain the **truth** of what is said in the statement.

■ **Example**: The personnel manager (**P**) says she dismissed the worker (**W**) because the supervisor (**S**) saw **W** clocking another worker's card. Only **S** and **W** can tell the truth about what happened. **P** got it second-hand (hearsay) so can't therefore corroborate **F**'s evidence in the same way as a witness to the event could. So the evidence is a straight conflict between **S** and **W**.
But
P can say that as a result of a report she got from **F**, she dismissed **W**. She is not testifying to the truth of the report – she is simply saying what she did. You would
1. object to the evidence
2. cross-examine on whether **P** fully investigated the report
3. remind the tribunal in summing up that this evidence is hearsay.

The key to cross-examination is knowing when to leave a point alone. Once you have from one witness the kind of statement you are looking for, and the Chairman has a note of it, move on. Do not beam proudly and repeat the statement for added impact – you can do this in summing up, and exaggerated emphasis on it will put the witness and the other side on alert. Nor should you ask any other witness the same question (apart from perhaps one of your own side who will say the same thing), as any change will detract from the impact you have achieved.

Summing-up

This is your chance to talk directly to the tribunal. You (or your representative) will sum up your case and where there is a difference in the evidence you will say why your story should be preferred, and why the other side's is unreliable. You can also deal with the law and show any Acts, codes and cases that help you. You can also quote law textbooks, and DE Guides. Although the views expressed are not binding, they will often be very influential.

Finally, you should say what remedy you are looking for if you win – for example, reinstatement or compensation, equal pay, promotion, etc. If you are claiming compensation for unfair dismissal, go for all the items set out on page 479. At least give the tribunal the basis on which they should assess compensation, such as the amount of weekly earnings.

The decision

The tribunal may give you your answer that day, in which case they will retire to discuss it and announce it on returning. Or they may 'reserve' their decision, which means you will have to wait, sometimes for as long as 12 weeks. It can be a unanimous or two-to-one majority decision. Tribunals tend to reserve decisions too often. They usually do so if they cannot agree, or if there is a lot of conflicting evidence, or if the law is complicated. Sometimes you may get a decision on the day, with the reasons following in writing. In *all* cases you or your representative gets a copy of the decision, and the written reasons for it, by post. It is then a public document. Printed at the end is the date on which the decision was entered in the register of decisions at Central Office and copies sent to the parties. This is the date from which the time limits for appeals and reviews run.

Enforcement

If your employers refuse to comply in full with a reinstatement order, you can apply to the tribunal for additional compensation. If they refuse to pay any compensation awarded, apply to the county court (or sheriff court in Scotland) for an order. You can get Legal Aid for this. The court will enforce the order and order your employers to pay costs.

Review

An application for review is a simple way of getting the case brought up again, and even of having an appeal of sorts. It arises in a limited set of circumstances: the tribunal staff have made a mistake, new evidence has become available or a party did not know of the hearing. It can also arise when 'the interests of justice' (Regulation 10) require it, so you should phrase your application for review in these terms.

If granted, the tribunal (or if not practicable another tribunal) will re-hear the whole or part of the case and the previous decision can be set aside or varied.

You must make your application within 14 days of the date the decision was sent to you. There is no special form, but you must set out the grounds in full.

Appeals

An appeal from a tribunal decision can be made on a **point of law only** to the Employment Appeal Tribunal. You have to show that the tribunal made a legal mistake, or followed the wrong cases. This does not mean that matters of fact can never be raised, because if the tribunal based their decision on facts that did not exist, or evidence of facts which could not possibly be true, this can itself be a question of law – that no reasonable tribunal could have decided the issue in the way this one did. The EAT has power to refuse to hear any appeal that does not show a question of law.

The Appeal Tribunal sits permanently in London and Glasgow and can hold hearings anywhere. When hearing a case it consists of a High Court judge, and a present or former trade union official and employers' representative. It has most of the powers of the High Court except that it deals only with appeals, and not cases heard for the first time. In this respect it differs from the National Industrial Relations Court (1971–74), but otherwise it is what the NIRC was intended to be.

Your appeal must reach the EAT **within 42 days** of the date the tribunal decision was sent to you. Addresses on page 511.

Anyone can represent you at the EAT, or you can do it yourself. You can get Legal Aid for legal representation. Despite the fact that lawyers do not have a monopoly, the proceedings and the correspondence are quite formal and geared to legal representation. Trade union officials and individual workers do appear quite frequently. Expenses are not paid to the applicant and people attending, as they are for an industrial tribunal. Only if a witness is ordered to be there will expenses be met.

Costs can be ordered against a losing party, and this power is used more often than in industrial tribunals. The EAT can order payment only if one party has acted unreasonably or the proceedings are improper or vexatious.

The EAT can dismiss your appeal, or can overturn the industrial tribunal decision. In the event it can itself make the decision you want, such as a calculation or the interpretation of an Act; or it can send the case back to the same or a differently constituted tribunal for a new hearing. It would do this if there were some facts, or a question of reasonableness, still to be decided.

Quite often the EAT says it would probably have decided the case differently from the tribunal. This doesn't entitle it to overturn the decision. Provided there was *some* evidence on which the tribunal could make a decision, the EAT can't interfere. This is in contrast to appeals against **wrongful dismissal,** where the appeal court can make a completely fresh decision on its own view of the facts.

Appeals from the EAT go to the Court of Appeal or the Scottish Court of Session Inner House.

In the six counties of Northern Ireland appeals from industrial tribunals go to the Northern Ireland Court of Appeal. There is no EAT.

Appeals on points of law of general public importance in the UK go to the House of Lords.

Summary

1. Most employment rights can be enforced in an industrial tribunal, but negotiation and direct action are more reliable methods.

2. You can get advice and representation from your union. State Legal Aid is not available for representation at a tribunal, but you can get advice and assistance from many solicitors on the £40 green form scheme.

3. There is in practice no chance that you will have to pay the other side's costs.

4. Time limits for making claims are strict, but tribunals have discretion in exceptional cases to extend the deadline.

5. At the hearing, you or your representative can bring witnesses, cross-examine and make opening and closing speeches.

6. You can get a tribunal to review their decision in some situations where the interests of justice require.

7. Appeals to the EAT must be on a point of law and be filed within 42 days of the written decision.

Workers' rights checklist

Right	Chapter	Continuous employment required	Time limit for claim
Race discrimination	8	—	3 months from act;* 6 months if Commission sues; 5 years after non-discrimination notice
Sex/marriage discrimination	8	—	as above
Spent convictions	3, 10	—	3 months (for unfair dismissal)*
Victimisation for TU activities	13	—	3 months from act
Dismissal for TU membership or non-membership	13	—	3 months from termination*
Equal pay	9	—	While employed or up to 6 months after leaving
Time off for ante-natal care	7	—	3 months*
Statutory sick pay	4	None, but must earn more than 'lower earnings limit'	6 months from first day of sickness*
Exclusion or expulsion from TU where a closed shop operates	14	Employment is not a requirement	6 months from exclusion/expulsion
Illegal deductions (Truck Acts)	3, 6	—	6 years
Minimum conditions (Wages Councils)	3, 13	—	6 years
Payment if employer insolvent	11	—	—
Consultation over redundancies and protective award	11, 18	—	3 months*
Protection of employment conditions on transfer of employer's business	11, 18	—	3 months*
Time off for union duties (lay officials)	13	Normally work 16 or more hours a week	3 months*

Workers' rights checklist

Right	Chapter	Continuous employment required	Time limit for claim
Time off for union activities (members)	13	as above	3 months*
Time off for public duties	3	as above	3 months*
Itemised pay statement	3	as above; entitled from first pay day	3 months*
Minimum notice	3, 10	1 month	6 years
Guarantee pay	5	1 month	3 months*
Medical suspension pay	4	1 month	3 months*
Dismissal connected with medical suspension under EPCA section 64	4, 10	1 month	3 months*
Written particulars of contract	3	13 weeks	While employed or up to 3 months after leaving
Written statement of reasons for dismissal	10	6 months	3 months*
Unfair dismissal	10	1 year (2 years in firms with fewer than 21 employees)	3 months*
Redundancy pay	11	2 years	6 months*
Time off to look for work/training before redundancy	11	2 years	3 months
Maternity pay	7	2 years by 11th week before confinement	3 months*
Return to work after pregnancy	7	as above	3 months (6 months if redundant)

* time limit can be extended if it is reasonable, or just and equitable.

Note: continuous employment means you are normally employed on a contract for 16 or more hours a week and have been employed for 5 years or more. There are exceptions – see Chapter 19.

Casual or temporary workers employed on fixed-term contracts of 3 months or less are excluded from medical suspension and guaranteed pay and consultation over redundancies. Workers hired for specific jobs not expected to last more than 3 months are also excluded from these rights, and from notice pay. In any event you

ORIGINATING APPLICATION TO AN INDUSTRIAL TRIBUNAL

	For Official Use Only
IMPORTANT: DO NOT FILL IN THIS FORM UNTIL YOU HAVE READ THE NOTES FOR GUIDANCE. THEN COMPLETE ITEMS 1, 2, 4 AND 12 AND ALL OTHER ITEMS RELEVANT TO YOUR CASE, AND SEND THE FORM TO THE FOLLOWING ADDRESS	Case Number

To: THE SECRETARY OF THE TRIBUNALS
CENTRAL OFFICE OF THE INDUSTRIAL TRIBUNALS (ENGLAND AND WALES)
93 EBURY BRIDGE ROAD, LONDON SW1W 8RE   Telephone: 01 730 9161

1   I hereby apply for a decision of a Tribunal on the following question. (**STATE HERE THE QUESTION TO BE DECIDED BY A TRIBUNAL. EXPLAIN THE GROUNDS OVERLEAF).**

Unfair dismissal and/ or redundancy pay; written reasons for dismissal, sex
discrimination

2   My name is M̶r̶/Mrs/M̶i̶s̶s̶ Surname in block capitals first):—
SMITH   Jane

My address is
247 BEECH AVENUE, LEICESTER

.... Telephone No. ....18297............
My date of birth is ..15 June 1948...................

3   If a representative has agreed to act for you in this case please give his or her name and address below and note that further communications will be sent to your representative and not to you *(See Note 4)*

Name of Representative:— Ms. S. JOHNSON

Address:— DISTRICT OFFICER, CLERICAL WORKERS' UNION

18 FRONT STREET, LEICESTER .... Telephone No. ...19643....

4   (a) Name of respondent(s) (in block capitals) ie the employer, person or body against whom a decision is sought *(See Note 3)*

PLASTIC PACKAGING LTD.

Address(es) ....UNIT 6, COUNTRY TRADING ESTATE, BROWNS ROAD, LEICESTER...............
.... Telephone No. ....48721............

5   Place of employment to which this application relates, or place where act complained about took place.
......as above..................

6   My occupation or position held/applied for, or other relationship to the respondent named above (eg user of a service supplied in relation to employment).
................telephone sales clerk...........

7   My employment began on ..21 March 1979............. and *(if appropriate)* ended on ..24 June 1983....

8   (a) Basic wages/salary ....£110 per week.............................
   (b) Average take home pay ....£78 per week............

9   Other remuneration or benefits ....quarterly bonus £30 approx...............

10 Normal basic weekly hours of work ..37½.......

11 (In an application under the Sex Discrimination Act or the Race Relations Act)
Date on which action complained of took place or first came to my knowledge ....24th June 1983.................

Please continue overleaf

IT 1(Revised September 1981)

510 Rights at work

12 You are required to set out the grounds for your application below, giving full particulars of them.

I worked in the telephone sales department at Plastic Packaging for four years. There are three other clerks who are all men.

On 24 June at 2.30 p.m. Mr. Phillips, the general manager, said that orders were falling due to the recession and I was surplus to requirements.

He said I was unreliable because I have two children under 6 years old. I asked why I was being dismissed and he just said "You Know". I was the longest serving person in the department.

I consider I was unfairly dismissed and was subjected to sex discrimination. I have no reply to my request for written reasons for my dismissal.

13 If you wish to state what in your opinion was the reason for your dismissal, please do so here.

14 If the Tribunal decides that you were unfairly dismissed, what remedy would you prefer? (Before answering this question please consult the leaflet "Unfairly dismissed?" for the remedies available and then write one of the following in answer to this question: reinstatement, re-engagement or compensation)

Reinstatement and Compensation

Signature _Jane Smith_ Date 30 June 1983

	Received at COIT	Code	ROIT	Inits
FOR OFFICIAL USE ONLY				

Useful addresses

Advisory, Conciliation and Arbitration Service

Northern Region
Westgate House, Westgate Road, Newcastle upon Tyne NE1 1TJ

Yorkshire and Humberside Region
Commerce House, St Alban's Place, Leeds LS2 8HH

South East Region
Clifton House, 83 Euston Road, London NW1 2RB

South West Region
16 Park Place, Clifton, Bristol BS8 1JP

London Region
Clifton House, 83 Euston Road, London NW1 2RB

Midlands Region
Alpha Tower, Suffolk Street, Queensway, Birmingham B1 1TZ
    Nottingham Sub-office, 66 Houndsgate, Nottingham NG1 6BA

North West Region
Boulton House, 17 Chorlton Street, Manchester M1 3HY
    Merseyside Sub-office, 27 Leece Street, Liverpool L1 2TS

Scotland
Franborough House, 123 Bothwell Street, Glasgow G2 7JR

Wales
Phase 1, Ty Glas Road, Llanishen, Cardiff CF4 5PH

Central Arbitration Committee

1 The Abbey Garden, Great College Street, London SW1

Central Office of the Industrial Tribunals

England & Wales
93 Ebury Bridge Road, London SW1W 8RE

Scotland
St Andrew House, 141 West Nile Street, Glasgow G1 2RU

N. Ireland
2nd Floor, Bedford House, Bedford Street, Belfast BT2 7NR

Certification Officer

15–17 Ormond Yard, Duke of York Street, London SW1Y 6JT

Companies House

England & Wales
55 City Road, London EC1
Crown Way, Maindy, Cardiff CF4 3UZ

Scotland
102 George Street, Edinburgh 2

N. Ireland
43–47 Chichester Street, Belfast 1

Commission for Racial Equality

Elliot House, 10–12 Allington Street, London SW1E 5EH

Employment Appeal Tribunal (England & Wales)

4 St James's Square, London SW1

Employment Appeal Tribunal (Scotland)

249 West George Street, Glasgow G2 4QE

Equal Opportunities Commission

Overseas House, Quay Street, Manchester M3 3HN

Equal Opportunities Commission Northern Ireland

Lindsay House, Callender Street, Belfast BT1 5DT

Fair Employment Agency

as above

Health and Safety Commission

Baynards House
2 Chepstow Place, London W2

Department of Health and Social Security (leaflets)

PO Box 21, Stanmore, Middlesex HA7 1AY

HMSO

Cornwall House, Stamford Street, London SE1

Independent Review Committee

Congress House, Great Russell Street, London WC1B 3LS

Labour Relations Agency

Windsor House, 9–15 Bedford Street, Belfast BT2 7NU

Labour Research Department

78 Blackfriars Road, London SE1 8HF

Legal Aid

England & Wales
PO Box 9, Nottingham NG1 6DS
Scotland
Legal Aid Central Committee, PO Box 123, Edinburgh EH3 7YR

National Council for Civil Liberties

21 Tabard Street, London SE1 4LA

Scottish Council for Civil Liberties

146 Holland Street, Glasgow G2 4NG

Scottish Trades Union Congress

Middleton House, 16 Woodlands Terrace, Glasgow G3 6DF

Trades Union Congress

Congress House, Great Russell Street, London WC1B 3LS

Workers' Education Association

9 Upper Berkeley Street, London W1H 8BY

Further reading

General

B. Hepple and P. O'Higgins, *Employment Law*, 4th edn, 1981 and *Encyclopedia of Labour Relations Law* (3 vols, loose-leaf, updated), Sweet & Maxwell

C. Drake and B. Bercusson, *The Employment Acts 1974–1980* with commentary, Sweet & Maxwell 1981

C. Drake, *Labour Law*, 3rd edn, Sweet & Maxwell 1981

C. Drake and F. Wright, *Law of Health and Safety at Work: the new approach*, Sweet & Maxwell 1983

I. T. Smith and J. C. Wood, *The Law of Industrial Relations*, Butterworths 1983

R. J. Harvey, *Industrial Relations and Labour Law*, Butterworths (2 vols, loose-leaf, updated)

D. Lewis, *Essentials of Employment Law*, IPM 1983

J. McMullen, *Employment Law under the Tories*, Pluto 1981

R. Lewis and B. Simpson, *Striking a Balance? Employment Law after the 1980 Act*, Martin Robertson 1981

N. Selwyn, *Law of Employment*, 4th edn, Butterworths 1982

D. N. Pritt, *Law, Class and Society Book 1: Employers Workers and Trade Unions*, Lawrence & Wishart 1970

NCCL, *Your Rights at Work* 1981

K. Wedderburn, R. Lewis, J. Clark, *Labour Law and Industrial Relations: Building on Kahn-Freund*, Clarendon 1983

The Department of Employment publishes a set of *Guides* to specific aspects of employment law. All free from local offices or General Office, Information 4, DE, Caxton House, Tothill Street, London SW1H 9NF.

Incomes Data Services, 140 Great Portland Street, London W1 publish a series of very detailed practical legal guides on specific subjects.

Sweet & Maxwell publish a *Law at Work* series of low-priced books on specific subjects.

The TUC and Labour Research Department, 78 Blackfriars Road, London SE1 8HF regularly publish guides to changes in the legislation. Regular bulletins, news and case reports are published by Industrial Relations Services, 67 Maygrove Road, London NW6 2EJ, Incomes Data Services and Labour Research Department.

Chapter 1

B. Weekes, *Industrial Relations and the Limits of Law*, Blackwell 1975

A. Sachs and J. H. Wilson, *Sexism and the Law*, Martin Robertson 1978

Chapter 2
The Legal Systems of Britain, HMSO 1976
J. A. G. Griffith, *The Politics of the Judiciary*, 2nd edn, Fontana 1981

Chapter 3
M. R. Freedland, *The Contract of Employment*, Oxford 1976

Chapter 4
Statutory Sick Pay, LRD 1982
Employer's Guide to Statutory Sick Pay, DHSS 1982 (free)
Employee's Guide to Statutory Sick Pay, DHSS 1983 (free)

Chapters 7–9
T. Gill and A. Coote, *Women's Rights*, 3rd edn, Penguin 1981
J. Coussins, *Maternity Rights for Working Women*, 2nd edn, NCCL 1980
Home Office, *Guides* to *Sex Discrimination; Racial Discrimination*.
EOC and CRE, *Guides* to aspects of the legislation.
D. Wainwright, *Discrimination in Employment*, ABP 1979
A. Grant, *Against the Clock*, Pluto 1983
N. Hadjifotiou, *Women and Harassment at Work*, Pluto 1983
S. Adams, *Sex Discrimination*, Sweet & Maxwell 1980
S. Read, *Sexual Harrasment at Work*, Hamlyn 1982
Bear, Jeffrey and Munyard, *Gay Workers: Trade Unions and the Law*, NCCL 1981

Chapter 10
J. McGlyne, *Unfair Dismissal Cases*, 2nd edn, Butterworths 1979
R. Upex, *Dismissal* (*Law at Work* series), Sweet & Maxwell 1980
Chapeltown CAB, *Sacked? Made Redundant?*, NACAB 1981

Chapter 11
C. Grunfeld, *The Law of Redundancy*, 2nd edn, 1980
C. Bourn, *Job Security* (*Law at Work* series), Sweet & Maxwell 1980
P. Davies and M. Freedland, *Transfer of Employment*, Sweet & Maxwell 1982

Chapter 12
A. Ogus and E. Barendt, *The Law of Social Security*, Butterworths 1982
T. Lynes, *Penguin Guide to Supplementary Benefits*, 4th edn, Penguin 1981
Supplementary Benefits Handbook, HMSO
S. Ward, *Social Security at Work*, Pluto 1982
F. Bennet, *Your Social Security*, Penguin 1982
M. Rowland and R. Smith, *Rights Guide to Non-Means-Tested Social Security Benefits*, 5th edn, CPAG 1982
J. Albeson and J. Douglas, *National Welfare Benefits Handbook*, 12th edn, CPAG 1982

Chapter 13
Disputes Principles and Procedures, TUC 1979
G. Morris, *Union Members* (*Law at Work* series), Sweet & Maxwell 1980

Chapter 15
C. Hird, *Challenging the Figures*, Pluto 1983

Chapter 17
L. Grant *et al*, *Civil Liberty: The NCCL Guide to your Rights*, Penguin 1978
Trouble with the Law: The Release Bust Book, Pluto, 1978

Chapter 20
J. McIlroy, *Industrial Tribunals*, Pluto 1983
D. Williams and D. Walker, *Industrial Tribunals – Practice and Procedure*, Butterworths 1980
J. Angel, *How to Prepare Yourself for an Industrial Tribunal*, IPM 1980 (+1983 supplement)

List of statutes, regulations and codes

Statutes

Characters of Servants Act 1792
Unlawful Combinations of Workmen Act 1800
Combination Laws Repeal Act 1824
Combinations of Workmen Act 1825
Truck Act 1831
Master and Servant Act 1867
Trade Union Act 1871
Criminal Law Amendment Act 1871
Conspiracy and Protection of Property Act 1875
Truck Act 1896
Trade Disputes Act 1906
Trade Union Act 1913
Emergency Powers Act 1920
Trade Disputes and Trade Union Act 1927
Public Order Act 1936
Disabled Persons (Employment) Act 1944
National Insurance Act 1946
Companies Act 1948
Agricultural Wages Act 1948
Mines and Quarries Act 1954
Copyright Act 1956
Terms and Conditions of Employment Act 1959
Wages Councils Act 1959
Payment of Wages Act 1960
Factories Act 1961
Offices, Shops and Railway Premises Act 1963
Contracts of Employment Act 1963
Industrial Training Act 1964
Trade Union (Amalgamations) Act 1964
Redundancy Payments Act 1965
Prices and Incomes Act 1966
Race Relations Act 1968
Transport Act 1968
Employer's Liability (Defective Equipment) Act 1969
Employer's Liability (Compulsory Insurance) Act 1969

Merchant Shipping Act 1970
Equal Pay Act 1970
Industrial Relations Act 1971
Immigration Act 1971
Attachment of Earnings Act 1971
Contracts of Employment Act 1972
Counter Inflation Act 1973
Health and Safety at Work Act 1974
Trade Union and Labour Relations Act 1974
Rehabilitation of Offenders Act 1974
Social Security Act 1975
Remuneration, Charges and Grants Act 1975
Social Security Pensions Act 1975
Sex Discrimination Act 1975
Industry Act 1975
Employment Protection Act 1975
Trade Union and Labour Relations (Amendment) Act 1976
Supplementary Benefits Act 1976
Race Relations Act 1976
Patents Act 1977
Unfair Contract Terms Act 1977
Criminal Law Act 1977
Industrial and Provident Societies Act 1978
Employment Protection (Consolidation) Act 1978
Wages Councils Act 1979
Companies Act 1980
Social Security Act 1980
Social Security (No. 2) Act 1980
Industry Act 1980
Employment Act 1980
Local Government, Planning and Land Act 1980
Employment and Training Act 1981
Social Security and Housing Benefits Act 1982
Employment Act 1982

Regulations
Employment Appeal Tribunal Rules SI 1976 No 322
Safety Representatives and Safety Committees SI 1977 No 500
Industrial Tribunals (Rules of Procedure) Regulations SI 1980 No 884 (and
    885, Scotland)
Transfer of Undertakings (Protection of Employment) Regulations SI 1981 No
    1794
Statutory Sick Pay (General) and (Adjudication) Regulations SI 1982 Nos 894,
    1400

Codes of Practice
Industrial Relations – DE Code issued under the Industrial Relations Act
Disciplinary Practice and Procedures in Employment – ACAS Code No 1
Disclosure of Information to Trade Unions – ACAS Code No 2
Time off for Trade Union Duties and Activities – ACAS Code No 3

Safety Representatives and Safety Committees – HSC Code and Guidance Notes

Picketing – DE Code

Closed Shop Agreements and Arrangements – DE Code revised 1983

Code of Practice for the Elimination of Racial Discrimination and the Promotion of Equality of Opportunity in Employment – CRE

Glossary of legal terms

a week's pay: *see* week's pay.

Act: written law passed by both Houses of Parliament and signed by the Queen.

arbitration: system for settling disputes by reference to a person or persons whom the parties to the dispute empower to make a decision.

associated employer: any two employers are associated if one is a *company* of which the other (directly or indirectly) has control, or if both are companies of which a third person (directly or indirectly) has control.

attachment-of-earnings: a court order requiring your employer to deduct a fixed sum each week from your wages to pay maintenance or a fine.

bankrupt: *see* insolvency.

Certification Officer: official responsible for giving certificates of independence to trade unions and checking union accounts.

check-off: system by which an employer, with your written authority, deducts union contributions from your wages and forwards them to your union.

code: document produced by official body, for example ACAS, to give guidance and which must be considered in any legal proceedings.

collective agreement: agreement or arrangement made by or on behalf of trade unions and employers or employers' associations relating to any of the list of subjects on page 313.

collective bargaining: negotiations relating to any of the list of subjects on page 313.

common law: used in this handbook to mean binding *judges' rulings*. Contrast statute law, made by Parliament.

conciliation: method by which an independent person attempts to get a dispute settled by agreement of the parties. ACAS's main function, and a step available in all tribunal applications.

constructive dismissal: action taken by management which shows they have no intention of abiding by your contract and as a result of which you leave.

contract: legally binding agreement, made in writing or orally.

Court of Appeal: court which hears appeals on law from the High Court and County Courts and on law or fact from a Crown Court in England and Wales.

Court of Session: Scottish equivalent of English High Court (Outer House) and Court of Appeal (Inner House).

Crown Courts: locally-based courts staffed by judges and, in appeals from magistrates, lay magistrates. They try mainly criminal cases with a jury, but some civil work is done. The Old Bailey is the City of London Crown Court.

Crown employment: employment by a government department.

damages: compensation ordered by a court designed to put the innocent party in the same position s/he would be in if his/her contract had been carried out as agreed, or, in tort cases, as if the injury had never occurred.

dismissal: sacking, with or without notice, or constructive dismissal.

employers' association: organisation of employers (or a federation of such organisations) whose principal purposes include regulating relations between employers and workers.

fixed-term contract: contract of employment which ends on a specific date even if it can be ended by either side giving notice before that date.

frustration of contract: automatic termination of a contract of employment due to some unforeseen event which makes it impossible to carry out the contract.

guarantee payment: daily payment employers must make to workers laid off.

High Court: court for hearing *civil* claims for more than £5,000; commercial, tax and many matrimonial cases; and appeals from magistrates.

indemnity: promise to make good any direct losses arising when a person assumes a legal obligation.

independent contractor: worker, often self-employed, who is employed on a contract to render services, as opposed to an employee who works on a contract of service.

independent trade union: *see* trade union.

industrial tribunal: comprises a legally-qualified Chairman, with two lay members chosen from a panel nominated by employers and the TUC. Hears complaints under most of the legislation dealing with individual industrial rights, and appeals under the Health and Safety at Work Act. Does not have the powers of a court, for instance, to fine, or enforce orders.

injunction: temporary or permanent civil court order requiring a person to do or refrain from doing something which adversely affects someone's rights.

insolvency: inability to pay one's debts. Insolvent individuals and partnerships are bankrupt (sequestrated in Scotland). Insolvent companies are put into the control of a liquidator or receiver and *wound up*.

interdict: Scottish injunction.

liquidation: winding up of a company – *see* insolvency.

mitigation: after a breach of contract or an injury you must take all reasonable steps to reduce (mitigate) the losses you suffer.

negligence: failure to do something that a reasonable person would do, or doing something a reasonable person would not do. It must result in damage or injury to someone whom you should expect to be affected by what you do or do not do. Negligence is a tort.

originating application: written complaint to an industrial tribunal giving details of your complaint. Usually use Form IT1 (see page 509) but not compulsory.

patent: government licence giving you the exclusive right to make or sell a new invention.

protective award: sum of money which a tribunal can order management to pay to you if they have made you redundant without properly consulting your union.

receiver: *see* insolvency.

redundancy: lessening or cessation of an employer's need for employees to do work of a particular kind.

repudiation of contract: action or words showing a refusal to abide by a contract – *see also* constructive dismissal.

restraint of trade: illegal restrictive practice preventing an employee or former employee carrying on his/her trade or occupation.

social security benefit: (in this handbook) benefit payable as of right to people who suffer a specified hardship.

statute: *see* Act.

statutory instrument: law passed by a minister who has been given authority by an Act of Parliament.

stipendiary: salaried full-time legally qualified magistrate.

summary dismissal: sacking without proper notice or wages in lieu.

tort: civil wrong giving rise to civil proceedings between two parties, for which the courts order damages to be paid by one party to the other. The same wrong can be both civil and criminal, e.g. assault.

trade union: organisation of workers (and a federation of such organisations, for example the TUC) whose principal purposes include the regulation of relations between workers and employers; includes organisations of workers such as shop stewards' committees. TU on the Certification Officer's *list* gets tax relief. A *listed* trade union can apply to become an *independent* trade union if it is not under the domination or control of any employer and not liable to interference from any employer.

trade union official: lay or full-time officer of a union, branch or section, who is elected or appointed according to the union's rules to represent members, for example, a shop steward.

Truck Act: statute forbidding payment in kind (truck) to manual and other workers.

union membership agreement: agreement between an employer and one or more independent trade unions which makes union membership a requirement for all employees, that is, a closed shop.

vicarious liability: rule of law by which someone is responsible for the wrongful acts of another, for example, an employer is liable for torts committed by employees in the course of employment.

a week's pay: the minimum payment you are entitled to under your contract. Used as the basis for calculating pay for most statutory rights—such as redundancy, unfair dismissal, maternity pay, guarantee pay.

worker: person who works, normally works, or is seeking work under a contract of employment, or for a government department or as a self-employed person. In this handbook worker usually means employee and Crown employee.

Index of cases

Industrial law cases are reported in at least five different series of law reports. Most main libraries have Weekly Law Reports or All England Law Reports. It may be more difficult to find a library with the main series of industrial cases reports. Universities, polytechnics, and major city libraries should have these.

Main page references are given in bold after each case.

Abbreviations

AER: All England Law Reports
ICR: Industrial Court/Cases Reports
IRLR: Industrial Relations Law Reports
ITR: Industrial Tribunal Reports (1965–1978)
KB: King's Bench Reports
WLR: Weekly Law Reports

AER, KB and WLR have more than one volume for each year. All cases are cited by name, year, volume, law report, page.

For example:

North Riding Garages Ltd v Butterwick is reported in volume 2 of the Weekly Law Reports for 1967 at page 571.

Index

Other Pluto Handbooks

Michael Cunningham
Non-Wage Benefits

'a readable and worthwhile guide' *Daily Mail*   £3.50

Jack Eaton & Colin Gill
The Trade Union Directory (new edition, 1983)

'essential reference material for trade unionists'
Labour Weekly   £7.95

Maurice Frankel/Social Audit
Chemical Risk
a workers' guide to chemical hazards and data sheets

'an excellent guide for trade union safety representatives'
Labour Research   £1.95

Alan Grant
Against The Clock — work study and incentive schemes

'excellent and much-needed' *Labour Research*   £4.95

Patrick Kinnersley
The Hazards of Work

'essential reading for every shop steward'
The Guardian   £1.95

Dennis MacShane
Using The Media

'an excellent handbook' *New Statesman*   £3.95

Sue Ward
Pensions

'No trade unionist who is concerned with pensions can afford to be
without this book' *Labour Research*   £4.95

Sue Ward
Social Security At Work

'a cut above some of its cheaper contemporaries... a useful reference
work' *The Landworker*   £4.95

John McIlroy
Industrial Tribunals

More and more workers are having recourse to industrial tribunals, seeking individual redress and maximum compensation; most shop stewards and full-time officials will at some time in their lives be involved in such cases. **Industrial Tribunals** is a timely guide and textbook that is detailed, authoritative, accessible and comprehensive. Its subject matter has never been covered before in such depth from the workers' point of view. It will be essential reading for trade union officers and lay representatives, for public interest groups, as well as for the many workers who feel they might have a case but would like to make sure of it before making the first moves. The book will also be essential reading for management and for the legal profession.

John McIlroy is staff tutor in industrial relations at the University of Manchester.

0 86104 368 5   paperback   £5.95

Pluto books are available through your local bookshop. In case of difficulty contact Pluto to find out local stockists or to obtain catalogues/leaflets (Telephone 01-482 1973).
If all else fails write to:

> **Pluto Press Limited**
> **Freepost** (no stamp required)
> **The Works**
> **105A, Torriano Avenue**
> **London NW5 1YP**

To order, enclose a cheque/p.o. payable to Pluto Press to cover price of book, plus 50p per book for postage and packing (£2.50 maximum).